How to be Led by the Spirit of God

Maturing in the Spirit

Bruce Williams

with

Alta Ada Williams

Lititz Institute
Publishing Division

Published by Lititz Institute Publishing Division
P.O. Box 7808, Lancaster, PA 17604-7808
www.lititzinstitute.org

Author's edition, August 8, 2008
First edition, February, 2009

Printed in the United States of America

Library of Congress Cataloging-in-Publication Data

Williams, Bruce.
How to be led by the Spirit of God: maturing in the spirit / Bruce Williams

p. cm.

ISBN-13: 978-0-9820014-0-0 (paperback)

1. The spiritual and physical universes. 2. God, man, and the devil. 3. The interrelations of the various parts of man. I. Title.

All Scripture quotations are taken from *The Authorized King James Version of the Holy Bible*.

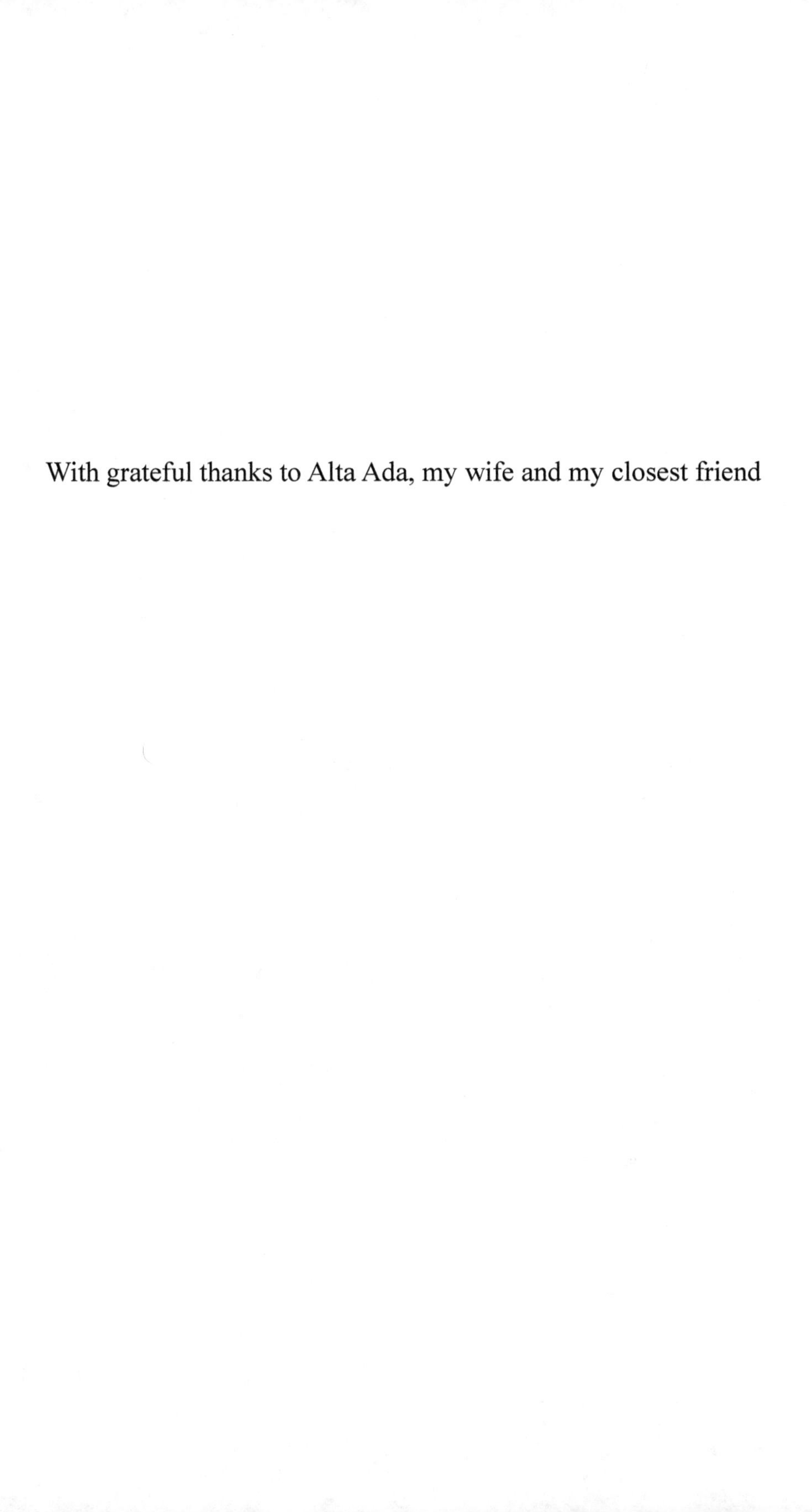

With grateful thanks to Alta Ada, my wife and my closest friend

ACKNOWLEDGMENTS

First and foremost I want to give thanks to Almighty God—God the Father, God the Son, and God the Holy Spirit. I thank God the Father for creating this earth and for wanting all of His children to have an exciting part in His plan for the ages. I thank God the Son for coming to earth, dying for our sins, and forever serving as our High Priest. I thank the Holy Spirit for drawing me to the Lord and for guiding me into truth and teaching me all things.

The Lord brought the subject matter of this book to my attention more than 35 years ago when I was a young Christian. He drew me to desire from the bottom of my heart to learn to be led by His Spirit. Over the years the Holy Spirit has indeed been my teacher. The Lord led me to read Watchman Nee's *The Spiritual Man* and several other authors; but He has taught me primarily from His Scriptures.

I should also like to thank my wife, Dr. Alta Ada Williams, for her work in editing, for help with the Hebrew and Greek languages, and for her many suggestions concerning content. I thank her for her patience during the many evenings I have spent at the computer. She really has coauthored this work; the Lord made us a complement to each other.

I would like to thank those of you who have read the author's edition and have given me helpful feedback and to those who will read this book and give me feedback. Thanks also to our family and friends who have prayed for me and encouraged me in this work.

Dr. Bruce Williams
Lititz, PA
February 2009

FOREWORD

The book is intended to be a manual for study. A workbook is available for help in meditating on and applying the principles contained in this book. We have intended the book primarily for believers. Since Christendom uses the word *believer* in many different ways, we need to define it. By using the word *believer*, we do **not** mean "intellectual assent." The Bible tells us: "Thou believest that there is one God; thou doest well: the devils also believe, and tremble" (James 2:19). When we use the term *believer*, we are indicating a person who has understood that he is a sinner, separated from God because of his sin, and cannot earn his way back to God. He has understood that Jesus the Messiah, the second Person of the Trinity, was incarnated, lived a perfect life, and died to pay for the sins of mankind. The believer has responded to this information by trusting in Jesus for his salvation and confessing Him before men (Romans 10:9-10). When an unbeliever reads this book, it is our prayer for at least two things to happen—for him to desire the benefits of living in the power of God's Holy Spirit and, thus, to come to saving faith as a result. For those who have no spiritual background, but who are analytically minded, the book will place spirituality on less of a mystic plain and more on a reasoned basis. It will bring an understanding of how man functions and will help them to understand how emotional diseases interact with spiritual illness.

Our primary audience, then, is that group of people who have entered into a saving relationship with God through faith in Jesus (those who have been through the second birth). It is not a book that can be used for light, devotional-type reading. One must want to live in the Spirit with a steadfast intensity. The book demands that one think in a way different from that which has been presented in most Christian groups. The basic premise is very simple: one is, at any particular moment, sowing to the flesh or sowing to the spirit. They are mutually exclusive. The book will teach a person how to sow to the spirit. It goes into a lot of detail as to what constitutes body, soul, spirit, heart, conscience, inner man/new spirit, mind, and will. Understanding these parts of man helps one to begin to co-operate with God in living always in the spirit. We believe the Holy Scriptures are the divinely inspired Word of God, without error in the original languages. Therefore, we have based all our conclusions on the Word itself. For example, when considering the soul, we printed every verse in the Bible in which that word occurred in the original language. Then we meditated on each verse until we could see what God was saying about the soul. We can support every statement in the book with Scripture, except in those cases in which I state a personal conclusion (those are clearly indicated). Our prayer is for this book to serve those who have been through the second birth by helping them to grow in spiritual maturity. The writings cannot bring that maturity through reading and grasping the material with the mind. In order for growth to occur, an individual must come into a close and intense relationship with God the Father, God the Son, and God the Holy Spirit. This book will help the reader to understand how this can occur and will challenge him to commit himself to God.

Some readers may want to read Chapter 20 first. It is, in general, a summary; but reading it will show some of the main ideas of the book.

Several notes need to be made. All Scripture quoted is from *The Authorized King James Version of the Holy Bible*. When a word does not appear in the original language but is supplied by the translator, that word is put in italics. I have left those italics as in the translation. When I add italics for emphasis, I note this by stating, "emphasis added."

An explanation is necessary concerning a grammatical point. In Standard English, pronouns must agree in number and gender with their antecedents. Whenever the gender could be either male or female and when the word is singular, Standard English uses the male. Thus, the following sentence would be correct: "Each believer must decide for himself what he will do." Since *believer* is singular and since the gender is not specified, the masculine is used. Modern "politically correct" writers frequently avoid this situation by making the pronoun plural: "Each believer must decide for themselves what they will do." Alternately, some writers use the awkward "Each believer must decide for himself or herself what he or she will do." Neither of these attempts to avoid using the masculine pronoun is acceptable, the former one being incorrect grammar and the latter being very awkward. Thus, in this book we have used the traditional English grammar form, the masculine, when the gender is not specified. Obviously, any statement concerning a believer or an individual should be understood to apply equally to males and females except where context specifically precludes this reading.

Good syntax tends to use the passive voice as rarely as possible. We have used it more then we would normally use it for one reason. Much of the development in the life of the beleiver is not due to action on his part. Rather, God does the acting to or upon the believer. The fact that a believer can do nothing in and of himself is emphasized by the use of the passive voice.

Finally, when we refer to the inner man or to man's spirit (these are the same), we use the words *he/him* and *it* interchangeably.

TABLE OF CONTENTS

Part V

Part VI

Introduction

Not following the Spirit of God is so serious a sin that Paul addressed the impact in a very sobering manner in Romans 8:13: "For if ye live after the flesh, ye shall die: but if ye through the Spirit do mortify the deeds of the body, ye shall live."

In verse 13 the word *die* is translated better as "being in a state of death." Paul is telling us that, if we as believers follow the flesh, we will be in a state of death. The Greek word is not *thanatos*, which stands for the second death. If we follow the Spirit, we will be in a state of life while in our carnal fleshly body. Paul then tells us in verse 14 that as many as are led by the Spirit of God, they are the sons of God. The Greek word for *son* is *huios*. This word denotes a degree of maturity as opposed to *nepios* in Hebrews 5:13, where the writer describes people as babes. God desires us to grow and to become mature sons and daughters. This is a significant reason for learning how to be led by the Spirit of God. We do this by feeding on His Word, being in His presence, acting in faith on His *rhema* and *logos*, and following His Spirit.

Another significant reason is found in Isaiah 11:1-4, as Isaiah refers to the future Messiah: "And there shall come forth a rod out of the stem of Jesse, and a Branch shall grow out of his roots: And the spirit of the LORD shall rest upon him, the spirit of wisdom and understanding, the spirit of counsel and might, the spirit of knowledge and of the fear of the LORD; And shall make him of quick understanding in the fear of the LORD: and he shall not judge after the sight of his eyes, neither reprove after the hearing of his ears: But with righteousness shall he judge the poor, and reprove with equity for the meek of the earth: and he shall smite the earth with the rod of his mouth, and with the breath of his lips shall he slay the wicked."

This indicates that Jesus did not use knowledge from His natural senses to draw conclusions. He relied on impartation of knowledge into His spirit from the Spirit of God. He always followed the Spirit and did not follow worldly wisdom. We are not greater than our Master; and, therefore, if we are to do greater works than He did (John 14:12), we must also follow the Spirit of God.

Let us be aware of how seriously God expects us to meditate upon His Word. The Lord Jesus rebuked the Sadducees (who did not believe in the resurrection of the dead) for not realizing that God is a God of the living (referring to God's stating that He is the Father of Abraham, Isaac, and Jacob [Exodus 3:15]). This Scripture supports the resurrection from the dead. Reading the Scripture superficially and even meditating on it as deeply as the Sadducees had done did not result in their believing in the resurrection. God speaks very precisely and without agenda so that we in our sin must try to place ourselves in His reference frame in order to understand Scripture. The same applies to the passage in Romans 11 regarding Israel's being the root into which the Church is grafted. Many have run shipwreck on this passage because they look at the externals and try to reinterpret what God means when God is quite clear in the plain wording of the passage that the Church does not ever replace Israel.

Another area for potential shipwreck is found in the gospels where the Lord Jesus talks about His body in terms of the communion. There are vast differences in Christendom on how these passages are understood. Yet with the Holy Spirit teaching us and leading us into all truth, if we will be sensitive to His leading, there is only one interpretation of these passages, when they are all examined carefully and associated with the miracles of the feeding of the two multitudes.

Part I

1
THE PHYSICAL (NATURAL) UNIVERSE AND THE SPIRITUAL UNIVERSE

In this chapter we will examine the interrelationship of the spiritual universe and the physical universe. Understanding this relationship is absolutely necessary for a person to function in both spheres. It will become clear in later chapters why a person must be able to function in both spheres. The Lord Jesus states that, although we are in the world, we should not be of the world (John 17:14-16). A person who is spiritually reborn has to learn to operate his spiritual senses, just as a child must learn to operate natural senses.

The physical universe can be defined readily as that with which we can interact through our natural senses. It will include that with which we interact through engineered extensions of our natural senses. These include such things as seeing atoms with the assistance of an electron microscope or seeing distant galaxies with the aid of a powerful telescope. Our natural senses include sight, smell, touch, hearing, positional sense, and taste.

Most people are familiar with the operation of these natural senses. Some people may lack one or more of them, such as those who are blind or deaf. A similar principle applies in the spiritual realm. Man, as God created him, was able to operate with the use of both spiritual and natural senses. With the fall of man in the Garden of Eden man was left with a vestigial residue of the spiritual senses, and consequently he has very limited ability in the spiritual universe. People who are not "born" into the spiritual world are left with this condition. People who are "born" into the spiritual world by the second birth have the potential to develop their spiritual senses. We will elaborate on this principle throughout this book.

Jesus spoke about the natural and the spiritual universes in John 3:1-8: "There was a man of the Pharisees, named Nicodemus, a ruler of the Jews: The same came to Jesus by night, and said unto him, Rabbi, we know that thou art a teacher come from God: for no man can do these miracles that thou doest, except God be with him. Jesus answered and said unto him, Verily, verily, I say unto thee, Except a man be born again, he cannot see the kingdom of God. Nicodemus saith unto him, How can a man be born when he is old? Can he enter the second time into his mother's womb, and be born? Jesus answered, Verily, verily, I say unto thee, except a man be born of water and *of* the Spirit, he cannot enter into the kingdom of God. That which is born of the flesh is flesh; and that which is born of the Spirit is spirit. Marvel not that I said unto thee, Ye must be born again. The wind bloweth where it listeth, and thou hearest the sound thereof, but canst not tell whence it cometh, and whither it goeth: so is every one that is born of the Spirit."

Jesus is telling Nicodemus that he must be "born again" to be able to enter the kingdom of God and that this new birth is "of the Spirit." We will see that at the time of being "born again" God gives us a new spirit and a new heart. This new spirit replaces a dead (dying) spirit that we inherited at our physical birth. This passage deserves constant meditation for months to penetrate into our souls. It is quite beyond any written statement outside the Scripture to be able to do justice to all that is contained in it. We will examine some of the implications now. In order to do this, we must first study the interrelationship of the spiritual universe and the physical universe.

SUPREMACY OF THE SPIRITUAL UNIVERSE

When we read the early chapters of the book of Genesis coupled with the first chapter of the Gospel of John, we clearly see that the physical universe was created from the spiritual universe. Neither makes an attempt to define the details, but obviously God existed in some structured situation before He created the physical universe. As we read the Scriptures, we see that the physical universe has a set of laws under which it operates; and we see that these physical laws are subject to the operation of a higher set of spiritual laws. A very good example of this is when God made the sun to stand still (Joshua 10:12-14). In some way, using mechanisms into which we do not have insight, God accomplished this. Since this happened in history, the impact is discernible. There are people who have written about this singular event and are able to describe currently examinable evidence for it. Around the world people groups described in their lore a day when the sun/moon stood still (depending on in which hemisphere they were residing).

There are countless other instances of the spiritual universe's governing the operations and the events of the physical universe. That God has prophesied the history of the end of the physical universe and that He has shown how He can influence the events between the beginning and the end to suit His purposes show that the spiritual universe dictates the operations and workings of the natural realm.

One example that is instructive to review is the Israelites' battle with the Syrians described in 2 Kings 6:13-18: "And he said, Go and spy where he *is*, that I may send and fetch him. And it was told him, saying, Behold, *he is* in Dothan. Therefore sent he thither horses, and chariots, and a great host: and they came by night, and compassed the city about. And when the servant of the man of God was risen early, and gone forth, behold, an host compassed the city both with horses and chariots. And his servant said unto him, Alas, my master! how shall we do? And he answered, Fear not: for they that *be* with us *are* more than they that *be* with them. And Elisha prayed, and said, LORD, I pray thee, open his eyes, that he may see. And the LORD opened the eyes of the young man; and he saw: and, behold, the mountain *was* full of horses and chariots of fire round about Elisha. And when they came down to him, Elisha prayed unto the LORD, and said, Smite this people, I pray thee, with blindness. And he smote them with blindness according to the word of Elisha."

In this passage we see that the Lord had unseen forces from the spiritual universe that were going to prevail in the outworking of the battle in the natural realm. In addition, the Lord answered the prayer of Elisha on two occasions. In the first He showed Elisha's servant details in the spiritual universe, and in the second instance He smote the Syrians with blindness. There are literally hundreds of passages that show the underlying order of the natural universe as being subject in all things to the spiritual universe. The ultimate outworking of this is the fact that God the Father has placed all things in subjection to the Lord Jesus Christ, His Son.

We have illustrated now the supremacy of the spiritual over the natural universe. The natural universe was created within the spiritual universe, and the laws under which it operates are subject to higher spiritual laws. We will see how these spiritual universe laws operate as we learn to function in the spiritual realm after a second birth. This is similar to learning how the natural universe laws operate through growing up in the natural universe. When one is reborn into the spiritual world, he must begin a growth process that is akin to that in the physical world. In order to do this, one must stop relying on his natural senses to discern truth. Most readers will find that they cannot imagine how this can be accomplished. An example may help. In treating illness most of us take natural medication and go to a physician who is trained in natural observations of the world. God criticized King Asa of Judah for not asking Him for healing and instead turning to a physician first (2 Chronicles 16:12). A core reason for this book is for people to learn how to transition from living their life in a state in which the natural world dictates their decision making to a state in which they function first and foremost as a spiritual being living in a natural body of flesh. One must first develop a vision for the need to make this transition; then he has to go through a paradigm shift in his beliefs, attitudes, and behavior for it to come about.

The Impact of Spiritual Universe Supremacy on the Individual

Truth is a concept that philosophers may argue about. We will define absolute truth as the revelation of God as He portrays Himself in the Scriptures. This view accepts absolute truth as the person of the Lord Jesus Christ. He stated that He is the Truth. We elaborate on this in Chapter 2. It is an obvious point that a person's success in life is in large part going to depend on his application of knowledge of the truth of how the world and universe operate. Here we should note that "success in life" should not be measured by world standards but by service for God.

We will not join in any debate in this book regarding a defense or apologetic for the Christian faith. There are many good works in this area already. We will assume that the Scriptures are inerrant and that the only consistently correct interpreter of the Scriptures is the Holy Spirit. This underscores the extreme importance of learning how to work with the Holy Spirit as a disciple and then as a bond servant. In order to work with the Holy Spirit, we must learn how to recognize His communications with us; and then we must learn to be obedient to His requirements for our service.

Therefore, an individual responding to this knowledge that the spiritual universe is supreme to the natural universe would need to recognize that he must go through a revolutionary change in his understanding of life and that he must go through a complete metamorphosis of his person in order to live out this knowledge. It is not enough to understand the concept, for this is readily understood. Understanding the concept in the framework of the natural mind serves only to stunt further or to prevent spiritual growth. The spiritual growth that is required comes only through living in the spiritual universe by faith. This book will help a person to begin to grow in his spirit and hence will lead to the ability to develop spiritual senses.

Beginning to Transition from the Natural to the Spiritual Universe

Spiritual growth can occur only after spiritual birth takes place at the time that God gives us a new heart and a new spirit. God does this when we repent of our past sinful life that was lived in rebellion toward Him. In addition we must believe in our heart that Jesus Christ, the Son of God, is our Lord and Savior. We must be willing to subject ourselves to His authority as Lord. We also must confess Him before men as our Lord and Savior. Once we have come into a relationship with Jesus Christ as our Savior, then we will obtain that new spirit in a spiritual birth. After this birth, by subjecting ourselves as bond servants of the Lord Jesus Christ, our spirit will begin to grow; and the sensory modalities will grow along with the spiritual (renewed) mind. The Apostle Paul tells us to put on the new man and to consider the old man as dead. This is critical if we are to experience spiritual growth. Our growth in the spiritual realm will be subject to the completeness with which we fulfill the Apostle's command.

For this putting on of the new man to occur, the individual must renew the mind after he receives a new spirit at the new birth. That is not easy to do, as we will see later. In fact, we will learn that from the moment of new birth an individual should start tearing down all preexisting learned behavior in a systematic and comprehensive manner. This will be a real battle in the thought life and will need to be continued on a daily basis and, indeed, on a thought-by-thought basis. Unfortunately, we have become subject to the world system and to the demonic powers in our life before rebirth. This took place without our being very much aware (although not unaware) of the captive net being placed around us. Unless we undergo a systematic, conscious, and deliberate process of renewing our mind, we can never hope to take even baby steps in terms of renewing our minds. A major current initiative in the armament of the powers of darkness is that of leading us to think that once we have heard a concept in a lecture, seen it in writing, or encountered it in some other format, we assume that we understand it. This leads us to think that we have accomplished it. This is no more than a thought pattern that the world system has built up in our souls through the modern day system of learning in which we attend classes, take tests, regurgitate facts, and get a diploma. We will label this pattern that of intellectualism. Note that this pattern is centered wholly in the mind and not in the spirit. It is our spirit that remains alive after we are dead. This fact of the spirit's being the only part of us that survives death should alone underscore the supremacy of spiritual things to the natural things.

Later, we will contrast natural learning with spiritual learning. Note we saw above that Elisha's servant could not have seen into the spiritual realm had not God granted him a temporary sight. In the same way, God must give spiritual learning, at least until our spiritual senses have developed and we can observe spiritual phenomena. We cannot obtain it deductively. We will see in the chapter on the mind that there is a place for the mind within the soul to deduce the correctness of information coming to it from the heart. This occurs after we learn how to sense what is of the spirit and what is of the flesh. A simple example will help the understanding of this. We read about Elisha's servant having his spiritual vision opened by God. He then understood the issue about the battle in a new way through revelation given to him by God. On the other hand, Elisha already had this spiritual vision and could deduce that the angels of God would be present without necessarily seeing them. We will see later that God gives us revelation into our spirit. He does this both for natural and for spiritually reborn people. The problem is that most of us are so poorly developed in our spirit that we cannot discern what is of God, what is of the world system, and what is of the powers of darkness.

In order for spiritual growth to take place, we must meditate day and night upon God's Word; and we must let our hearts be changed in order to grow in the spirit. Without this we can remain functioning only in the natural. In this case we build little for God's kingdom, and we remain in darkness throughout our days. We are in so much darkness that we do not even see our plight. It is therefore imperative, if we are to understand the difference in the spiritual and the natural universes, that we learn it through the Holy Spirit by revelation. Note that Jesus said that the Holy Spirit would lead us into all truth. We must not rely on learned concepts or on concepts of how to learn from the natural to try to grasp the spiritual. It just does not work this way. We must understand that this is like putting the natural above the spiritual. To emphasize this, let us look at the mathematics of Set Theory. Let us assume that A and B are sets of laws that govern operations of two systems. We will define Set B as a subset of Set A. If we reason from Set B laws, we cannot grasp the whole concept of what Set A is all about. We may see evidence of the impact of some of the Set A laws, since they all will impact Set B laws; but we will not in a complex set be able to grasp much of the interrelationship of the various set A laws and their impact on Set B laws. We may not see anywhere near all of the hierarchy of the Set A laws. We will probably come away seeing very vaguely what Set A is all about, if our only understanding of Set A is from deductions based on Set B laws. This is even more an issue as the relative size of Set A and Set B becomes increasingly large. An example is looking at the issue that we discussed above about the sun being made to stand still. This is not an everyday occurrence. Indeed, we have a lot of occurrences in Scripture to show the impact of the spiritual on the natural universe but not nearly enough for us to understand easily the laws of the spiritual universe without profound meditation and revelation from God. Indeed reading a book like this cannot make one grow in the spirit at all. All this book can do is to give a roadmap and point out the possibilities. By the end of the book we would hope that at least the roadmap will be clearer and that the reader would see that the need to undergo spiritual growth is of paramount importance.

To illustrate the points in the last paragraph, we will look at the following example. We know that the natural laws of physics cannot explain the standing still of the sun. Albert Einstein could not in the theory of relativity explain this. We have to approach the understanding of this event and its reason by turning to God and asking Him to give us insight into why the spiritual laws that He governs allowed it to be a natural event. Depending on our purpose for seeking to understand this, God may be pleased to reveal to us His purposes in it. Obviously, if we are to understand the phenomena of the physical natural universe, we must have a deeper understanding of the spiritual. We will examine how we may grow in our spirit to acquire deeper understanding of the spiritual. It must be obvious that to do this, we have to believe God's Word about the interrelationship between the two; and we must begin to live by it. Intellectual assent and understanding (intellectualism) will never compel God to release spiritual revelation to us. As we grow in the spirit, God will give us more authority and power. He will also release more of His desires through us. We will try to understand this later as we examine some of the spiritual laws that God uses in the spiritual universe.

To get the most out of this book, one must approach it with the understanding that the spiritual universe is supreme to the natural universe and that God's Word is foundational truth. In regard to God's Word being foundational truth, we must believe that this means Jesus Christ is foundational truth. This means that to understand truth, we must first look at all the words and thoughts of Jesus and all that He is. Outside Jesus there is at best a distant glimmer of truth that will be out of focus and only partially correct. We will explore how this fits together with our going to school and learning natural concepts such as reading, writing, and arithmetic. We will attempt to explore this in later parts of this book. Let us accept the premise about the order of the spiritual and the natural, agree to meditate on it and pray about it, expect to receive from God on it, and move into the next area.

Part II

2
WHO IS GOD?

In this chapter we will study about who God is. This study will focus on just a few areas of who God is, and those very briefly. John 21:25 states: "And there are also many other things which Jesus did, the which, if they should be written every one, I suppose that even the world itself could not contain the books that should be written. Amen."

We are going to try to show how far above us He is in all of His workings and in all His thinking. The statement John made (John 21:25) could not possibly apply to any other individual. With all of our technology for recording, one could imagine a baby at birth having everything he did recorded on video and audio. If this were to continue throughout his life even to age 100, the recordings would occupy a relatively small volume of space. Even if these videos were transcribed with exaggerated detail embellishing every act performed by this person and then transcribed onto hard copy, one could not envisage even a large warehouse being filled. God himself tells us in the Scripture that His ways are above our ways and His thoughts are above our thoughts.

God reveals Himself to us primarily in three ways. He reveals Himself to us through the creation, as He tells us in Romans 1 and in Job 38-41. Secondly, He has revealed Himself to us in His written words recorded in the Bible. In that account He gives Himself many names to reveal various facets of His character and personality, and He records His deeds throughout history. Names in Hebrew indicate character. Thus, when God reveals one of His names, He is revealing something about His character. Finally, He revealed Himself more completely and fully in the incarnation of the Lord Jesus Christ who stated that "he who has seen me has seen the Father" (John 14:9). It is important to understand and examine the various ways that we learn about God from these revelations.

GOD'S REVELATION OF HIMSELF THROUGH HIS CREATION

In the creation God's personality and thinking are revealed, at least to the extent that we can observe from the creation. It is of great concern that we do not find very much discussion about this anywhere in our churches, synagogues, or other places of worship. We do not find people in normal daily conversation discussing it. I cannot recall the last time that I heard anyone holding even a casual conversation about it, let alone an in-depth discussion. This is indeed unfortunate, because it was God's first revelation of Himself to man, excluding the very direct relationship that He had with Adam and Eve and their immediate descendants. He revealed Himself to Job, as we read in Job 38-41, primarily by referencing His power in the creation.

Our generation actually learns about the creation in a very distorted way. We are taught observations about it that may have an evolutionary slant, depending on who is teaching. We are taught about the laws by which nature appears to function. We are taught very little, however, if anything, about God's purpose for it. We are not taught to observe and to ponder. God created us in His image as a vital part of His creation. We have to meditate on this to understand it more fully. We learn this fact in our church settings at an early age, but how little do we hear discussions of it and the truths that flow from it! Unless the truths that flow from this become a part of our core, we cannot hope to learn how to relate to God at a personal level in the way that He intended.

A foundational truth is that God made the earth for man to rule over it. In Genesis 1:26-28 we read: "And God said, Let us make man in our image, after our likeness: and let them have dominion over the fish of the sea, and over the fowl of the air, and over the cattle, and over all the earth, and over every creeping thing that creepeth upon the earth. So God created man in his *own* image, in the image of God created he him; male and female created he them. And God blessed them, and God said unto them, Be fruitful, and multiply, and replenish the earth, and subdue it: and have dominion over the fish of the sea, and over the fowl of the air, and over every living thing that moveth upon the earth." We learn in later passages that God created man to rule with Him in future ages (Revelation 5:10).

A second foundational truth is that God made man in His image (Genesis 1:26). We will need to think about the implications of this second truth. There are many implications from God's creating us in His image.

The way our minds work, the way our emotions operate, and the ways that we purpose and will to accomplish goals are all a distillation of His own personality. If we look around us, we may have trouble seeing that, if we do not factor in the massive casualties that mankind has suffered at the hands of the devil and his princes. Nonetheless, one can still see the "ruins of the castle through the trees," so to speak, and gain some inkling of how man would have functioned in a setting in which he had not fallen from his original state.

There is a massive tension in our understanding of man's individual responsibility for his own action before God and how much of man's actions are preordained by the way God set up the operation of the universe. Not to have grappled extensively and not to have meditated upon it appropriately are to have missed entirely the issues involved. One cannot relate to God properly on a personal level without settling this in his own mind. This is obvious since, if one believes that he has no influence over his own actions, he will relate to God in exactly the same manner as an unrepentant criminal will relate to his victim. On the other hand, if one believes that he has responsibility to God for all of his actions, then he will function as if he has missed the efficacy of Christ's atonement. He will always be working for his salvation or sanctification instead of following his spirit. He will have no rest. We must come to the point of knowing that God chose this particular history and that He was able to give us free will as well. God did not create robots, but He wants us of our own free will to choose His way. The fact that God could have chosen another history for the creation is demonstrated by Matthew 11:23.

God's mandate to rule over the earth was the original charter that man was given. After man fell into sin, the right to rule over the earth became Satan's. In Matthew 4:8-9 we read: "Again, the devil taketh him up into an exceeding high mountain, and sheweth him all the kingdoms of the world, and the glory of them; and saith unto him, All these things will I give thee, if thou wilt fall down and worship me." Jesus' response to this shows that He acknowledged Satan's dominion as rightfully his to give.

We, therefore, have to try to understand the creation in light of this change of rule in terms of God's revelation to us; yet also it is clear from Scripture that God knew in advance man would fall into sin and made allowance for it in that the "Lamb was slain before the foundation of the world" (Revelation 13:8).

The fact that God knows history in advance tells us much about His intellect in comparison with ours. We must try to understand history from God's perspective by trying to identify with His goals. We may do this very imperfectly; but if we do not attempt this, we will be woefully egocentric in our understanding of events that occur in our daily lives. We need, therefore, to ponder God's genius.

God numbers the hairs on our heads. This is for every one of the billions of people who have ever lived and who will ever live. He also numbers the stars. He can do such things as when he told Abraham that his descendants would be like the number of grains of sand (Genesis 22:17). No sparrow falls to the ground without God's knowledge (Matthew 10:29). God works all things for good to those who are the called (Romans 8:28). This is not just one thing or a few things but every single event in every microsecond of His children's lives. This means that God is processing an enormous amount of information at enormous speeds to keep everything in perspective so that He can make sure that His promises are kept. All of the above facts reveal a God who is integrally involved in the events of our lives and who is a genius.

We should then consider that God is the creator of the entire universe and is able to keep it running by the words of His mouth (Hebrews 1:3) When we think about the enormous power involved in the release of energy from just one star, we understand that this power far exceeds even the most devastating nuclear weapon that man has devised. God can stop the sun and suspend the natural laws that He established just by His word. The far reaches of space and the enormous gravitational forces that operate throughout the universe are all His handiwork.

We must become more personally involved with the wonderful emotions that He has made as a part of us so that we may enjoy His works. We can ponder the beauty of a lonely sunset, the sweeping vistas of mountain ranges, and the intricacy of a snowflake. We must realize that God knows the details and the placement of every blade of grass throughout our whole earth. As we ponder His greatness, we will begin to get a better perspective of our own place in this universe. We must begin to break down the enormous anthrocentricity that has been fostered in us by the powers of darkness. We are not even aware of the work of these powers, so much have we as a people chosen to shut out the light that is around us. As we grope in darkness, unfortunately we are deluded into thinking we have great light, because our generations have been able to determine to a small degree of how God has set up some of the operating natural laws.

All of our genetic knowledge, all of our nuclear knowledge, all of our metallurgical knowledge, our space age technology, and all other learned facts do not even begin to approach the higher planes of spiritual knowledge that have laws which govern all of the physical universe. Without understanding spiritual laws, we cannot understand the physical laws with all of their anomalies except approximating (as Isaac Newton did prior to Albert Einstein, who in his turn has only approximated future understanding). We must bow before revelation that we have in the natural universe of this great and mighty, awe-inspiring God. If we do not try to meditate deeply upon such facts, we throw away an incredibly large part of revelation knowledge. As we meditate more about these things, God in turn reveals more of Himself to us.

Having stated these things and hopefully having internalized them by prolonged meditation, let us turn to examine the things that God has revealed to us about why He chose to do things the way that He did. God clearly explains that we are to rule and reign with Him in the ages to come (Revelation 5:10). The concept of individual freedom to choose becomes a guiding fundamental. If God had chosen to create people without the ability to choose, then they would not have been made in His image. They would have been less than He desired. In deciding to create individuals with choice, He knew in advance that not all of the individuals would choose to relate to Him in the way that He wished.

How often we hear someone make a statement that a "good god would not allow his children to suffer permanently in the hell described in the Scriptures." There are many variations on this theme. The position that this statement carries is one of trying to abdicate the responsibility to understand what God has done and merely to react to this. God clearly tells us that He is not willing for any to perish (2 Peter 3:9). He also tells us that He takes no pleasure in the death of the wicked (Ezekiel 18:23). However, once He determined to set up the universe in the way that He did, there was no turning back. He must keep His word. He is unable not to keep His word, because truth is a fundamental core attribute of His person (John 14:6). He has chosen to create us in a way that we can understand what He tells us and in such a way that we can understand the expectations that He has for us. We are completely responsible for all of our own actions in this life. God tells us that at the end of this age all of the things whispered in the ear and all of the things done in darkness will be shouted from the rooftops and will be made light (Luke 12:3). What God tells us is always absolutely true. This fact holds for creation (when there were no witnesses outside the Godhead), for unseen acts and thoughts in this life, and for events that will occur in the future. However, He does not always tell us everything (Deuteronomy 29:29). There are some things so deep that we cannot understand all the implications in this life. There are some things that are hard to understand. Examples of this are the times He mentions such things as having created some vessels as vessels of wrath (Romans 9:22), such concepts as His hardening Pharaoh's heart (Exodus 7:13), or statements such as His having hated Esau and loved Jacob (Romans 9:13). Concerning the secret things, God does have some mysteries. There were certain mysteries, for example, that were not revealed to the people in the Old Testament times; but they were revealed under the New Covenant (Colossians 1:26). God also states that He tells His prophets what He will do (Amos 3:7). Nevertheless, there are still matters that He does not choose to share with man.

We must see that our lifespan in this world is for training for a future age. This must motivate our behavior and expectations in this age. God tells His children to "see Him (His hand) in **all** that happens to us." This means that we must be assessing constantly from moment to moment what God's purpose for us is. He also tells us in all circumstances to be content, for this is His will for us (Philippians 4:11). That means that we must see Him and be consciously aware of His controlling millions of variables for millions of people constantly throughout the lives of these people. The purpose is to conform us to the image of Christ (Romans 8:29-30) and to fit us to rule and to reign in future ages (Revelation 5:10). Thus, we need to understand our environment; we need to understand people; we need to understand spiritual powers; and we need to understand God. God expects us to understand Him. All of this is a tall order, and we will discuss in later chapters how we can accomplish it. It cannot be accomplished by a passive mind. We need to have an active mind that wrestles with continually changing circumstances and which cooperates with God to gain revelation knowledge about these issues. We can never grasp this without God's revealing it to us in the various circumstances. For example, we could ask what God's purpose for our aches and pains is. We must understand this issue, if we are to cooperate with God in our circumstances. We should similarly ponder the death of a loved one, a crushing loss of a home due to a flood, the loss of a job, the failure to keep a marriage intact, the breakdown of an automobile at an inconvenient time, and many other issues. It is only by gaining a strong understanding of how God uses the physical universe to teach us, to get our attention, to conform us to Christ's image, and to fit us for future ages that we will be partners with Him in the process.

GOD'S REVELATION OF HIMSELF THROUGH HIS WORD

God has left us a legacy in the Bible that reveals Himself to us in a very systematic manner. Let us consider how we can use the Bible to learn about God. It is really quite similar to learning about anyone in history whom we do not know. If a historian wishes to understand the past, then he must learn about the details that are recorded and try to read any writings that the individual has left. The historian will want to understand the motivations of the individual. These can be inferred from known actions in various circumstances. Individuals such as Hannibal, Alexander, Dr. Johnson, various rulers, and past presidents have left a certain trace in history that can be examined for understanding.

In a similar manner God has given us a very detailed account of His actions, and He has given us understanding of His motivations in various circumstances. He has revealed a huge amount of what He is like and of His expectations for us in the written Word. Like any other historical account we must read it and meditate upon it to understand God. This works as it does with other persons in history, when we read God's Word from this perspective. Hannibal, *e.g.,* did not sit down and leave us written documents about himself in order for us to understand him. We must look at what others said about him, and we must get the context of the time period in which he lived in order to understand him. It is the same with God. Many people throughout history have written about Him from their knowledge of Him. People like Josephus (a Jewish historian) gave their own observations. His Spirit inspired others, such as the writers of the Scriptures, to write what they did. There are some parallels with Hannibal. Hannibal had a spirit that inspired others to write about him. That spirit influences those interpreting him even to this day, if they try to observe his spirit through his actions and words. This should not surprise us, for we have been created in God's image; and, therefore, the spirits of past persons still can speak through their recorded words and actions. We should note, however, that people who have written about Hannibal are fallible; thus, we must interpret what we read with this in mind. In studying the Scriptures, we should be aware that God's Spirit inspired the writers to use their own words but that the end result is that there is no error in the original manuscripts. Thus, the truth of the document stands in contrast to all other writings, even those about God, and to all other historical writings.

In addition, the Holy Spirit interprets God's Word when one is reborn. This is akin to having the author communicating directly to us and telling us what the various written words are meant to convey. It is foundational to understanding God and to knowing God that we learn, keep before our mind constantly, and continually meditate on God's word. God tells us that His Word is living and active in Hebrews 4:12. This is again vastly different to reading an historical account of a person such as Julius Caesar. Since God's Word is living and active and all of it is profitable for our instruction (2 Tim 3:16), we must seek to interact with it with an active mind just as we would if someone were to be conversing with us in a room. We must always seek to determine what it is telling us about ourselves and about our circumstances. We should never read God's Word passively, since it would be like being present in a room with someone who is talking to us and our ignoring him. This would be extremely rude, to say the least.

Some people recommend a "Quiet Time," since the discipline of setting aside a time to spend with God is helpful. However, this can become quite a point of fleshly pride in keeping such a time, and the lack of spontaneity may become a hindrance to active interaction with God's Word. It is more important to submit to God the timing of formal prayer and to learn to be in constant prayer with Him (we will discuss how this works later in the book).

We must interact with God's Word and seek to understand the hierarchy of it. God is quite familiar with the intellectual assent of this age. We read facts, recall them, and then conclude that we have understood them. This does not really work in any area and especially not in the Scriptures. This intellectual assent is a reaction to a "Spirit of Knowledge" that is very active in this age. People are driven to react to this spirit in one of two ways: a) building up a fleshly pride or b) being driven by a fear of lacking knowledge. A very good example of this lack of depth of understanding is revealed when one asks a professing Christian what it means to be led by God's Spirit *per* Romans 8:14. I have yet to find anyone who can answer more than summarily; usually the answer is in terms of repeating of the question, and sometimes the answer is totally wrong. When one asks how this process tales place, one is usually met with some spluttering and finally an admission of not knowing. This is awkward, since God tells us in the passage in Romans 8 that those who are led by His Spirit are mature (study of the Greek word for *sons*). Obviously one cannot be led by God's Spirit in the manner promoted in this passage, if one cannot explain how it takes place. We will discuss in this book how this process takes place. If it takes a large amount of work that involves intensive study and intensive discussion with the Holy Spirit to come to an understanding of just one short passage, then one can see that reading God's Word without meditating on it (intensively studying it and having long discussions with the Holy Spirit on it) is not going to build us up in the understanding of God's Word. It is not a task for the mentally lazy. God is not impressed by anything short of diligent work. We must not forget that God is good to reveal His truth as we grapple with His Word. We cannot understand in any but the most superficial manner any of His Word without discussing it with Him.

I have been pleased to observe in people that I have treated that some people who are intellectually less gifted than others have a very deep understanding of God's Word. That tells me that God meets us at our point of need. Those who are more gifted intellectually are more hampered in their understanding of God's Word frequently than those less gifted, since they tend to try to master it alone; of course, without the discussion with God this will not work. We must also note that, compared with God's intellectual capacity, there is very little difference across the human IQ spread from the lowest to the highest scorers. God states in His Word that the wise (after the wisdom of the flesh, not natural ability; this speaks of those who have a lot of learning in the ways of the world) will find it very difficult to inherit His Kingdom (1 Corinthians 1:26-27). If you are a person with some degree of worldly wisdom and are more intellectually gifted than the average person, you may wish to ponder this statement over a period of several weeks before the Holy Spirit until you understand the implications for you and how you must get around the hindrances. There is enough material in this one verse to write several books. Do not fall for a form of intellectual assent. This intellectual assent, so rampant in this age, will not give you any understanding of what God is telling you. Ask a series of questions of yourself about this verse; and as you meditate before God on these questions, you will begin to see how this verse ties into your whole understanding of who you are, how you work, and how God deals with you.

God knows that true knowledge comes about only by revelation from Him. As we read and interact with His written Word, He will start to explain it to us. He will help us to understand how the different parts fit together. He will help us to understand ourselves in the light of it. He has chosen to hide much in His Word by the manner in which it is written. He has made it such that we must bring together a little from here and a little from there in order to get a comprehensive grasp of His Word. Isaiah

28:10 instructs us to learn "line upon line and precept upon precept." It is only as we really wrestle with the ideas that we begin to understand and internalize them through use whereby they become a part of our heart.

In order to understand completely, we must use God's Word. This is how we develop faith. Imagine a pilot's learning how to fly an airplane from just reading and discussion. The first time he flies, he starts to learn much more about how flying really works. He may read about how to correct for wind in a general way; but each aircraft is different, each flight is different, and the aircraft varies from flight to flight in mild ways in its performance characteristics due to factors such as fuel weight, air pressure, engine tuning, and a hundred other variables. Only as he actually spends time flying does he begin to master the craft. The Lord Jesus promised that the Holy Spirit would be our teacher and that He would guide us into all truth (John 16:13). When we are guided into truth, we will begin to understand how the spiritual universe operates. We address how important faith in God's Word is in a later chapter.

It is only as one practices using God's Word in faith that he can begin to understand it in any depth, and this understanding continues to deepen with use. As we walk in deeper understanding, we start to build up a new structure within us that impacts our inner being. We will see more of this as we practice walking before God in a manner that depends on the truth of His Word.

We cannot choose to depend on just parts of His Word for our spiritual maturation; this will not work. It is akin to trying to survive physically without the intake of all of the necessary vitamins and minerals. If we have an unbalanced diet, we would stop growing as children; and we would lose the ability to repair our tissues as an adult. In any case disease would quickly appear. It is the same with our spiritual maturation. We cannot have a partial walk with God. We might take some degree of pride that we are trying to do what God wants. It does not work. Our growth in spiritual maturity is not going to come about through intellectual assent but only as we yield to God and let Him teach us directly as we make daily decisions in faith. We will find that He knows how to lead us in order for us to grow in the areas in which we are deficient. To allow God to teach us, we must know how to hear His voice. This involves faith. One cannot interact with God without having faith that he can talk to Him and hear back from Him. This interaction, in turn, removes barriers to the interaction; and then one can build up understanding and knowledge of how God speaks to us and of how God works with us to bring us to spiritual maturity.

God speaks in metaphor and in example continually in order for us to understand. We see how the tabernacle showed the future salvation through Jesus in the structure of it. As just one example, God had the Israelites camp in certain groups that, when viewed from the air, formed a cross. All of the facets of the tabernacle, in fact, are types of Jesus and His salvation for us. We mention this to show that a quick reading of the setting up of the tabernacle would not show us what God wants to reveal about His plan and about His Son. This again underlies the need for very detailed knowledge of God's Word. We must approach the study of His Word and communication with Him as the most important thing in our lives.

All of the above discussion is to show how the Bible is essential for us to see the revelation of God. There are many ways to absorb this revelation. One is through following the principles given above for seeing His character revealed while we are studying or reading the Bible. There are some other, more integrated, ways. A study of the tabernacle mentioned above would be one example of the more integrated way. As mentioned earlier in this chapter, God revealed facets of His character in His word through the use of names. It would take many volumes to study all the names of God. It will suffice to give a brief sketch of two groups of names. An in-depth study of this group of names can be found in our book *The YHWH-Compound Names of God: A Revelation of God's Character and of His Plan for the Ages.*

There are seven primary YHWH-compound names of God. These are names in which YHWH is followed by another name of God. There are many places in the Bible in which YHWH is used and a descriptive word follows, but in the strictest sense there are only seven compound names. In Hebrew thought numbers have meaning. Seven is the number of completion. Thus, this study gives a complete picture of God's character. They also show, if studied in the order they are introduced in Scripture, the plan of God for the ages.

YHWH is first used in Genesis 2:4. It is first used when God is showing a personal interaction with man (*i.e.*, at creation). Later, it is used primarily when God is in a covenant relationship with man. Many people are familiar with God's revealing of this name to Moses at the time of the burning bush experience. Many are also familiar with the usual translation of Exodus 3:14: "And God said unto Moses, I AM THAT I AM: and he said, Thus shalt thou say unto the children of Israel, I AM hath sent me unto you." This is not a perfect translation, but it is attempting to show what is behind God's name.

Hebrew does not have tense in the same sense that the Indo-European languages do. Time is usually shown by a relation with other words. The word used here is the basic word for pure existence. Thus, God is saying that He is outside of time and that He is existence. It is a very hard concept for us to grasp, with our reliance on time and boundaries. Nevertheless, the idea with the compound names is that God's essence is the second word and that it is always true, outside of any time considerations. Thus, when we look at the second one, YHWH Rapha, we see that God is saying that He is the God who heals. His character is such that he ***always*** heals. This idea in itself refutes the argument sometimes heard in evangelical circles that God has somehow quit healing in our age.

The seven YHWH (Jehovah)-compound names of God, their meanings, and the location of each one's first use in Scripture follow:

1. (Gen.22:13-14) Jehovah Jireh—the God Who sees (the sacrifice) or Who provides—more specifically the God who provides an atonement for sin, thus making the way for man to have a relationship with Him

2. (Exodus 15:26) Jehovah Rapha—the God Who heals

3. (Exodus 17:8-15) Jehovah Nissi—the God Who is our banner

4. (Judges 6:24) Jehovah Shalom—the God Who is our peace (Note that peace comes only after we establish a relationship with Him.)

5. (1 Samuel 1:3) Jehovah Sabaoth—the Lord of Hosts, or the God Who fights for us (He fights the battles for us that we face in life.)

6. (Jeremiah 23:6) Jehovah Tsidkenu—the God Who is our righteousness

7. (Ezekiel 48:35) Jehovah Shammah—the God Who is present (Eternally, we will live with Him.)

Until we master the meaning of these names and their reflection upon the character of God, we have not even begun to know God. Although this is just an outline of this study, it should serve to show how far we are from the depth of knowing God and understanding His character. These are God's covenant names in the Old Testament. The New Covenant does what it frequently does and that is to summarize the past into the new. The new revelation of God's name is found in Matthew 28:19: "baptizing them in the name of the Father, and of the Son, and of the Holy Ghost." This new name is the completed revelation of God's name in history.

GOD DESIRES A CLOSE INTERACTION WITH US

Psalm 81:8–14 speaks of the intensity of God's desire for communication with us. He is very personal with His people and expects us to learn how to distinguish His voice from other voices coming into our mind. We will learn much about this in the last two sections of this book. It is critical for the increasing of our faith in God that we are able to talk reliably to and fro with Him. Maturation in our spirit cannot occur without this.

GOD'S SELF REVELATION THROUGH THE LORD JESUS CHRIST

Jesus stated that "he who has seen me has seen the Father" (John 14:9). Jesus' behavior, motivation, and personality portrayed the Father. We can study the Scriptures to see what made the Lord Jesus the person that He is. We can also let the Holy Spirit teach us about the Lord Jesus as we pray and wait for His words to us. We can learn about God from how He interacts with us as we become more trusting of Him and as we draw closer to Him. We must focus on learning how to interact with Jesus. It is completely unacceptable to learn about Jesus and never learn how to have a direct relationship with Him in which to and fro communication on a daily basis is the norm.

It is helpful to meditate upon the humanity of Jesus. I was surprised when I visited the Holy Land to see how rugged the cliffs at Nazareth are. It was here that the crowd tried to throw Him over the cliff. I was impressed by the thought of how physically fit Jesus and the disciples were to be able to walk all over the land. It will help us considerably to focus on the physical aspects of His life while growing. It will help us to appreciate how difficult it must have been not to sin.

It is also helpful to study and meditate upon the fact that Jesus was God incarnate, the only begotten Son of the living God. We really have to study both of these aspects of Jesus to learn about Him and to get to know Him on a personal, interactive basis. Praying is talking with God. Many people pray to God and do not know how to hear His voice in return. We have to focus on preparing ourselves to hear God's voice. We shall go into how to do this in much detail in later chapters, particularly in chapter 20. First we must cleanse iniquity from our hearts. If we repent of those sins of which God convicts us, then He will cleanse us from all unrighteousness (1 John 1:9). We will learn later that we must work to get our consciences into shape, and then we will be in better shape to work actively with God in getting to know Him personally. There are many sins and sinful states of which God wants us to rid ourselves (Chapter 20) in order to communicate with Him better. The problem for us when we have sin patterns (or regard iniquity) is that the devil has a right to accuse us, and there is a basis for his accusations. Unfortunately, his voice tends to drown out other voices; and it makes it hard to hear what God is saying to us when we have evil spirits accusing us and literally screaming and shouting at our spirit in the spiritual realm (Ephesians 2:6).

Some of the issues that need to be cleared in order to communicate with God are:

1. Lack of faith in the communication process (God is not pleased by a lack of faith [Romans 14:22 and Hebrews 10:38])
2. Holding anything against a brother (Matthew 5:22-24)
3. Regarding iniquity (Psalm 66:18) in one's heart—pride, lust of the flesh, and lust of the eyes (1 John 2:16)
4. Being double minded (James 1:6-8)
5. Not loving one's spouse (Ephesians 5:33)

There are others that are listed in Chapter 20.

CONCLUSION

These thoughts are a small part of what we need to contemplate in order to know the "Majesty on high." Meditate daily on His majesty—high and lifted up, filling the temple—far greater and richer than any earthly king or president. At the same time He is tenderly approachable and desirous of an intimate relationship with the people that He created. As we study His Word and talk with Him, we gradually have those barriers in our heart, the high places and evil imaginations, broken down. The false images that we have worshipped in our past days become dim and distant. Gradually, a new and true image forms within us that we see with the eyes of our spirit. Paul talks about this new image in Galatians 4:19: "My little children, of whom I travail in birth again until Christ be formed in you." The old things have gone; and all things become new again, as the abiding presence of the Lord Jesus is formed within our spirit. Note that this has to be formed by effort. It is only after considerable war against the flesh and evil spirits that the true image of the Lord Jesus will be formed in us so that, when in the spirit, we are always aware of His presence. We will focus on this later in the last two sections of the book and in the chapters on the mind and the heart.

3
WHO IS MAN?

MAN

What is man that thou art mindful of him (Psalm 8:4)? To understand ourselves, we must come to an understanding of what God's understanding of us is. There is no truth in anything that is not in Christ Jesus. Therefore, to understand ourselves, we must learn from God about ourselves in specific detail and about mankind in general.

We can learn about mankind and ourselves from the same three sources about God that we used in Chapter 2. These are:

1. The creation
2. God's written Word
3. The Lord Jesus Christ

In order to become spiritually healthy, we must align our self concept to be in agreement with God's view of us. God's view is truth, and anything short of this is at best partial truth. In this chapter we will try to see how we must be changed in order to understand more fully how God sees us. We are not going to follow through these three sources separately but will integrate them as we proceed

THE CREATION

We read in Genesis of God's intention to let mankind oversee the creation. We see how God partnered with Adam to help him to name the animals. God brought the work to Adam and waited to see what he would do. We note that God designed the creation for man to manage. We read in Genesis 1:26-28: "And God said, Let us make man in our image, after our likeness: and let them have dominion over the fish of the sea, and over the fowl of the air, and over the cattle, and over all the earth, and over every creeping thing that creepeth upon the earth. So God created man in his *own* image, in the image of God created he him; male and female created he them. And God blessed them, and God said unto them,

Be fruitful, and multiply, and replenish the earth, and subdue it: and have dominion over the fish of the sea, and over the fowl of the air, and over every living thing that moveth upon the earth." The task was complex enough for this to be a challenge. It would cause growth in abilities, in that man had to replenish the earth and subdue it. In Genesis 2:5 we read: "And every plant of the field before it was in the earth, and every herb of the field before it grew: for the LORD God had not caused it to rain upon the earth, and *there was* not a man to till the ground." God had work created for man before He created man. Man and his work are central in the creation. In Genesis 2:15-17 we read: "And the LORD God took the man, and put him into the garden of Eden to dress it and to keep it. And the LORD God commanded the man, saying, Of every tree of the garden thou mayest freely eat: But of the tree of the knowledge of good and evil, thou shalt not eat of it: for in the day that thou eatest thereof thou shalt surely die."

We see that God in the creation placed man in a small garden to dress it and keep it. This presumably was the beginning place of learning how to replenish and subdue the whole earth.

In Genesis 2:18-20 we read: "And the LORD God said, *It is* not good that the man should be alone; I will make him an help meet for him. And out of the ground the LORD God formed every beast of the field, and every fowl of the air; and brought *them* unto Adam to see what he would call them: and whatsoever Adam called every living creature, that *was* the name thereof. And Adam gave names to all cattle, and to the fowl of the air, and to every beast of the field; but for Adam there was not found an help meet for him." The translation of *help meet* (literally *help fit*) reveals that the term is used to mean an individual with abilities that are complementary to the other person's. The two are needed for either to succeed.

In this account in Genesis we see God working with Adam in the creation. Much later Paul tells us that before the foundation of the world God chose each person for a unique work (Ephesians 2:10). Therefore, the wording in Genesis about Adam's not finding a fit help is not describing an afterthought of God.

Let us digress at this point to ponder why God chose this manner of conveying the information about his decision to create Eve. We realize that it was Moses who wrote the book of Genesis. Moses would have had to use revelation from God together with tradition passed down through Noah and his family. We accept, as a basic assumption, that the Holy Scripture was divinely inspired by God and that it is without error. Therefore, we must conclude that God's purpose is to show that He could not create the kind of helper that He wanted for Adam out of the dust of the ground. Instead, God had to create this helper from a part of Adam in order for it to be right. Adam was now missing a part of his flesh because of this procedure; for it to be made whole, it had to be made back into one flesh through a marriage union that would make Adam whole again. Without marriage to the right person God cannot use a person in the work that He intended, since that union will be forever wrong. Eve had to be a perfect complement for Adam. All that she had was lacking in Adam; and similarly, all that he had retained was lacking in Eve (Genesis 2:25: Therefore shall a man leave his father and his mother, and shall cleave unto his wife: and they shall be one flesh). We must realize that it was in the context of helping Adam in the work that God had set before him that the helper was required. Therefore, we can conclude that it was the purpose of God to set before Adam and Eve tasks that they would complete only as they were joined in a union to become one flesh. There are, however, certain people that God chooses to set aside for Himself whom He does not intend to marry (1 Corinthians 7).

Why did He choose to do it this way in the creation? That becomes the next issue to ponder. Certainly He could have chosen a different way of creating man, but we must recall the very significant fact that He made man in His image. Therefore, the very heart of this way of creating Adam and Eve is answered in the likeness of this to the image of God. God is one God and yet is comprised of three distinct persons—The Father, The Son, and The Holy Spirit. The closeness and attributes of these three persons in God are mirrored in ways that we poorly understand in the making of Adam and Eve in His image.

We also note that the spirit breathed into Adam was carried to Eve without any need for God to breathe directly into Eve's nostrils.

Therefore, we can conclude that, once God gave spirit to mankind, He did not need to repeat the process. This shows us that spirit is carried in the cells of the body, including the germ cells, and that spirit is genetically transmitted along with fleshly features. This should not surprise us because we can observe that all of the cells of an individual are capable of life independently at least for a period of time; that is because they are imbued with life energy that God gave to them. As an aside, recent genetic research confirms that there were two ancestors common to mankind. Research shows that all of genetic differences aside, there is evidence to support just one man's and one woman's being present initially. All mankind descended from this couple, confirming what many have accepted in faith from the beginning.

SIN ENTERS

After God created man with the ability to choose his ways freely, Adam and Eve directly disobeyed Him in the matter of the one thing that He had told them not to do. God had commanded Adam and Eve not to eat of the fruit of the tree of knowledge. They did this after the devil tempted them. God had warned them not to do this for their own well being. For some reason the Lord had an agreement with the devil; and once he had enticed Adam and Eve to disobey God (sin) through not trusting him in faith, then the devil was now allowed to rule the earth in this age.

God anticipated before the foundation of the earth that mankind would fall into sin and that the devil would have dominion over the earth. God had already provided a means for saving mankind from the dominion of the devil. Adam and Eve, with one act of disobedience, caused all of their descendants to inherit sin genetically. Satan, according to some covenant to which we are not given the details, has dominion over men who choose to remain in a state of sin. We may have questions about why God did this, but we do not have sufficient material to answer all of them. It is not difficult to see that it was God's decision to create mankind with the ability to make decisions independent of Him that allowed for the possibility that not all would follow His instructions. If all had followed His instructions, the likelihood is that there really was no free choice.

God made provision for this dilemma by creating a pathway by which mankind could negate the sin into which it entered and perpetuated. In this pathway God reveals the truth that He does not want any to perish as they must, in that the penalty for Adam and Eve's action was eternal death. Since mankind has freedom to choose, not all will avail themselves of the remedy provided by God. If they all did, this would again indicate that we are not free to choose.

Why did God knowingly create some who would suffer eternal torment? Eternal torment is the penalty for not accepting God's remedy for the sin issue. The stakes have to be high; or, again, there is really no choice. One can surmise that God felt that it suited His purpose to have creatures who were made in His image and who could therefore learn to become loving children as a free choice. Constraining man to follow a path because he is made to by pressure or by design is not God's nature (Matthew 26:53); therefore, since we are made in His image, we cannot be different. Once the decision was made to create a people who could relate to God in a manner that would be like a family, full of love for each other and full of joy, then the rest must follow; or these people are no more than automatons.

Now we turn to see how God sees us. We must know how He sees us, or we cannot see ourselves clearly. We see God creating us in His image with all of His personality, emotions, reasons, decision-making capacity, and intellect—but in a limited version. God was interested in a relationship that would be two-way. He enjoyed working in the garden with Adam, forming the animals and bringing them to Adam to name. Unfortunately, this was soon lost. Sin entered into mankind, and God judged the sin worthy of death. God's Word makes it clear that He is not pleased to see any man die in sin and that He wills that all would be saved from His judgment with its penalty of spiritual death with perpetual torment. However, not all will accept the only provision that He made for avoiding this penalty.

If one reads about the horror of hell in the Scripture, it is difficult to understand why anyone would choose to go there. The problem is that people do it incrementally, and gradually they lose the ability to change their mind. God has revealed to all men that they have a choice; and at some point each individual has chosen to remain in sin and therefore earns his judgment (Romans 1). God tells us that He is impartial, that we have all sinned, and that all are worthy of spiritual death. (We will discuss what spiritual death means later in the book. It obviously does not mean either the end of suffering or the end of conscious awareness.) It is very important to let this concept of eternal suffering and the concept of sin soak into our fiber so that we feel it. It has to be meditated on, acted on, and believed at the very core of our being.

Sin at its root is disobedience to God. It results in a broken trust and a broken fellowship. It introduces something to our being that God is not. It makes us different to the way that He created us in that we are no longer completely in His image. (In Genesis 5:3 we see that after the Fall Adam's children were now born in his [Adam's] image—not in God's image.) Something has been added. It is clear that God abhors sin. He cannot tolerate it. It is against His very nature. It is like anti-matter is to matter. God's nature and the sin nature are diametrically opposites. In God there is love, peace, and joy. In the sin nature there is hate, turmoil, and fear. God displays His nature through a description of Himself in the creation, in His word, and in the Lord Jesus Christ. We have a description of the devil at the antipodal pole. Everything that God is, the devil is not and vice versa. Men are somewhere in between. When we have any sin in us, God looks at us just the same if we have one sin or if we have 10,000 sins (Matthew 5:48). Both situations bring the same judgment because of God's standard for us to be perfect. To understand then how God looks at us, we must realize that God's emotions are millions of times more intense than ours. His strength and His determination are millions of times greater than ours. He hates sin with an indescribable passion. We must ponder and meditate about sin and about ourselves to the point that to sin induces in us an enormous reaction of self-hate and loathing. We must hate all of our sin patterns with an enormous passion. Unless we do, we cannot see our situation with any degree of accuracy. It will also completely undergird our determination to walk after the Spirit. If we try to save ourselves from addressing the full horror that we are in our unclean hearts, then we can never walk completely after the Spirit; nor can we even begin to purpose to do so. We must bring ourselves to the point of shuddering with the emotion of hate toward our sins. We have to come to this enormous emotional acceptance of how tainted we are before we can even approach truth about the sin issue. It is only as we approach this that we can see and relate to truth, for this is how God views sin. If we are to become like Him, our thoughts and emotions must line up with His.

With a full understanding of this at a core level, how then can we stand before God? When we see ourselves as God sees us in our state of sin and when we realize the very real and fearful punishment that is ours, there is only one way out. It will be to reach toward the salvation provided by the death of the Lord Jesus on the cross. We will reach for this salvation with true tenacity only when we address the sin issue. God is good to give us salvation when we repent of our sinful state, but this is not enough for walking after the Spirit. We must keep our initial repentant state perpetually, as we continue in this life. To do this, we must learn by real wrestling with the sin issue how God views our continued sin after salvation. It is only as we actually grasp this that we are freed of the hold of sin and can enter into the rest God describes in Hebrews 4. It is impossible to "fake" this rest before those with spiritual discernment. They will perceive a different smell in the spiritual olfactory senses, due to having put in the necessary hard wrestling to see sin from God's viewpoint (which means walking in truth). (Remember that proper sacrifice is a sweet odor to God; and, as we live in the spirit rather than the flesh, we are conformed again to His image and, therefore, will be able to detect spiritual odors.) We can walk in God's Spirit only as we walk in truth. Partial truth will not get us there. We will learn later that it is only by submitting to God and accepting His power that we can come to the correct viewpoint in our spirit about experiencing this hate for our own sin.

We will discuss it later, but getting these spiritual truths into the fiber of our own spirit takes a very great amount of energy. It is not going to be something that one can gain without real spiritual work and accepting the power of God. This involves energy, perseverance, commitment, and faith. It will not come to those who are lazy and who are not trying to seek the Lord in all things, since this truth has to be revealed progressively to one's spirit by the Lord Himself.

The next issue is to understand what happens to one who sees himself in such a wretched state. The salvation that God offers also gives the answer to this. By faith we accept the Lord Jesus as our Savior. We then accept the new state that God sees for us. We also have to see how our accepting God's plan to save us from our sins changes His view of us. As soon as we accept the Lord Jesus' death as a substitute for ours, we begin to see repairing of the damage done by the original sin of Adam and Eve. After the second birth we now have a trust relationship with God. We trust Him; and He can trust Jesus to keep us (John 17), once we have made the commitment to Him. We also have to see how great is the salvation that faith in the Lord Jesus provides us. God sees that we have accepted Him as our Lord and Savior. He then no longer keeps an account of our sins and welcomes us as members of His family and as siblings of the Lord Jesus. We become seated with God in the heavens (Ephesians 2:6). We are a vital and treasured part of a royal family. There is great spiritual authority that God will entrust to us as we walk in and grow in His ways. After salvation, while abhorring any present sin, we must also forget those past sins (since God does and we will as we become like Him), repent of present sins, and focus on seeing ourselves as sitting in the heavens with great spiritual authority—eventually to judge angels. We will get this only by believing it and walking in faith. To walk in faith in this issue, we have to balance both our origin before salvation and our renewal since salvation in perspective. We will discuss later how to grow as we learn how to walk in the Spirit. As we walk in the Spirit, we will see that we undergo a metamorphosis just like a grub does as it becomes a butterfly. We turn from the lowest of worms through death of self and accepting our salvation through Jesus to the highest of princes in the royal family of the ages. We learn to rule and to reign with the Lord Jesus, as we make this transition. What a marvelous and incomprehensible thing as we make this incredible transition! It is not an intellectual understanding of cold facts that we seek but a true and heartfelt integrated walk into the character of Jesus as we "put on the new man."

4
WHO IS THE DEVIL?

In this chapter we will see how important it is to understand the attributes and the personality of the devil and his cohort of fallen angels. There are several reasons for this. Since we cannot walk by the Spirit of God if we are being influenced by any demonic influence, we must understand how Satan works and who he is. We also need to know his methodologies to help us to differentiate more easily between his voice, God's voice, and our own inner voice. Unless we can make this distinction, we will not be able to walk in the Holy Spirit in a consistent way.

We have to look first at the creation and the subsequent fall of this creature. We must keep in mind the statement in Deuteronomy 29:29: "The secret *things belong* unto the LORD our God: but those *things which are* revealed *belong* unto us and to our children for ever, that *we* may do all the words of this law." Our information in the Bible is sketchy. We may, and should, learn what God has revealed to us; but we must not add to this information. God has given us all we need to know in dealing with this enemy.

One of the most important points is to notice that we do not live in a dualistic universe, as some religions insist. That is, we do not live in a universe in which the forces of good are lined up on one side and the forces of evil are lined up in opposition. There is one God only (1 Timothy 6:15-16); He has created everything outside Himself in the universe; He has set the "rules of engagement"; His final victory is assured (1 Corinthians 15:25-28); and our only reason to study the subject is to help fight our own battles that we face in this lifetime.

There are many names given to Satan in the Scriptures, most of them describing his depraved character. We have one name, at least, that appears to antedate his fall, Lucifer. We will use this name, especially when discussing him before his fall. We have discussed the fact that, in Hebrew thought, names indicate character; and thus there is a reason for these names. The meaning of the name *Lucifer* is discussed in the next section.

THE CREATION OF ANGELS

First, we must see who the angels are. Angels are associated with stars. Some have speculated that each angel was assigned to a star or celestial body. This group would suggest that Lucifer was assigned to the earth. We cannot determine that for sure; but Lucifer, or Satan, does seem to have a certain relationship with the earth. It is possible that the relationship is due to his successful tempting of Adam and Eve on earth. Job 38: 6-7 suggests the close relationship of the angels with stars: "Whereupon are the foundations thereof fastened? or who laid the corner stone thereof; When the morning stars sang together, and all the sons of God shouted for joy?" The phrase "sons of God," *ben ha-Elohim* or *ben Elohim*, always means "angels." It can refer to fallen or to unfallen angels. This term is used in the Job 1:6: "Now there was a day when the sons of God came to present themselves before the LORD, and Satan came also among them." The words "sons of God" are exactly the same as in Job 38. We see from the passage in Job 38 that the angels saw the part of creation that occurred after their creation and that they sang for joy. Some scholars have suggested that they might have been created the fourth day of creation, the same day that the stars were created. That is speculation, however; we *do* know that they were not fallen at that point in time, because, after God had completed creation, He observed: "And God saw every thing that he had made, and, behold, *it was* very good. And the evening and the morning were the sixth day" (Genesis 1:31). He would not have pronounced His creation "very good" if Lucifer had introduced sin at this point.

WHO LUCIFER IS

We have two primary passages in the Bible that indicate some of the characteristics of Lucifer before and leading up to his fall, Isaiah 14:12-17 and Ezekiel 28:12-19. Although the passages are lengthy, it is instructive to look at them in their entirety.

How art thou fallen from heaven, O Lucifer, son of the morning! *how* art thou cut down to the ground, which didst weaken the nations! For thou hast said in thine heart, I will ascend into heaven, I will exalt my throne above the stars of God: I will sit also upon the mount of the congregation, in the sides of the north: I will ascend above the heights of the clouds; I will be like the most High. Yet thou shalt be brought down to hell, to the sides of the pit. They that see thee shall narrowly look upon thee, *and* consider thee, *saying, Is* this the man that made the earth to tremble, that did shake kingdoms; *That* made the world as a wilderness, and destroyed the cities thereof; *that* opened not the house of his prisoners?

Isaiah 14:12-17

Son of man, take up a lamentation upon the king of Tyrus, and say unto him, Thus saith the Lord GOD; Thou sealest up the sum, full of wisdom, and perfect in beauty. Thou hast been in Eden the garden of God; every precious stone *was* thy covering, the sardius, topaz, and the diamond, the beryl, the onyx, and the jasper, the sapphire, the emerald, and the carbuncle, and gold: the workmanship of thy tabrets and of thy pipes was prepared in thee in the day that thou wast created. Thou *art* the anointed cherub that covereth; and I have set thee *so*: thou wast upon the holy mountain of God; thou hast walked up and down in the midst of the stones of fire. Thou *wast* perfect in thy ways from the day that thou wast created, till iniquity was found in thee. By the multitude of thy merchandise they have filled the midst of thee with violence, and thou hast sinned: therefore I will cast thee as profane out of the mountain of God: and I will destroy thee, O covering cherub, from the midst of the stones of fire. Thine heart was lifted up because of thy beauty, thou hast corrupted thy wisdom by reason of thy brightness: I will cast thee to the ground, I will lay thee before kings, that they may behold thee. Thou hast defiled thy sanctuaries by the multitude of thine iniquities, by the iniquity of thy traffick; therefore will I bring forth a fire from the midst of thee, it shall devour thee, and I will bring thee to ashes upon the earth in the sight of all them that behold thee. All they

> that know thee among the people shall be astonished at thee: thou shalt be a terror, and never *shalt* thou *be* any more.
>
> Ezekiel 28:12-19

Although both of these passages begin by addressing earthly kings, scholars are unanimous that the passages go far beyond the first layer of meaning. They can describe only Lucifer. From these passages we learn the following about Lucifer.

1. One of his names is Lucifer (meaning "light-bearing"), and that apparently describes one of his duties, to shed light in the throne room of God. "Son of the morning" refers to this task, (Isaiah 14:12).
2. He was created without sin (Ezekiel 28:15). We earlier showed that God's pronouncement at the end of creation shows the same thing.
3. He is a cherub (Ezekiel 28:14). We know the following about cherubim (Hebrew plural for cherub):
    a. They are spirit beings.
    b. At times they are used as God's servants.
        (1) The Scriptures tell us that, at times, God "rides" upon a cherub and is said to fly (2 Samuel 22:11 and Psalm 18:10).
        (2) They were sent to Ezekiel to give him a commission from God (Ezekiel 1).
        (3) They were sent to guard the east entrance of the Garden of Eden after man's expulsion (Genesis 3:24).
        (4) They offer eternal praise to God day and night (Revelation 4:6-11).
    c. Their likeness covered the ark in the tabernacle and the temple (Exodus 25:17-22 and other passages give instruction for this), thus looking upon the mercy seat (a type of Messiah's future sacrifice). This duty seems to echo one of the original tasks of Lucifer, "the anointed cherub that covereth" (Ezekiel 28:14). We learn in Hebrews that the tabernacle was a picture of the throne room in heaven

(8:5 and 9:23-24 with 4:14). Presumably Lucifer had some duties covering the most sacred place. The adjective *anointed* is related to the word for "Messiah." It indicates a special commission.

   d. Cherubim are not the same as the seraphim mentioned in Isaiah 6. Cherubim appear to be related to the holiness of God as outraged by sin (Genesis 3:24, Revelation 4:6-11, *et al.*).

4. His original duties include the covering discussed above. His duties as the anointed cherub involved his being in one of the highest places in the heavens, upon the holy mountain and in the midst of the stones of fire (Ezekiel 28:14).
5. He apparently was part of the heavenly choir (Ezekiel 28:13b). Certainly, we saw in Job 28 that the angels sing.
6. His beauty was dazzling, and he was full of wisdom (Ezekiel 28:12).
7. He was created with the most precious of gems covering him (Ezekiel 28:13).

Thus, Lucifer was one of the most beautiful, wise, and dazzling creatures to be created by God. We will see that his very excellence contributed to his fall.

THE FALL OF LUCIFER AND OTHER ANGELS

The above passages from Isaiah and Ezekiel give us the only information about Lucifer's original sin. Both passages make it clear that his first sin was wicked thought within himself, not some overt action. Ezekiel states that he was "*perfect in thy ways from the day that thou wast created, till iniquity was found in thee*" (28:15 [emphasis added]). In a similar vein Isaiah states: "How are thou fallen from heaven….For thou hast said in thine heart…" (14:12-13).

Some particulars of his sin can be gleaned from these passages. Isaiah indicates that, although Lucifer was created as one of the chief of created beings, this was not enough for him. He wanted God's place. His desire to exalt his throne above the stars of God (v.13) indicates that he wanted to be not one of the stars or angels, but above that rank. His desire to sit upon the mount of the congregation indicates a desire to rule in areas outside his provenance. Finally, he reveals his true desire, to be like the most High (v.14).

Ezekiel lets us see some of the reasons that Lucifer sinned in this way. He tells us that, because of his great beauty, wisdom, and brightness, he became proud ("thine heart was lifted up") and sinned.

Ezekiel also tells us that Lucifer was stripped of some of his heavenly duties—he was taken out of the mountain of God and from the midst of the stones of fire. These places appear to be in the governing areas of the highest heaven. He and his fellow fallen angels were not forbidden access to the presence of God, as such passages as Job 1-2, 1 Kings 22:19-23, and Revelation 12:10c show. Revelation 12:10 indicates that at a future time Satan will be cast out of heaven. Verse 6, taken with the rest of the larger context indicates that this will be at the middle of the Tribulation. Verses 9-12 tell us: "And there was war in heaven: Michael and his angels fought against the dragon; and the dragon fought and his angels, And prevailed not; neither was their place found any more in heaven. And the great dragon was cast out, that old serpent, called the Devil, and Satan, which deceiveth the whole world: he was cast out into the earth, and his angels were cast out with him. And I heard a loud voice saying in heaven, Now is come salvation, and strength, and the kingdom of our God, and the power of his Christ: for the accuser of our brethren is cast down, which accused them before our God day and night." John adds in verse 12 that, at that point in history, Satan will work very hard, since he knows that his time is limited.

We know, from the numerous Scripture references to the fallen angels, that there were many angels who participated in Lucifer's rebellion and thus are condemned with him. Apparently, one third of the angels rebelled (Revelation 12:4).

THE FINAL STATE OF LUCIFER AND THE FALLEN ANGELS

As we have seen, Lucifer and his angels will be expelled from heaven during the middle of the Tribulation period. They will work very hard in the 3½ years remaining to them, because they know their time is short (Revelation 12:9,12). At the end of this time, the beast and false prophet (we will not discuss their identities, as that is not relative to the discussion about Lucifer) will be cast into the lake of fire burning with brimstone (Revelation 19:19). Lucifer and apparently most of the fallen angels [the ones already in Tartarus are left in the heart of the earth until after the Millenial reign of Christ] are then chained for a thousand years in a different place, the bottomless pit, so that they cannot deceive the nations during this time (Revelation 20:1-3). God is going to show that man's heart is indeed desperately wicked (Jeremiah 17:9) and that even after a 1000-year perfect reign of Christ, there will be numerous people who will follow Satan when he is finally loosed from his pit. The number will be as the "sand of the sea" (Revelation 20:7-9). At the end of this period God will come down from heaven, devour the rebels, and Satan and his demons will be cast into the lake of fie and brimstone, where the beast and false prophet will be (Revelation 20:10). It is interesting that the Bible, in telling that Satan is put into the lake of fire 1000 years after the beast and false prophet were put there, says that he is put where the beast and false prophet "*are*," indicating that in 1000 years they had not been annihilated. Thus, those put in this lake will live eternally in torment. Unfortunately, following Satan's being put into the lake, all those people who did not accept Jesus Christ as their Lord and Savior during their lives are judged and put into the same place. Jesus makes it clear, however, that the lake was created for Satan and his minions, and not for man (Matthew 25:41); but men who reject Jesus, by their own choice, will also spend eternity there.

Satan's Work between His Fall and His Eventual Doom

Now that we know who Lucifer/Satan is, we need to understand his methods of working during the time in which God has allowed him to work. We need to study this so that we can equip ourselves to fight the battles against him. One of the most important Scriptures relating to Satan's work is found in John 10:10a: "The thief cometh not, but for to steal, and to kill, and to destroy." Satan does not come unless he tries to steal, kill, or destroy. This is crucial to understand.

There are several areas we need to examine, although there is some overlap between sections 2 and 3:

1. Satan's program from a historical perspective
2. His methods and activities against God's people and institutions
3. The tools God has given us to defeat him

Satan's program from a historical perspective

After Satan's fall, he first appears (as related in the Bible) in the Garden of Eden. He appeared indwelling the most subtle creature on earth, the serpent (Genesis 3:1ff). He caused Eve to doubt the word of God and appealed to her in the same three areas in which sin always operates: the lust of the flesh, the lust of the eyes, and the pride of life (1 John 2:16). Genesis 3:6 tells us: "And when the woman saw that the tree *was* good for food, and that it *was* pleasant to the eyes, and a tree to be desired to make *one* wise, she took of the fruit thereof, and did eat, and gave also unto her husband with her; and he did eat." Verses 7-13 describe the ensuing tragedy—the eyes of both Adam and Eve being opened to their sin, their hiding from God, His addressing them, and both of them trying to pass the blame to others (Adam to Eve, and Eve to the serpent). In verse 14 God addresses the serpent and pronounces the curse upon it. In verse 15, however, God both pronounces a curse and also gives the first hope for fallen mankind. He says: "And I will put enmity between thee and the woman, and between thy seed and her seed; it shall bruise thy head, and thou shalt bruise his heel." A bruise on the heel is not fatal, but a head injury frequently is. Thus, God was saying that Lucifer, who had indwelt the serpent, would be able to bruise the heel—*i.e.*, inflict a non fatal injury—to the seed of the woman; but the woman's seed would fatally injure him. The word *seed* is interesting; it is *zera*, which normally refers to a man's seed or sperm. This is an early indication of the virgin birth of Jesus.

From that point Lucifer did all he could to prevent the birth of this seed. That is the spirit behind the murder of Abel (Genesis 4:8ff) and the cohabitation of demons with women, thus trying to cause all humanity to be tainted with this strain (Genesis 6:1-7). Once God called Abraham to be a separate race and one through which the seed would come (Genesis 12, 15, 17, *et al.*), Satan concentrated on that group of people. Thus, the plot to get Sarah into Pharaoh's harem, thus tainting the line, and the plan for Abraham to conceive by Sarah's maid Hagar were elements to stop the seed's coming through Abraham in the way God had ordained. Once God revealed that the seed would come through Judah, there were many plots to destroy this line. At the beginning the line of Judah almost died and might have except that Judah's former daughter-in-law became pregnant by Judah (Genesis 38). Athaliah's slaying of all the royal seed of Judah would have accomplished this, except that Jehosheba hid her nephew Joash until he could be crowned (2 Chronicles 22:10-12; 2 Kings 11:1-3).

There were many other plots, but these serve to show Satan's hatred for the Jewish people and for members of the tribe of Judah. At times his hatred has been expressed for the entire Jewish race. He attempted to get Balaam to pronounce a curse on the people, but God prevented it (Numbers 22-24). He used Haman to try to destroy the entire race during the Persian empire (Esther); but, again, God prevented it. Down through history men and nations have tried to destroy the Jewish people and nation, but all have failed—from Sennacherub and the Assyrians (2 Kings 19; 2 Chronicles 32; Isaiah 37) to Hitler and the Third Reich. In the early twenty-first century many rulers and nations are "promising" to eradicate the Jewish nation and people. They, too, will fail.

Once it became obvious that Jesus was the Messiah, Satan did all he could to foil His work. He tried to kill him shortly after his birth by having Herod kill all children in Jesus' age group (Matthew 2:16-18). He tempted him to avoid the cross (Matthew 4; Mark 1; Luke 4). He tried to have him killed on many occasions (*e.g.* Luke 4:29-30). Since he entered into Judas Iscariot to cause him to betray Jesus, he must have thought that having Jesus killed would foil God's plan. Instead, of course, the cross became the very place that Satan's defeat was accomplished (Colossians 2:14-15).

Once Jesus died and rose again, Satan's ire has been directed toward God's people. He tries to attack their message, their credibility, and their effectiveness in living the life in the Spirit. Since losing the battle of the ages at the cross, Satan has tried to neutralize the effectiveness of the Church, Christ's body, in the world. His goal is always to destroy mankind and take as many to the lake of fire with him as he can. Some people have theorized that Satan knows that there are a certain number of individuals who will become believers and that he thinks he can delay his eventual doom by slowing the number of people who come to Jesus in saving faith. Be that as it may, he tries to destroy the effectiveness of believers in reaching unbelievers, and he tries to keep the unbelievers from coming to a saving faith in Jesus. His personality is antithetical to that of God's in all ways. There is an absolute lack of any love in Satan, whereas God is eternally love. Satan wants to destroy any vestige of the image of God in man. Even though he has lost the final battle, he is still intent on winning as many of the continuing skirmishes as he can. We will look at his many devices in the next section.

Finally, when Satan sees signs that the end of the age is approaching, he will work furiously. We saw in Revelation 12:12 that when Satan is cast out of heaven at the middle of the Tribulation, he will "come down unto you, having great wrath, because he knoweth that he hath but a short time." He will make war with the Jewish remnant, being especially angry with this group (Revelation 12:17).

His methods and activities against God's people and institutions

We are given many glimpses in the Scriptures of Satan's methods of attacking God's people. One of the first principles to remember is that Satan himself is transformed into an angel of light (2 Corinthians 11:14) and that his ministers are transformed as the ministers of righteousness (2 Corinthians 11:13, 15). Thus, he always deceives. He is able to make his plan and program look good. Believers and unbelievers alike follow him down this road. He appeared in this way to Eve, and his methods have not changed. It will be hard to distinguish a particular tempting by Satan without the ability to discern what spirit is behind the situation. This makes it extremely hard for anyone, even the elect, to detect that he is active in a given situation. It is only through the use of spiritual discernment that the elect will not be deceived in the end times of this age. Satan is a formidable foe, and we as men are completely unable to combat him successfully. It is only through prayer and being led by God's Spirit that we can stand against the devil and begin to allow God to take victories in the spiritual war of this age. The problem is that most people have not developed the ability to walk after God's Spirit; and, therefore, they do not detect the initial spiritual nudge or small word from the devil to set up a particular pathway for them. Soon the human spirit picks up and takes over a small undetected demonic suggestion or emotion that was deliberately and cunningly inserted at an opportune time. The believer picks it up in his own spirit and quickly amplifies it; and instead of walking after God, he walks after the lust of his eyes, the lust of his flesh, or the pride of life (1 John 2:16). We should remember that God tells us that in the closing times of this age even the elect will need to be extremely careful not to be deceived (Mark 13:22).

Secondly, we know that he is very active in pursuing God's people. Peter tells us that the devil (Satan) walks about like a roaring lion, seeking someone to devour (1 Peter 5:8). This passage is addressed to believers; thus, we must ever be vigilant. In a similar way we learn in Revelation 12:10b that "the accuser of our brethren is cast down, which accused them before our God day and night." We must notice that Satan accused the *brethren*, *i.e.*, believers. He has done that and will do that until he is cast out of heaven during the middle of the Tribulation. The picture seems to be that he accuses us continuously. Obviously, we have no defense for this; presumably, the Lord Jesus makes intercession for us in this matter, as in others (Hebrews 7:25). Although the Lord does make intercession, God allows Satan to wreak havoc on us at times. The devil accuses us before God's throne. Sometimes the accusation is false, as in the case with Job. When, however, he accuses us and we have committed any sin of either omission or of commission, then he apparently has some basis. If we walk in any detail outside of faith, then God is not pleased. This means that when we are not being led by His Spirit, we are opening ourselves to demonic interaction in which the demons gain a foothold of power over us. It is sobering to realize to what degree our actions and life are lived in subjection to the demonic forces of evil. The very name *Satan* indicates this work of his. The word is a Hebrew word meaning "the hater or the accuser." This supernatural hate and Satan's work in accusing the brethren go hand-in-hand. Since names indicate character in Hebrew, we should take note that Satan's character is one of hate and standing against God's people.

We have mentioned that Satan will be cast out of heaven permanently during the middle of the Tribulation period. He has access to heaven and to God Himself until that time. Occasionally, one hears someone say something like, "God and Satan cannot exist in the same place. Therefore, Satan cannot enter heaven." [Note: This argument is used by some to say that believers cannot be demon-possessed. These people say that, since a believer is filled with the Holy Spirit and since God and Satan cannot exist in the same place, then a believer cannot be indwelt by a demon. There are other arguments for and against the premise that a believer can be demon-possessed; but this particular argument cannot stand.] This statement has no basis in the Scriptures. We see in Job 1 and 2 that Satan and his fallen angels have full access to God. In fact, Satan's attacks on Job are a result of God's challenge to Satan regarding Job. We see fallen angels in the heavenly councils in 1 Kings 22:13-23, when there is a discussion of how the Lord will get Ahab to go down the road to his death. This council is described as "the LORD sitting on his throne, and all the host of heaven standing by him on his right hand and on his left" (v. 19b). From comparison with other Scriptures, we know that one group on the right hand and one on the left refer to not fallen and fallen angels, respectively. The Lord showed Zechariah a scene in heaven in which Satan was standing before the Lord and in which Satan was acting as the accuser of the brethren, preparing to accuse the high priest Joshua (Zechariah 3:1-2). What we should understand from this information is that during this period of history, Satan has access to God's presence and, apparently, is cognizant of some of God's plans. It should come as no surprise that he is able to attack us in the area of our being in the Spirit and fulfilling God's plans for our lives.

I asked the Lord one day why the devil is able to interrupt my thoughts, even in prayer, and why he is able to try to confuse me with an answer to a prayer. The Lord promptly reminded me in His own voice that Satan is in heaven and hears and sees most of what is going on. He has incredible powers compared to us. We should not even think that we are any match for Him, except hidden in the cleft of the rock and coming out only as led by God's Spirit. We know that he influences unbelievers in this way, almost automatically. Actually, the case is that they have no filters to be able to recognize his whisperings. David prays for Satan to influence a wicked man, who would in turn condemn one of David's enemies: "Set thou a wicked man over him; and let Satan stand at his right hand" (Psalm 109:6).

We know, in addition, that Satan has his minions superintending the movements of some nations on earth. The answer to a prayer of Daniel was delayed for 21 days, because the angel sent with the answer was thwarted by a demon who was over the kingdom of Persia (Daniel 10:12-13). Michael had to come to the rescue of that angel. This passage shows that there are different levels of power within Satan's minions. Apparently, the angels were created at different ranks and with differing amounts of power. That does not change for fallen angels. Thus, Michael (a higher angel than the one over Persia) had to deal with him. The angel over Persia, in turn, was mightier than the one sent to answer Daniel's prayer. Even the powerful Michael, one of the chief princes (Daniel 10:13) and also an archangel (Jude 9), was not able to withstand Satan alone when they were disputing over the body of Moses; he had to call on the Lord Jesus to accomplish this (Jude 9). [Michael may be the *only* archangel, as he is the only one so named in the Scriptures, and he is called "the archangel" (Jude 9).] The apostle Paul mentions these various degrees of rank and power in Ephesians 6:11-12: "Put on the whole armour of God, that ye may be able to stand against the wiles of the devil. For we wrestle not against flesh and blood, but against principalities, against powers, against the rulers of the darkness of this world, against spiritual wickedness in high *places.*" Paul alludes to these various ranks in Romans 8:38-39: "For I am persuaded, that neither death, nor life, nor angels, nor principalities, nor powers, nor things present, nor things to come, Nor height, nor depth, nor any other creature, shall be able to separate us from the love of God, which is in Christ Jesus our Lord." We mention these ranks for a purpose. If various angels need to get help from angels of higher rank to conquer a particular foe, we are foolish to assume that we can best these powerful creatures by ourselves. We will discuss the tools that God has given us to defeat the foe in the next section, but we will note that in the passage in Ephesians Paul proceeds to tell us about the armor we should wear for protection. In the passage in Romans he also gives us the key to victory: "…in all these things we are more than conquerors through him that loved us" (Romans 8:37). It is only as we appropriate what God has given us in grace that we are able to defeat this enemy.

We also know that Satan has a highly developed organization of principalities, powers, and rulers through which he operates to try to increase his authority and control over mankind. It is only as God allows the devil to take the power that he can use it. God has Satan completely at His disposal and uses his attacks to hold up a mirror in which we can see our situation before Him. Satan can take power against us and use it to harm us in both physical and spiritual areas. We see from the book of Job how this works. There we see that Satan was allowed to inflict disease and anguish on Job. He was allowed to kill Job's family and animals. We do not know the rules and limits that God has set for the devil; but we do know that, as we sin and continue in lack of faith, we open ourselves for the devil to accuse us successfully before God. This ties God's hand in ways that we do not understand. As a result, for example, some of the people in Corinth had fallen sick, and some had died when they took communion in an unworthy manner (1 Corinthians 11:28-30).

We do not know the details of how God makes decisions when Satan correctly accuses us, but we can infer that we fall into various forms of discipline, including premature death (1 Corinthians 11:30). We must get out of the trap of thinking that our salvation covers everything in terms of sin. It covers us only when we repent of our sin. Most believers know God's Word so poorly that they do not even know when they commit major sins. People look at the external sins such as adultery and murder and focus on these and actually take pride in the fact that they are not like their neighbor. It is the internal sins of the individual that are the really serious ones. Proverbs 6: 15-19 lists the seven sins that God hates most: "These six *things* doth the LORD hate: yea, seven *are* an abomination unto him: A proud look, a lying tongue, and hands that shed innocent blood, An heart that deviseth wicked imaginations, feet that be swift in running to mischief, A false witness *that* speaketh lies, and he that soweth discord among brethren." Only one, murder, is an overt sin. Three are sins of the tongue, and three are mental attitude sins. We do not even begin to look on sin as God does.

Lack of faith is a major issue that inhibits our relationship with God, and yet few see it as a sin. However it completely smashes the first and second commandment into pieces and tramples on the spilled blood of our Lord. It is an incredibly serious sin. It is so easy to have a lack of faith. People think that they walk in faith because they made a decision to trust Jesus for their salvation. This is not so. Walking in faith is a moment-by-moment process that can occur only when we allow ourselves to be led by God's Spirit. When we do not walk moment by moment under the leadership of God's Spirit, we are not putting God first in all things. We must forever get past the notion that, because we made a single point-in-time decision to follow Jesus for salvation or even to commit ourselves more fully to Him, we are doing well. We are not, until we allow ourselves to be led by His Spirit from moment to moment. When we do this, we can be cleansed from all unrighteousness by repenting of our known sins (1 John 1:9). The problem with most of us is that our consciences are hard toward the things of God; and, therefore, we do not repent of things of which we know we should repent. Most believers know that they should be putting God first in all things. If they continue a sin pattern, they have not repented of it. Repentance is more than a cheap, "Oh yeah, I did wrong today, and I am sorry." It is a heartfelt, meditated decision to turn in the opposite direction, followed by plans to ensure that the change is kept. The gospel has been so cheapened that people do not come to true repentance the way that they should. Because people do not come to true repentance, they stay in a state of unforgiven sin patterns that open them up to demonic attack. Thus, Satan succeeds for a time as the accuser of the brethren.

The history of mankind is one of war. Satan's rulers, principalities, and powers see to it that they prey upon men in order to foment continuing strife, misery, and destruction. The devil is able to keep most people even from thinking that he is real, but he does have his own followers who recognize him and worship him. Through the ages these people have been praying to the devil and worshipping him. In return, he shares some of his power with them. These people frequently try to assault the Church directly and also try to bring about death. There are large numbers of these people working in places such as intensive care units, where they can bring about a spirit of discouragement and death to people who are fighting for their life. We have personal testimonies from individuals who have seen these phenomena. The devil rejoices in death, because it increases his apparent victory, and it prevents a life from fulfilling its God-ordained purpose.

The Scriptures list the fruit (result of the work of) these spirits in various places. One such place is Galatians 5:20-21, where we read that the works of the flesh are “idolatry, witchcraft, hatred, variance, emulations, wrath, strife, seditions, heresies, Envyings, murders, drunkenness, revellings, and such like.” These works of the flesh are the result of the fall of man into sin and the acquiring of the “sin nature.” These spiritual actions and emotions come from the personality described by Jesus as “from your father, the devil” (John 8:44). The demons are able to tempt men to sin and, in fact, have a rather easy time of it when a person is not mounting a defense using the armor that God has provided. God reassures us and also convicts us in His word about this matter by telling us that He will not allow us to be tempted beyond that which we are able to withstand (1 Corinthians 10:13). One of the requirements for walking after God’s Spirit is to recognize that God expects us to play our role in all activities. We must always be careful with any planned action to weigh what God says He will do, and what He tells us that we must do.

The devil seems to tempt through the mind when dealing with intellectuals. He will tempt a person with natural abilities to assume too great a role in any work that God wants to perform. This type of individual then runs ahead of the Lord’s program, performing work that he has reasoned out. There are seldom any miracles in this type of work; and while God may bless it in a general way, He cannot give specific blessing to it, since it is a self-righteous act that He has not ordained. The opposite is also true of many people who are on the side of being a little lazy spiritually. They pray to God and ask Him to do something for them or show them something, and then they leave it up to God and do not go through their part of keeping the armor on, seeking counsel, visiting the prophets, and analyzing the situation from all viewpoints. They do not fulfill their part; and, therefore, they do not receive a blessing.

God wants partnership, just as a father in an earthly business wants partnership with his children. This involves actively working together. In this case God must do all of the initiating of the works, but He will not initiate them unless people pray and ask for them. God will not act independently of men, since He has given the earth to man over which to have dominion. God sees further and more accurately than we can, and so the planning of activities must be done by Him. We see the ultimate example of this with Jesus, who stated that "the Son can do nothing of himself, but what he seeth the Father do" (John 5:19b). If Jesus had to operate this way, then we must also.

The demons try to attack this balance of work to interrupt God's work and plans. They do so by bring a variety of weapons against men, "the fiery darts of the evil one" (Ephesians 6:16). A negative spiritual force exerted against an individual at the correct time will result in anger or some other negative emotion. The devil has at his command only the negative spiritual forces. In his capacity of deceit, posing as an angel of light, he does have analogues of the positive spiritual forces that God has. He can "fake" these forces on occasion. For example, Satan cannot love; but he can fake love in order to deceive men. There is always something askew, however, in these deceptions; and the believer who is walking in the Spirit can discern them.

The devil attacks men in several ways:

a) Through the body
b) Through the mind
c) Against the spirit

a) The attacks against the body include the bringing about of illness and death.

b) The attacks through the mind occur by appealing to those sin patterns common to all people—the lust of the flesh, the lust of the eyes, and the pride of life. We will learn much more about this in the ensuing sections of this book.
c) The attacks against the spirit come in the form of a weight that is much stronger and more persistent than an emotion. It is like a heavy weight on the spirit. The devil seems to reserve this for occasions in which he has failed or fears failing to succeed in attacks against the body or the mind.

Attacks through the mind consist of arousing negative emotions by interjecting a thought that plays to the wrong attitudes, beliefs, and behavior patterns that we have built up in our soul. The demons are smart enough to hit at the right moment against the right person to get their greater agenda performed. For example, Hitler was often communing with the evil spirits before any major action; and this allowed them to play directly to his evil patterns that had never been changed by the Scriptures. In a leader the demons are able to affect far more people with such things as physical oppressions, slavery, wars, and other negative conditions.

We have already seen that the demons are arranged in hierarchical form, just as God created governments. Satan always opposes the things of God; and, in order to do it, he must build a counter to God's organizations on earth. The demons try to influence elections and the placement of high officials in various countries. They always try to bring men into bondage to evil rulers and do so by influencing people in key positions, using their own demonic hierarchy. We saw that Daniel had the answer to a prayer delayed by the demonic prince of Persia. God allowed Satan to entice David to number Israel in direct violation of God's will (1 Chronicles 21:1). There were national implications from this, as 70,000 men were killed as a result. We can look to see what kind of government rulers and leaders we have in order to see if God is giving a country over to the lusts of its people or whether He is blessing that country. God will change His actions, as He says: "If my people, which are called by my name, shall humble themselves, and pray, and seek my face, and turn from their wicked ways; then will I hear from heaven, and will forgive their sin, and will heal their land" (2 Chronicles 7:14). Thus, we see that the devil is well organized and can be extremely deceptive in carrying out his agenda, which is always to bring men into bondage under an evil system in which they will fall under the judgment of God, just as he did. We should recall once more Jesus' statement in John 10:10a: "The thief cometh not, but for to steal, and to kill, and to destroy." The last half of this verse is instructive: "I am come that they might have life, and that they might have it more abundantly." Thus, we *cannot* have the more abundant life, *i.e.*, the walk in the Spirit, if we do not understand the first part of the verse and take up our armor against this foe.

The tools God has given us to defeat him

God has not left us defenseless. One of the most important verses in the Bible to remember is 1 Corinthians 10:13: "There hath no temptation taken you but such as is common to man: but God *is* faithful, who will not suffer you to be tempted above that ye are able; but will with the temptation also make a way to escape, that ye may be able to bear *it*." This verse tells us that God will never allow us to be tested (tempted) by anything—Satan or anything else—more than we are able to bear. We can be victorious in each circumstance in our lives. Knowing this should enable us to face any attacks from Satan more easily.

Secondly, Paul in Ephesians 6: 10-16 instructs us as to offensive and defensive weaponry that we need to use if we are to defeat him: "Finally, my brethren, be strong in the Lord, and in the power of his might. Put on the whole armour of God, that ye may be able to stand against the wiles of the devil. For we wrestle not against flesh and blood, but against principalities, against powers, against the rulers of the darkness of this world, against spiritual wickedness in high *places*. Wherefore take unto you the whole armour of God, that ye may be able to withstand in the evil day, and having done all, to stand. Stand therefore, having your loins girt about with truth, and having on the breastplate of righteousness; And your feet shod with the preparation of the gospel of peace; Above all, taking the shield of faith, wherewith ye shall be able to quench all the fiery darts of the wicked."

We see that it is with the *armor of God* that we can stand against Satan. We should remember the examples given above of the archangel Michael and the messenger to Daniel and accept that we cannot defeat him in our own strength. We must rely on God's armor and call on the Lord Jesus when necessary. We quoted above Romans 8:37, the key to victory: "…in all these things we are more than conquerors through him that loved us." Thus, we see again that we cannot defeat Satan by ourselves; we are conquerors only as we are covered by our Lord, the One who loves us. It is only through prayer and being led by God's Spirit that we can stand against the devil and begin to allow God to take victories in the spiritual war of this age.

As we look at the passage in Ephesians 6:10-16 more closely, we see that we have to be diligent in many important areas. If we are not doing all of these things moment by moment, we are going to be wounded or killed in the battle. If we do not know God's Word extremely well as a result of frequent reading, hearing, and meditation, we are not going to have our loins girded with truth. If we are in Christ, we are righteous so far as salvation is concerned; but if we step outside the covering momentarily or extensively due to a sin pattern—including wrong attitude, wrong belief, or wrong behavior—then we become a target. If we are not in a state of spiritual peace as a result of our allowing ourselves to be led by God's Spirit in a moment-by-moment fashion, then we will be barefooted. If we are not covering ourselves by confining all of our actions to be based on faith in God's written and His *rhema* words, then we have at best a rather tattered shield that will easily be penetrated by a fiery dart. All believers should have assurance of their salvation, since God tells us that we can have that assurance (1 John 5:13). If we do not have that confidence, then we have our head bare; and we can be easily attacked. Again, reliance on the word, both written and spoken, is essential to mount any form of defense or even a Spirit-led attack using the sword of the spirit. We must walk with God closely enough to discern His voice always. "My sheep will know my voice" (John 10:14). There are many voices that come into our minds, including our own and those of mimicking demons who would try to deceive us into thinking that we hear our Lord's voice. If we are spiritually afar from our Lord, we may not hear His voice clearly. This happens when we are running under emotional and intellectual pressures. To know God's voice is critical to being led by the Spirit of God, and we will learn this only as we mature in spiritual things. Imagine a neonate surrounded by a multitude of voices, all telling him that they are his father. How long do you think it would take that child to learn the voice of his own father, especially if some of those voices were quite good at mimicking? It is the same in spiritual matters; and yet to fight in the spiritual war, we must know God's written Word extremely well, and we must be able to discern His voice to pick up a *rhema*. There are ways of learning this process more easily, and we will cover them later. If a believer is not doing these things actively and constantly or if he thinks that the above does not apply to him, he will find himself on the sidelines, out of the battle, useless to the Lord, or, even worse, dead.

As we have seen, God stays in control and allows the devil to act only to a degree. God's major purpose in all things has always been to protect man's freedom to choose which way he will go. God is not willing that any perish, and He is not pleased by the death of any evil person or unbeliever. Nevertheless, God protects our freedom to accept Him and to love Him above all else or to reject Him wholly or in part.

As a result God has set up the operation in the spiritual world in such a way that neither He nor the demons are able to overwhelm man and force man into a non-free choice. The balance is delicate. We see that God uses evil forces in such a way that they act as a mirror into which we can look to see how our attitudes, behaviors, and beliefs conform us to the image of His Son, Jesus. We must always be assessing this in all things that occur to us. It is only as we do this painstakingly and comprehensively in all situations that we will be able to begin walking after His Spirit. This alone is not sufficient for us to walk after His Spirit, but it is a prerequisite.

God uses evil forces to bring discipline and to alter the course of history. The judgments given to the Egyptians involved the use of the forces of evil (Exodus 7-15). We saw above how God sent a lying spirit to be in the mouths of advisers to King Ahab (1 Kings 22:19-23). We see how God allowed the devil to enter into Judas in order to precipitate the arrest of the Lord Jesus (Luke 22:3; John 13:2). We can look and clearly discern what is happening in our own countries today, as God holds up the mirror of judgment through the forces of evil. God does not rely on the forces of evil alone to bring judgment. He will use his own angels, especially in the end times, both leading up to and during the Tribulation.

We have seen above how the demons are organized into several administrative layers for the purpose of winning their war against God. In a sense they know that they must obey God. We see the demons subject to Jesus during His advent. However, they are also at war against Him, because they have been judged; and they are in rebellion and carry intense supernatural hatred. They will try to attack God directly at the end of the age; and, in the meantime, they try to attack God through marring His image as reflected in mankind. Their attack is extremely well-organized and focused in comparison to any ability that man has to do the same. This stems from the fact that man was created a little lower than the angels (Psalm 8:5; Hebrews 2:7). The angels have more power and capability than man does in this age. In the age to come, however, man will judge the angels (1 Corinthians 6:3).

In order to withstand the demonic assault on our body, mind, and spirit, we must learn God's Word in a functional way. No longer will it work to read the Word in a passive way. We must now interact with it, meditate upon it, and then integrate it into areas that apply to different aspects of our functioning. We must use the Word to build our faith. We must become spiritually mature in order to acquire spiritual sensitivity and discernment. These will come only from walking in a living, submitted, and close relationship to the Lord Jesus Christ. Without this walk one cannot even begin to stand against the enemy. The Lord wants us to stand in faith, and this alone can gain Him advantage over the enemy. We must study the Scripture thoroughly to learn all there is about spiritual warfare, since our battle is not against flesh and blood in this life.

We cannot attack the demonic without the leadership of Jesus. All we can do is stand in faith until He outlines His campaign for a particular skirmish. This is parallel to Israel's taking her land. The children of Israel had to begin to move into the Promised Land in faith and then had to work with the Lord in each battle. We see different strategies that the Lord required in various battles. One battle against Jericho is documented in Joshua 6, and a second battle against Ai is documented in Joshua 7:1-5. In this battle against Ai the Israelites did not seek the Lord's specific guidance. They lost this first battle. In Joshua 7:6-8:29 we read of the success of a second battle against Ai when they asked God for His plans. The Israelites, even after this, did not always seek the Lord's specific instructions; and when they failed to follow the Lord's commands, they did not do well. God asked them to take the land completely, but they never did take the land completely. We see that they thought that they knew better. It cost them dearly in the end, and they never did take the land in the way that the Lord intended. The people they left became snares and traps (Joshua 23:13) as the Lord predicted. In the same way we must advance only under the direction, authority, and covering of the Lord Jesus. The orders may come directly to us or through a prophet (friend, advisor, or formal prophet). We must always test the spirit of a friend, advisor, or prophet before obeying. If one thinks that he has a direct order, this needs to be tested carefully, or better still, to be subjected to the spirits of the prophets (1 Corinthians 14:32); one should never go alone into battle. It is forbidden, and one will be sorely chastised for putting oneself and possibly others into danger. The demonic is not something to be taken without great gravity, and one should make sure that his spirit is one of work to do and not one of excitement or self enhancement when battling evil powers.

5
SUMMARY OF PRECEDING CHAPTERS

In the preceding four chapters we have tried to give some thoughts about preparation for beginning to learn how to walk after God's Spirit. It is critical to get the relationship of the three major parties in this age into a true perspective. We have discussed that the true perspective comes from seeing and believing how the Lord Jesus created the universe and this age and to see what He tells us, what he asks of us, and how He speaks of and views the parties in this age.

The parties are:

1. The Holy Trinity
2. The demonic kingdom
3. Man

We must learn how to relate to these three parties in truth; and as we mature in the growth of our spiritual understanding, we will be able to do this in spirit also. In order to get the relationships right, we must put God first in all things. To do this, we must know what He tells us in His word about doing this; and we must take this as a most sober responsibility. We must come to see that the only way to spiritual maturity is to know God in such a way that we can converse with Him as with a person across the room. We must know that the progress toward spiritual maturity is measured only in how much of our attitudes, beliefs, behaviors, spiritual authority, and spiritual ability parallel that of the Lord Jesus. Putting God first means learning how to replace self as first in our life and then crucifying self, regardless of the cost. We must come to love Him truly, something that can come only from talking with Him and watching what He does in us and through us. It cannot come from reading and studying the Word alone. This can only whet our appetite for depth in our relationship with God. Our relationship must be such that the deep calls to the deep (1 Corinthians 2:9-16).

The last four chapters may or may not speak to a particular individual. They are not meant to be exhaustive by any means. They are intended to form a basis for encouragement for one to devour and then to devour again the written Word, all the time applying every bit of it day by day. While you are doing this, talk to the Lord. You will begin to get a feel for His majesty as you read and believe His word. You will get nowhere, if you do not believe every syllable completely and utterly. As you believe and devour and act continually to apply the Word to your attitudes, beliefs, and behaviors, you will begin to get a glimpse of the depth and majesty of God. You must commune through talking with Him and believing that He will answer you. You have to listen until you can pick His answering voice out from the crowds of demonic counterfeits. Only then can you talk directly with Him, always on His terms. He will come to you to talk sometimes at what seem like unlikely times. As you work with Him and watch Him work in your life to change you, patiently bearing your faults, you will find that there is a growing bond of real love and affection that comes out of great appreciation for what He has done for you.

In the next sections of this book we will try to bring you to an understanding of the dynamics of attaining to these ideals. It really is not complex, if you will come to it as a child; for then God will work with you. If you will discard much of your earthly learning and wisdom, you will begin to learn the ways of the spiritual world. If you are intent on hanging onto your learned behaviors, attitudes, and beliefs, you will not be able to be taught the deep things of the Lord. Is it worthwhile? Yes, it is an exciting and thrilling adventure, but one must be prepared to give up all that he is in order to participate fully.

An individual must be prepared to undergo a radical change from the world view under which he has operated in order to transition to what God wishes him to become. He will operate under a new reality in which he sees everything that occurs in his life as ordained by God for molding him into God's desires for His child. When he embraces this, all suffering can become truly joyful, as one works with God to mature in the eternal family. Material possessions of the world will no longer be attractive, except as tools for achieving God's purpose. The individual will be able to separate the spirit from the flesh and maintain righteousness, peace, and joy (Romans 14:17) internally, despite the tempests that the evil angels try to cause against him through adverse conditions in the flesh. Philippians 3:8 states: "Yea doubtless, and I count all things *but* loss for the excellency of the knowledge of Christ Jesus my Lord: for whom I have suffered the loss of all things, and do count them *but* dung, that I may win Christ." This can be said with truth and joy when one has the correct heart attitude. One does not have to grit the teeth and "suffer" with an artificial fortitude. In 2 Timothy 3:12 we read: "Yea, and all that will live godly in Christ Jesus shall suffer persecution." We will so yield to the Lord that He will be supplying His power, and we will be empowered in the inner man by Him and thus be able to stand against the demonic foes. They are made higher than us; and, therefore, without joining to other believers and to the Lord we cannot overcome them. God's Word tells us how we can be victorious. We also learn to speak things into being by decree, as we are led by God in our inner man.

As we mature, it is critical that we learn to trust God, in faith, for maturation to take place. We are not expected to walk blindly. We have to learn to know when He is speaking to us in the many ways that He speaks. We have to learn to be obedient to Him; and, as we do this, we will find that His Word will be fulfilled. Life becomes a growing experiential process of maturation in understanding supernatural phenomena and working in these areas to allow God to use us to take back the works of the devil. We do not battle the devil with weapons of the flesh (Ephesians 6:10-18). We cannot battle the devil with natural means. When we operate in the flesh (and we do when we are paying attention to the flesh because of pain or adverse worldly circumstances), we will lose. God's Word tells us the correct way to fight. To fight, we must be joined to and subject to the head (the Lord Jesus Christ).

Have the authors achieved this state? By no means, but the Lord has shown us much that we feel that He wishes us to communicate. We hope and pray that what you are about to study will be as true to His desires as we can write, given our still limited understanding of spiritual things. We would anticipate revision as we learn more in the future, but we do believe that the Lord will protect us from major error. Since we are embarking on a journey of learning to be led by the Spirit of God, we will begin in the next chapter to study and see what the Lord means when He writes about spirit in His Word.

The next two sections of the book, Part III and Part IV, cover topics in Scripture that show us how our spiritual body is made and how the components interact. In order to live in the spirit, we *must* have a comprehensive understanding of these topics.

In Parts V and VI, the prior parts of the book are brought into a functional summary of how an individual can change from having a mixed carnal and spiritual walk with the Lord into having a more mature and more comprehensively spiritual walk with the Lord.

Part III

6
HOW DOES SCRIPTURE DEFINE SPIRIT?

TYPES OF SPIRIT(S) IN THE BIBLE

Before we study how to be led by God's Spirit, we must first understand what God's Word tells us about His use of the word *spirit*. We first reviewed every instance in the Scriptures where the word in Hebrew or Greek is translated as "spirit." After examining all of this information, we meditated upon it, sought the mind of the Lord on it, and eventually developed the following understanding of what spirit is and what spirit does. In the chapters which follow this, dealing with the anatomy and with the physiology of the spirit, it will become much clearer why we arrived at this conceptual model of spirit.

A list of the types of spirit(s) that occur in scripture follows:

1. The Holy Spirit
2. The Spirit of God
3. The human spirit
4. Angelic beings—both evil and good
5. Geographic spirits (not individual evil spirits such as the Prince of Persia)
6. National spirits
7. Animal spirits
8. Spirit associated with God's words
9. An anointing spirit from God
10. Spirits sent to groups of people by God
11. An impartation of a special spirit from God to a man

When we look at these uses of the word *spirit*, we note that the Holy Spirit, the Spirit of God, the human spirit, angelic spirits, and animal spirits are intelligent. To have intelligence, these spirits must be considerably complex. This complexity will be studied in chapter 7. We shall discuss the intelligence of the human spirit in chapters 7, 9, and 11.

We shall define the following terms that we will use—emanation, impartation, and anointing.

1. An emanation is that which is transferred between spiritual beings, including man, as a means of spiritual communication. It is like a radio wave radiating out to all in the immediate area. It is not analogous to a radio wave in that the intended recipients will receive much more information than others in the vicinity. This is because they have their spiritual receptors tuned to receive it. Thus, it is like a directed energy transmission.
2. An impartation is the transfer of spiritual energy (power) and knowledge from one spiritual being to another. This is usually a permanent transfer. It results in spiritual energy and knowledge being added to the recipient's spirit.
3. An anointing is that which is given by God for a purpose such as to equip an individual to judge a situation or to prophesy. This can be spoken of as a mantle, such as with Elisha's getting Elijah's mantle. It can be represented by a "pouring out on." An anointing is not always permanent. (An anointing was on King Saul but was removed.)

The Holy Spirit and the Spirit of God

We read in the scriptures that God is spirit. We read of the triune God the Father, God the Son, and the Holy Spirit. The Spirit of God is often mentioned, and it is uncertain whether this always refers to the Holy Spirit or whether at times it refers to the Spirit of God the Father. In all practicality, it makes no difference to the conclusions that we reach in this book. Therefore, we will be content to have ambiguity with respect to whether God is always referring to the Holy Spirit as a distinct person or whether He is sometimes referring to a more limited emanation for a particular purpose of a particular spirit(s) from Him.

Geographic and National Spirits

In various scriptures God talks about pouring out a particular spirit over a geographic area, such as Egypt; in some passages of Scripture He talks about pouring out a spirit over a people group in a specific area (*e.g.*, Isaiah 29:1-10). God uses these spirits to accomplish some of His purposes.

Spirit Associated with God's Words

In Scripture we read that God's words are spirit and life (John 6:63). Since we are held accountable for all of our own words and because we are made in God's image, our words also must have spirit. The Scripture does not expressly state this, but it does state God weighs all of the spirits emanating from people associated with behaviors and motivations. In Proverbs 16:2 we read: "All the ways of a man are clean in his own eyes; but the Lord weigheth the spirits." Speaking is a behavior (or way) of man.

Anointing Spirits and Impartations of Spirit

In different passages of Scripture we see God speak of placing His Spirit upon or over someone. This is to effect a certain impact—frequently for prophecy, sometimes for judgment. In Joel 2:28-29 He states that He will pour out His Spirit over all flesh. This will result in dreams and prophecy.

In other Scriptures God talks of placing a spirit into someone, as an impartation, that will remain resident with him. He usually does this to cause special skills and knowledge to be resident in an individual. This spirit presumably joins with the individual's spirit to become a part of it. Exodus 28:3 is an example.

Spirits sent to groups of people by God

One example of a spirit sent by God is the occasion in which a lying spirit volunteered to go and be a lying spirit in the mouths of King Ahab's prophets (1 Kings 22:22-23).

TRANSMISSION OF SPIRIT

We read of God's breathing spirit into Adam in order for him to become a living soul (Genesis 2:7).

We read of the Holy Spirit's being given from the laying on of hands (1 Timothy 4:14).

We are warned in Scripture not to accept casually the laying on of hands, since presumably evil spirits can also be transmitted in this manner (1 Timothy 5:22).

We read of Elisha's receiving a double portion of the spirit of Elijah, when he saw Elijah taken up by God (2 Kings 2:9).

WHAT THEN IS SPIRIT?

HEBREW AND GREEK WORDS

When one looks at the original languages for the term *spirit*, there is an association with wind and breath. God breathed into Adam's nostrils, and he became a living soul. Jesus, in describing the spirit (John 3:8), likened it to the wind. No one sees spirit, but one can see the effects of it—just like wind or breath.

The Holy Spirit is also portrayed in Scripture as oil. We see this in the anointing of Aaron and his sons as priests. We see it in the lampstand in the tabernacle. We see it in the New Testament as described by Jesus and recorded in the Gospels in the parable of the ten virgins and the oil for their lamps.

FORM OF A SPIRIT

Jesus stated that a spirit does not have flesh and bones. We read that Jesus stated that we cannot see the Spirit but that we can see the effects of the Spirit (He was referring to the Spirit of God). He likened the Spirit to a wind. Many passages in Scripture, as we have read above, mention a spirit's being poured out (Joel 2:28-29). The anointing on the prophets was viewed as a mantle.

These passages lead us to conclude that to the natural eye a spirit is invisible, but the impact of it can be seen. It also tells us that from the natural perspective a spirit is formless like a liquid or a gas, or at most it can be draped like a mantle (like a flowing solid). We cannot go beyond this and state what a spirit would appear like with spiritual vision, but we do know that God has given men glimpses into the spiritual universe and that demonic and angelic spirits have many forms—*e.g.*, seraphim with six wings, the cherubim, and others similar to a man. However, we do not know whether God portrayed them in an anthromorphic manner for our understanding only or whether these are the true spiritual forms. In addition, we note that, since the effect of a spirit can be observed, a spirit can perform work.

COMPONENTS OF A SPIRIT

Perhaps the key passage in all of Scripture in helping us to define what a spirit is, in terms of being able to grapple with the concept, is in 2 Timothy 1:7, where we read that "God hath not given us a spirit of fear; but of power, of love, and of a sound mind." This shows us that our human spirit has three components to it. These are:

a) Power the ability to perform work in the spiritual and natural universes
b) Emotion—love when reflecting what God has given (but our spirit can and does contain the ability to express all of the emotions and states, such as being contrite, that God has created)
c) Control—Sound Mind when it expresses what God has given (but in a more general sense it contains knowledge or information)

When we try to look at all the Scriptural use of the term *spirit* and then try to organize it into information that we can use, this passage is most helpful. We are going to draw conclusions here from our own study of spirit in the Scriptures.

What God is telling us in this passage is that the new spirit that He gave to us at the second birth is capable of expressing His power, His love, and His mind. It is obvious that our spirit does not always do this. In fact it rarely does it. This is God's "gold standard" for the spirit that should emanate from us.

Power

In 1 Corinthians 2:4 Paul tells us: "And my speech and my preaching *was* not with enticing words of man's wisdom, but in demonstration of the Spirit and of power." We see Jesus walking through the crowds at the Nazareth cliffs and in the temple where nobody was able to touch Him or see Him because it was not His time. We see in the garden of Gethsemane that the soldiers fell back when he announced who He is. We see the power to work the miracles over nature, illness, and demons during Jesus' earthly ministry. Paul states that all things are now placed into subjection to Jesus (Ephesians 1:21). He has ultimate power. He shares His power with us as we are in need of it and if we are ready to be responsible with it (Ephesians 3:16).

The Holy Spirit strengthens us with might (power) in the inner man (spirit or spirit man [Ephesians 3:16]). The human spirit has power. When we subject our soul (and consequently our spirit) as a servant of God, He will give us special powers such as He gave the disciples—authority over illness and demons. The human spirit can, therefore, express power of its own. It can express power from God. Unfortunately, as in the example of the Gadarene man, we see that it can also express demonic power.

In our testing of our spirit we must always ask ourselves whether our spirit is demonstrating these three components that God gave to it—*i.e.*, God's power, God's love, and God's mind. If it is not, it is because our flesh or an evil spirit is modifying the expression or because we have allowed our heart to be impure and our spirit to be polluted. Until these three components are constantly demonstrating God's Spirit to be present in what is overflowing (emanating) from us, then we have not reached the maturity of spirit that God calls us to reach.

Emotion

Our spirit can emanate a full range of emotions and emotional states that are the same as those that God experiences. We will learn later that there are two sets of emotions, spiritual and soulish. These are similar in certain respects, but in other respects they are quite different. When the Holy Spirit sheds an emotion abroad in our heart by witnessing with our spirit, this is a pure and Godly emotion. As this spirit traverses our heart into the flesh and the mind, it will be contaminated by our fleshly emotions, which reside in our heart. These fleshly emotions are associated with various learned behavior patterns throughout our lives. It becomes an impure or soulish emotion. This impure emotion contaminates the spirit emanating from us. Only as we purify our hearts, with God's help, will the spirit become more purely that of the Holy Spirit. We will discuss this whole concept in great detail as we proceed through this book.

God is telling us that He has given us a spirit of love. This means that when our spirit is pure, it will express all emotions subjected to a hierarchy in which love is the pinnacle. We will learn more about this later, but an example of the ordering of the emotions in such a hierarchy is shown by the difference between righteous anger and soulish anger. An individual may be righteously angry about a situation that is harming God and/or one of his neighbors. This would be anger subject to love. A soulish emotion would be a reflex anger when one's ego is thwarted. In the second situation, self is elevated above God's standard for love. God's standard for love is complete self sacrifice, such as the Lord Jesus' actions in undergoing the emptying of self (*kenosis*) described in Philippians 2:5-9.

Knowledge or Information

A spirit, when flowing from one individual spiritual being to another spiritual being, always conveys information about a situation. It conveys a structured knowledge. God has given us in our new spirit the ability to have a sound mind. This means the ability to apprehend absolute truth pertaining to a situation. If our spirit conveys what the Holy Spirit gives to it, then we will speak absolute truth. Our spirit will have the ability to know when God is imparting something to it. Those who are prophets experience words coming into their spirit from the Holy Spirit. If they pronounce these as detected, they are speaking absolute truth. They must also capture adequately the inflexion. A prophet might feel an urge to explain and interpret information due to a fleshly pressure. If the prophet succumbs to this pressure, then the sound mindedness of the communication will be lessened.

We can see that sound mindedness is really having the mind of Christ. This we are asked to develop.

CONCLUSIONS

Let us then bring together a concept of what spirit is. We have not examined yet the factual basis for the conclusions expressed here, but we will cover this in subsequent chapters. Spirit is the essence of life that is imparted into the creation and the created creatures by the Lord. It always has three aspects in various combinations:

1) Power
2) Emotion
3) Information

Spirit imparted by God in keeping with these three aspects can be in the form of a unique individual such as an angelic being or a man. In these forms there is a unique expression of spirit emanating from the being at any one time. The individual is capable of changing the spirit emanating from himself continuously. The gamut of power, emotion, and information that can be expressed by a man's spirit is as full as that which God expresses, since man is made in the image of God.

In what is probably the simplest form of spirit, a spoken or written word, we note that the author of that word is putting some power (the physics definition is quite appropriate here, which is a sustained flow of energy over time) into it. The author has probably formed the word within a broader message but even the use of the word *no* can have many emotional tones. The word *no* is expressed in a context of the passage of information from one intelligent being to another. A single word is probably the smallest element containing spirit; and, as discussed, it conveys power, emotion, and information.

When we look at the spirit of a man in the next few chapters, we will see a very complex spirit that really is the seed that will be released from the body of corruption into eternal existence at the point of death. This seed is clothed in a new spiritual body that is incorruptible. Our soul shapes and molds this new human spirit obtained at the second birth. After the first death this spirit is our spiritual seed sown into eternity. We need to dwell on how important it is, therefore, to teach and train our spirit man to be all that it should be before the Lord God.

The human spirit has an intelligent mind, has a full set of emotions, and carries knowledge that is derived from revelation by God. It is tainted by the earthly experiences of the soul to various degrees. The Apostle Paul tells us to cleanse ourselves from all filthiness of the spirit in the context of talking with people who have gone through the second birth (2 Corinthians 7:1).

Our human spirit is capable of expressing through our impure hearts thousands of beliefs, attitudes, and behavior patterns that it can energize. God looks on all of these as spirits that He weighs (Proverbs 16:2 states: "All the ways of a man *are* clean in his own eyes; but the LORD weigheth the spirits"). At any one moment we express a limited number of these, which are perceived by others at the level of their spirit.

Psychologists talk about non-verbal communication. They are actually describing the power and emotional parts of the spiritual communication. The words which people speak are the information part of the spiritual communication. Whenever we communicate with God, other men, or other parts of the creation, we are releasing spiritual force (again the physics definition is a good parallel). This spiritual force is always comprised of a degree of strength, a particular emotion, and the imparting of information. The fact that it acts over time to produce a result means that the spiritual strength actually causes a result or work, and in this sense it is also a parallel to the physics concept of power.

As we examine the structure and functioning of the human spirit and of the human soul in subsequent chapters, we should see the factual basis in God's Word that has led us to this overview. We will see how the various components of man interact. We will see examples of the spiritual impact of the human spirit on other spirits and on God. We will see how we are made to function, and then we will look at the impact this knowledge can have on us for our future plans and life.

For many people the thoughts expressed above will represent a new paradigm. This will need to be examined closely. It has great implication for all of us. We will understand the importance of it more clearly if we recall the earlier chapters on the supremacy of the spiritual world over the physical world. We have to believe this and then live this to allow the full impact of the above understanding of spirit to be useful to us.

Spirit is a life energy that is structured by God to be in the form of individual lives (beings—angels or people) contained within a confined body. The whole of the creation is fundamentally spiritual. Any spiritual individual has a continuous communication with the spiritual universe and at all times expresses some aspects of its own character in the continuous communication. Spirit is what it is, just as God is "I AM." Spirit has no guile; but our soul, heart, and mind contrive to make people have guile. They can mask the purity of spiritual communications and thus bring deceit into a communication. As our hearts are purified and our spirit is cleansed, we emanate a cleaner spirit that is closer to the Holy Spirit's qualities, as our spirit bears witness to the Spirit of God. Our spirit is always in communication with the spiritual universe and is seen by the enemy. Our spirit reveals the state of our heart to God (completely) and to the enemy (to some extent—see how well Satan knew Job).

We see that the spirit of man is in continuous communication with God, who can integrate all that He is seeing, hearing, and feeling constantly. Individual spiritual beings cannot apprehend the amount of information that God can understand. We should keep in mind that we are constantly emanating spiritual communications, even in our sleep. There is no communication between spiritual beings, including man, which is not primarily spiritual. In man there are communications that are always going on that are a mixture in various parts of spirit and soul in origin. The spiritual and the soul parts will add up to one hundred percent. In a man who has not been reborn, the soul part overwhelms the spirit part. In a reborn man it is God's desires for there to be a maturing of the inner man (new spirit) so that greater and greater parts of the continuous communication come from a clean spirit that is transmitted through a purified heart.

7
STRUCTURE OF THE HUMAN SPIRIT

It is very important for us to understand the structure of the human spirit and of the human soul, if we are going to follow God's desire for His people to be led by His Spirit (Romans 8:14). This seems to be a rather obvious statement, and so let us begin to explore the concept of the structure of the spirit.

To understand the structure of anything, be it person or organization, we must study the structural sub-components and their spatial interrelationship. We will explore the working of the human spirit and of the human soul in subsequent chapters. The studies of the working of the human spirit and soul will show how the components work and function together.

THE STRUCTURE OF THE HUMAN SPIRIT AND SOUL

Location of the Human Spirit within the Soul

Genesis 7:22 shows that the human spirit is located in the flesh. We will define the flesh in Chapter 12, and we will see in that chapter that the flesh defined in the Scriptures is more than our physical body. Job states in Job 27:3 that "all the while my breath (spirit) is in me." This shows that the location of the spirit is within our corporal body. In James 4:5 we read that "the spirit that dwells in us lusts to envy." Therefore, the Scriptures tell us that our spirit is contained within our physical body. In Daniel 7:15 we read: "I Daniel was grieved in my spirit in the midst of *my* body, and the visions of my head troubled me." This clearly indicates that Daniel perceived that his spirit was different from his mind and was in his midst. The *midst* probably indicates the area of the upper abdomen and lower thorax.

Complexity of the Human Spirit

We will examine the various moods and emotions of our spirit in

Chapter 8 and will see that our spirit can have many various moods and emotions. Since the spirit is subject to moods and emotions, it must be just as complex an entity as our flesh and soul. We need to stop thinking, if we ever did, of the spirit as just a little internal emotion or feeling. That concept will never get us to a point of allowing us to be led by God's Spirit. We see, perhaps, the most overwhelming evidence for great complexity in our spirit in reading 1 Corinthians 15:45, where Paul states that the first man Adam was made a living soul, and the last Adam was made a quickening spirit. The "last Adam" always refers to the Lord Jesus.

Location of the Spirit within the Soul and Flesh

In Ezekiel 1:20-21 we read that the spirit of the living creature was in the wheels. This tells us that the spirit of these creatures spirit was definitely located in a specific part of them. This suggests that in man there is a specific location for the spirit.

We get more understanding of the inner structure of the soul when we read Romans 2:29: "he is a Jew, which is one inwardly; and circumcision is that of the heart, in the spirit, and not in the letter; whose praise is not of men, but of God." Thus, the human spirit resides in the heart (not the physical cardiac organ). This Scripture is easy to misinterpret and for one to think that the heart is in the spirit, but other Scriptures place the spirit in the heart. This verse is written in a journalistic style. There is other Scripture that tells us that the Holy Spirit also dwells in our heart when we are born of the Spirit at the second birth.

The Hidden Man

Ephesians 3:16 tells us that Paul is praying that "God would grant you, according to the riches of His glory, to be strengthened with might by His Spirit in the inner man." This tells us that our unseen structure includes an inner man, or a "hidden man."

In Hebrews 4:12 we read that "the word of God is quick, and powerful, and sharper than any two-edged sword, piercing even to the dividing asunder of soul and spirit." This shows us that the soul and spirit are distinct parts of us. It indicates also that we are easily confused about what is from our soul and what is from our spirit in terms of being led by God. We need for the *logos* (word) of God to make these areas distinct. If we do not undergo this surgical procedure by the Word of God, then the Holy Spirit can never consistently lead us. We will always be led by a mixture of soul and spirit drives.

Another key passage of Scripture for understanding the internal structure of the soul is found in 1 Peter 3:4: "but let it be the hidden man of the heart, in that which is not corruptible, even the ornament of a meek and quiet spirit, which is in the sight of God of great price." This seems to tell us that the hidden man of the heart is our spirit. This is consistent with the new man that Paul talks about in Ephesians 4:22-24. We receive this new spirit at the second birth. After our physical death it is given a spiritual body at the resurrection. Until the physical death the new spirit is clothed with the old body, and the new man remains hidden in the heart. We know that a spirit is not flesh and bone, so we are not able to say with certainty just what the difference is between the new man and the new spirit. The use of the term *new man*, as opposed to just *new spirit*, probably results from God's giving us new flesh in the form of a new heart at the second birth. It is not a new cardiac organ but rather part of the spiritual structure that is replaced as a new heart or added to the flesh as a new heart. The intersection of the spiritual heart and the organic body is not well defined by Scripture, but we will get some further insights later in the chapter pertaining to the heart.

Let us look further at the hidden man of the heart mentioned by Paul in Ephesians 3:16. Here we read of an inner man who can be strengthened by the Spirit of God. We see again that this inner man is found in our heart. God often speaks allegorically to us and also frequently shows us how something works by comparing something that we can see to something that is unseen. For example, there are many examples in the construction of the tabernacle to show us the story of our eventual salvation through the cross. The visible things spoke to the ancient Israelites of a future that was as yet unseen. In terms of allegory in the area of the spirit and the flesh God chooses to use the concept of a seed's being sown. To understand this better, we can note that a very important thrust in Scripture is the fact that it is our spirit (not our soul) that is saved in the final judgment. Our spirit does get a resurrection body. The first part is illustrated by Scriptures such as 1 Corinthians 5:3-5. Here we see that Paul told the Corinthian church to "deliver such a one unto Satan for the destruction of the flesh, that the spirit may be saved in the day of the Lord Jesus."

To understand further this issue of the spirit and the hidden man, we will return again to 1 Corinthians 15:45. This shows us that the spirit is really our eternal being that can be clothed with a spiritual body. In Luke 24:37-39 Jesus tells the disciples in an appearance after His resurrection that a "spirit hath not flesh and bones." Spirits can be clothed with a natural or a spiritual body. After the first birth into the world our spirits are clothed with a natural body of flesh. After our resurrection we will receive a spiritual body. The Lord was in a resurrection body that clothed His spirit after His resurrection. It is evident that before His incarnation the Lord Jesus made many appearances to people such as Abraham, Jacob, and Job—to name a few. Presumably, He was using a spiritual body at those appearances. A spiritual body is not subject to death and decay as a fleshly body is. It is noteworthy that 1 Corinthians 15:45 has the word *made* translated twice from different Greek words. The first time, referring to Adam, it refers to the making of Adam into a living soul which occurred when God breathed the spirit into Adam. The fact that within the same verse a different word is used for the Lord Jesus becoming a quickening spirit should alert us to a distinctly different process. The making of a soul obviously results in a different product to the making of a life-giving spirit. However the important point to grasp in this is that the making of the Lord Jesus into a life-giving spirit was not part of the creation. The Lord Jesus had no need of creation since He was there as God before the foundation of the world, and He is the Creator. Therefore, this second use of the word *make* refers to a process that took place within the realm of time. Since the Lord Jesus is the first of many brethren (who will be made into life-giving spirits), this process is presumably one that those who are brethren of the Lord will undergo. As a quickening Spirit He is able to give eternal life to those who accept Him as their Lord and Savior.

CONCLUSION ABOUT THE STRUCTURE OF THE SPIRIT

We will now review the structure of the human spirit. Our spirit is located in the heart, and it is developed from the time of the new birth throughout our lifetime into that part of our being that goes into eternal life. It is separated from the natural body of corruption in a process similar to a seed's being planted into the ground. Our spirit is given a new and incorruptible body after our resurrection. Therefore, our spirit is who we will be in eternity. It is obviously just as complex as our flesh, and even more complex. Note carefully that our spirit is not our soul and that we must learn to distinguish what is coming into our minds from the soul and what is coming from the spirit. This is clear from Hebrews 4:12. We can be led consistently by the Holy Spirit only if our spirit leads us in our decision making and subsequent behavior. Our spirit combined with our flesh produces our soul. This is a basic formula that God gives us in Genesis 2:7 "And the LORD God formed man *of* the dust of the ground, and breathed into his nostrils the breath of life; and man became a living soul." The flesh was created from dust, and God breathed the spirit into Adam. This combination made a soul.

In using the term *inner man* God seems to be telling us that the inner part of us that is essential for maintaining us as a distinct being after our physical death has the key attributes of a man. The new things God gives us at the second birth include the giving of a new heart and a new spirit. It is the concept of a new heart combined with a new spirit that makes it a new man as opposed to being a new spirit only. We cannot see the spiritual shape without God's giving us a spiritual vision; otherwise, our only revelation is His written Word. We know from what Jesus said (quoted above) that spirits do not have flesh or bones. The phrase that Peter uses in 1 Peter 3:4, "in that which is not corruptible," refers to the fact that this new spirit will not die. The old man of flesh is going to die, since the sin caused by the flesh led God to judge the flesh.

Now that we have learned about the structure of the human spirit, it is an appropriate time to examine the structure of the soul. This will lead us to a deeper understanding of what God expects of us in this life.

THE STRUCTURE OF THE HUMAN SOUL

Two key passages of Scripture enable us to understand the fundamental issues in the structure of the human soul.

"That ye put off concerning the former conversation the old man, which is corrupt according to the deceitful lusts; And be renewed in the spirit of your mind; And that ye put on the new man, which after God is created in righteousness and true holiness" (Ephesians 4:22-24).

"Lie not one to another, seeing that ye have put off the old man with his deeds; And have put on the new man, which is renewed in knowledge after the image of him that created him" (Colossians 3:9-10).

In these passages the Apostle Paul directs us to put off the old man and to put on the new man. This immediately tells us that as a soul we have a choice to make about who we are going to be, the old man or the new man. Our soul is able to make a decision. This is because both the old man and the new man share the same mind. When we are given a new heart and a new spirit at the time of rebirth, we become different from those who have never been through this rebirth. Before rebirth we were at enmity with God, and our father was the devil. We had no means of changing this. God gave us by His grace a way of becoming His children, through faith in His Son as our Lord and Savior.

The Scriptures tell us to renew our mind after rebirth. We are asked to take every thought captive for the Lord Jesus. God places a new heart and a new spirit into us at the time of rebirth. The Scriptures do not seem to indicate whether the old heart and the old spirit are removed or remain. In terms of what God expects of us, it is not of any functional consequence whether they remain. What we had before the second birth is a spirit that was doomed to eternal separation from God. Now God has placed a new spirit into us at the second birth that is created in righteousness and holiness, as the passage quoted above from Ephesians 4:22-24 tells us. Since Paul uses the terms *old man* and *new man* and since God is always accurate, we will, therefore, need to understand these terms. Galatians

2:20 tells us: "I am crucified with Christ: nevertheless I live; yet not I, but Christ liveth in me: and the life which I now live in the flesh I live by the faith of the Son of God, who loved me, and gave himself for me." This indicates that it is the new spirit that gives us life after the second birth. We now live because of our new spirit which was given to us when we accepted the atonement of the Lord Jesus. Thus, the old spirit is either gone or not functioning, and we can disregard it for further discussion. There is never any mention in Scripture regarding the old spirit and the old heart, so my interpretation is that the Lord removed them after giving us the new spirit and heart at the second birth. A passage that strongly supports this view is 1 Thessalonians 5:23 where Paul prays that "your whole spirit and soul and body be preserved blameless unto the coming of our Lord Jesus Christ." This verse indicates that functionally the new man is made of three major interrelated components—flesh, spirit, and soul. These could not be preserved, wholly blameless, if the old heart and spirit were still present. An interesting consideration arises as to the order in which this took place. Did God place the new before removing the old, or did He remove the old first? If He removed the old first, then we were technically dead at least momentarily; and then the above Scripture from Galatians 2:20 can be seen in a very different light. I do not think that we can be sure, and idle speculation without more fact is an intellectual exercise that is inclined to inflate the flesh. The order in which this occurred does not have any impact on the concepts in the rest of this book. If one really wants to know this, then he should pray to God and ask for His revelation on the topic.

The term *old man* indicates the flesh with all of the learned patterns of sinful behavior and the lusts that remain after the second birth. It is this flesh which has to be crucified daily. The flesh is combined with the new spirit to make the *old man*. Similarly, with the term *new man* it is apparent that this is the new spirit and the new heart clothed in the original flesh. The new spirit and new heart and old flesh also result in the *new man*. The *new man* has to be put on by the soul, and the *old man* must be crucified by the soul. This is done partly by the renewing of the mind. The flesh cannot be renewed, and remains dying, but actively at war against the new spirit. The spirit and the flesh are always (constantly in every thought and action) at enmity. We will discuss this in greater detail in the chapters about the working of the spirit and the working of the soul. As we progress through the chapters on how the various components of the soul work, we will see in much detail how this transition from the old man to the new man can be accomplished.

After the new birth our mind can receive information from the new spirit which is in our new heart, and it can receive information from the flesh. In Genesis 2:7 God tells us that He breathed spirit into Adam's flesh and that he (Adam) became a living soul. This tripartite structure that we have is foundational for much of our understanding of our soul's structure. We see that "PHYSICAL FLESH + SPIRIT = SOUL." This is a foundational concept for understanding the spiritual structure of man.

We shall now turn our attention to looking briefly at the sub-components of our soul. The various areas of the soul to which the Scriptures refer are the mind (as opposed to the structural brain), the heart, the conscience, the will, the spirit, and the flesh.

SPIRIT

We have learned much about God's portrayal of spirit in Chapter 6. Spirits, like flesh, vary in complexity. Just as in the natural there are simple amoeba and complex men, so in the spiritual there are very simple spirits and very complex spirits—such as the Holy Spirit, the spirit of man, archangels, and demons. The more complex spirits, including the spirit of man, are intelligent. God views our new spirit as being an *inner man*. Thus, our new spirit is very complex, and we will learn later that it is more intelligent than our soul. 2 Corinthians 7:1 tells us to "cleanse ourselves from all filthiness of the flesh and spirit, perfecting holiness in the fear of God." This shows that our new spirit, while clean at the time of the new birth, becomes polluted and has to be cleaned. This cleaning process can be performed by an act of our will and is under our conscious control and within our power to perform—God would not command us to do something that was unnecessary or that we could not accomplish.

MIND

Within the mind are areas that think, that remember, and that make final decisions. The soul develops beliefs, forms attitudes, and adopts behaviors. These form in the mind as a result of our past experiences and as the result of our understanding of the future. In the spiritual universe we have a mind that is different from the brain. The brain is the fleshly part that provides a framework for our mind. We have a fallen mind, and after spiritual birth we can renew our mind. Both our flesh and our spirit use our mind. In Ephesians 4:3-4 Paul tells us after the second birth to be renewed in the "spirit of our mind." We will discuss this in detail in Chapter 11. When using the term *mind* so far, we have been alluding to what we shall term *the mind of the soul*. We will find out that our soul has four minds—those of the spirit, the heart, the soul, and the flesh. They all communicate in such a manner that the mind of the soul has the power to make final decisions for the soul over the other minds within the sub-components of the soul.

Our heart is the core of our soul that contains the spirit. In the new man the Holy Spirit is also resident in the heart. The Old Testament Scriptures tell us that our hearts are wicked and that only God can see the depths of them. In the new man we have a new heart, but it is surrounded by the old man. We see that our heart includes at least a part of our mind, since it is out of our mouths that the thoughts and intents of our heart are expressed. This illustrates that the heart must contain at least a substantial part of our mind, since it has thoughts and intents. God writes His laws on our hearts.

CONSCIENCE

The location of the conscience is uncertain. Our conscience requires purifying when the new spirit is given. The scriptures tell us that a conscience can be defiled.

WILL

The will is within the mind. The bedrock decisions made by the will and the adhering to them make us the person that we become.

FLESH

The flesh is the natural body and the learned processes that we retain in the non-renewed mind. These learned processes consist of sinful lusts, memories, beliefs, attitudes, and thought patterns. Our motives for acquiring knowledge structure what we learn and remember. Sin falls into three categories—the lust of the flesh, the lust of the eyes, and the pride of life. The flesh is the source of all three of these sin areas in the new man.

We will now look at some of the other parts of our structure that are derived from these core parts of the soul.

OTHER PARTS OF THE SOUL

An important part of our soul is communication both in the natural world and in the spiritual world. In 1 Corinthians 12:1-13 we read "he that speaketh in an unknown tongue speaketh not unto men, but unto God: for no man understandeth him; howbeit in the spirit he speaketh mysteries." This tells us that our spirit can speak and that we can mobilize our voice both by our spirit and by our soul. The mobilization by the soul is through the mind.

2 Timothy 1:14 shows that the Holy Spirit also dwells within the corporeal flesh of those who are "born again" and is, of course, distinct from the human spirit: "that good thing which was committed unto thee keep by the Holy Ghost which dwelleth in us." In addition, in 1 Corinthians 6:17-20 we read: "He that is joined to the Lord is one spirit ... he that committeth fornication sinneth against his own body. What? Know ye not that your body is the temple of the Holy Ghost? Ye are bought with a price: therefore glorify God in your body and in your spirit, which are God's."

It is important also to see what our spirit is not. In 1 Timothy 4:12 we read: "be thou an example of the believers, in word, in conversation, in charity, in spirit, in faith, in purity." This shows that the spirit is not conversation, not charity, not faith, and not purity alone. All of these are linked, and a person will not be perfected in one without being perfected in the other areas.

Our corporeal bodies can be separated from our spirits, and many Scriptures tell us that this results in our corporeal death. One of these Scriptures is poignant in another way: James tells us in 2:26 that "as the body without the spirit is dead, so faith without works is dead also." The parallel here is that works are the "spirit" that sustain our faith and keep it alive. If we take away our works, then our faith is dead. Many people tend to look at this in reverse and state that, if we have faith, works will follow, since we will do works out of our faith. It is the very opposite. As we are obedient to God to do the work that He asks us to do, then our faith will live and grow. If we are not obedient to God and demonstrate this in action, then we will not get faith. This is entirely consistent with other Scripture that tells us that "faith comes by hearing and hearing by the [*rhema*] word of God." When God speaks a personal request to us and we act in obedience to it, our faith grows. We could, at our own peril, not act on His individual word to us; and then we would not develop or increase our faith. The growth in faith comes from seeing God keep His promises.

SPIRITUAL SENSES

In Revelation 4:2 John states: "I was in the spirit: and, behold, a throne was set in heaven, and one sat on the throne." Clearly, John is talking about seeing in a spiritual vision that which was revealed to him. Paul also talks about an incident when he was seeing supernatural things and notes that he did not know if he was in his body or out of it (2 Corinthians 12:1-4). It is not clear exactly what Paul means, but it is clear that we have different senses in our spirits. In Mathew 22:43 Jesus asks: "How then doth David in spirit call him Lord?" This indicates that David in his spirit was able to call him Lord, indicating a perception and a reasoning process in his spirit. In Mark 2:8 we read that "Jesus perceived in His spirit."Jesus' perceiving in His spirit indicates the ability to sense in the spirit.

In 1 Corinthians 5:3–5 Paul says: "For I verily, as absent in the body, but present in spirit, have judged already. As though I were present." This indicates that the spirit, while resident in our hearts and in the inner man, is not constrained to sensing in the same way that the corporeal body is limited. In other words a spiritual sensing is able to cover physical distances that a corporeal sense is not able to.

CONCLUSIONS

1. The spirit of a man is closely linked to the inner man, and the inner man is hidden in the heart.
2. The spirit is able to sense and then to reason and understand information that it receives and which may come over large geographic distances.
3. The spirit is always at enmity with the flesh; and to be led by the Holy Spirit, one must have a separation of the soul and of the spirit.
4. We have a responsibility to keep our spirit from being defiled.

Therefore, the structure of the spirit is quite complex; and in order to present our spirits to God in purity, we must see to it that they are cleansed in their structure and operation.

A quickening spirit is a life-giving spirit. When Jesus was able to overcome death because there was no sin in Him, then He was able to transmit that life to those who accept Him as Lord and Savior. Our mortal bodies, when sown into the ground, have a spiritual seed in them that has been placed there at the time of our rebirth. This seed. when raised, has a new spiritual body. By implication our spiritual seed that is sown determines who we are in the eternal kingdom. Therefore, it seems that our spirit that is presented to the Lord during our earthly tenure is the genetic material in a sense that determines our heavenly persona. We certainly have very complex spirits.

8
THE EMOTIONS AND MOODS OF THE HUMAN SPIRIT

In this chapter we will learn what God means by the following terms that He uses in Scripture: lead/led, paths, lusts, desires, and visions.

BACKGROUND

We have discussed that the three components of a spirit are power, emotion (or state of the heart), and a control (or information) element. If we look at the physical universe and how it is structured, we see bodies (masses) from sub-atomically small to astronomically large. These are held in place by forces and are moved by forces. As these masses are moved, there is a release of power from one body's acting on another. We can see in this an analogy to the three components of a spirit in which the masses are the packets of information ranging from very small, such as an individual idea that one person holds, to the very large, such as a major philosophy to which many people adhere. The forces acting on these individual ideas and philosophies are the emotions. I shall not push this analogy further in this book, since it is not the focus of this work. It is of interest and may help some people to develop a greater appreciation of the God who created all things and to see how He speaks to us in the physical sciences, if they wish to study this more rigorously.

Also in the life sciences we can get an understanding of the role of spiritual maladies interacting with the psychological functioning of people and how this can lead to psychiatric states developing. We see how they may be approached for healing, as we look at the implications of what follows, and how the understanding of "spirit" brings great insight into such situations.

It is very important to understand how a soul (person) is led into performing his actions and developing and holding his attitudes and beliefs. The study of being "led" applies to the soul. We shall now look at the above mentioned words.

LEAD/LED

We shall study the verb *lead* and other tenses and forms of the word. These are used in the Scriptures just as they are in regular use. They speak of an individual or groups of souls following a leader.

God as leader

Frequently the Lord is the leader, as in Genesis 24:48: "And I bowed down my head, and worshipped the LORD, and blessed the LORD God of my master Abraham, which had led me in the right way to take my master's brother's daughter unto his son." We read in Deuteronomy 8:2: "And thou shalt remember all the way which the LORD thy God led thee these forty years in the wilderness, to humble thee, *and* to prove thee, to know what *was* in thine heart, whether thou wouldest keep his commandments, or no." Psalm 68:18 says, "Thou hast ascended on high, thou hast led captivity captive: thou hast received gifts for men; yea, *for* the rebellious also, that the LORD God might dwell *among them*." Psalm 107:7 states: "And he led them forth by the right way, that they might go to a city of habitation." Note here that there is a right way in which God will lead us. God will sometimes lead us into a way that does not have a seemingly good end immediately in order for a greater lesson to be learned, as in Ezekiel 39:28: "Then shall they know that I *am* the LORD their God, which caused them to be led into captivity among the heathen: but I have gathered them unto their own land, and have left none of them any more there."

How God leads us

God has different expectations of how we are to be led by Him. These depend on our "spiritual maturity." In Hebrews 5:13 the term *babes* is used to describe those who have been through the second birth. In Romans 8:14 the term *sons* is used to describe those who have been through the second birth and who are being led by the Spirit of God. God wants us to mature in our walk with Him. This is to our own eternal good that we should do this. In 2 Timothy 2:20 we see one of the major reasons we should wish to know God more closely, love Him as we should, and consequently be a vessel of usefulness to Him. We should aspire to be a vessel of gold for the Lord. As we go through this chapter, we shall examine the various ways that God leads us and then dwell at greater length on how we can prepare to be led by the Spirit of God. This will necessitate our learning the different spiritual states of our heart and, therefore, the various emotional states that our heart can display and emanate.

In Psalm 25:5 we read: "Lead me in thy truth, and teach me: for thou *art* the God of my salvation; on thee do I wait all the day." The Lord leads in truth. If we do not walk in truth, we are not following the Spirit of God. The Lord also leads us in a plain path. We read this in Psalm 27:11: "Teach me thy way, O LORD, and lead me in a plain path, because of mine enemies." A plain path is described as a "way of plainness." This is in contrast to an exotic or twisted path. We see that the way of the Lord is straight, as in Isaiah 40:3-4: "The voice of him that crieth in the wilderness, Prepare ye the way of the LORD, make straight in the desert a highway for our God. Every valley shall be exalted, and every mountain and hill shall be made low: and the crooked shall be made straight and the rough places plain." The path of the Lord is straight; where He goes, we go; and, therefore, our way will not be devious but very straight, plain, and truthful.

In Psalm 139:24 we read: "And see if *there be any* wicked way in me, and lead me in the way everlasting." God will lead us in the way everlasting. If our way is not building for the future eternity, then the leading we are following is not of God.

God will lead us into the land of uprightness: "Teach me to do thy will; for thou *art* my God: thy spirit *is* good; lead me into the land of uprightness (Psalm 143:10)." If we are not walking in uprightness, then we are not being led by God.

God's commandments (not just the ten, but all of His Word) will lead us as described in Proverbs 6:22: "When thou goest, it shall lead thee; when thou sleepest, it shall keep thee; and *when* thou awakest, it shall talk with thee." If we are obedient to God, we are led by Him. If we are disobedient, then at those times we are not led by Him and can end up in terrible spiritual trouble because of our following some other spirit.

In Proverbs 8:20 we read: "I lead in the way of righteousness, in the midst of the paths of judgment." God will lead us into the way of righteousness. If our contemplated behavior is not in the area of righteousness, then God is not leading us at that point. We are told here that the path of righteousness is surrounded by paths that lead to God's judgment.

Isaiah 49:10 tells us: "They shall not hunger nor thirst; neither shall the heat nor sun smite them: for he that hath mercy on them shall lead them, even by the springs of water shall he guide them." God will lead us in a path that is refreshing, and we will not hunger or thirst (spiritually). We cannot expect to have no physical hunger or thirst; that would be inconsistent with many other Scripture passages.

In Jeremiah 31:9 we read: "They shall come with weeping, and with supplications will I lead them: I will cause them to walk by the rivers of waters in a straight way, wherein they shall not stumble: for I am a father to Israel, and Ephraim *is* my firstborn." Again, we see that God leads in a straight way. We also see other reasons for why He will lead us.

God will not lead us into temptation. James 1:13 states: "Let no man say when he is tempted, I am tempted of God: for God cannot be tempted with evil neither tempteth he any man." Matthew 6:13 states: "And lead us not into temptation, but deliver us from evil: For thine is the kingdom, and the power, and the glory, for ever. Amen." If we are tempted to do something (that is, we are experiencing temptation), then we know that this path is not of God. James continues: "But every man is tempted, when he is drawn away of his own lust, and enticed. Then when lust hath conceived, it bringeth forth sin: and sin, when it is finished, bringeth forth death (James 1:14-15)." We need to discern the spirit of temptation so that, when we recognize it, we need to not yield to it. It may come in quite subtle forms and variations, but it will be recognizable and will become more easily discerned through practice. The choice may not be unrighteous in its own right but will be in context with all other issues. An example would be that of the Pharisees. They circumvented the Lord's command to support their needy parents by pledging their resources to the Lord (Mark 7:11).

In Psalm 32:8 we read: "I will instruct thee and teach thee in the way which thou shalt go: I will guide thee with mine eye." God will not compel us in a leading. He will give us wisdom. If we are feeling compelled to do something by the spirit associated with the choice, then this is not of God. God's leading is gentle and with reasoning.

In Isaiah 30.21 we read: "And thine ears shall hear a word behind thee, saying, This *is* the way, walk ye in it, when ye turn to the right hand, and when ye turn to the left." We have to learn to hear the voice of God in order to be led properly. If we do not learn to distinguish His voice from other voices speaking to our mind of the soul, then we will always have trouble being led by God. We will discuss hearing the voice of God in greater depth in later chapters.

In summary, we should look at the consequences of our beliefs, attitudes, and behaviors in terms of our walk before the Lord. If our reasons for doing what we do are not plain and straightforward, righteous, building for eternity, obedient to His commands, based in truth, gentle, spiritually refreshing, and spiritually nourishing, then we should wait until we are absolutely sure that we are hearing from God. In addition, we absolutely must learn to distinguish His voice from all those voices speaking to the mind of our soul.

Why God will lead us

We can entreat the Lord to remember His Word and lead us as He has promised in Psalm 31:3: "For thou *art* my rock and my fortress;

therefore for thy name's sake lead me, and guide me." He has promised to do it; and, therefore, He will do it for His name's sake.

We see in Psalm 43.3: "O send out thy light and thy truth: let them lead me; let them bring me unto thy holy hill, and to thy tabernacles." God will send light and truth to us to lead us to Him.

In Psalm 61:2 we see that God will lead us to Himself when we cry out for His help when our heart is overwhelmed: "From the end of the earth will I cry unto thee, when my heart is overwhelmed: lead me to the rock *that* is higher than I." Our heart must be overwhelmed and in a state of self abandonment. God will answer us when we have lost all self sufficiency.

Jeremiah 31:9 adds: "They shall come with weeping, and with supplications will I lead them: I will cause them to walk by the rivers of waters in a straight way, wherein they shall not stumble: for I am a father to Israel, and Ephraim *is* my firstborn."

God leading

Most of those Scriptures we have reviewed above do not specify a particular member of the Godhead as leading people but some Scriptures denote a specific member of the Holy Trinity to be the one leading us. For completeness we will review some of these briefly without attempting to elaborate on them.

God the Holy Spirit leading

Then was Jesus led up of the Spirit into the wilderness to be tempted of the devil (Matthew 4:1). Romans 8:14: "For as many as are led by the Spirit of God, they are the sons of God." Galatians 5:18: "But if ye be led of the Spirit, ye are not under the law." There are consequences as to whom we allow to lead us.

God the Son leading

Luke 24:50 tell us: "And he led them out as far as to Bethany, and he lifted up his hands, and blessed them."

God delegates leading

God spoke to Moses and delegated leadership of His people to Moses. This is a great privilege that God gave to Moses. We read about it in Exodus 32:34: "Therefore now go, lead the people unto *the place* of which I have spoken unto thee: behold, mine Angel shall go before thee: nevertheless in the day when I visit I will visit their sin upon them."

Others as Leaders

Enemies can lead someone by force, as seen in 1 Kings 8:48: "And *so* return unto thee with all their heart, and with all their soul, in the land of their enemies, which led them away captive, and pray unto thee toward their land, which thou gavest unto their fathers, the city which thou hast chosen, and the house which I have built for thy name."

Kings can lead, as we see in 2 Chronicles 25:11: "And Amaziah strengthened himself, and led forth his people, and went to the valley of salt, and smote of the children of Seir ten thousand."

Isaiah 9:16 shows a wrong way to be led: "For the leaders of this people cause *them* to err; and *they that are* led of them *are* destroyed."

Matthew 26:57 states: "And they that had laid hold on Jesus led *him* away to Caiaphas the high priest, where the scribes and the elders were assembled."

In Matthew 15:14 we read: "Let them alone: they be blind leaders of the blind. And if the blind lead the blind, both shall fall into the ditch." The Lord tells us that those who are blind (to spiritual truth) will not be able to lead someone else into spiritual truth.

2 Timothy 3:6 describes one type of evil leader and how that type of leader exerts power over those who follow him.

It requires Power to Lead

In 1 Corinthians 9:5 we read: "Have we not power to lead about a sister, a wife, as well as other apostles, and *as* the brethren of the Lord, and Cephas?" This is a very important concept, for it tells us that all leading is performed by power. In order to lead, one spiritual being has to have greater power than the other. With people the difference in power will be situational. One person may be able to lead in teaching a class, but not in deploying troops. However, since men are lower than angels, they cannot lead angels. It is for this reason that we have to seek covering under the Lord to prevent ourselves being forcefully led by Satan and his angels. Power can be released by the holder when he chooses, and it need not be ostentatiously evident. God has omnipotent power but controls the release of it carefully, as He wills. Some people have a stronger inner man than others, because they have been built up in might in the inner man (Ephesians 3:16).

We read more about the differences in spiritual power that God gives to various people and His reasons for it in Romans 13:1-7:

> Let every soul be subject unto the higher powers. For there is no power but of God: the powers that be are ordained of God. Whosoever therefore resisteth the power, resisteth the ordinance of God: and they that resist shall receive to themselves damnation. For rulers are not a terror to good works, but to the evil. Wilt thou then not be afraid of the power? do that which is good, and thou shalt have praise of the same: For he is the minister of God to thee for good. But if thou do that which is evil, be afraid; for he beareth not the sword in vain: for he is the minister of God, a revenger to *execute* wrath upon him that doeth evil. Wherefore *ye* must needs be subject, not only for wrath, but also for conscience sake. For for this cause pay ye tribute also: for they are God's ministers, attending continually upon this very thing. Render therefore to all their dues: tribute to whom tribute *is due*; custom to whom custom; fear to whom fear; honour to whom honour.

In this passage God is talking about the organization of government that He has instituted to keep law and order in our societies. We must be very careful to fulfill this Scripture obediently, if we are going to follow the Spirit of God. He will not lead us against this, unless the government itself becomes corrupt, in which case we must make a stand; but it well may be at huge personal cost, for this also is ordained of God. When God gives power to a man, such as King Nebuchadnezzar, He may not stop the man using the power wrongfully, but He will judge him for the wrong use.

1 Timothy 2:1-3 explains how God implements His wishes for these powers: "I exhort therefore, that, first of all, supplications, prayers, intercessions, *and* giving of thanks, be made for all men; For kings, and *for* all that are in authority; that we may lead a quiet and peaceable life in all godliness and honesty. For this *is* good and acceptable in the sight of God our Saviour." If we do not obey God, then He cannot do His part on our behalf; for He has ordained man to lead on earth. That is why we are asked to pray for "His will to be done on earth as it is in heaven."

Mixed Leading

A person or people can be led by more than one source. We see this in Deuteronomy 32:12: "*So* the LORD alone did lead him, and *there was* no strange god with him." Here in this passage the Scripture emphasizes that the LORD alone led him (referring to Jacob's descendants). The implication is that people can be led by more than one god in what amounts to a mixed walk, such as the Corinthian church had.

Guiding

God also guides us as He leads us. We shall now look at a few Scriptures that illustrate this. Some worth looking at are Exodus 15:13, 2 Chronicles 32:22, Psalm 25:9, Psalm 78:52, Proverbs 11:3, Isaiah 49:10, and Isaiah 51:18. In Psalm 31:3 we read: "For thou *art* my rock and my fortress; therefore for thy name's sake lead me, and guide me." Here we see that guiding is a complementary process to leading. Guiding is a fine tuning of leading. Leading is along a path, and guiding is to get us around obstacles and pitfalls along the path. In Psalm 32:8 we read:

"I will instruct thee and teach thee in the way which thou shalt go: I will guide thee with mine eye." God will counsel us about the way we should choose. He will not compel us. Another Scripture that states a similar idea is Psalm 73:24: "Thou shalt guide me with thy counsel, and afterward receive me *to* glory." God guides with counsel. Again, we must learn to know His voice and to recognize when He is speaking to us through other people.

In John 16:13 we read: "Howbeit when he, the Spirit of truth, is come, he will guide you into all truth: for he shall not speak of himself; but whatsoever he shall hear, *that* shall he speak: and he will shew you things to come." This passage shows that the Holy Spirit is the guide to those people who have been through the second birth.

Men as spiritual guides

We can guide ourselves. Proverbs 23:19 says: "Hear thou, my son, and be wise, and guide thine heart in the way." A soul has to guide and shepherd his own heart.

In Matthew 23:16, 24 we read that the Lord accused the Pharisees of being blind guides. Men can be guided by other men, but the quality of the guiding depends on their spiritual understanding. Contrast this with Acts 8:31: "And he said, How can I, except some man should guide me? And he desired Philip that he would come up and sit with him." In this Scripture we see that a man of spiritual understanding can guide another man. Note that the connotations of good and bad guiding are based on God's revealed truth as a foundation for what is truth.

PATH(S) AND PATHWAYS

In Scripture paths are the direction of a life.

God leads on paths

God set darkness in Job's paths (at least Job thought so [Job 19:8]). David states that God will show him the path of life (Psalm 16:11). We can ask God to keep us in His paths so that our feet do not slip (Psalm 17:5).

Note the following verses as examples: "He restoreth my soul: he leadeth me in the paths of righteousness for his name's sake (Psalm 23:3)." "Shew me thy ways, O LORD; teach me thy paths (Psalm 25:4)." "All the paths of the LORD *are* mercy and truth unto such as keep his covenant and his testimonies (Psalm 25:10)." "Teach me thy way, O LORD, and lead me in a plain path, because of mine enemies (Psalm 27:11)." "Thou crownest the year with thy goodness; and thy paths drop fatness (Psalm 65:11)." All of these describe good paths on which God leads us. We observe some conditions for being on these paths.

A Scripture that reinforces well our need to know God's Word thoroughly is Psalm 119:105: "Thy word *is* a lamp unto my feet, and a light unto my path." This shows that we need to know God's Word in order to see where we are putting our feet and in what direction we should be walking.

God surrounds our path, knows all our ways, and knows when we need to rest (Psalm 139:3).

God keeps paths of judgment and preserves the ways (paths) of His saints (Proverbs 2:8). In Proverbs 8:20 He tells us: "I lead in the way of righteousness, in the midst of the paths of judgment." This gives us a picture of the path of life being in the midst of all of the paths of death. It is a path that is not filled with excesses; it is very plain and straight, as other Scriptures indicate.

A similar Scripture is Proverbs 3:6: "In all thy ways acknowledge him, and he shall direct thy paths." If we give God the glory for leading us and if we follow His Spirit, then He shall direct our paths.

In Proverbs 4:26-27 God instructs us: "Ponder the path of thy feet, and let all thy ways be established. Turn not to the right hand nor to the left: remove thy foot from evil." We are to think deeply about, deliberate on, and decide carefully where to place our feet each step of our life's pathway. God does not want us to be careless in even the small details.

In Isaiah 42:16 we read: "And I will bring the blind by a way *that* they knew not; I will lead them in paths *that* they have not known: I will make darkness light before them, and crooked things straight These things will I do unto them, and not forsake them." God's paths are straight and light-filled. If a path is not like this, then we should not venture onto it.

Good Paths

Proverbs 2:9 speaks of some of the good paths: "Then shalt thou understand righteousness, and judgment, and equity; *yea*, every good path." Proverbs 2:19 speaks of paths of life. Note that there is more than one path of life—this is not speaking of the door to life, who is the Lord Jesus Christ; it describes our journey through this life. Proverbs 4:11 speaks of the way of wisdom as being a good path.

Proverbs 4:18 tells us: "But the path of the just *is* as the shining light, that shineth more and more unto the perfect day."

In Jeremiah 6:16 we read: "Thus saith the LORD, Stand ye in the ways, and see, and ask for the old paths, where *is* the good way, and walk therein, and ye shall find rest for your souls. But they said, We will not walk *therein*." If you are walking in the path of the Lord, there will be rest—contrast with that with Isaiah 59:8, discussed in the next section.

In Matthew 3:3 we read: "For this is he that was spoken of by the prophet Esaias, saying, The voice of one crying in the wilderness, Prepare ye the way of the Lord, make his paths straight." The Lord's paths are straight. Therefore, when we are walking after His Spirit, our paths will be straight. If our path is not straight in a particular area, we should be careful to discern if we are still in the Lord's path.

In Hebrews 12:13 we read: "And make straight paths for your feet, lest that which is lame be turned out of the way; but let it rather be healed." The Lord clearly tells us here to make straight paths for our feet. Being on the Lord's path brings spiritual healing. If we do not stay on the Lord's path, then we become spiritually lame; and we may be turned out of the way.

Proverbs 12:28 states similarly: "In the way of righteousness *is* life; and *in* the pathway *thereof there is* no death." Lameness, or lack of wholeness, is related to death—both products of sin

Wrong Paths

Job 6:18 tells about people who practice deceit: "the paths of their way are turned aside; they go to nothing, and perish." There are people who do not abide in the paths of light (Job 24:13). The devil sets their paths (Psalm 17:4). Proverbs 2:18 speaks of paths that lead to death.

In Isaiah 59:8 we read: "The way of peace they know not; and *there is* no judgment in their goings: they have made them crooked paths: whosoever goeth therein shall not know peace." A wrong path has no spiritual peace on it. If your path is not peaceful, get out of it; for it is not of God. Read Jeremiah 6:16 to contrast this.

Summary

There are pathways to death, and in the middle there is a pathway of life. It is straight, plain, and peaceful. If your walk is producing other spirits within you, then you are off the pathway on which you should be. The Lord wants us to watch every footstep. He will guide us when we commit to Him in all of our ways (Psalm 37:4-5). We need to know the written Word of God thoroughly, for it is a lamp for our feet and a light for our path (Psalm 119:105). With His Word we can see ahead and avoid pitfalls along the way.

LUSTS

The word *lust* is used in the Old Testament only eight times. It is apparent that lusts occur in the heart. The Israelites lusted for meat in the desert and tempted God in their heart (Psalm 78:18). Psalm 81:12 shows us that God gave His people up to their own hearts' lust, and they walked in their own counsels. Proverbs 6:25 warns us not to lust after the beauty of a woman in our heart. The New Testament expands on lust.

Who is responsible for lusts?

The soul is responsible for lusts. Earlier we quoted James 1:14-15: "But every man is tempted, when he is drawn away of his own lust, and enticed. Then when lust hath conceived, it bringeth forth sin: and sin, when it is finished, bringeth forth death." In this Scripture we clearly see the relationship between lust and sin. The soul has to choose whether to let lust conceive sin. We need to be especially careful not to dwell on anything that is not pure (Philippians 4:8). We must crucify it. Lust gives rise to temptation and enticement by evil spirits. This leads to sin, if we yeild to the temptation. However, regard the Lord's warning as mentioned in Matthew 5:28. It is the responsibility of the soul not to be in situations where lust might occur; to purify the heart to prevent a seed of lust; and to crucify any leading of lust from the flesh, eyes, or pride of life. This must be done before lust is allowed to birth and grow.

Origin of lust

Lust is derived from the commandment, "Thou shalt not covet (Romans 7:7)." It comes from the flesh and the eyes (1 John 2:16 and Ephesians 2:3) and is of the world (1 John 2:17). If our father is the devil, we will have the same lusts and will follow them (John 8:44).

Location of lusts

Lusts occur in the heart (Romans 1:24 and Psalm 81:12).

Sin

Sin is derived from lusts (Romans 6:12 and James 1:14-15). Therefore, do not let sin reign in the body of flesh (Romans 6:12). The old man is corrupt due to deceitful lusts (Ephesians 4:22). In 1 Peter 4:3 we see that lusts are described along with other ungodly behaviors: "For the time past of *our* life may suffice us to have wrought the will of the Gentiles, when we walked in lasciviousness, lusts, excess of wine, revellings, banquetings, and abominable idolatries." The interesting thing to note is that some of these situations, if not all, are also due to a prior lust having conceived. Once there is a sin pattern established, then the Scripture no longer calls this lust. Lust is the precursor to the sin pattern that becomes established.

Antidote to lust

Lust is countered by "putting on the Lord Jesus (Romans 13:14)" and not making provision for the flesh. If we "walk in the spirit," we shall not fulfill the lust of the flesh (Galatians 5:16). We can crucify the flesh with the affections and lusts when we are Christ's (Galatians 5:24).

Being led by lusts

In the last days (we are in them now) scoffers will walk after their own lusts (2 Peter 3:3). Others (murmurers, complainers, and mockers) walk after their own ungodly lusts (Jude 16, 18). Those people who walk after the flesh walk in lusts of uncleanness (2 Peter 2:10). People have several lusts (2 Timothy 3:6, Ephesians 4:22, and 1 Timothy 6:9). Titus 3:3 speaks about a person led by lusts, and Paul describes them: "For we ourselves also were sometimes foolish, disobedient, deceived, serving divers lusts and pleasures, living in malice and envy, hateful, *and* hating one another." James 4:1 indicates that, when we are led by lusts, we have lusts at war in our flesh. This ends up with our fighting and warring among the brethren. We see this today to some degree as denominationalism in the Church.

Some things after which people lust

1. Looking on a woman (Matthew 5:28)
2. Cares of this world and deceitfulness of riches (Mark 4:19 and 1 Timothy 6:9)

3. Concupiscence (1 Thessalonians 4:5)
4. Fruits, dainty and goodly things (Revelation 18:14)
5. Youthful lusts (2 Timothy 2:22)

Lusts can stop answers to prayer

In James 4:3 we read: "Ye ask, and receive not, because ye ask amiss, that ye may consume *it* upon your lusts."

Lusts can be overcome

We see this from 1 Peter 1:14, 2:11, 4:2 and 2 Peter 1:4. This is good news for us that we can succeed with the Lord's help. We must ask God to fill us with power in our inner man when we face lusts, before they conceive sin. We must learn to recognize a pre-lust condition and ask God's protection and help, making sure that we are asking without being double-minded. We must learn to flee temptation.

Summary

People who have not been through the second birth are led by lusts of many types for various persons and things—this is the primary way they make decisions. A lust is a spiritual force (not an individual spiritual being) that is resident in the heart as a result of past experiences. Individuals over time acquire many lusts after things that appeal to the flesh, eye, or pride. Souls who have been through the second birth can be led by lusts if they are led by the flesh, the eyes, and the pride of life. Lusts pertain to external things, situations, and people that are presented to the soul by the world system for pleasure, power, or enhancement of the self. Lusts are a craving for the thing or person lusted after. They never originate in the inner man. They are precursors to sin and the establishing of sin patterns. They dwell in the heart and need to be rooted out with the Lord's help in purifying the heart. With the Lord's strengthening power in our inner man we can defeat, and to some extent eradicate, lusts; and we can lead a victorious life, being led by the Spirit of God.

DESIRES

There are many Scriptures that talk about desires. As opposed to lusts, desires can be Godly; or they can be of the flesh. People are led by desires and lusts. They are the energizing spiritual powers behind our beliefs, attitudes, and behaviors. Let us look at an example in the world system. Suppose we have a soul who is fond of works of art by a limited number of painters. A new painting becomes available, and the individual reads about it in the news. The individual has found that collecting these paintings has been pleasurable, places him in a position of being admired by others, and gives him a knowledge that few others have. That individual is going to develop an intense desire, based on his past experience in collecting these objects, which will become a lust. It may lead to sin, if he has to be dishonest, or worse, to acquire the object. Desires are not as strong a spiritual force as a lust. A desire may convert to a lust, which in turn can lead to sin. A desire is a longing for.

In Genesis 3:6 we read: "And when the woman saw that the tree *was* good for food, and that it *was* pleasant to the eyes, and a tree to be desired to make *one* wise, she took of the fruit thereof, and did eat, and gave also unto her husband with her; and he did eat." This is the first desire in the Scriptures, and it led to sin.

Desired people and things mentioned in Scripture

1. Wisdom to have God's knowledge (Genesis 3:6)
2. To a husband (Genesis 3:16)
3. To serve the Lord (Exodus 10:11)
4. Land (Exodus 34:24)
5. Neighbor's wife (Deuteronomy 5:21)
6. Silver and gold (Deuteronomy 7:25)
7. A place the Lord chooses (Deuteronomy 18:6)
8. A beautiful woman for a wife (Deuteronomy 21:11)
9. A king (national desire—1 Samuel 12:13)
10. Things of the Lord (2 Samuel 23:5)
11. Timber (1 Kings 5:8)
12. A son (2 Kings 4:28)

13. Buildings (2 Chronicles 8:6)
14. Many wives (2 Chronicles 11:23)
15. To fear the name of the Lord and prosper (Nehemiah 1:11)
16. To reason with God (Job 13:3)
17. Not to have the knowledge of God's ways (Job 21:14)
18. To dwell in the house of the Lord (Psalm 27:4)
19. Harm to enemies (Psalm 54:7; 59:10)
20. The hurt of another (Psalm 70:2)
21. Young men (Ezekiel 23:23)
22. Mercies from God (Daniel 2:18)
23. To speak with the Lord Jesus (Matthew 12:46)
24. To see a sign from heaven (Matthew 16:1)
25. To be first (Mark 9:35)
26. To have the highest seats in the synagogues (Luke 20:46)
27. To hear the Word of God (Acts 13:7)
28. For the Apostle Paul to leave a city (Acts 16:39)
29. For Israel to be saved (Romans 10:1)
30. Spiritual gifts (1 Corinthians 14:1)
31. To be clothed with our heavenly house (to be with God after death [2 Corinthians 5:2])
32. To be in bondage (to the law [Galatians 4:9; 4:21])
33. Vain glory (Galatians 5:26)
34. To die and be with the Lord (Philippians 1:23)
35. To be filled with the knowledge of the Lord's will (Colossians 1:9)
36. The office of a bishop (1 Timothy 3:1)
37. The sincere milk of the Word (1 Peter 2:2)
38. To die (Revelation 9:6)

Parts of man where desire is located

1. Mind (of the soul [Deuteronomy 18:6; Ephesians 2:3])
2. Soul (2 Chronicles 15:15)
3. Heart (Psalm 10:3; 21:2)
4. Flesh (the flesh and our mind can have desires that are not Godly [Ephesians 2:3])
5. Eyes (Ezekiel 24:16)

Special Scriptures showing God's leading us through desire

In Psalm 37:4 we read: "Delight thyself also in the LORD; and he shall give thee the desires of thine heart." This is a very special promise for being led by our desires. The key condition for us to meet for the Lord to lead us in this way is that we delight ourselves in the Lord. This condition is rarely, if ever, met by anyone; for it is similar to loving the Lord with all of our heart, mind, soul, and strength. It must be done twenty-four hours a day, seven days a week. We must always put God first. Then we can enjoy seeing all of those things that we desire coming to pass, because our desires are according to His will. Similar to this is Psalm 145:19 where David tells those who fear God that they will have their desire. The desire of the righteous is only good (Proverbs 11:23).

Mark 11:24 reads: "Therefore I say unto you, What things soever ye desire, when ye pray, believe that ye receive *them*, and ye shall have *them*." This is a wonderful promise, but the precondition to believe is receiving a *rhema* from the Lord with an absolute faith in the heart that it will come to pass. One has to be in communication with God and know, not just hope, for the thing to be received. A similar Scripture is 1 John 5:15: "And if we know that he hear us, whatsoever we ask, we know that we have the petitions that we desired of him." Some of the preconditions for knowing that God hears us are discussed in Chapter 20.

Miscellaneous Scriptures about desire

In Psalm 112:10 we read that the desire of the wicked will perish. Their desires have no place in heaven.

Wisdom is more precious than rubies, and all things that can be desired are not comparable (Proverbs 3:15).

Proverbs 13:12 states: "Hope deferred maketh the heart sick: but *when* the desire cometh, *it is* a tree of life." If one has a Godly desire that is delayed, he may be ill at heart; but when the desire finally is fulfilled, it will be healing and even greater, in that growth to life will result.

Ecclesiastes 6:9 declares: “Better *is* the sight of the eyes than the wandering of the desire: this *is* also vanity and vexation of spirit.” Solomon tells us that one should be occupied with what he can see rather than to have idle daydreams which only vex our inner man.

Who has desires?

The Lord Jesus had desires (Luke 22:15).

Satan has desires (Luke 22:31).

Angels have desires (1 Peter 1:12).

Souls have desires (many Scriptures listed above).

Degrees of desire

Romans 15:23 speaks of a great desire (desires have degrees) for many years (and can last a long time). In 2 Corinthians 7:11 we read of a vehement desire along with zeal.

Summary

As we review the above listed thirty-eight points in Scripture about desires (this is not an exhaustive list), we should note that they can be Godly, evil, or relatively neutral in spiritual direction (such as the desire to see an individual). This is quite different from the way in which Scripture uses lust.

Souls have to have spiritual energy to move in a given manner. This energy for life comes from the inner man and is modified by the heart. The heart, in turn, modifies the output of spiritual energy (power) from the inner man. This is like a feedback loop between the heart and the inner man. The energy that flows into enabling action by the soul is modified by structures in the heart that have been erected as high places. These are the foundation and walls of our attitudes and beliefs. These flows of energy can be released from external events that generate reflexive actions based on our beliefs and attitudes. These reflexive actions can be modified by the mind of the soul, as they are monitored and as new information comes into the mind of the soul from the world or from the inner man. These flows of spirit, in turn, translate into actions (or a decision to not act) that are termed by the Scriptures to be lusts and desires. Lusts are a stronger form of desire and are always evil. Thus, all behavior is due to a lust or a desire to cause an expected (or hoped for) result.

It is of interest that the Scripture does not have desire linked with inner man in a single verse. In the soul that has experienced the second birth, however, the inner man is at unity with the Spirit of God; therefore, it does have desires and transmits them into the heart. There they are mixed with other desires. The heart at any time has many lusts and desires that are resident and are "on hold" until an appropriate time for their release into a behavior.

BEING LED BY THE SPIRIT OF GOD

We need to observe the spirits that are coming into the mind of the soul in order to discern when God is leading us. That means we need to learn to recognize the presence of God's power, the states of the heart, and the emotional states that are associated with God's presence. Conversely, we need to learn those states of the heart and emotions that are not from God. We can learn these things by analyzing our thoughts and speech. It takes time and effort; but, like anything else, we gradually become more proficient with practice.

We will review the various emotions and states of the heart in Chapter 10. There are many of them and it will take time to learn them all experientially. You can ask God to help you learn them; and as you observe and give Him praise and thanks, you will begin to see how He brings you into situations that will increase your spiritual knowledge. It is particularly important to discern the fruit of the Spirit in Galatians 5:22-23 and the works of the flesh in Galatians 5:19-21. It is also very important to know experientially the Lord's love, joy, and peace as opposed to fleshly lust (a counterfeit for love), excitement (a counterfeit for joy), and absence from turmoil after closing on a decision (a counterfeit for peace). These are fundamental states of the heart that one must learn to recognize through experience. We also need to learn how to distinguish the emotion in the heart that is associated with offending the conscience from a false guilt that Satan will place in the heart to counterfeit offending the conscience. He desires to do this because, when he is successful, our walk before the Lord becomes a legalistic observance of rules. It produces a confusion of leadership, instead of our being free in our spirit. Only a strong insight in the spirit into the whole Word of God will free us in this area.

In observing and testing spirits in the mind of our soul, frequently we first notice the emotional component of the spirit coming from the heart before we really examine for message content or power. It is also the easiest of the three components of spirit to test accurately, because we have a limited set of emotions to learn (from experience). If the spirit does not contain an emotional element of the fruit of the Spirit, such as those mentioned in Galatians 5:22-23, then it will not be a message from the Lord and should not be followed. The power element of a spirit is sometimes difficult to test immediately, and the information element can be exceedingly diverse—thus, more difficult to test.

VISIONS

We shall examine visions to see how they impact us in being led by God. We can receive visions from God and from the evil spirits. Visions are a fundamental way of communicating between spiritual beings. We need to learn the difference in the visions from evil spirits and from the Lord. There are many types of visions that are mentioned in the Scriptures.

Visions from God

In Genesis 15:1 we read: "After these things the word of the LORD came unto Abram in a vision, saying, Fear not, Abram: I *am* thy shield, *and* thy exceeding great reward." God considers a vision to be part of His speaking to a person. We, therefore, need to learn how to differentiate a vision from God, from our own heart, or from an evil spirit. Genesis 46:2

states: "And God spake unto Israel in the visions of the night, and said, Jacob, Jacob. And he said, Here *am* I." We see that God speaks to people in dreams, but we need to learn to distinguish the source of our dreams. God considers that a dream He gives is His speaking.

Numbers 12:6-8 tells us more: "And he said, Hear now my words: If there be a prophet among you, *I* the LORD will make myself known unto him in a vision, *and* will speak unto him in a dream. My servant Moses *is* not so, who *is* faithful in all mine house. With him will I speak mouth to mouth, even apparently, and not in dark speeches; and the similitude of the LORD shall he behold: wherefore then were ye not afraid to speak against my servant Moses?" God speaks to prophets in visions and dreams, but to His friends who are faithful He will speak much more directly. Moses still saw just a similitude of the Lord, but that was much more intimate than a vision or dream.

In Numbers 24:4 we read: "He hath said, which heard the words of God, which saw the vision of the Almighty, falling *into a trance*, but having his eyes open." This is a more open vision from the Lord as He speaks to people. It is called a trance.

Likewise, the Prophet Samuel heard the Lord speak while he was awake. In 1 Samuel 3:10 we read: "And the LORD came, and stood, and called as at other times, Samuel, Samuel. Then Samuel answered, Speak; for thy servant heareth." Samuel saw the Lord and heard Him speak directly.

People today still receive all of these levels of communication from the Lord. We have to be ready for any of them. Visions were very frequent for the Apostles. Peter experienced a trance at Joppa (Acts 10:9-16). Paul saw a vision at his conversion (Acts 9:1-9) and many others during his ministry (*e.g.*, 2 Corinthians 12:2).

The Book of Revelation was written as the result of God speaking in visions to the Apostle John. The Scriptures were written by men under the leadership and guidance of the Holy Spirit, as God guided them in their memory. God frequently brings memories to our mind in order to speak to us; all memories brought into our mind have to be tested to see which spirit is bringing them.

Interpreting Visions and Dreams

In Daniel 1:17 we read: "As for these four children, God gave them knowledge and skill in all learning and wisdom: and Daniel had understanding in all visions and dreams." God needs to give one skills to interpret the visions and dreams of others. It is a special anointing. In dreams and visions that I have had, the Lord has always given me the interpretation of them when I have asked. He could conceivably have me go to someone else, if that suited His purpose, for an interpretation. Always ask God to interpret what you receive, if there is no explanation with the vision or dream. Daniel asked God to interpret the King's dream, and God gave a dream to Daniel (Daniel 2:19) with the interpretation. In Daniel 2:28 we read: "But there is a God in heaven that revealeth secrets, and maketh known to the king Nebuchadnezzar what shall be in the latter days. Thy dream, and the visions of thy head upon thy bed, are these." Note that Daniel gave credit to God for the interpretation of the King's dream. Also note that there are no secrets from God in any of our thoughts. In the last days all thoughts will be revealed.

Lack of vision from God

In Proverbs 29:18 we read: "Where *there is* no vision, the people perish but he that keepeth the law, happy *is* he." We also see in 1 Samuel 3:1: "And the child Samuel ministered unto the LORD before Eli. And the word of the LORD was precious in those days; *there was* no open vision." When God stops speaking into a situation, then there are very serious consequences and problems.

In Isaiah 29:10-11 we read: "For the LORD hath poured out upon you the spirit of deep sleep, and hath closed your eyes: the prophets and your rulers, the seers hath he covered. And the vision of all is become unto you as the words of a book that is sealed, which *men* deliver to one that is learned, saying, Read this, I pray thee: and he saith, I cannot; for it *is* sealed." God ceased giving visions because of the rebellion of the people. They lacked guidance and were at the mercy of their enemies.

Isaiah 28:7 states: "But they also have erred through wine, and through strong drink are out of the way; the priest and the prophet have erred through strong drink, they are swallowed up of wine, they are out of the way through strong drink; they err in vision, they stumble *in* judgment." We see here that alcohol causes people not to be able to hear properly from God. They will err in their vision (hearing from God).

False Prophesy

Jeremiah 14:14 tells us: "Then the LORD said unto me, The prophets prophesy lies in my name: I sent them not, neither have I commanded them, neither spake unto them: they prophesy unto you a false vision and divination, and a thing of nought, and the deceit of their heart." We see that, when a prophet has fallen into sin, he will prophesy out of the content of his heart. The Lord did not say that these were not His prophets but rather that they were not accurate. Therefore, to hear and see accurately from the Lord, we must keep our hearts pure. Prophets were false in the Old Testament if their message was not accurate. It does not mean that they were not a prophet. Balaam was a true prophet but was demonically or fleshly inspired to give counsel against Israel that was not God's desire. In Jeremiah 23:16 we read: "Thus saith the LORD of hosts, Hearken not unto the words of the prophets that prophesy unto you: they make you vain: they speak a vision of their own heart, *and* not out of the mouth of the LORD." The prophets were making the people vain (which means spiritually empty). God did not say they were not prophets but that they were not listening to Him.

Discerning visions from God and from evil spirits

This is part of testing the spirits in all situations. It is no different with visions than with other communications. Examine the three parts of the spirit. In our experience we can discern a lot from content and the intention behind the vision. Frequently, those that are from God are "soft, gentle, and not forceful." They do not induce fear. Those from the enemy are the opposite. It takes a little practice to start recognizing visions for what they are. Many people may dismiss them as from their imagination. However, that means they are not testing their thoughts to discern the origin. Start watching but never, ever, try to force a vision; or it will be from your flesh or even an evil spirit. The timetable for getting a vision is up to the Lord and not up to you as an individual. You can ask God to start teaching you about visions; then wait on His timetable, and do not expect an immediate response. You may have to wait quite some time, but the Lord will reward your waiting. You will also know that the vision is from God, for it will almost certainly carry that awareness with it as part of the structure and content of the spiritual flow. God's teaching carries an authority and has a character that you can learn to recognize.

Summary

God is the same yesterday, today, and tomorrow. He has always spoken in dreams, visions, trances, audible sounds, inner voices, and diverse other ways. We always have to test the spirit in any communication; but we should live expectantly, rejoicing that our God enjoys communicating with His people. We have to purify our hearts and abstain from alcohol to hear most clearly from God. Since God may speak at any time, the total abstinence from alcohol is wise. (There is much in Scripture to support this statement, but this is not the place to go into it. However, an individual could certainly do his own study—looking at all references to wine, strong drink, and other similar beverages in Scripture and then prayerfully ask God to bring order to the study.)

Expect God to communicate with you, and start accepting in faith that He will. Start examining every thought and picture (vision) that comes into your mind; and test it to see if it is from your own heart desires, from God, or from an evil spirit. We will discuss the testing in much detail in the last two sections of this book I first started to realize that God speaks to us a lot in internal visions (pictures) when working in the office. I would see a patient who had an upper respiratory infection such as a cold or "flu." I would then have a picture in my mind of my becoming ill with this. It would be a picture that would try to pressure me. I began to understand that the devil was trying to get me to accept this vision as truth so that I would be led by it. I started to realise just how much God is also talking to us through these images that come into the mind. We have to test the origin of the spirit. If we are daydreaming about a nice sports car, that is probably the lust of the flesh. All of us frequently get these leadings from the heart and spirit. We have to watch them, refute those of the flesh and evil spirits, and follow those of God. Until our heart is pure, the visions will often be mixed with a little of God and a lot of the flesh. Just keep on working with God to purify the heart, and gradually it will be more of God and less of the flesh. We all receive this type of leading.

There is also a vision of the inner man that God will sometimes open up for us, so that our inner man sees into the spiritual realm. This is a different type of vision, and one can learn to recognize it and ask God His purpose for it. It is understood with the mind, but it does not come from the mind. All of this may seem a little far fetched to many readers, but beginning to work with it is no different from learning any new skill. One has to practice.

FINAL SUMMARY FOR THE CHAPTER

We shall go into the details of how to be led by the Spirit of God in the later chapters of the book. This chapter is meant to frame some of what will be covered later, and the concepts will be helpful for starting to become more aware of what spirits are coming into the mind of our souls.

Part IV

9
WORKINGS OF THE HUMAN SPIRIT

In this chapter and the next few chapters we will examine the spiritual components of man that we identified in Chapter 7. We also studied the structure of the human spirit in Chapter 7. We have seen the various uses of the word *spirit* in the Scriptures. We will now focus on the flow of spiritual energy (power, emotional state, and information) into and out of the human spirit. It is to and from this human spirit that flows of spirit occur. In order to make it easier to follow when we are talking about the new spirit that God gives us at the second birth, we will refer to it as the inner man or human spirit. When we are talking about a flow of spirit between different spiritual beings—such as God, another person, or an evil spirit—then we shall use just the term *spirit*. We shall also study the flow of spirit within the soul among the different areas of the spiritual man. We will cite appropriate Scripture so that you can see the Biblical support behind this information. We will also learn how the components of spiritual man communicate within the natural and within the spiritual universes with other people and with other spirits.

There is a lot of material to cover before one can gain a comprehensive understanding of the workings of spiritual man. One may ask why we would even do this. The answer is that all of God's Word is to be meditated upon day and night, and all of it is profitable for instruction (Deuteronomy 6:6-9; 2 Timothy 3:16). It is God's command to us that we understand these things. It may not be easy, but with prayer and the reliance upon the Holy Spirit as the teacher who will lead us into all truth we shall come to an understanding. It is critical, if we are going to be of service to God, that we learn to follow His Spirit, just as the Lord Jesus did. To follow His Spirit means to be in constant communication with God and to be waiting to see His leading in all of our circumstances.

In the table below the components studied in the next seven chapters are listed. The right column of the table gives the areas to and from which the flows of spirit go to each of the components.

Component	Flows of spirit
Human (Inner Man) Spirit	A. God
Heart (Spiritual)	B. Other people
Mind	C. Other spirits
Flesh	D. Other parts of man The Flesh
Soul	The Soul The Heart (Inner Man)
Conscience	The Mind The Conscience
Will	The Will

We saw in Chapters 6-8 that all spiritual interactions between spiritual beings consist of communications carrying the three elements—power, emotion, and information. These spiritual flows are bi-directional between individual spirits. There are differing sensitivities in the mind of the soul among individuals for perceiving the three elements of a flow. There is no such thing as a one-way spiritual communication. The incident in which the Lord Jesus perceived in His Spirit that an ill woman had touched the hem of His garment (Luke 8:43) demonstrates this.

We will examine under each of the above sections spiritual flows into and out of that component which we are discussing. In this chapter will look at the first component, the human spirit.

DEFINITIONS OF THE COMPONENTS OF SPIRITUAL MAN

We have defined *spirit* in a Chapter 6. We have also studied the structure of the human spirit in Chapter 7. As we study the workings of the human spirit and soul in this and following chapters, we will develop a greater level of comfort for the new concepts that were introduced in Chapter 6. As we read through the examples from Scripture pertaining to all of the spiritual flows between the areas of spiritual man (heart, soul, conscience, etc.) mentioned above, we will draw inferences that will also help in our coming to understand what spirit is. We have to understand that without our human spirit we die. Therefore, our human spirit supplies us with our life energy (power) to perform all of the acts of living. We will see that our human spirit will give us power over our will (if we have gone through the second birth). We will also see that our soul is expected to rule our human spirit and to shape and mold it (Proverbs 25:28 tells us: "He that *hath* no rule over his own spirit *is like* a city *that is* broken down, *and* without walls").

The **flesh** is that which God made from the dust of the ground. It comprises all of our physical structure, biochemistry, and workings. In addition, it includes all of our thought patterns, memories, learned emotional responses, beliefs, and attitudes that we had prior to our second birth and that have not been passed through a valid mental renewal that the Scriptures command under the phrase "the renewing of the mind."

The **soul** is formed from the union of the spirit with the flesh. God breathed into the nostrils of Adam, and he became a living soul. We will expand this in Chapter 13, which discusses the soul in more detail.

The **mind** is the reasoning, remembering, and calculating part of man. The mind of the soul (as opposed to the mind of the heart) is the place from which the self awareness of who we are stems. The mind itself has a spirit. We see in Ephesians 4:23–24 that Paul commands us to "be renewed in the spirit of your mind." This spirit of our mind was not part of what was given to us at the time of the second birth when God gave us a new heart and a new spirit. We are not commanded to renew these, but rather we are commanded to take every thought captive and to be renewed in our minds. We will see that the spirit of our minds is energized by the new spirit that God gave as at the second birth.

The **conscience** is that set of laws that God gives us internally to guide us as to right and wrong. It is not a failsafe guide, for we can have a defiled conscience that will be in need of renewal. The location of the conscience is not completely clear from the reading of Scripture, but it seems to be on either the inner or outer surface of the spiritual heart.

The **will** is that part of our soul that makes our decisions stand firm. It can be viewed as the ultimate decision-enforcing center of the mind and soul. Most of the time we make more or less reflex decisions, based on learned behavior, without bringing information to a state of conscious decision making. The will can be influenced heavily by God, who can place various spiritual forces on it. The will can be influenced by our spirit. In Exodus 35:21 we read "every one whose heart stirred him up, and every one whom his spirit made willing." This reveals that the will is subservient to the spirit and that a healthy spirit can help us to will. When people are unable to set a determined course of behavior in which they persevere, they have a spiritual malady.

The **emotions** are a complex set of forces that act on and within our souls. We know that God created us in His image. Our emotions are derivatives of God's emotions. There are also many spiritual states of the heart which we must carefully distinguish from emotions, such as the state of being proud. We have discussed the emotions and the states of the heart in Chapter 8 and will discuss them further in Chapter 10.

In sinful man our emotions are skewed and different to those experienced by the inner man who bears witness to the Holy Spirit. This is because they are released from a heart that is impure. The pure emotions of the inner man are polluted by the filth in the spiritual heart. We have to learn what emotions are appropriate for expression in various circumstances. Emotions are purpose-driven; *i.e.*, they have an objective, as we saw in Chapters 7 and 8. They, together with the power behind them and the purpose for them, comprise a flow of spirit.

Emotions are short time "spiritual" forces. States of the heart are built up over much time and reflect the additive effects of prior emotions. Both the soul and the human spirit have emotions. These emotions of the human spirit are deeper and more pure in the sense that the information from them is genuine and reflects the state of the flow of spirit from the Holy Spirit in one who has been through the second birth. Emotional flows from the heart and soul may be masked and difficult to interpret, since the individual soul may be attempting deceit, either consciously or unconsciously.

The **inner man** was described in the Chapter 7 under the structure of the spirit. The inner man resides in the heart, and the human spirit is the inner man.

The **heart** is completely different from the inner man and from the heart of the flesh which pumps our blood throughout our body. The spiritual heart is our deep core. We receive a new heart and a new spirit at the new birth. The heart contains the inner man (human spirit), the Holy Spirit after the second birth, and the Lord Jesus' presence under some circumstances. We shall learn much more about this very important component of the spiritual man in Chapter 10.

FLOWS INTO THE SPIRIT

We saw in Chapter 6 that the flow of spirit is always comprised of three things in its interactions with other components of man and with other spiritual entities, including other people. These are a flow of power, a flow of emotion, and a logical structure resulting in the flow of information (knowledge). Just as there are always outflows from the human spirit, there is an equivalent flow of information into the human spirit. These flows of power and emotion into our human spirit come from the following sources:

a) God
b) Other components of the man as mentioned above
c) Other people
d) Other spirits

We will examine how these spiritual beings bring information and energy into a person's spirit. Before doing this, we will look at a key Scripture for understanding the Biblical basis for the flow of spirit from one being to another. In Proverbs 16:2 we see this very important concept: "All the ways of a man are clean in his own eyes; but the Lord weigheth the spirits." This is a critical verse, for it confirms the concept that we discussed earlier of all of our actions, including verbal communications, being spiritual in nature and carrying power, emotion, and knowledge with them. We can infer the following points from this Scripture as a result of our understanding of our spiritual structure:

a) All of our actions have a spirit causing (associated with) them.
b) These spirits are spiritual outflows from our human spirit, for only spirit gives birth to spirit.
c) God can discern the spirit (power—His, ours, or demonic; emotion; and intent-structured information) behind each of our actions.

Since we are made in God's image, we can also expect, therefore, to discern the spirit behind someone's action, if our spiritual discernment has been developed. It takes some maturation of our spirit for this to operate. Proper growth in our human spirit, we will see later, is only taking place as we feed on God's words (*logos* and *rhema*). Just as physical growth is coordinated by God through our genetic heritage, so also must spiritual growth be coordinated by God. There is no short cut to spiritual maturity, unless God accelerates the process.

This Scripture, Proverbs 16:2 (above) opens our understanding and leads us to see that the human spirit of a person sends flows of spirit into all of his actions—including speaking, listening, working, praying, and many other actions. For action to take place there have to be information, emotion and energy coming from the human spirit, since God deems it needful to judge each spirit flow emanating from our inner man. The fact that David states before God that he can have a right (or wrong) spirit confirms this (Psalm 51:10). Therefore, the outflow from our spirit has a moral "fruit or seed" to it. This fruit is discernible to God. We have read (2 Timothy 1:7) that God has given us a spirit of power (Godly), of love (Godly), and of a sound mind (filled with truth, acting in divine truth, and able to control). If all three of these characteristics are not present in any spirit emanating from our inner man, then the spirit is not from God and does not measure up to His standards. We will study in more detail later the definitions of power, love, and sound mind.

GOD

Spiritual flows from God to our human spirit and back to God

There are many Scriptures which relate God's filling a person's spirit with information to perform certain tasks, power to accomplish these tasks, and a desire (emotional drive) to fulfill the tasks. A good example of this is found in Exodus 28:3, where we read: "And thou shalt speak unto all *that are* wise hearted, whom I have filled with the spirit of wisdom, that they may make Aaron's garments to consecrate him, that he may minister unto me in the priest's office." In Exodus 35:21-22 we read: "And they came, every one whose heart stirred him up, and every one whom his spirit made willing, *and* they brought the LORD'S offering to the work of the tabernacle of the congregation, and for all his service, and for the holy garments. And they came, both men and women, as many as were willing hearted, *and* brought bracelets, and earrings, and rings, and tablets, all jewels of gold: and every man that offered *offered* an offering of gold unto the LORD."

Exodus 28:3 relates God's filling people's spirits with wisdom (knowledge or information) for the purpose of being able to make special garments. The power to accomplish the Lord's desire accompanied this impartation into the people's spirits. We also see God's filling these men with the desire (emotional drive) to accomplish these tasks (they did accomplish the tasks). Thus, all three components of spiritual flow that God imparted to these people in their human spirits were present—power, emotion, and information. In all such impartations from God into a human spirit there are the three components of power, knowledge, and emotion. We see this process again in Exodus 35:21-22. In this Scripture we see that the Spirit made them willing (power). We see that the heart was stirred up (from the Spirit we will learn later). This is the emotional drive. The Spirit also imparted the knowledge of what to do, that is, to bring offerings.

In all of the following examples we will see these three components. We will now review a number of examples of God's imparting something to a person's spirit, with a resulting impact on the heart, since the spirit is located within the heart.

In Deuteronomy 2:30 we read: "But Sihon king of Heshbon would not let us pass by him: for the LORD thy God hardened his spirit, and made his heart obstinate, that he might deliver him into thy hand, as *appeareth* this day." To harden a person's human spirit, the Lord had to impart something into the spirit that made it view incoming spiritual information in a certain light. Therefore, God imparted information to King Sihon's spirit. He also gave power with the information so that he could will to act in the way that he did. There was also emotion involved in that the King disliked the idea of Israel's going through his land.

In Judges 3:10 we read: "And the Spirit of the Lord came upon him, and he judged." There are many times when the Lord speaks of putting a spirit upon someone for a particular purpose. Many times it is for the individual to prophesy. In this case it was for the person to judge a situation. We are not told whether these spirits come into the heart; but we can infer that they do, since they alter behavior. To do this, they must interact with the rest of man in the same way that the person's own human spirit does. In a sense they usurp the otherwise routine functioning of a person's human spirit. These examples of a spirit's coming upon someone are different to one's being given an impartation into his human spirit, since they are given to accomplish a one-time limited act. They are more akin to an anointing that God gives for a specific and limited purpose. This anointing may or may not be permanent. It is much more a situation of God overtly controlling the behavior through power from the Holy Spirit or some other spirit that He has commanded to perform His will in the circumstances. These spirits cause power to be released for a particular purpose, in this case to judge. There is also a desire (emotion) to judge, and there is knowledge for judging. Thus, an anointing of a spirit from God is structured to interact with the spirit of man in the same manner as an impartation into the spirit of man. The major differences between the two are the length of time and the breadth of the mission (purpose) for which the impartation or over which the anointing functions. The impartation seems to be permanent; and the anointing, shorter lived. The impartation seems to cover a broader set of behavior than the anointing.

God stirred up the spirits of Pul, king of Assyria, and Tilgathpilneser, king of Assyria (1 Chronicles 5:26). He did this for the purpose of disciplining the Israelites, who had followed after other gods. It led to Israel's being taken captive. This shows that the stirring up of the spirit of a man by God leads to certain consequent emotions and behaviors. It results in a complex series of events that are sustained over time. Thus, there is a filling with certain emotional energies and knowledge to accomplish a task. The individual is not necessarily aware of being "stirred up in his spirit." God later punished people for going against Israel, so He held these kings accountable for their actions. This indicates they had the control over themselves to resist acting in the way they did. Therefore, even when God moves to do something in the human spirit of a person, that individual is still responsible for his actions.

In Jeremiah 51:11 we read: "The Lord hath raised up the spirit of the kings of the Medes: for His device is against Babylon, to destroy it; because it is the vengeance of the Lord, the vengeance of His temple." Again, we see the Lord doing something to the spirits of these kings to accomplish His purposes.

In Ezra 1:5 we read: "Then rose up the chief of the fathers of Judah and Benjamin, and the priests, and the Levites, with all them whose spirit God had raised, to go up to build the house of the Lord which is in Jerusalem." We see a sequence of events unfolding over time, as a result of God's raising up the spirits of these people. It resulted in certain actions that required God to have transferred knowledge, emotion, and power into the spirits of these people.

In a similar vein we read in Haggai 2:5: "And the Lord stirred up the spirit of Zerubbabel the son of Shealtiel, governor of Judah, and the spirit of Joshua, son of Josedech, the high priest, and the spirit of all the remnant of the people; and they came and did work in the house of the Lord of Hosts, their God."

Job 32:8 states: "But there is a spirit in man: and the inspiration of the Almighty giveth them understanding." This is a very important concept to consider in comparing **learned knowledge** to **inspiration**

knowledge. Elihu was conveying the concept that his thoughts had come from the inspiration of God into his human spirit. We will study the differences between learned knowledge and inspirational knowledge later.

David asks God to "create in me a clean heart, O God; and renew a right spirit within me" (Psalm 51:10). This shows that David prayed in the will of God for a clean heart and a right spirit. God is able to place a right spirit in a person, and then He is able to renew it if it goes astray.

God discerns information about our spirits and then acts upon it. Isaiah says: "I dwell in a high and holy place, with him also that is of a contrite and humble spirit, to revive the spirit of the humble, and to revive the heart of the contrite ones" (Isaiah 57:15). In this case the action is to revive our spirit, if it is humble, and our heart, if it is contrite. God looks at the heart and the spirit. Note again the association of heart and spirit.

In Isaiah 66:2: we read: "For all these things hath mine hand made, and all those things have been, saith the Lord: but to this man will I look, even to him that is poor and of a contrite spirit, and trembleth at my word." Again, this shows the Lord looking at the condition of the spirit and acting on His observation.

God puts a new spirit into His people. In Ezekiel 36:26 –28 we read: "A new heart will I give you and a new spirit will I put within you: and I will take away the stony heart out of your flesh, and I will give you a heart of flesh. And I will put my spirit within you, and cause you to walk in my statutes, and ye shall keep my judgments." God is speaking to Israel here, but the same thing happens to a person at the time of his second birth. God is able to put a new spirit into a person.

The New Testament lists many activities of the Holy Spirit and also the work of God in our spirits.

Matthew 4:1 recounts the Spirit of God leading Jesus into the wilderness.

Matthew 10:1 and Mark 6:7 show that Jesus is able to give us power (in our spirit) to cast out demons.

Luke states that John the Baptist had the spirit and power of Elias (Eliajah). God had given him the same spirit as He had given to Elijah (Luke 1:17).

Luke 2:25-30 tells of Simeon's being led by the Spirit into the temple, where he saw the infant Savior.

In Luke 4:1 we read of Jesus' being full of the Holy Spirit. This tells us that it is possible for a person to have the Holy Spirit within but not to be full of the Holy Spirit. This is something to keep in mind when we are examining our own human spirit. We will learn to make assessments of our spiritual condition and, therefore, to diagnose when changes are needed.

Jesus explains that the Spirit of the Lord was on Him for a purpose (Luke 4:18). God does not do things without a distinct purpose. Since this is part of the spirit that He gives to us and since we are made in His image, we always must have a sound mind in our spirit; or we will not be walking in the Spirit of God. We made this point above in reference to the Lord weighing our spirits.

In Luke 8:54-55 we read of Jesus' having the power to restore the spirit to a dead person.

Jesus tells us that the words that He speaks to the people are spirit and life (John 6:63). Words from God are life-giving to man, and they are spirit. In the same way, since we are made in the image of God, our words are spirit; but they are not always life. In fact probably very few of our words are life. It is because words are spirit that they are judged by God. At the end of the age the things whispered in the ear will be shouted from the roof top. Words are spirit since they carry information, have an emotional purpose, and have power to cause change. Therefore, they can be judged by how they fulfill the mandate for Godly power, Godly love, and a Godly sound mind.

We learn that Jesus can give us the Holy Spirit by breathing on a person (John 20:22). Compare this to the creation of Adam.

We will receive power when we are baptized with the Holy Spirit, and after that we will be witnesses for the Lord, according to Acts 1:8.

In Acts 2:17-18 we read that God will pour our His Spirit upon all flesh; this will result in prophesy, visions, and dreams.

God allows the act of laying on of hands by the Apostle Paul to be a means of giving someone the Holy Spirit (Acts 19:6).

In Romans 5:5 we read that the love of God is shed abroad in our hearts by the Holy Spirit. We recall that the Holy Spirit becomes resident in our heart at the second birth.

Romans 11:8 states that God has given a spirit of slumber to Israel. This is an example of a national spirit that we mentioned in the Chapter 6, where we defined spirit. So far we have read of impartations of spirits into our heart from God. We have also seen examples of a spirit being placed on someone as an anointing to achieve a certain purpose. Now we see a third situation in which God impacts many spirits in a geographic or national area. We see here an example of a spirit affecting a people. Spirits do not have flesh and bones. God uses terms such as "pour out His Spirit (Joel 3)." We get a sense that a spirit has similar properties to the natural properties of being liquid or gaseous. We cannot go further than to accept the analogy, for the Word of God does not seem to support further inference along these lines. We just read that a spirit can be transmitted by touching a person and by breathing onto a person. We are beginning to get more understanding of spirit(s) as we look at Scripture.

In Romans 15:13 we read that through the Holy Spirit we can abound in hope and can be filled with all joy and peace in believing. We are temples of God, and the Holy Spirit dwells in us (1 Corinthians 3:16).

1 Corinthians 15:45 tells us that God made Jesus a life-giving (quickening) spirit.

In Galatians 4:6 we read that God gives the Spirit of His Son into our hearts. Thus the spirit of the Lord Jesus, the Holy Spirit, and our own new spirit reside in our new heart after we go through the second birth. In addition, the grace of Jesus is with our spirit (Galatians 6:18). Paul adds that the Lord Jesus will be with our spirit (2 Timothy 4:22).

In Ephesians 3:16 we read that God can grant us a petition to be strengthened with might by His Spirit in the inner man. You should now be seeing the structure of the inner man more clearly, as you review these Scriptures. It becomes more apparent that the inner man is the human spirit of a man contained within the heart. We have discussed this in more detail in the Chapter 7 on the structure of the spirit and of the soul.

Hebrews 4:12 is a key passage of Scripture. We see that the Word of God can divide our soul, flesh, and spirit. This is a process that only God can perform, and He will do this only as we offer ourselves as a living sacrifice. It takes great time, spiritual battle, and going through one's own *kenosis*. It is an utter and complete emptying and sacrifice of one's own will. It has to happen before we can be led by God's Spirit in a manner in which we are fully cooperative. Very few believers will make the sacrifice to go through the process, although God desires it for every person. With it comes great blessing in the spiritual realm, because one can enter into a working relationship with the Lord. It is the only path to lasting peace and joy. It is only after this that one develops an awareness of Christ Jesus' living in one. Even after this major step there are many further steps in growth to follow in which God imparts increasing authority and responsibility as one walks after His Spirit. He wants this for everyone, but very few make themselves willing to go through the rigorous self denial and turning away from the world system. Resident power and the higher levels of ministry that are given by a call from the Almighty God Himself (as opposed to the call of men) confirms this. God does not squander His name on those who will not allow themselves to be made worthy. One does not become sinless in this life (1 John 1:10)—despite such a deep separation of soul, flesh, and spirit. The flesh is forever at war with the spirit, but there is a rest because we recognize and deal with the old sinful desires more easily. In addition, God, being more powerfully present in the spirit, gives protection from demonic pressures on the spirit.

Hebrews 12:9 states that God is the Father of our spirit as opposed to our earthly father who gave the former spirit and the flesh (Genesis 5:3). God works with our human spirit to correct and to mature it.

John describes himself as being in the Spirit on the Lord's Day (Revelation 1:10). He wrote the book of Revelation from his experience in the Spirit. The Lord can at His discretion give us supernatural senses and perceptions in the human spirit. We cannot will this but rather have to be willing to receive it as God determines it to be needful. We should not try to bring on such an experience, or the enemy may place a counterfeit in our heart.

Flows from our spirit to God

There are many examples that we can examine in Scripture that show that our human spirit emanates to God. The foundational one is Proverbs 16:2. We looked at this above: "All the ways of a man are clean in his own eyes; but the Lord weigheth the spirits." This shows us that God is receiving information from our spirit continuously in order to weigh the various spirits emanating from it.

Another example is from Ezekiel 13:3 where we read: "Thus saith the Lord GOD; Woe unto the foolish prophets, that follow their own spirit, and have seen nothing!" This shows that God sees which spirit a person is following from the emanation from it. We can also note that the foolish prophet does not realize that he is following his own spirit.

FLOWS OF SPIRIT BETWEEN PEOPLE

In Genesis 41:38 we see that Pharaoh could discern that Joseph carried within him the "Spirit of God." We see, therefore, Joseph's spirit communicating the presence of God in him to Pharaoh.

Similarly, in 2 Kings 2:15 we read: "The prophets saw that the spirit of Elijah was on Elisha." These other prophets could discern the spirit of Elijah emanating from Elisha.

We shall look at another example from Numbers 5:30 that is not direct spirit-to-spirit but is an impact from the spirit of one person onto another *via* an intermediary in the spiritual world. This passage talks of a spirit of jealousy coming over a man if his wife is unfaithful. This can occur without any external evidence of infidelity in the physical world. Therefore, if an individual sins in a hidden manner, an intermediary spirit of jealousy can come against another individual, thereby causing him to become jealous. Thus, in the spiritual realm sin opens the way for the persons impacted by the sin to "find out," in a sense. An individual could be jealous for other reasons and falsely accuse another individual. Therefore, in judging these matters, one would need spiritual discernment or a physical world investigation. Obviously, we need to be very careful of our words and actions at all times; for the Lord tells us that what is whispered in the ear will be shouted from the rooftops, and what is done in darkness will be made light. In addition, there is the old saying: Be sure that your sin will find you out. One, therefore, really can do nothing in secrecy. for it is transparent spiritually. This is a key concept to grasp and use in the maturing of our own spirit.

In Psalm 106:33 we read that ".... they provoked his spirit, so that he spake unadvisedly with his lips." This refers to Moses' actions in the wilderness, during the wanderings of Israel. Men's actions had an impact in Moses' spirit. We learn that all of a man's actions are initiated in his human spirit. This is another example of spirits flowing between individuals.

Ecclesiastes 10:4 tells us: "If the spirit of the ruler rise up against thee, leave not thy place; for yielding pacifieth great offences." Here we see that a spirit in a ruler can rise up against a person and that, in addition, that person can adopt a course of behavior (all of a man's behavior originates in a man's spirit) to mitigate against the problem. This, again, shows two human spirits having flows between them.

FLOWS FROM OTHER SPIRITS

This is a key concept in being led by the Spirit of God. Obviously, in any position that one seeks to be led, then one must decide which of these four spirits is trying to lead—God, the human spirit of the individual seeking to be led, the spirit of another person(s), or an evil spirit. In this section we will look at some Scriptures that illustrate the way that the Holy Spirit leads us and how evil spirits seek to lead us.

In John 13:12 we read: "And supper being ended, the devil having now put into the heart of Judas Iscariot, Simon's *son*, to betray him." This shows that an evil spirit can infiltrate a human heart. An evil spirit can become resident there. Judas did not have the Holy Spirit resident in his heart. There is no Scripture that indicates an evil spirit can co-share a human heart with the Holy Spirit. However, an evil spirit can certainly come against a human heart through the flesh and through the individual's operating under a spirit of fear. A person who has had the second birth can certainly have his new spirit become impure (2 Corinthians 7:1). This impurity results from evil ways that the individual adopts, causing evil structures to be erected in the heart. However, there is nothing to indicate that a person who has had the second birth can harbor an intelligent, named, individual power resident within his heart. Such powers may come into his soul and come against his heart and human spirit to the extent that deliverance is required. In a person before the second birth there can be powers possibly resident within his heart. Thus, if such powers are present at the time of the second birth, they may subsequently need to be cast out. It really does not make any difference functionally whether such powers are in or are surrounding the heart.

We get more information about this situation in Acts 5:3: "But Peter said, Ananias, why hath Satan filled thine heart to lie to the Holy Ghost, and to keep back *part* of the price of the land?" Satan had certainly filled Ananias's heart with evil structures and thought patterns. Thus, an evil spirit is able to fill a believer's heart. This is not the same as a power living in the new heart that the believer has been given.

In Romans 5:5 we read: "And hope maketh not ashamed; because the love of God is shed abroad in our hearts by the Holy Ghost which is given unto us." Here we see that the Holy Spirit is located within our heart as is our new spirit. The Holy Spirit resides only with those who have been through a second birth. Romans 8:27 also shows this: "And he that searcheth the hearts knoweth what *is* the mind of the Spirit, because he maketh intercession for the saints according to *the will of* God." God searches the hearts of His people and, in so doing, notes the mind of the Holy Spirit with respect to those people. This again supports the location of the Holy Spirit within the heart of a man who has gone through the second birth. 2 Corinthians 1:22 also attests to this: "Who hath also sealed us, and given the earnest of the Spirit in our hearts."

We can read in 1 Kings 22:22-23 of how the Lord allowed King Ahab to be misled: "And the LORD said unto him, Wherewith? And he said, I will go forth, and I will be a lying spirit in the mouth of all his prophets. And he said, Thou shalt persuade *him*, and prevail also: go forth, and do so. Now therefore, behold, the LORD hath put a lying spirit in the mouth of all these thy prophets, and the LORD hath spoken evil concerning thee." Thus, evil spirits can influence the words of the mouth. This means that a lying spirit impacted the hearts of these prophets, since Scripture states that the words of the mouth come from the heart.

FLOWS BETWEEN OTHER PARTS OF MAN AND THE HUMAN SPIRIT

FLESH

In Leviticus 17:11 we read: "For the life of the flesh *is* in the blood: and I have given it to you upon the altar to make an atonement for your souls: for it *is* the blood *that* maketh an atonement for the soul." It is the spirit that gives life to the flesh; and this illustrates again the semi-solid, liquid, or gaseous nature of the spirit that is seen throughout the Scriptures. Spirit power circulates in the blood to the individual cells. This flow of spirit carries power, emotion, and information at a microscopic level. Cells are in constant communication with the human spirit, relaying needs; and they are fed by the energy of the human spirit being dispersed through the blood. We can appreciate this better if we reflect on King Solomon's statement in Ecclesiastes, when he states that "there is nothing new under the sun." From this statement we can conclude that anything under the sun in the natural creation has a predecessor in the spiritual realm. This is obvious, since the physical realm is born out of the spiritual realm. The systems in the natural realm have to have an equivalent in the spiritual realm. The Lord Jesus is a life-giving spirit. This life circulates among the people who make up His body (cells). Spiritual flows maintain the life of these cells. "The life which I now live in the flesh I live by the faith of the Son of God," according to the Apostle Paul (Galatians 2:20).

It is noteworthy that the Israelites differentiated that God is the God of the spirit as opposed to the God of the soul or of the flesh. We see this in Numbers 16:22: "And they fell upon their faces, and said, O God, the God of the spirits of all flesh, shall one man sin, and wilt thou be wroth with all the congregation?" In Jeremiah 32:27 we read: "Behold, I *am* the LORD, the God of all flesh: is there any thing too hard for me?" God is the God of the whole creation; and, of course, this includes all flesh and all spirits.

In Deuteronomy 12:23 we read: "Only be sure that thou eat not the blood: for the blood *is* the life; and thou mayest not eat the life with the flesh." Here we see that God forbade the eating of blood, where the spirit is. The symbolism is very important to understand.

When Sampson was thirsty and thought that he was dying, the Lord gave him a drink; his spirit came again; and he revived (Judges 15:19). This shows that the state of the flesh and its feelings influence the spirit, even to the extreme of near death. This may seem surprising, but it is important to make the observation. We see another example of this in 1 Samuel 30:12.

When the Queen of Sheba had seen all of Solomon's riches and wisdom, there was no more spirit in her (1 Kings 10:5). This is an example of observations made in the natural world by the senses of the flesh impacting the spirit. This example is not a case of the nearness of physical death, but more a case of "emotional" stunning. It is akin to the human spirit's being stopped in its flow of life-giving power, emotion, and knowledge by the impact of the external flows into it.

In Job 4:15-17 we read: "Then a spirit passed before my face; the hair of my flesh stood up: It stood still, but I could not discern the form thereof: an image *was* before mine eyes, *there was* silence, and I heard a voice, *saying*, Shall mortal man be more just than God? shall a man be more pure than his maker?" This shows that Eliphaz could use the senses of the flesh to detect the presence of a spirit being presented in a vision to him. We have seen that Elisha's servant had his eyes opened by the Lord after Elisha prayed (2 Kings 6:17), and he saw the spiritual world arrayed to help in battle. This situation with Eliphaz seems different. It is important to see that our flesh can, under certain circumstances, apprehend the spiritual world. It seems that God has to open our physical senses in order for us to perceive this, and He does this seemingly in only special circumstances.

Proverbs 15:4 tells us that a perverse tongue is associated with a breach in the spirit. A breach is a serious malady that opens the way to emotional and physical illness. Keep in mind that the spirit, heart, and soul come into a consonant state over time; and any differences in their emotional states and content states are transient. Therefore, an abnormality in one component is quickly is transmitted to the other areas.

The Lord uses *flesh* to describe the total of humanity at the period in history that is discussed in Joel 2:28: "And it shall come to pass afterward, *that* I will pour out my spirit upon all flesh; and your sons and your daughters shall prophesy, your old men shall dream dreams, your young men shall see visions." The Spirit of the Lord covers that flesh, apparently like an anointing in this circumstance. The Spirit communicates with our human spirit in the heart, and the mind apprehends it.

In Matthew 16:17 we read: "And Jesus answered and said unto him, Blessed art thou, Simon Barjona: for flesh and blood hath not revealed *it* unto thee, but my Father which is in heaven." The revelation to Peter from God the Father was a direct revelation to the human spirit of Peter. No person or physical observation by Peter's flesh (flesh or blood) had played a role in his perceiving this truth.

In Matthew 26:41 we read: "Watch and pray, that ye enter not into temptation: the spirit indeed *is* willing, but the flesh *is* weak." We see the contrast between the flesh and the human spirit that became more sharply defined in the writings of the Apostle Paul. The flesh does not have the same agenda as the spirit of a person, even before the giving by God of a new spirit at the second birth. After God gives a new spirit, the believer's human spirit is always at enmity with his flesh (Galations 5:17).

Jesus contrasts a soul which is "spirit in flesh" with a spiritual being such as an angel, who does not have flesh in Luke 24:39: "Behold my hands and my feet, that it is I myself: handle me, and see; for a spirit hath not flesh and bones, as ye see me have."

We see a foundational law of the spiritual and physical universes in John 3:6: "That which is born of the flesh is flesh; and that which is born of the Spirit is spirit." One kind cannot give birth to a different kind. A fleshly motivation cannot ever become transformed into a spiritual motivation. We must lay hold of this principle when learning to walk after the Spirit of God. Regardless of how good the motivation, if the flesh conceived it, then it will never be of value to God.

In John 6:63 we read: "It is the spirit that quickeneth; the flesh profiteth nothing: the words that I speak unto you, *they* are spirit, and *they* are life." Here we see God's view of the flesh, emphasizing what we discussed above. The flesh does not ever, ever, ever cause God or a man any profit. We also see Jesus emphasizing that His words are spirit and, as such, give life.

Jesus tells us in John 8:15-16 that we judge with the senses of the flesh, whereas He judges with revelatory knowledge from His Father: "Ye judge after the flesh; I judge no man. And yet if I judge, my judgment is true: for I am not alone, but I and the Father that sent me." The Father's knowledge is, of course, true. This further underscores how we can place no stock in the flesh. The purpose of this book is to teach us how we can allow God to mold us into perceivers in the spirit and how we can then follow our human spirit, as it hears from the Spirit of God, instead of our fleshly senses.

The Apostle Paul states in Romans 7:18: "For I know that in me (that is, in my flesh,) dwelleth no good thing: for to will is present with me; but *how* to perform that which is good I find not." In Romans 7:25 he adds: "I thank God through Jesus Christ our Lord. So then with the mind I myself serve the law of God; but with the flesh the law of sin." These passages show how appositional the flesh is to the soul that has a new spirit. They are operating under completely different spiritual world laws. This is further accentuated by the apostle in Galatians 5:17: "For the flesh lusteth against the Spirit, and the Spirit against the flesh: and these are contrary the one to the other: so that ye cannot do the things that ye would." *Lust* is a present active indicative verb. This means that the action is in the present, and it is continuous. In other words, this is the condition of the flesh. It is what the flesh is like. We have to plumb the depths of our sinfulness by practicing the walk after the Spirit to learn just how we can never change this by our will. It is just what our flesh is; and we have always to be aware of this, as we learn to walk after the Spirit.

We learn in Romans 8:1: "*There is* therefore now no condemnation to them which are in Christ Jesus, who walk not after the flesh, but after the Spirit." If we walk purely after the Spirit of God, there will be no condemnation. The Lord Jesus achieved this. We do not achieve it. To the extent we are led by our fleshly lusts, which sadly to say is probably 99% of the time, we come under condemnation; but we do not lose our salvation. At the final judgment our works from the flesh will be burned, and we will be saved "yet so as by fire" (1 Corinthians 3:13-15). This shows why it is so important to learn how to walk after the Spirit of God as opposed to walking after our fleshly lusts.

In Romans 8:4 we read: "That the righteousness of the law might be fulfilled in us, who walk not after the flesh, but after the Spirit." As we walk after the Spirit, we are free from the law of sin and are doing righteous works (this is different to the righteousness that is ours for salvation as a gift from God). When we fall back to walking after the flesh, our deeds become unrighteous (as filthy rags in Isaiah 64:6). We are still righteous for salvation, based on the Lord Jesus' atoning death, if we have accepted Him as our Lord and Savior.

In Romans 8:5 we read the explanation for this statement in Romans 8:4: "For they that are after the flesh do mind the things of the flesh; but they that are after the Spirit the things of the Spirit." We see that, when we walk after the Spirit, our actions are consistent with God's purposes and not our own fleshly purposes. Ponder that deeply when you do not know what action to take. Wait for clarification of any action, even the smallest action; for, if you walk after the flesh, you are like filthy rags in God's sight; and He cannot use your works done in the flesh. He is not pleased by them at all, as we see in Romans 8:8: "So then they that are in the flesh cannot please God."

In Romans 8:13 we read: "For if ye live after the flesh, ye shall die: but if ye through the Spirit do mortify the deeds of the body, ye shall live." It is crucial for one who has had the second birth to see that the flesh cannot deliver the flesh. This is one of the most profound and liberating truths of the whole gospel. It can and must be thoroughly understood through experience only. Intellectually, it cannot be grasped, because the intellect in all probability has not been renewed adequately. To eliminate a recurring sin pattern in our lives, such as alcoholism, we cannot will by an effort of the flesh to overcome it. It is only removed as a recurring problem by confessing it as sin and asking the Lord to deliver us of it, which He will accomplish in His time. He may do it immediately, or He may do it gradually; but if that prayer was prayed in faith, believing that it would be answered, then that sin pattern will be eliminated. God is holy and would never leave a sin pattern that we have, when we desire in our heart to eliminate it. If we have not been delivered, then God is telling us that we are still under discipline; and we have to be led by the Spirit to discern why and then to correct the issues that the Spirit points out. Again, this correction must be under the leadership of the Spirit. We must have confessed the behavior as sin and repented of it, and we must have asked for deliverance from it.

We should realize that if we are not led by the Holy Spirit, then we are led by death and led into death.

Romans 13:14 states: "But put ye on the Lord Jesus Christ, and make not provision for the flesh, to *fulfil* the lusts *thereof*." This is a command to the soul to put on the mind of Christ and to subject our will to His will in all things, both great and tiny.

In 1 Corinthians 5:3 we read: "For I verily, as absent in body, but present in spirit, have judged already, as though I were present, *concerning* him that hath so done this deed." This is a good example of the difference between physical and spiritual sensing and communications. Paul in the flesh (body) was limited to a precise geography. When receiving information from the Lord in the spirit, he could be with the Corinthians, although geographically separated. The spiritual universe is far more powerful than the physical in all ways.

Paul instructs the Corinthian believers in 1 Corinthians 5:5: "To deliver such an one unto Satan for the destruction of the flesh, that the spirit may be saved in the day of the Lord Jesus." Paul was telling the believers that with their spirits and his spirit (with the power of the Lord Jesus) they must turn this sinner over to the devil to be killed in order for the spirit of this sinner to be saved at the final judgment. [This passage may raise in some minds concerns about the possibility of losing one's salvation, but note that Paul does not say that the believer would lose his salvation if not turned over now. It may be the intent of the Lord in the situation to remove a very diseased member. This situation is similarly seen in Paul's statement that those who had taken communion in the wrong manner had died early (1 Corinthians 11:30). Those who died early died because of the particular sin pattern.] This passage shows the spiritual power that the Lord will release to Paul for this purpose. Paul was writing under the influence of the Spirit of God when he penned these words. We see the dichotomy of the spirit and the flesh in the believer and also a picture of the issues we discussed regarding Romans 8:4-5.

In Colossians 2:5 we see another example of Paul's being present in the spirit but not in the flesh (body).

A new spirit that God has given at the second birth can be polluted and filthy. In 2 Corinthians 7:1 we read: "Having therefore these promises, dearly beloved, let us cleanse ourselves from all filthiness of the flesh and spirit, perfecting holiness in the fear of God." This serves to show further that we must learn how we are structured in the eyes of God. It will help us in learning how to walk after His Spirit. This cleansing is to be undertaken through reliance on Him to do it with our permission and cooperation. If we do it ourselves in a self-willed manner, then we will only cause further pollution.

In Galatians 1:16 we read: "To reveal his Son in me, that I might preach him among the heathen; immediately I conferred not with flesh and blood." Here there are two important points to note. The first is that the Apostle Paul after his second birth did not seek his learning from men but rather relied on withdrawing unto God. All of his knowledge was revelation knowledge that the Holy Spirit taught him. The second point to note is that there are many Scriptures that separate flesh from blood. Since the life is in the blood, then we can view the blood as a transporter throughout the flesh of spiritual life both before and after the second birth. The spiritual life in the blood is not the same as the human spirit man that is hidden in the heart. However, the blood circulates spiritual life energy to the body. Thus, the spirit of man releases a life energy or force into the blood that circulates and nourishes all of the individual members and cells of the body. In a similar way the Holy Spirit circulates and nourishes all of the members of the Body of Christ.

Once we have gone through the second birth, we are dead in our mortal body; but we still live because of the life of the Lord Jesus that now resides in our body. Our spirit is bearing witness to His Spirit. This is seen in Galatians 2:20 which reads: "I am crucified with Christ: nevertheless I live; yet not I, but Christ liveth in me: and the life which I now live in the flesh I live by the faith of the Son of God, who loved me, and gave himself for me." Romans 8:11 reads: "But if the Spirit of him that raised up Jesus from the dead dwell in you, he that raised up

Christ from the dead shall also quicken your **mortal** bodies by his Spirit that dwelleth in you" (emphasis added). Further, in 2 Corinthians 4:11 we read: "For we which live are alway delivered unto death for Jesus' sake, that the life also of Jesus might be made manifest in our **mortal** flesh" (emphasis added). Overall, the thrust of these Scriptures seems to indicate that, after we have gone through the second birth, the flesh has been put to death with Jesus by crucifixion. However, we are still always delivered unto death, indicating that in God's view we are seen as dead by crucifixion with Jesus; but we still have to live in this life. The power for that comes from the resurrection life-giving Spirit of which Jesus is the first. Since our flesh has not changed, God always continues to put circumstances into our lives to deliver our flesh to death for the Lord Jesus' sake.

Therefore, if we are to follow the Spirit, we will indubitably find that circumstances occur that require us to put our flesh to death. The flesh must be dead, in other words, for us to walk after the Spirit of God. This death must be positional, as in Galatians 2:20, and also daily, as in 2 Corinthians 4:11. The critical point is, that to walk after the Spirit, we must cause our flesh to be dead both historically by our acceptance of Jesus as our Lord and Savior, and in daily life. If it is not occurring in daily life, then we cannot walk after the Spirit. Therefore, in learning how to walk after the Spirit, we must learn how to cooperate with God's work of always putting our flesh to death. In Galatians 5:16-17 we read: "*This* I say then, Walk in the Spirit, and ye shall not fulfil the lust of the flesh. For the flesh lusteth against the Spirit, and the Spirit against the flesh: and these are contrary the one to the other: so that ye cannot do the things that ye would." This supports what we have just concluded. The flesh is always at enmity and lusting against the Spirit of God. To the extent that our spirit has been kept undefiled, then our spirit will lust against the flesh.

Paul rebukes the Galatians for beginning to follow again the flesh again after initially beginning in the Spirit in Galatians 3:3: "Are ye so foolish? having begun in the Spirit, are ye now made perfect by the flesh?"

In Galatians 6:8 we read: “For he that soweth to his flesh shall of the flesh reap corruption; but he that soweth to the Spirit shall of the Spirit reap life everlasting.” This is a key passage for learning how to walk after the Spirit. It is a foundational spiritual universe principle. Every word, thought, belief, attitude, action, and behavior that we have and perform sows either to the flesh or to the spirit. We have a constant fight against the flesh that will never cease in this life. It is the major war in which we are involved. The devil will try to sidetrack us with external concerns; but if we refuse to be sidetracked and continue to fight this constant battle, the Lord will bring us to a place of rest when the devil will flee from us (James 4:7). We must view this as a war, taking every single thought captive before it leads to any action. All thoughts must be conformed to the mind of Christ. We must die to the flesh (self). We must perform this continually and actively. A passive mind that has been entertained by the media is very poorly equipped to perform this fight. We have to train for it and buffet the body (flesh) to sow to the spirit and to the Holy Spirit.

Philippians 3:3 explains: “For we are the circumcision, which worship God in the spirit, and rejoice in Christ Jesus, and have no confidence in the flesh.” Paul is telling us that we are the “circumcision” when we do the following:

1. Worship God in spirit
2. Rejoice in Christ Jesus
3. Have no confidence in the flesh

When these things come about in our lives, then our hearts have been circumcised. Note that we must have no (absolutely not even a drop) confidence in the flesh (old mind, old behaviors, physical perceptions, old knowledge, and so forth).

SOUL

When an individual uses the term “I” or other form of self reference, he is referring to his “soul.” The soul is the whole self and all that this embodies. It is the sum of the spirit and the flesh, but the combination of these two components is much greater than the individual parts. The soul, we will see, makes the call as to what is sown to the flesh and to what is sown to the spirit. It is the seat of the will where our decision making is carried out. The energy of the soul comes from the spirit, which gives the life energy to the soul.

We will now look at a conceptual model of how spirit, soul, flesh, and will work together. A model is an abstraction of the whole in order to make the information understandable and usable. A meteorologist models weather patterns in order to make predictions. He measures at a few points and then interpolates data between those points. A mathematical equation of acceleration models a more complex behavior for ease of understanding. In the same manner the model that follows captures the truth of the Scriptures and provides a framework for understanding the more complex whole.

As we progress through this section on soul, what will emerge is represented by the following model.

Our flesh and spirit form our soul (we cover this in much detail in Chapter 13, showing that the Bible always presents the formula: flesh + spirit = soul). We have seen that our spirit is located in the deepest part of our soul, the heart. We know that we have both physical and spiritual senses. In Ephesians 1:18 we read of Paul praying that the "The eyes of your understanding being enlightened; that ye may know what is the hope of his calling, and what the riches of the glory of his inheritance in the saints." We see Elijah asking God to give his servant a vision of the spiritual forces around about him prior to a battle. These are examples of someone praying for spiritual vision. There are other examples of spiritual senses in the Scriptures. One is when the child Samuel heard the still, small voice of the Lord; and Eli did not. We read in Job of the sense of spiritual touch.

We will see that our flesh and spirit are contained within the soul that they form. They are contained within it functionally, if not physically. Our flesh communicates with the natural world; and our spirit, with the spiritual world. It is our spirit, above that of the soul, from which God values communications (1 Corinthians 2:10-15), although the Scripture asks us to glorify God in our spirit, soul, and body. Unless we worship God in spirit and truth as the Scripture commands (John 4:24), we cannot glorify God. We will see that our decision-making apparatus, the will, resides within the soul and that we can will to develop our flesh or our spirit. We develop one at the expense of the other, for we have seen that the flesh and the spirit are always at enmity. In essence, our soul is in charge of our course through life; and it can choose (we can choose) to grow in spiritual knowledge, strength, and development; or we can pursue a mixed spiritual and fleshly course, which we will see leads to emptiness and frustration. We can also choose to have a totally fleshly walk without any heed to spiritual growth.

We shall learn that information comes to us (our soul) from the natural world as observations by our physical senses of natural events and of people. These observations from our physical senses go into the mind and then into the heart, where they interact with our human spirit. The mind forms a response to this information, as does the spirit (in the mind of the spirit). These responses may include internal change within the spirit, heart, and soul in response to new unique information. There may also be a response back into the natural world from the soul and into the spirit world from the spirit. These responses from the spirit and the soul may be disparate, either deliberately when deceit is intended or involuntarily under emotional pressure to save face or for some other reason. Whenever there is a dichotomy in the responses in the natural and spiritual realms, deceit is present. The inward flows of spirit or physical information may cause the individual to produce outward spiritual flows to God in prayer—spiritual, soulish, or both. A beautiful sunset may induce a response from the soul of gratitude to God for the beauty of the creation. A spirit of anger emanating from an evil person making a threat may induce fear and a prayer for protection to the Lord. Most people have very little ability to sense things in their spirit. They will act in a seemingly spiritual manner because they see visual cues from a person's countenance and posture or hear tones that convey information to their human spirit through the fleshly senses.

Information also comes to us from God, from God's angels, from other people's spirits, and from evil spirits. This information is apprehended first in the spirit with our spiritual senses. This can then stimulate spiritual flows into our heart, then into our soul, and subsequently into our flesh. Our soul can emanate spirit to other spiritual beings based on these impartations into our spirit.

It is our soul that chooses (wills) what flows of information to apprehend and to which to respond. Our soul also decides on the type of response and to which spirits the response will go. It also decides whether a response is to be made in a physical manner in the natural world.

As we progress through the following examples, we will get a much better understanding of the relationship of the soul to the spirit; and then at the end of the examples we will draw some conclusions. We have seen above that God weighs the spirit of all of our acts and thus holds us (soul) accountable for how we interact with the natural world, with the spiritual world, and with Him. The Scripture portrays us as being quite accountable for all of our actions in the soul, mind, flesh, spirit, and will. We shall now look at Scriptures that will help us to see the Scriptural evidence for the above model. In order to make it easier to fit the Scriptures into the model proposed, we have frequently used a bold type to show how a Scripture works toward the development of the model.

In Psalm 31:5 David states: "Into thine hand I commit my spirit: thou hast redeemed me, O Lord God of truth." David is showing the ability of his soul to control his spirit so that he can make this commitment. This is a key foundational concept for our understanding of these inter-relationships. Recall that the spirit is the seed that is within our heart that will go into eternity. The development of the information and personality of this seed is within our control, as we make decisions in this life in our soul. The following example in Psalm 32:2 confirms to us that God judges us for the condition in which we maintain our spirit. **This shows the will in the soul controlling the spirit**.

Psalm 32:2 states: "Blessed is the man unto whom the Lord imputeth not iniquity, and in whose spirit there is no guile." God is telling us here that He will judge us by how we keep our spirit with respect to its characteristics. In this case it is in respect to guile. This indicates that we can control the state of our spirit by the decisions that we make in the soul. Similarly in Psalm 34:18 we see that God is telling us that we can make our spirit contrite. **These passages show the will in the soul controlling the spirit.**

In Psalm 143 we read: "For the enemy hath persecuted my soul; he hath smitten my life down to the ground; he hath made me to dwell in darkness, as those that have been long dead. Therefore is my spirit overwhelmed within me; my heart within me is desolate." This clearly spells out that the impact of persecution of the soul in causing the spirit to be overwhelmed. Note that this is not the result of a single or casual interaction, but rather a series of events over time. **This shows flows of spirit and natural observations into the flesh and then the soul. It results in a flow into the heart, and then spirit that brings about internal change.**

Psalm 77 tell us: "I cried unto God with my voice, *even* unto God with my voice; and he gave ear unto me. In the day of my trouble I sought the Lord: my sore ran in the night, and ceased not: my soul refused to be comforted. I remembered God, and was troubled: I complained, and my spirit was overwhelmed. Thou holdest mine eyes waking: I am so troubled that I cannot speak. I have considered the days of old, the years of ancient times. I call to remembrance my song in the night: I commune with mine own heart: and my spirit made diligent search. Will the Lord cast off for ever? and will he be favourable no more?" This passage shows a complex set of events occurring in the life of Asaph. He was clearly very stressed in this day of his trouble. He felt that the Lord was keeping him awake. He had physical problems in the flesh with a discharging sore. He "communed or searched" his heart, apparently trying to understand the reason(s) for and the solution(s) to the problems. In communing with his heart, he activated his spirit into making a diligent search. Therefore, we see in this case the dynamics of how an issue is perceived in the flesh, thought through in the mind, and then dealt with in the very depths of the soul, *i.e.*, in the heart of the man. In the heart the spirit pours "energy" into a diligent search. **This shows flows of spirit and natural observations into the flesh and then the soul. It results in a flow into the heart, and then spirit, which brings about internal change and also results in prayer to God and a search of the soul.**

Another very important Scripture for our understanding of these relationships is found in Proverbs 16:32. We read: "He [when the Scripture uses *he*, it is a synonym for the whole person, which, of course, is the soul] that is slow to anger is better than the mighty; and he that ruleth his spirit than he that taketh a city." We must make an immediate observation from this Scripture. Under warfare in Solomon's day it was rarely easy to take a city. In fact, it was probably very difficult with some cities and relatively easy with few cities. The Lord gives us praise, if we will make the effort to go through the battle that will ensue to rule our spirit. The Scripture indicates that it is not easy to control our spirit; but in order to follow God's Spirit and to mature in our life with Him, we must succeed in ruling our spirit. Certainly, with a new spirit as the result of a second birth, the issues are different in scope and magnitude; but the new spirit still must be ruled by the soul. In Proverbs 25:28 we then read: "He that hath no rule over his own spirit is like a city that is broken down, and without walls." In the New Testament we will see that the flesh is always at enmity with the spirit. The flesh must be controlled to minimize the impact of these constant and persistent attacks on the spirit. Persistent constant attacks that are not defended leave the spirit in a broken state like a city without walls. The city is then easily attacked by spiritual enemies. **This shows the role of the will in the soul's controlling the spirit. It is not an easy task.**

These above Scriptures demonstrate clearly that the inner spirit man is subject in development and function to the will of the soul. These issues will be discussed in Chapter 15 on the will. The picture that we have acquired is from the Old Testament Scriptures. These people did not have the benefit of a new spirit. At the second birth we get a new heart and a new spirit. This new spirit should be able to work with God much more effectively than the old dying spirit. This ideal, however, does not occur as well as it should, since in our present age the devil, in his persistent war against mankind, has so polluted the new spirit (2 Corinthians 7:1) that it frequently is in need of cleansing until it can be brought back into conformity with what God expects. This is an action that we can will to do in our soul that will result in changes in our spirit. The changes come within an individual with a new spirit, as the soul wills to use the power of the new spirit (strengthened by God with power as needed) to dominate the flesh. **This shows the will in the soul controlling the spirit. It also shows that our new spirit is subject to pollution**.

Solomon states in Ecclesiastes 2:11: "Then I looked on all the works that my hands had wrought, and on the labor that I had labored to do: and, behold, all was vanity and vexation of spirit, and there was no profit under the sun." Solomon is reflecting on a long time period of his works (all). In Ecclesiastes Solomon is observing life from the natural realm (under the sun), and not from God's viewpoint. Therefore, the conclusions he draws would be applicable to either an unbeliever or a carnal believer. He concludes that "all" was vanity and vexation of spirit. If "all" was vanity and vexation of spirit, we must, therefore, conclude that doing work of mixed motives over time will vex the spirit. This is understandable, since the mixed walk of a carnal believer results in erratic spiritual development (alternately sowing to the flesh and to the spirit); thus, it becomes frustrating. Note, of course, that the work is in the physical realm; and the spirit of it flows inward to impact the spirit. Thus, spiritual growth is hampered, slowed down, and stopped by a mixed walk before the Lord. It is only as we serve Him first in all things that we begin to develop in the power, strength, emotions, and knowledge of spiritual things. **This shows that a mixed carnal/spiritual walk results in vexation of spirit**.

Solomon adds in Ecclesiastes 8:8: "There is no man that hath power over the spirit to retain the spirit; neither hath he power in the day of death: and there is no discharge in that war." This Scripture shows that we have one obvious limitation in our ability to control and direct our spirit, *i.e*, at the point of dying. **This shows one exception to the soul's controlling the spirit. However, the Lord Jesus in His soul made the decision to give up His Spirit on the cross (Luke 23:46)**.

In Isaiah 26:9 we read: "With my soul have I desired thee in the night; yea, with my spirit within me will I seek thee early:" This tells us that the soul uses the spirit to seek God. The soul is obviously in command of the spirit in this Scripture. We read in the New Testament that true worshippers will worship God in spirit and in truth. We must make sure that the soul is using the spirit, not the flesh, to seek and worship God. It is only too easy for Christians to mistake the soul's other areas that can worship, if they have not undergone the separation of spirit and soul that is described in Hebrews 4. If they cannot tell what is coming from their spirit as opposed to their flesh, then they will worship in a mixed spiritual/non-spiritual (fleshly or soulish) fashion that is vexing to the spirit (as we have seen in Ecclesiastes 2:11). **This shows the will in the soul controlling the spirit. It also shows that the soul uses the spirit to communicate with God. In addition, it is God's desire that we worship Him in spirit and in truth**.

Ezekiel 21:7 portrays a complex inner interaction. We read: "And it shall be when they say unto thee, Wherefore sighest thou? That thou shalt answer, For the tidings; because it cometh." This is a response that resulted from news that Ezekiel heard. The news caused him to sigh. The passage goes on to say "and every heart shall melt, and all hands shall be feeble, and every spirit shall faint, and all knees shall be weak as water: behold it cometh, and shall be brought to pass, saith the Lord God." Thus, Ezekiel is showing the reaction that the Israelites would have to future news.

This later part of the passage describes the news reaching the mind when the Israelites would hear and perceive the news. After this it would go into the heart, causing it to melt, along with the spirit fainting. The news also would cause the hands to be weak and the knees to be weak. All of these things might occur almost simultaneously. Such emotionally strong news will reflexively cause the hands and knees to become weak. This process goes from the flesh into the heart and then into the inner man, causing a reaction which will feed back through the heart and the soul and into the flesh. In the case of such bad news it probably is a reflex reaction from the heart and spirit feeding back into the flesh, through the soul, without the mind of the soul assessing and modifying the response.

This shows a flow of spirit and natural information into the flesh through the sensory organs and into the spirit through the words heard by the ear. When the external disaster strikes *via* the natural world, this sensory input will traverse the flesh into the mind of the flesh and into the heart and, thence, into the spirit. It results in a reaction in the spirit and heart that flows back into the soul and then into the flesh, causing weak knees. This illustrates the accuracy of the modeling that was described above.

In Isaiah 26:9 we read that the prophet's soul had desired God in the night and that, parallel to this with his spirit, he would seek God early. Note that Isaiah has a choice of how to seek God, so that he specifies that it will be with his spirit. We note that in the Church Age God expects true worshippers to worship him in spirit and in truth. **We note that the soul can choose to seek God in the spirit, or it could do it in the natural mind as a soulish seeking. There is a choice the will can make**. Another example of this is seen in Matthew 22:43: "How then doth David in spirit call Him Lord...." This tells us that David could choose between using the flesh or the spirit. The Scripture distinguishes between flesh, soul, and spirit here.

In 1 Timothy 4:12 we read that Paul commands Timothy to be an example for the believers in word, in conversation, in charity, in spirit, in faith, and in purity. This means that Paul expects Timothy to control his spirit, his soul, and his flesh by willing to do so and then doing it. **This shows the control God expects of the soul, which in turn controls the spirit and flesh *via* the will**.

God pronounces woe unto the foolish prophets who follow their own spirit instead of following God's spirit (Ezekiel 13:3). This tells us that we can will to or that we can be deceived into following our own spirit with our soul. This is a key concept, for of the three spirits—human, God's, or demonic—we must follow one in order to have any power. **This tells us that we can be led by our own spirit instead of His spirit. It also tells us that the human spirit leads our will, as we conform our decision making to the spirit. These "foolish prophets" were not using their soul to control the spirit; and, as a result, their spirit was**

leading their soul. They were like a city with broken-down walls. That is why we are told to rule our human spirit (so that it will not lead our soul). We must keep our spirit waiting before God's Spirit in a worshipful, meek, and quiet manner (1 Peter 3:4). If our soul is not in charge of which spirit we follow, we will walk in error. This Scripture tells us that the prophets did not perceive their error. Now we must be careful here to not look down on these "foolish prophets," for almost certainly most of us are not even trying to discern which spirit we are following. The devil is an angel of light in this arena; and it is very easy to be deceived, unless we are prayerful about all of our words and actions, taking each of them captive for Christ. Our generation is so weak that we are almost all in spiritual infancy.

In Ezekiel 18:30 we read: "Cast away from you all your transgressions, whereby ye have transgressed; and make you a new heart and a new spirit: for why will ye die, O house of Israel?" **This again shows that God expects our soul to control our spirit, even before the second birth. He requires this so much more after the second birth to the extent that He now expects purity of spirit, as we read above**.

Malachi 2:14-16 reports God's telling the Israelites to take heed of their spirit that they deal not treacherously. Therefore, God expects the people to monitor their spirit and change their behavior if their spirit is wrong. **This shows that the soul can monitor the condition of the spirit and that the soul can will to change that condition**.

In Matthew 10:20 we read of Jesus' telling His followers that "it is not ye that speak, but the Spirit of your Father which speaketh in you." This shows that the Holy Spirit bears witness with our spirit and gives us actual words to state in extreme circumstances. This shows how our spirit uses the flesh and the soul to give expression to other persons. **This indicates an impartation from God into our spirit, resulting in a spiritual flow into the heart—then the soul, mind, and flesh. Our behaviors result from this flow**.

Jesus tells the disciples in Matthew 26:41: "Watch and pray, that ye enter not into temptation: the spirit indeed is willing, but the flesh is weak." This passage is similar to Scripture that tells us that the spirit is always at enmity with the flesh (Galatians 5:17). We are willing to serve God with our renewed minds; but there is always a battle with the flesh, caused by physical fatigue, lust of the flesh or of the eyes, fear in various forms, or pride in all its varied forms. In following God's spirit, we must sow to our spirit in order both to strengthen it and, at the same time, to weaken our flesh. We see a similar thought in John 6:63: "It is the spirit that quickeneth; the flesh profiteth nothing…." **These scriptures indicate the conflict between spirit and flesh**.

In Luke 1:46-47 we read of Mary's response to God. In faith she chose by will to believe the word of the angel. Because of her faith "there shall be a performance of those things which were told her from the Lord." Mary then distinguishes separate but similar responses from her soul and from her spirit. She states that: "My soul doth magnify the Lord, And my spirit hath rejoiced in God my Saviour." It is the spirit that generates the emotional responses, power, and wisdom that flow into the heart and then into the rest of the soul. The action of her will to believe led to the magnification of God from her entire being (soul).

Jesus rebuked the disciples for not recognizing that the spirit that was flowing from them did not come from Him (Luke 9:51-56). They had seen something and had responded to it in an ungodly way from their spirits. Thus we see a flow of information into the flesh, soul, and then spirit and a conditioned response from the spirit back into the soul and flesh to give voice to the spirit within. Since all words have spirit, we always speak from our spirit. It is very important to recognize and understand this concept in taking every thought captive. **We need to remember always to discern the spirits before talking or acting**.

Paul stated that the city of Athens was "wholly given to idolatory" (Acts 17:16). When Paul perceived this (presumably in the flesh, although it could have been in the spirit), his soul reacted; and information flowed into his spirit causing it to be "stirred" in him.

Paul stated in Romans 1:9 that he served God with his spirit. Paul chose to serve God with his spirit. It was a choice. God does not want us to serve him with our flesh. When we offer up a sacrifice from our flesh, it is displeasing to God, for He has judged the flesh; and it is sinful. There is no good in our flesh. The sacrifice that God expects and desires of us is obedience (2 Corinthians 10:5-6 and 1 Peter 1:2, 14). It does not matter what the end goal of fleshly behavior is, regardless of how altruistic it is; this is still unacceptable to God, just as Cain's sacrifice was unacceptable. We can be obedient only when our spirit hears God's Spirit speak to it. Therefore, we can be obedient to Him only when we have learned in the mind of our soul how to distinguish His voice coming into our spirit and thus learn His desires for us. **This again shows that the soul is expected to control the spirit (and, of course, the flesh)**.

In Romans 7:6 we are told to serve in newness of spirit and not in the oldness of the law. We must, therefore, learn how to serve in newness of spirit. This is done by learning how to be led by God's spirit. **This again shows that the soul is expected to control the spirit**.

In Romans 8:1-16 we see the key passages that led to the writing of this book. Let us begin to explore this looking at some of the verses in more detail. We note that there is no condemnation (ever, now, or in the future) to those who are in Christ Jesus, who walk after the Spirit of God (v. 1). There is by default condemnation for the other two classes, *i.e.*, those who are not in Christ Jesus (they cannot even hear from the Spirit unless God does something special in their lives) and those who are in Christ Jesus but who do not walk after the Spirit. In his letters to Corinth Paul describes this latter group of people as having a mixed walk. This is the walk of many people most of the time and a few people some of the time. There is no one other than the Lord who can claim to have approached the sinless state of walking completely after the Spirit at all times. We noted above that this mixed walk was described by Solomon as leading to vexation of spirit. Our acts of disobedience have eternal consequences for us and for others who are caught up by the effects of our actions. God will never work with our sacrifices of the flesh that arise from actions that do not come from the following of His Spirit. They have an unsavory aroma and appearance to Him (Isaiah 64:6). We can move on with the Lord only when we repent of our flesh-led actions. We have to hate them as much as He does. This is not easy to do, since most of them appear to us to be so good. We will do this only as we see how small we are before our mighty God. God will discipline us to train us to walk after His Spirit. That is His goal for us in our daily and continual walk before Him. **This again shows that the soul is expected to control the spirit**.

The law of the spirit of life in Christ Jesus makes one free of the law of sin and death (v. 2). This tells us that God has created the spiritual universe in such a way that, when one is being motivated to act in the power, love, and sound mind of Him through His Spirit, he cannot be subject to the law of sin and death. He is freed from that lesser law. Under the lesser law he had to keep it perfectly, or he failed it. No one apart from the Lord has ever kept it perfectly. Those who follow the Spirit imperfectly will be subject to the impact of their sin and will reap current and eternal consequences of it. Sin must not be regarded lightly, whether it is overt or less overt (such as disobedience by trying to follow the Lord by fleshly means). Jesus in His death provided the legal means for those who have been through the second birth not to be condemned eternally for those sins into which they continue to fall. Sin in not following the Spirit of God is so serious that Paul addressed the impact in a very sobering manner in verse 13 of this chapter. Here we read: "For if ye live after the flesh, ye shall die: but if ye through the Spirit do mortify the deeds of the body, ye shall live."

In this verse the word *die* should better be translated as being in a "state of death." Paul is telling us that if we as believers follow the flesh, we will be in a state of death. The Greek word is not *thanatos* which stands for the second death. If we follow the Spirit, we will be in a state of life while in our carnal fleshly body. Paul then tells us in verse 14 that as many as are led by the Spirit of God, they are the sons of God. The Greek word for son is *huios*. This word denotes a degree of maturity as opposed to *nepios* in Hebrews 5:13 where the writer describes people as babes. God desires us to grow and to become mature sons and daughters. We do this by feeding on His Word, being in His presence, acting in faith on His *rhema* and *logos*, and following His Spirit. As we mortify the flesh by walking after His Spirit, take all thoughts captive, ponder all spoken words, renew our minds, we grow in spiritual stature. Our growth is coordinated by following the Spirit of God. We can never plan this growth by willing our actions, which would be a work of the flesh. We must rather sit back, relax, and let God bring circumstances to us that will cause us to grow in the spirit. We must continually observe and assess the spirit emanating from us and judge it ourselves. We must continually train our spirit to express only the attributes that God demands—power, love, and a sound mind. We must take all thoughts captive constantly to renew our minds. In this way without planning it we will be trained by God, and He will do it in such a way that our spirit will mature enough to allow Him to separate it from the flesh (Hebrews 4:12). This will result in the ability of our soul to distinguish between flesh-, soul-, and human spirit-led initiatives.

In Romans 12:11 Paul tells us that we should not be slothful in business and that we should be fervent in spirit. These are choices that we must make. Paul would not tell us to be these things, if we could not will to be this way and then carry it through to success. **This again shows that the soul is expected to control the spirit**.

1 Corinthians 2:7-16 is a very important passage about the spirit of man: "What man knoweth the things of a man, save the spirit of man which is in him?...Even so the things of God knoweth no man, but the Spirit of God." This shows us that our human spirit knows all there is to know about us, even more than the soul, which does not even know the heart completely. It is the spirit which God weighs. He has already judged the flesh. This illustrates why it is so important for us to learn how to hear and interact with our spirit. We have all learned to listen to the flesh with its urges to eat, rest, and so on. We think in terms of worldly wisdom by the reflexes built up in our fleshly mind. After receiving our new spirit at rebirth, we have to learn to listen to the communication from this human spirit. We have to cleanse it from the pollution that has built up from our ignorance of what we should be doing. As we renew our minds, we can discern the desires of our spirit and act on them rather than heeding the flesh. We have to discern the mind of our spirit as it receives information from the Holy Spirit. This takes time and practice. It does not come easily. It must be learned before we can walk after the Spirit of God consistently. Too many believers think that, because they have a good

Bible study or a good time of prayer, they are spiritual people. These are just small beginnings. We must take those good feelings and realize that they should not be transient but a permanent residual in our spirit that exudes peace, joy, patience, long suffering, and all of the other fruit that the Holy Spirit wishes to develop in us. This must be our state in the spirit in all circumstances. Just as a piece of fruit on a vine cannot grow and mature if it is separated from the vine, we cannot mature if we are not linked closely to the Lord Jesus Christ in a relationship in which we hear from Him regularly and He hears from us regularly. We must learn to recognize His voice; we must know His written Word in great depth; and we must wait on Him in our spirit. (Isaiah 40:31 reads: "But they that wait upon the LORD shall renew *their* strength; they shall mount up with wings as eagles; they shall run, and not be weary; *and* they shall walk, and not faint.") He does not do things on our terms. We must learn to ignore our ideas that come from the fleshly lusts and distinguish them from the things placed in our heart by impartation from God's Spirit. We do not control the timing. God will make us wait and wait and wait to bring about patience. We must stop making our own plans that are not based on a vision imparted to us by God into our spirit. Even with a vision we must wait on God for the timing of implementation.

Our spirit's intellect is far, far greater than the mind of the flesh. It is hard to accept this without pondering it; but as we ponder from where ideas and images that flit into our minds come, then we will see that our minds are not quite as logical as we would hope. Who, after all, can control even what comes into his mind? As we focus on discerning the mind of our human spirit, we will begin to understand more spiritual things; and we will begin to discern the spiritual universe out of which came the physical. Which is greater, the physical or the spiritual? Just so it is with our spirit's mind versus the mind of our flesh. As we renew our mind, it begins to acquire understanding of the spiritual; for as we understand the spiritual and then walk in obedience to God, our mind is conformed to that of the Lord Jesus. This is the essence of having a sound mind, that is, walking with the mind conformed to the mind of Christ. We now can avail ourselves of how He thinks about issues.

If the Lord has determined that something is going to happen, He will share it with His prophets (Amos 3:7). We want to know what the Lord wants us to be doing so that we are not working against Him. Working against Him is futile. Therefore, let us learn to listen to our spirit as it reveals His mind to us. We will be much more intelligent people, but the world will not recognize that and will think we are foolish. If the world is not regarding us as foolish, then we should evaluate our walk. When we are walking after God, it is impossible not to appear foolish to the world (1 Corinthians 2:14).

In 1 Corinthians 5:3-5 Paul relates that his spirit can discern at a geographic distance. This is due to the information that the Holy Spirit gives to his spirit. Paul was able to choose to be present in the spirit. Note that this was a choice that he made. He had chosen to build up his awareness of his spirit, and now he had a greater ability in his soul to discern information coming from his spirit.

We can choose in our soul to join ourselves to the Lord. 1 Corinthians 6:17 says: "But he that is joined unto the Lord is one spirit." **This again shows that the soul is expected to control the spirit.** This also illustrates how spirits are linked in the spiritual world. Our spirit and the Lord's spirit are joined.

We see evidence in 1 Corinthians 14:2, 12-16 that our souls are to control our spirits. Paul speaks of two types of praying—in the soul, that is in language understood by the people present; and in the human spirit, which can be expressed in an unknown tongue. We learn in this passage that when we talk in an unknown tongue, we talk to God and not to men. Paul adds that in the spirit he speaks mysteries. This illustrates how in the soul we can choose to talk to God either with the mind of understanding or in the spiritual language that we have been given. It is our spirit praying when we pray in an unknown tongue (1 Corinthians 14:14). Paul is telling us to pray both in the language of the soul and in the language of the spirit. The setting will determine which is best. Note that in terms of blessing another person, the content of the prayer has to be led by the Spirit of God and cannot be derived from the flesh or from the soul, regardless of whether the language is understandable by the hearer.

However, the soul chooses to let the human spirit be a blessing; and the human spirit will, in witness to the Spirit of God, choose which language to use to convey a spiritual blessing to the hearer. Paul suggests that in a service it is best to pray with the mind so that others will understand (1 Corinthians 14:17-19). **This again illustrates how the soul must decide whether to express through the spirit or through the flesh or through both the spirit and the flesh**. Note here that the spirit can pray both through the soul and directly to God. It is not that the soul is leading the worship; but rather the human spirit out of love for those other persons in the service leads the soul to choose to express in the spoken natural tongue as opposed to speaking a spiritual language out loud—the soul is in control still since it can decide whether to let the human spirit lead the prayer.

2 Corinthians 2:13 relates that Paul, when he could not find Titus suffered unrest in his spirit. **This shows an external event causing a spiritual reaction**.

2 Corinthians 11:4 shows that our soul can control which Jesus, which gospels, and which spirits we receive. For example, we could receive the Jesus of the Bible, the second person of the Trinity; the Jesus whom many cults respect as a prophet; the Jesus whom many secular people call a good man; or any number of other non-biblical persona. We can discern the real Jesus only in the spirit and by the fruit. We can have an idea from the mind, but only the spirit reveals truth. This is a good example of how the spirit is much more intelligent than the mind. We must forever rid ourselves of the use of our intellect as a primary way of getting wisdom, understanding, and knowledge. True wisdom is discerned by the spirit, not by the mind. The renewed mind can assent to true wisdom for the purpose of operating in truth in the flesh and soul.

We read of another foundational understanding for walking after the Spirit of God in Galatians 5:16-26. In this passage we read that, when walking in the spirit, we will not be fulfilling the lusts of the flesh. These are mutually exclusive. The lusts of the flesh and the works of the flesh are defined. They all fall into one or more of the divisions of lust of the eyes, lust of the flesh, and the pride of life. They are only in part enumerated here in this passage. If we walk continually after the Spirit of God, we will not be involved in these things. Walking in the spirit is mutually exclusive to walking in the flesh. They do not intersect. Paul goes onto define the fruit of walking after the Spirit of God. **This shows that the flesh and the spirit are always opposed. One can use this in discerning in the soul whether the spirit or the flesh is doing the leading. One can examine the potential fruit of a contemplated word or action and whether it sows to the flesh or the spirit. In this manner one learns with patience to follow the Spirit of God**.

We can, therefore, examine the spirit of every thought, word, and action that we are contemplating and discern the root of them. If we are sowing to the spirit, then the fruit of the Holy Spirit will be formed in us. If we are sowing to the flesh, then the lusts of the flesh will be formed in us. Therefore, as we do as we are commanded and take every thought captive for Christ, then we will walk after the Spirit of God, if we determine in advance what the root of the thought is. If the thought is of the flesh and leads to one of the fruits of it, then we must "will" to extinguish that thought. Gradually, as we do this, we will reprogram our minds, our hearts, our spirits, and our souls to walk after the Spirit of God. We read in Galatians 6:8 the foundational spiritual principle that we have noted before. This principle is that we choose that to which we sow, the flesh or the spirit; that is what we will reap.

In Galatians 6:1 Paul assumes that we can determine what a spirit of meekness is. We must learn this from the Spirit of God. It is not what we would automatically think when our minds have not been renewed. This learning what a spirit of meekness is comes by impartation, as we determine in our souls to will to walk after the Spirit of God.

We learn that we must be renewed in the spirit of our mind (Ephesians 4:23-24). This means in the source of power, the expression of spiritual emotion, and the precepts and structure of our mind's workings. If we do this by an act of will that is implemented by the soul, then we will put on the new man. The Lord Jesus by His death and resurrection as a life-giving spirit gives us the power to do this, as we allow ourselves to walk after the Spirit of God. We acquire it only by choice and action.

We have to do our part. God will initiate the desire in many; but while many are called, few will accept the call to become chosen. We read in Ephesians 5:18-19 that we should choose to be filled with the Spirit of God and speak to ourselves in psalms and hymns and spiritual songs. We are asked to sing and make melody in our heart to the Lord. **This shows again that the soul chooses a path for the spirit. It also confirms that our mind as an individual component within the soul has its own spirit**. The spirit of the mind will be the major power base that the mind uses, whether it expresses spirit-derived or flesh-derived emotions and whether it works with worldly knowledge or imparted knowledge.

In that great passage of Scripture in Ephesians 6 we read in verses 17-18 that we should take up the sword of the Spirit, which is the Word of God. This is both a defensive weapon and an offensive weapon. Note that this is the only way that you as a soldier in the spiritual war of the ages can make any progress on your own account or on behalf of others, including the Lord. Note well that your sword will only be as sharp, as long, as flexible, and as deadly to spiritual foes as your time in the Word that is spent meditating before the Lord. Learning Scripture is good to an extent, but it must be put into the correct hierarchy by the Holy Spirit. You cannot approach the reading of Scripture passively or learn it by rote and still expect your sword to be lengthened. It is only as you prayerfully read Scripture, pray about it in the presence of the Holy Spirit, and ask the Holy Spirit to teach you about it that you can be led into all truth and thereby gain a sword that will be worthy of the Lord's use. If, after reading Scripture, you have no new insight and no commitment to change, then you have almost certainly not interacted with it at the level of the human spirit or in the heart. It has been kept at the level of a reflex in the mind. The information still travels to the heart and human spirit but comes back in a reflexive manner that has been set up by prior beliefs and attitudes. No change is made; and no pondering takes place in the mind of the human spirit, heart, or soul. This can be used as a diagnosis of hardness of heart in respect to this particular issue.

In Philippians 3:3 Paul elaborates on the criteria for those of the spiritual circumcision:

a) Worship God in the spirit (as opposed to the soul or flesh).

b) Rejoice in Christ Jesus.
c) Have no confidence in the flesh (do not place any confidence in the unrenewed mind).

Note that all of these are willed choices that we must choose to do and to continue to walk in. **Again, the soul must make a choice to sow to the spirit or to the flesh**.

Paul states in Colossians 2:5 that, while he is absent in the flesh, he is present in the spirit. In the spirit he is able to joy and behold their order and the steadfastness of their faith in Christ. This shows the difference in the natural and the supernatural. This is a supernatural awareness given to Paul by the Lord in his spiritual perceptions.

Peter commends believers who have by an act of will purified their soul by obeying truth (Jesus) through the Spirit (1 Peter 1:22). Note that they had to do it through the Spirit. It would not be pure to do it through the flesh; it is then a work of man. One result of this purity is unfeigned love of the brethren. If it were a work of the flesh, it would appear somewhat similar; but it would be discernible to the spiritual man as feigned love of the brethren. Now Peter goes a step further and asks them to see that they love one another with a pure heart fervently. The steps of purifying the heart and becoming fervent are under the control of our soul. **This passage clearly reveals the spiritual emotion of unfeigned love and, by implication, the love of the flesh, which is feigned. The same applies to every emotion that the soul and spirit can express**.

This illustrates the point that all spiritual emotions can be counterfeited by those from the flesh. We have to learn to discern from which spirit an emotion emanates to determine whether it is of God.

In 1 John 4:1-6 we read some very important commands from God. He wants us to try the spirits to see whether they are from Him. We are asked to not believe every spirit. This means testing and evaluating with spiritual discernment all of the words, power, and emotion coming from an individual spirit or from a spiritual flow. We have to discern the emotion to see if it is feigned or unfeigned. We have to see from where the power is, *i.e.*, human spirit, evil spirit, or Holy Spirit. We have to see if it is of sound mind by seeing if it will stand up to analysis. We can know the spirit of truth and the spirit of error by seeing if someone is hearing us (1 John 4:6). He that knows God will hear us. He that is not of God does not hear us. A believer, however, who is in rebellion, may not hear us on a particular issue related to his rebellion; but he could hear us on other issues related to God. Therefore, this is not a simple test but rather one to be applied carefully. We can never rest on one verse from Scripture. We need to have a sound hierarchy of Scripture that has been taught directly to us by the Holy Spirit, who leads us into all truth. This hierarchy has to be supported by further Scriptures. All Scripture witnesses to other passages in a complex manner, as we discussed earlier in the book. This allows those to see who will see and those who will not see not to see.

MIND

There are not very many Scriptures that link spirit and mind directly. Many Scriptures link heart and mind, and there is a very frequent link between heart and spirit that we will examine further in Chapter 10. We will examine this link between the heart and the spirit closely to see how spiritual flows proceed through the heart into the soul, mind, and flesh from the spirit. In this section we shall examine just those Scriptures that directly link spirit and mind. We know that both the heart and soul have a mind. These minds are able to communicate with each other. The mind of the heart expresses itself through the mind of the soul into the physical realm. The mind of the soul expresses itself into the spiritual realm through the mind of the heart. All words and actions carry spiritual flow into the physical realm. All physical events carry spiritual flows into the flesh, heart, and spirit and thus impact the spiritual realm.

In Daniel 2:1-3 we read about Nebuchadnezzar's dreaming dreams that troubled his spirit. As a result of the trouble in the spirit his sleep "broke from him." These dreams occurred in the mind and resulted in an impact on the spirit. Of course, the soul is involved, because the mind is a part of the soul. We read in Daniel 2:29: "As for thee, O king, thy thoughts came *into thy mind* upon thy bed, what should come to pass hereafter: and he that revealeth secrets maketh known to thee what shall come to pass." This passage confirms that dreams occur in the mind. In Daniel 2:3 we read: "And the king said unto them, I have dreamed a dream, and my spirit was troubled to know the dream." Therefore, we see the impact of occurrences in the mind impacting the spirit.

The dream that the king had consisted of power (there was an energizing of the king to perform a work as the result of it); there was an emotion to it, since there was a sleep disturbance; and there was information with it. Therefore, we can see that this dream consisted of a flow of spirit from God into the mind of the king. There was a flow of spirit from the dream in the mind to the spirit of the king. We can assert confidently that all thoughts in the mind of the soul or in the mind of the heart travel as a flow of spirit back to the spirit itself.

Ephesians 4:23 tells us: "And be renewed in the spirit of your mind." This tells us that the mind of the soul has one gate-keeping spirit at the apex of a heirarchy of many spirits that we must renew. This apical spirit controls all flows of spirit into and out of the mind of the soul. It is set by our will, and it oversees what we will and purpose. It conforms all thoughts, thought processes, and activities of the mind of the soul to what we have willed to entertain. We see the outplay of this in a passage such as Philippians 4:8, where we read: "Finally, brethren, whatsoever things are true, whatsoever things *are* honest, whatsoever things *are* just, whatsoever things *are* pure, whatsoever things *are* lovely, whatsoever things *are* of good report; if *there be* any virtue, and if *there be* any praise, think on these things." Fulfilling the intent of this passage by an act of our will renews and stabilizes the spirit of our mind. When the spirit of our mind is set in this direction, then our mental processes and thought content are constrained in these areas.

In this case it is linked to putting on the new man and putting off the former corrupt conversation of the old man. The overall spirit of the renewed mind is toward having the mind of Christ. The spirit of the mind is like a gyroscope that is set spinning in a particular direction by our will. It can change, but not easily. We must bring much spiritual force into play to change the spirit of the mind. This spirit of the mind will energize our soul and our will to take certain actions, as opposed to other possible actions. These actions will be consistent with the spirit of the mind.

Under the power of this overall spirit the mind deals with ideas, concepts, memories, information from the human spirit, information from the physical world, and the imaginations. All of these individual entities have spirit associated with them. We see the play of power coming into spirit. The spirit of our mind is formed from a hierarchy of beliefs and attitudes. Suppose a new and Godly spiritual flow of wisdom that is empowered by the Holy Spirit comes into our mind from our human spirit. This flow of spirit will arrest the attention of a mind that has a spirit that seeks the things of God. It will have less chance of making such impact in a person whose mind has a spirit that is opposed to God.

We will see as we develop this study of being led by the Spirit of God that all spirit has a form of potential energy to bring about change. As spirit is able to flow from one individual to another or from the spirit of a person to the mind of the person, it has a power to perform a work of change. We will see that when God tells us to resist the devil, we must exercise spiritual force to do this. Spiritual force to resist the devil is increased or decreased by the structures that we choose to put into place in our mind, in our heart, and in our human spirit. Our prayers have spiritual power (force) associated with them, as they flow to God.

In Philippians 1:27 we read: "Only let your conversation be as it becometh the gospel of Christ: that whether I come and see you, or else be absent, I may hear of your affairs, that ye stand fast in one spirit, with one mind striving together for the faith of the gospel." Here we see that, as the believers at Philippi develop a unity in their spirit with each other, there is an expectation that they will have one mind with each other. The nature of spirit is such that, if the energies of the spirit are directed in different individuals to the same end, there will be oneness of mind. The key here is to have the spirits all aligned. It would take spiritual perception to know whether a group of people were really aligned in spirit over a particular issue. If they were not, then they would never be of one mind, since there would be spiritual flows from their spirits to their minds that would differ, with resulting impacts that would show as differences in thoughts about a particular issue. This passage emphasizes the fact that our human spirit sends information to the mind constantly in the form of spiritual flows. There is a constant back-and-forth communication that goes between the mind and the human spirit. It has to traverse the heart in each direction, and we will see later how this may influence the transmission of spiritual flows between the spirit and the mind.

It is worthwhile pondering 1 Corinthians 1:26: "For ye see your calling, brethren, how that not many wise men after the flesh, not many mighty, not many noble, *are called*." We note that the mind that has not been renewed is valued in low esteem by God. This tells us much about the need to renew our minds under the direction of the Spirit of God.

In conclusion, we can note that the spirit is always sending information to the mind through spiritual flows. The mind has an overall spirit that influences how these flows are apprehended and processed. This overall spirit can change, but it requires much spiritual power to change it. The mind processes the spiritual flows coming into it within the overall spirit of the mind and directs output to the soul, to the flesh, to other spiritual individuals, to God, and to other people. The mind also gets input from these sources and directs this, after it is processed within the context of the overall spirit of the mind. It will send spiritual flows to the spirit, to the heart, to the soul, and to the flesh. It will also send them, when appropriate, to other people, to other spirits, and to God.

CONSCIENCE

The Scriptures make no direct link between the spirit and the conscience. However, Hebrews 10:22 states: "Let us draw near with a true heart in full assurance of faith, having our hearts sprinkled from an evil conscience, and our bodies washed with pure water." This reveals that the heart contains the conscience. We are never told that it is part of the spirit. Since interactions of the heart are direct with the conscience, then those interactions of conscience with the human spirit are mediated through the interactions of the conscience with the heart. We will learn more of this when we study the heart. It is of interest to note that cleansing the conscience requires sprinkling (Hebrews 10:22)—which implies a much more directed, careful, and delicate process than, *e.g.*, the washing of the body necessitates. These people being addressed are relatively mature believers who are having their heart cleansed carefully and thoughtfully in order for their hearts to be true. This sprinkling operation, in this context, requires use of the mind's cooperating with the soul in order to determine what needs to be sprinkled. The mind certainly has to be renewed and actively working to determine what needs to be cleansed in the conscience.

When this is done, we will invariably find that the things that need to be cleansed from the conscience are those things which make us feel false guilt (in that they violate a concept of the freedom that we have to walk after the Spirit of God). It will be those things which the enemy can use to bring us back into partly serving the law. It is those things that Paul addresses in such passages as Colossians 2:21-23: "Touch not; taste not; handle not; Which all are to perish with the using; after the commandments and doctrines of men? Which things have indeed a shew of wisdom in will worship, and humility, and neglecting of the body; not in any honour to the satisfying of the flesh."

THE WILL

We shall examine Scripture to learn how the spirit and the will interact. In doing this, we learn some very interesting things. We shall study flows of spirit both from the spirit to the will and from the will to the spirit.

We can quickly see that there is a two-way spiritual flow from the spirit to the will and from the will to the spirit. Many Scriptures demonstrate this, but we will look at two of them. In Job 15:13 we read: "That thou turnest thy spirit against God." This indicates that the will controls what a man does with his human spirit. In Exodus 35:21 we read about "those coming" whose spirit made them willing to come. This Scripture shows that the human spirit can stir up the will. We see the fundamental interaction between the will and the spirit shown in these two Scriptures. We see that there is a feedback mechanism in place between the human spirit and the will.

The soul can command the spirit to turn away from God (Job 15:13). The soul wills to perform this action. The spirit would no longer communicate with God properly; and, as a result, the energy flows of spirit back to the soul (and will) would not provide pressure on the soul and will to desire communication with God. In order to restore a right communication with God, one would need to use significant spiritual power to alter the cycle into which he had fallen.

In Proverbs 25:28 we see that God expects us by an act of the will to rule our spirit: "He that *hath* no rule over his own spirit *is like* a city *that is* broken down, *and* without walls." We can see the symbolism of the difficulty of fighting against a walled city compared to ruling one's spirit. When we are not ruling our spirit, we are in a state in which we cannot mount much of a defense to spiritual attack—like a city without walls.

When we do not allow our human spirit to be ruled by the soul, it becomes independent of rule. Remember that we are responsible for maturing our human spirit; and that, until it matures, it is going to behave like a spiritual infant or child. Until we die the first death, our human spirit is being matured or broken down by our willed choices. We have learned that it always opposes the flesh. Our soul must work with God to conform our human spirit to the image of the Lord Jesus (Romans 8:29). We conform our human spirit by cleansing it from impurity and by supporting it by our will in order that it can dominate the flesh. The life energy that it supplies must be channeled in appropriate directions. Let us suppose that it has matured to the level of a five year-old child. We have been carefully grooming it, and now we stop doing this and leave it alone. Our human spirit supplies our life energy and is even more intelligent than our soul, but like a five year-old child it has not reached spiritual maturity. While it will not deliberately disobey God, it will not have the maturity to co-operate with Him. Our human spirit, when not ruled, will put power into various works that our heart may invoke and that the enemy may force on it. It will act in a reflexive manner just like an individual who has spoken carelessly without thinking. The spirit flows through the heart and energizes the flesh and soul to action, just as we saw in Exodus 35:21. Unless our heart is pure, it will contaminate all spiritual flows from the human spirit that energize the flesh and soul. We have to will which flows we release from the heart into the flesh and soul and, thence, to other people. We must not let the spirit act reflexively. It will already have learned to do this from our past behavior patterns that we retain after the second birth (Chapter 17). These old behaviors, stored in the heart as high places and evil imaginations, contaminate and defile the new spirit. We, therefore, have to will which behaviors, which thought patterns, which beliefs, and which attitudes we will allow our human spirit to energize and our soul to express. The power of the human spirit has to be harnessed (controlled) to build up those behaviors, thought patterns, beliefs, and attitudes that are appropriate for the new man.

It is the soul that wills to do something, and the power to perform it comes from the spirit. This is the link that we noted above. The performance of the thing willed strengthens the soul in this chosen course. The soul then reinforces to the spirit that this is desirable. The spirit learns and adapts to powering the thing willed. Left to itself, without any contravening spiritual power being applied by external physical world factors or by God as revelation into the spirit, this interaction of the spirit and will persists and grows stronger. We see in the example from Exodus 35:21 that God gave revelation and power into the spirits of people from whom He required a task. This is an example of a sufficient spiritual power coming into the spirits of these people to interrupt prior behaviors in order to do a new work.

Thus, the spirit provides power to do a work that the will chooses, and the will feeds back to the spirit the authorization to continue to release spiritual power into the thing chosen. This continues until interrupted by another spiritual flow from God, from another spiritual being, or from the environment. Further examples from Scripture will amplify and clarify this.

In John 1:13 we read: "Which were born, not of blood, nor of the will of the flesh, nor of the will of man, but of God." This reveals to us that the flesh has an independent will (recall that it is always at enmity with the spirit). We also see that the will of the flesh is not the same as the will of man. The will of man is the will of the soul. In like manner the spirit of man has a will of its own. The will of the flesh and the will of the human spirit must be subjugated to the will of the soul.

The soul, after the second birth, can have power over the will. 1 Corinthians 7:37 states: "Nevertheless he that standeth stedfast in his heart, having no necessity, but hath power over his own will, and hath so decreed in his heart that he will keep his virgin, doeth well." The fact that the Apostle Paul mentions it here in this context illustrates that not everyone who has been through the second birth has power over his own will. We can infer here, since power is involved, that this involves spiritual power, since there is no other source of power in this universe. Therefore, some have spiritual power to control their own decision making, while others of us do not. We see here the feedback relationship of the human spirit and the will more clearly. Unless an individual has sufficient spiritual power for a given course of action, he will not be able to will it to happen successfully. Man, in many situations, cannot strengthen his own spirit sufficiently to bring about a particular action; and he needs a filling of power from God for such a situation. In many of these circumstances he may desire something that is good, but he does not have the power from the human spirit flowing into the will to implement his desire. He then needs to pray and ask God to strengthen him in the inner man. God may seemingly delay the answer to this request until a certain amount of restructuring of the person's soul takes place. During this time the Holy Spirit will be working with that soul in order to assist the person to get the power he needs. The Holy Spirit will work to help bring about needed changes.

By inference we see that the will is comprised of a desire to do something and also a knowledge of what is to be done. There must be power to allow the desire and knowledge to be implemented. We see that principle in the garden of Gethsemane, when the Lord Jesus asked the disciples to pray with Him. They had the desire and the knowledge to perform a prayer; their human spirits were willing to pray; but they lacked power in the human spirit to resist the flesh. Later, they would be filled with power at Pentecost. Spiritual power can come from the spirit of man, an evil spirit, or from God—working through the spirit of man. Once the will has been energized by spiritual power, there flows spirit from it since there is now emotion (desire), structured knowledge, and power. This spirit flows, like all spiritual flows, both outward from the will to the soul and inward back to the human spirit. Depending on what other spiritual pressures are acting on the human spirit of the person, this feedback of spirit from the will may result in the reinforcing of the willed behavior or the diminishing or extinguishing of the behavior. In the case of the disciples in the garden of Gethsemane, their will sent information back to their human spirit, but the pressures from the flesh overcame the energy from their spirit and blocked their prayer. The Lord Jesus identified the culprit as being the flesh in this situation.

1 Corinthians 16.12 states: "As touching *our* brother Apollos, I greatly desired him to come unto you with the brethren: but his will was not at all to come at this time; but he will come when he shall have convenient time." Paul had a desire for Apollos to perform a course of action. Apollos did not do it; thus, the spiritual power flow from Paul into the spirit of Apollos was not of sufficient strength to displace whatever other flows were within the spirit of Apollos at that time. However, there was enough power for Apollos to agree to come at a more convenient time. This is an example of how these flows interacted within the will of these two people. Scripture does not reveal whether either one was specifically acting on or refusing to act on a directive from the Lord.

Paul states in Colossians 4:12: "Epaphras, who is *one* of you, a servant of Christ, saluteth you, always labouring fervently for you in prayers, that ye may stand perfect and complete in all the will of God." We note that Epaphras must labor in prayer for the Colossians to be able to stand perfect and complete in all the will of God. The Colossians' wills must be in alignment with that of God. This, by inference, cannot happen without God answering the prayers of Epaphras. Therefore, God must impart spiritual power into the spirits of the Colossian believers for them to have enough power to perform His will in this respect.

Other Scriptures that are useful to observe follow.

David was able by a willed action(s) to commit the course of his spirit. In Psalm 31:5 he says that "into thine hand I commit my spirit."

In Psalm 32:2 we read that God says that "Blessed is the man…in whose spirit is no guile." This tells us that by willing to do so, we can alter the state of our spirit. This requires sufficient spiritual power to make the change in one's spirit.

In Psalm 34:18 God tells us that we can will our spirit to become contrite. Similarly in Psalm 51:17 we see that God is looking for a broken (toward Him) spirit. (This is entirely different to a breach in a spirit.)

In Ephesians 6:6 we read: "Not with eyeservice, as menpleasers; but as the servants of Christ, doing the will of God from the heart." This tells us that a person can do the will of God from the heart or just from the soul. We saw an example of this with King Amaziah in 2 Chronicles 25:2 where we read: "And he did *that which was* right in the sight of the LORD, but not with a perfect heart." God judges an action in its relationship to the state of the heart.

CONDITIONS OF THE HUMAN SPIRIT AND OTHER INTELLIGENT SPIRITS —THE EMOTIONS/ATTITUDES/STATES

It is important for a soul to be content in its circumstances and to seek peace in the heart (Colossians 3:15) to be led by the Spirit of God. We shall list several emotions and attitudes that can be transmitted from one spiritual source to another. More than one transfer can occur at a time. It is instructive to see the parallels in this list and the conditions that Scripture lists for the condition of the heart.

Genesis 26:35: Grief of spirit
Genesis 41:8: Troubled spirit
Genesis 45:27: Revival of spirit
Exodus 6:9: Anguish of spirit

Exodus 35:21: Made willing
Numbers 5:14: Spirit of jealousy
Numbers 27:18: The Holy Spirit in him
Deuteronomy 2:30: Hardening of the spirit
Deuteronomy 34:9: Spirit of Wisdom
Joshua 2:11: Loss of courage in the spirit
Judges 3:10: Judging ability in the spirit
Judges 8:3: Anger in the spirit
1 Samuel 1:15: Sorrow in the spirit
1 Kings 21:5: Sad spirit
1 Kings 22:21: Lying spirit
2 Kings 2:9: Double portion of a spirit
1 Chronicles 5:26: God can stir up a spirit.
Job 6:4: A spirit can be drunk.
Job 20:3: Spirit of understanding in the mind
Psalm 51:10: A right spirit
Psalm 51:17: A broken spirit
Psalm 77:3: An overwhelmed spirit
Psalm 77:6: A spirit can make diligent search.
Psalm 106:33: A spirit can be provoked.
Psalm 142:3: A spirit can be overwhelmed.
Psalm 143:7: A spirit can fail.
Proverbs 11:13: A spirit can be faithful.
Proverbs 14:29: A spirit can be hasty.
Proverbs 15:4: A spirit can have a breach.
Proverbs 15:13 and 17:22: A spirit can be broken.
Proverbs 16:2: A spirit can be weighed.
Proverbs 16:18: A spirit can be haughty.
Proverbs 16:19: A spirit can be humble.
Proverbs 16:32: A spirit can be ruled.
Proverbs 17:27: A spirit can be excellent.
Proverbs 18:14: A spirit can be wounded.
Proverbs 25:28: A spirit can be unruly.
Ecclesiastes 1:14: A spirit can be vexed.
Ecclesiastes 7:8: A spirit can be patient.
Ecclesiastes 7:8: A spirit can be proud.
Isaiah 28:6: There can be a spirit of judgment

Isaiah 29:10: A spirit of deep sleep.
Isaiah 30:1: A spirit can be not of the Lord's.
Isaiah 54:6: A spirit can be grieved.
Isaiah 57:15: A spirit can be contrite and humble.
Isaiah 57:16: A spirit can fail before God.
Isaiah 57:16: A spirit can be heavy.
Isaiah 66:2: A spirit can be contrite.
Ezekiel 3:14: One can go in the heat of his spirit and in bitterness.
Ezekiel 21:7: A spirit can faint.
Daniel 2:1: A spirit can be troubled.
Hosea 4:12: There can be a spirit of whoredom.
Micah 2:7: The Lord's spirit can be straitened.
Micah 2:11: There can be a spirit of falsehood.
Habakkuk 1:11: A spirit can change.
Haggai 1:14: A spirit can be stirred up.
Haggai 2:5: The Lord promised that His spirit would remain with the people.
Zechariah 12:10: The Lord can pour out a spirit of grace and supplications.
Zechariah 13:2: There are unclean spirits.
Malachi 2:14-16: One can take heed of his spirit to deal not treacherously, and one can have a residue of the Holy Spirit.
Matthew 5:3: A person can be poor in spirit and blessed.
Matthew 12:18: God's spirit on Jesus allowed Him to judge the Gentiles.
Matthew 22:43: David in his spirit was able to call Jesus *Lord.*
Mark 2:8: Jesus perceived in His spirit.
Mark 8:12: Jesus sighed deeply in His spirit.
Mark 14:38: The spirit can be ready, but the flesh weak.
Luke 1:17: John the Baptist went in the spirit of Eliajah.
Luke 1:46: Mary's spirit rejoiced.
Luke 1:80: A spirit can wax strong.
Luke 9:51-56: Jesus told the disciples that they did not know what manner of spirit they had.
Luke 10:21: Jesus rejoiced in spirit.
Luke 13:11: A woman had a spirit of infirmity.
John 4:23-24: True worshippers will worship in spirit and in truth.

John 6:63: Jesus' words were spirit.
John 6:63: The spirit quickeneth, and the flesh profits nothing.
John 11:33: Jesus groaned in the spirit.
John 13:21: Jesus was troubled in spirit.
Acts 17:16: A spirit can be stirred.
Acts 18:5: A spirit can be pressed.
Acts 18:25: A spirit can be fervent.
Acts 19:21: Paul purposed in his spirit.
Acts 20:22-23: A spirit can be bound.
Romans 1:9: A spirit can serve.
Romans 11:8: God gave Israel a spirit of slumber.
1 Corinthians 4:21: A spirit can be meek.
1 Corinthians16:18: A spirit can be refreshed.
2 Corinthians 2:13: A spirit can have no rest.
2 Corinthians 4:13: A spirit can be of faith.
2 Corinthians 7:1: A spirit can be filthy.
Ephesians 1:17: A spirit can be one with wisdom and revelation in the knowledge of Jesus.
Ephesians 4:3-4: A spirit can have unity with another.
Ephesians 4:23-24: A mind has a spirit.
Philippians 1:27: People can stand fast in one spirit.
Colossians 2:5: A person can be absent in the flesh but with someone in the spirit and can see with the spirit.
James 4:5: A spirit can lust to envy.
1 Peter 3:4: A spirit can be meek and quiet (therefore, could be noisy).
1 Peter 4:14: A spirit of glory and of God can rest on one, if he is reproached for Jesus' name.

THE INNER MAN

The inner man (human spirit) is the spirit man. It is into the inner man that all flows of spirit (power, emotion, and knowledge) from both the physical and the spiritual universes come. It is in the mind of the inner man that these flows are perceived, analyzed, and reacted to with an outward flowing of spirit response. The spirit has a mind. We see the assumption for this made in such Scriptures as Psalm 77: "My spirit made diligent search." The human spirit must have an intelligent mind to make a diligent search. All of these flows, both to and from the inner man, come into the mind of the heart and the mind of the soul, or they go from the mind of the soul and the mind of the heart. The soul's mind has been given the overall capability for changing the condition of the heart and the human spirit by changing the mind of each. We shall look more closely at how these three minds interact in the chapter on the mind.

THE HEART

The Scriptures use the word *heart* frequently. It is used to describe what seems to be the core of an individual (soul). However, the soul has control of the heart and can will to change the condition of the heart. We shall look at Scripture in more detail in Chapter 10 in order to build up a more complete understanding of what the heart of man is and how it functions in man in relationship to the spirit. We now shall have a brief look at the heart.

As we study the Scriptures, we will see that a man can meditate within his heart. We will see that the words of the mouth reflect the thoughts of the heart. Therefore, serious thinking is able to occur within the heart. We have already seen that the heart of a man contains the inner man (human spirit). We will see that hearts can be associated with a variety of spiritual states, such as righteous, upright, contrite, and pure. Also, a soul can be whole-hearted in some or all of its actions. Hearts can contain a full spectrum of human emotion. They can fail with severe stress. The emotional and spiritual states of the heart dictate the emotional and spiritual state of the human spirit and of the flesh, but the heart can be changed by the will of a soul. At the second birth God gives a man a new heart and a new spirit. He writes His laws upon the heart. We will see that God looks closely at the state of the heart in a man. We also note that, while a soul can control the heart's state, even the soul does not understand the depths of wickedness within the heart. We will study flows of spirit into and out of the heart from the spirit of man and from the flesh and soul of man. We shall learn how the heart has the capacity to imagine.

Let us begin with Genesis 6:5: "And GOD saw that the wickedness of man *was* great in the earth, and *that* every imagination of the thoughts of his heart *was* only evil continually." Therefore, this passage is telling us that our thoughts that are not centered on God's revealed truth are always evil. *Imagination* is used in Scripture to denote a systematized structure within the thoughts of the heart that is frequently false in comparison to God's revealed truth.

In Exodus 28:3 we read: "And thou shalt speak unto all *that are* wise hearted, whom I have filled with the spirit of wisdom, that they may make Aaron's garments to consecrate him, that he may minister unto me in the priest's office." The direct impartation of wisdom from God into the spirit causes the heart of man to become wise.

Exodus 35:21 states: "And they came, every one whose heart stirred him up, and every one whom his spirit made willing, *and* they brought the LORD'S offering to the work of the tabernacle of the congregation, and for all his service, and for the holy garments." We see here the impact of a willing spirit's stirring up the heart of man, resulting in action. We see further in Exodus 35:4-36:1: "And he hath put in his heart that he may teach, *both* he, and Aholiab, the son of Ahisamach, of the tribe of Dan. Them hath he filled with wisdom of heart, to work all manner of work, of the engraver, and of the cunning workman, and of the embroiderer, in blue, and in purple, in scarlet, and in fine linen, and of the weaver, *even* of them that do any work, and of those that devise cunning work. Then wrought Bezaleel and Aholiab, and every wise hearted man, in whom the LORD put wisdom and understanding to know how to work all manner of work for the service of the sanctuary, according to all that the LORD had commanded." God sometimes uses the term *placed in the heart of* and sometimes amplifies the origination in the spirit. We know that the things in the spirit flow into the heart and vice versa. God gives us both a new heart and a new spirit at the second birth. It seems that at times He will place something into the spirit, and at times He will place it into the heart. We have seen from Genesis 6:5 that the heart contains structured thought patterns. We could conceive of these as a built-up structure of steel that will remain in shape and form, unless assailed by some strong spiritual force. When God puts something directly into the heart, He supplies a thought grid for the performance of His work. He may already have placed, or He may plan to place, the spirit impartation into the inner man that will act on this structure that He places in the heart. The structure that He places into the heart will not power the spirit, but it will act as a gate or a control to direct the flow of spirit.

Emotions reside in the heart. Leviticus 19:17 states this: "Thou shalt not hate thy brother in thine heart." We further see that this is a structured thought toward the brother that is accompanied by emotion (hate), and it is able to perform an action. Whenever there is an emotion in the heart, it has to be connected to a flow of spirit that will flow out of the heart of the individual to the spirit, to the flesh, and to the physical universe. God tells us to get rid of that thought structure in the mind of the heart that allows the spirit of hate to flow. Without the thought structure, there can be no flow of spirit. If the structure is left in place, then spirit can flow.

Deuteronomy 2:30 says: "But Sihon king of Heshbon would not let us pass by him: for the LORD thy God hardened his spirit, and made his heart obstinate, that he might deliver him into thy hand, as *appeareth* this day." Here we read about the Lord's hardening a spirit by impartation and, at the same time, making the heart obstinate. We can assume that the Lord had to put the thought structure into the heart of Sihon relating to Israel's request to pass through his land. In addition He placed an impartation of hardness into the spirit of Sihon, consisting of a negative emotion to Israel's going through the land. Therefore, Sihon had a hard spirit flowing into His heart toward Israel that came from his spirit. This spirit interacted with the thought structure that the Lord had put into Sihon's heart, resulting in an obstinate refusal to allow Israel to pass through the land.

We can understand that, for God to accomplish His purpose in a situation with an individual, there usually will need to be a change in both heart and spirit. There may be some circumstances in which a change in only one will suffice. We note that at the second birth the Lord gives a soul both a new heart and a new spirit. We can speculate that there is such closeness between the heart and spirit that, if one changed without the other, it would lead to blockage for any changes in the condition of a soul.

We can conceive various reasons why God might sometimes do something just to the heart or just to the spirit without a direct impartation to both. An example is 1 Kings 10:24: "And all the earth sought to Solomon, to hear his wisdom, which God had put in his heart." In this situation God had placed thought content and thought structure into the heart of Solomon at a given point in time. God had given this as a gift to Solomon. It was not associated at the time of giving with a change in spirit or an impartation of spirit, since that was not necessary. When Solomon later would be confronted with a situation that required the wisdom that was stored in his heart, then his spirit already contained the power and the desire to use this wisdom. That had to have been there when he asked for it. It is quite possible that God would impart something additional to Solomon's spirit in the future, when necessary, for a given work of His to occur. We see this linking of heart and spirit very closely in many Scriptures. In these a certain emotion in the heart is accompanied by a similar emotion in the spirit.

We read in 1 Chronicles 29:17: "I know also, my God, that thou triest the heart, and hast pleasure in uprightness." This Scripture shows us a key difference between the heart and the spirit. We note that God does not try the spirit. The human spirit, before the second birth, has already been tried and condemned. After the second birth the new spirit is of God and does not need judging. It is the heart that a man can change from being directed toward evil to being directed toward God. The thoughts and intents of the heart are what God judges, since the heart is a reflection of all that a person is. We will see that, as we proceed through Chapter 10. The old heart, before the second birth, becomes so hard through association with a dead spirit that at the second birth God gives an individual a new heart at the same time as a new spirit. When a person is given a new spirit, this spirit is going to live; and God does not judge it. It is true that the heart may pollute the spirit and that God may have to give impartations into this new spirit; but it is not in need of judgment, for it is of God. We have seen above how the heart influences the spirit to act. The heart teaches and trains the new spirit. The flesh may pollute the new heart and spirit so that we have to cleanse the new spirit. We have looked at this earlier and will study it further in Chapter 17. We have seen above how the heart gets power from the spirit. Without the spirit the heart is powerless to operate. Therefore, the new heart and the new spirit are closely linked; but it is only the heart that is tried by God. We see an example of this in 2 Chronicles 12:14 with Rehoboam, the King of Israel: "And he did evil, because he prepared not his heart to seek the LORD." We see that the soul and will can decide to prepare one's heart for a course of action. The will initiates a spiritual flow that is amplified by the spirit to power changes. God judges the lack of action by the king to change his heart. We see the opposite with Ezra in Ezra 7:10: "For Ezra had prepared his heart to seek the law of the LORD, and to do *it*, and to teach in Israel statutes and judgments."

God can directly change the structures of thought and the thought processes in a person in order to soften or harden a heart, either in general or for a specific purpose. Job 23:16 states this principle: "For God maketh my heart soft, and the Almighty troubleth me."

In Job 31:7 we read: "If my step hath turned out of the way, and mine heart walked after mine eyes, and if any blot hath cleaved to mine hands." This shows that the heart can be led by the flesh, as opposed to being led by the spirit. The leading of the soul by the flesh (eyes) results in a person's spiritual walk going in the wrong direction.

Again, we see a parallel between wisdom in the spirit and understanding in the heart. God asks Job "Who hath put wisdom in the inward parts? or who hath given understanding to the heart?" (Job 38:36). The thing to note is that there is always a difference between the heart and the spirit. The heart has a mind within it, and it has to meditate and ponder the flows out of the spirit. God imparts wisdom to the human spirit; and in order for an impure heart to understand the new flows from the human spirit, it must be prepared by God to understand it. Thus, the changes in the heart and spirit are parallel, in order for God's purpose to be accomplished.

The soul can configure the heart to have two separate agendas. "They speak vanity every one with his neighbour: *with* flattering lips *and* with a double heart do they speak" (Psalm 12.2).

In Psalm 34:18 we read: "The LORD *is* nigh unto them that are of a broken heart; and saveth such as be of a contrite spirit." Here we see again the parallel but different situations in the heart and spirit. A contrite spirit is parallel to a broken heart. The soul has to condition the spirit to be contrite by having the heart broken. The brokenness speaks of the changes in the heart that allow the spirit's attitude toward self promotion to change. Psalm 37:31 states: "The law of his God *is* in his heart; none of his steps shall slide." This illustrates how thought patterns and memory are organized in the mind of the heart." The Lord puts structures that are permanent into the mind of the heart to maintain an awareness of His law. This does not need to be echoed by a change in the spirit, since these structures must serve many spirits flowing out of a man's spirit throughout the years, in order to modify any spirit that is not of God.

In Psalm 77:6 we read: "I call to remembrance my song in the night: I commune with mine own heart: and my spirit made diligent search." Here again we see the link between spirit and heart. We see in this Scripture that the soul communes with its deepest part, the heart, to examine the structure of memories, thought patterns, emotions, and motivations within it. The soul wants to elicit a response from the heart, and this flow of spirit from the soul to the heart causes a flow into the spirit that will assist in the search for the solution to the current need in the soul. It is the spirit that provides the power to perform the search. In this case an intensive effort, communing with the heart, is met with an intensive response from the spirit (diligent).

Psalm 119:11 tells us: "Thy word have I hid in mine heart, that I might not sin against thee." Here we see that the soul can choose to place the Word of God into the memory places of the heart to build up a structure for further thought, emotion, and motivation. This is a structure that can serve any flow of spirit coming into the heart from outside or from the human spirit. Therefore, there is not a single change in the spirit that matches this change in the structure of the heart. However, with this structure in the heart the soul can mold the spirit into the characteristics that make it serve God.

David prays in Psalm 139:23: "Search me, O God, and know my heart: try me, and know my thoughts." We again see that God, in examining a person, does not examine the spirit, but rather the heart. We should also note that God's spirit is linked as one with the spirits of the elect who have been through the second birth (1 Corinthians 2:12; 6:17).

In Psalm 143:4 we read: "Therefore is my spirit overwhelmed within me; my heart within me is desolate." Here again is the parallel in the spirit and the heart. Note that, when these parallels are given, it refers to a specific event that is taking place. The change in the spirit powers the change in the heart, or vice versa, depending on whether the stimulus comes from God or from the outside world, respectively. Note that, if the spirit is overwhelmed, then the power is diminished. This would result in a noticeable loss of power flowing into the heart and a sense of deprivation or desolation. This Scripture gives an example of a change in the spirit leading to a change in the heart. We note, in context, that this change in spirit came from a series of actions by the enemy to cause the individual to be in spiritual darkness likened unto death. Earlier events that led to this might have been external and might have entered the soul and spirit through the flesh; however, now the spirit is in a state of being overwhelmed. We see the opposite situation in Proverbs 15:13: "A merry heart maketh a cheerful countenance: but by sorrow of the heart the spirit is broken." In this case the soul has allowed the heart to slide into a prolonged state of feeling sorrow. This prolonged state of sorrow continually causes spiritual flows into the spirit, which in turn cause the spirit to break because of the sorrow. The spirit goes on supporting life; but with respect to the case causing sorrow the spirit can no longer fight and, in this issue, is broken.

We see the interaction of the heart and the will directly in Proverbs 16:9: "A man's heart deviseth his way: but the LORD directeth his steps." The will is not able to overcome the heart's devising (inclination), unless there is a power that comes from the spirit to break it. Thus, an individual can will to do something; but he will not have the power to overcome the resistance in the heart, unless the spirit can bring about a change in the heart to allow the willed outcome to succeed. (This does not mean that the will is located in the heart, nor does it prove that it is not in the heart.) The heart and its condition determine the amount of spiritual power that is needed to bring about change or success in an endeavor that the soul would like to perform. Thus, the heart devises the way a man will walk; but the Lord can supply power to change the heart, or He can leave the heart as it is. By directing or withholding power to the human spirit, the Lord directs the steps that a soul will actually take.

Proverbs 17:22 shows a contrast between the condition in the heart of being merry and a condition in the spirit of brokenness: "A merry heart doeth good *like* a medicine: but a broken spirit drieth the bones." We note that both effects are seen in the flesh. Of course, the spirit impacts the flesh through flows of spirit through the heart. Such flows of spirit may induce changes in the heart.

In Proverbs 19:21 we read: "*There are* many devices in a man's heart; nevertheless the counsel of the LORD, that shall stand." The word *devices* can mean "thoughts, imaginations, or purpose." It means those "steel-like" structures of belief and attitude that a person builds up that become his core cause of behavior patterns. In Proverbs 20:5 we read: "Counsel in the heart of man *is like* deep water; but a man of understanding will draw it out." These Scriptures suggest that advice (counsel) given to man's heart (which has to come by impartation) will stand (in the sense to rise) when it is from the Lord. However, the advice imparted to the heart takes some effort to be drawn out. It is not immediately obvious. This is very important to understand. This difficulty shows one reason God asks us to meditate upon His Word. Meditation is very important for spiritual growth. It is not an idle afternoon of daydreaming that is described by meditation, but rather an agonizing search of the content of the heart and how it measures up to God's standards for content and process.

A key Scripture for understanding the role of the heart in the functioning of man is Proverbs 27:19: "As in water face *answereth* to face, so the heart of man to man." This tells us that the heart reflects the state of man's soul. It reveals who the man is. It reflects the emotions, thought patterns, behavioral patterns, imaginations, and the spiritual state of a soul. We need to reflect that all of the spiritual flows coming into the heart from the spirit and from the physical world are digested in the heart to set its attitudes, beliefs, and actions. Once the heart balances these, it releases spiritual flows both back to the spirit to mold it and back to the flesh and to other souls to produce desired actions. It is in the heart that all of the melding and sorting of spiritual flows take place. This, in turn, determines what the spirit will be like and what the person will be like. The soul has control of the heart to a degree, but God alone sees the depths of the heart. The soul can observe the outflows of the heart and meditate on them in the light of God's Word to see if the thoughts and intents of the heart should be changed. We need to remember that the content and environment in the heart is molding the inner man for eternity.

In Proverbs 28:26 we read: "He that trusteth in his own heart is a fool: but whoso walketh wisely, he shall be delivered." This is making the point that our hearts are desperately wicked. They are new after the second birth, but in our times they quickly become impure, as they pick up the ways of the flesh again. They again become deceitful and are not to be trusted. This is why the man of God must learn to follow the Spirit; he does this by perceiving the witness of his own human spirit. Thereby, the heart will be purified and the flesh daily put to the cross. If we do not walk by the Spirit of God, then, as we have seen above, we will walk by the flesh; and our heart will follow impure motives, thoughts, and emotions.

Solomon indicates that his soul decided to use his heart to seek and search for wisdom in Ecclesiastes 1:13: "And I gave my heart to seek and search out by wisdom concerning all *things* that are done under heaven: this sore travail hath God given to the sons of man to be exercised therewith." Wisdom, we will learn, comes from God into our human spirit as an impartation.

In Psalm 143:4 we read: "Therefore is my spirit overwhelmed within me; my heart within me is desolate." In the context external circumstances caused these conditions to arise in the spirit and in the heart, respectively. We see that conditions in the heart, in turn, moderate spiritual flows from the physical realm and from the soul to the spirit.

We see this clearly in Proverbs 15:13: “A merry heart maketh a cheerful countenance: but by sorrow of the heart the spirit is broken.” The Scripture is telling us that the condition of the heart causes a corresponding change in the spirit. Conversely, the human spirit, from its interactions with the spiritual world, impacts the heart through releasing outflows of spirit into the heart.

In Proverbs 15:13 we see that by sorrow of heart our spirit is broken. Thus, God can use repentance in the depth of our being, *i.e.*, a deep sorrow for sin, to break our spirit. Of course, deep sorrow for loss of an esteemed person or item that is not directed toward God could also break our spirit and not lead to repentance. The heart also has to be contrite toward God for Him to accept a broken spirit as a sacrifice (Psalm 51:17).

Solomon states in Ecclesiastes 1:17: “And I gave my heart to know wisdom, and to know madness and folly: I perceived that this also is vexation of spirit. For in much wisdom is much grief: and he that increaseth knowledge increaseth sorrow.” Solomon is telling us that, when we pursue in our heart both Godly (wisdom) and ungodly (madness and folly) knowledge, it will lead to vexation (frustration and anger) in our spirit. We need to wait on God to impart knowledge to us, as we grow enough in our inner man to assimilate the knowledge. Solomon is saying that fleshly pursuit of godly wisdom will result in disorder in the spirit and problems with spiritual growth.

In Ecclesiastes 8:11 we read: “Because sentence against an evil work is not executed speedily, therefore the heart of the sons of men is fully set in them to do evil.” God does not requite an evil work immediately. This delay allows an individual to build up a structure within the heart that is evil. If God dealt with an evil situation immediately, there would be less ability for an individual or nation to degenerate into evil paths. The behavior of people would be more forced, and men would not be as free to make choices. God created man with a freedom to choose a destiny, and this delay in both reward and punishment for attitudes and structures in the heart is in keeping with the bestowing of this freedom to choose.

We see crying for sorrow of heart and wailing from vexation of spirit (Isaiah 65:14).

In Jeremiah 9:14 we read: "But [they] have walked after the imagination of their own heart, and after Baalim, which their fathers taught them." The national heart of Israel was such that the people walked after their own imaginations (lack of reality and truth, thought structures and expectations that are untrue). As a result, God states that He would punish them. There is a false god after which they were walking, and this resulted in these people following a false spirit.

Jeremiah 17:9-10 tells us: "The heart *is* deceitful above all *things*, and desperately wicked: who can know it? I the LORD search the heart, *I* try the reins, even to give every man according to his ways, *and* according to the fruit of his doings." God is talking about the heart before the second birth. Only the Lord can know it. The reins are the mind. God tells us that He gives every man a reward based on what He plans for their service to Him and the carrying out by the individual of this planned work. This reward is eternal and is mitigated only by an individual's accepting the substitutionary righteousness of the Lord Jesus Christ. We note, from this Scripture, that an individual does not know the depths of his own heart.

In Ezekiel 11:19-21 we read: "And I will give them one heart, and I will put a new spirit within you; and I will take the stony heart out of their flesh, and will give them an heart of flesh: That they may walk in my statutes, and keep mine ordinances, and do them: and they shall be my people, and I will be their God. But *as for them* whose heart walketh after the heart of their detestable things and their abominations, I will recompense their way upon their own heads, saith the Lord GOD." This is a future promise to Israel made by God. It is similar to the promise made to those who submit to the Lordship of Jesus and who then go through the second birth.

Daniel 4:16 shows the ultimate power of God to change a human heart: "Let his heart be changed from man's, and let a beast's heart be given unto him; and let seven times pass over him." He changed

Nebuchadnezzar's heart to that of a beast, and He reversed this process after seven years.

The motivations and aspirations that a man has (his treasure) will dictate where his heart will be. In Luke 12:34 we read: "For where your treasure is, there will your heart be also." If a man in his heart chooses to place God's will above all other choices of action, then that man's spirit and heart will wait before God and will worship God. If a man chooses to seek self honor, then that man's heart will have structures built up (high places). Spirit flows from his human spirit through these constraining structures in the heart to the mind of the soul and builds up self honor.

In Romans 2:29 we read: "But he *is* a Jew, which is one inwardly; and circumcision *is that* of the heart, in the spirit, *and* not in the letter; whose praise *is* not of men, but of God." For a person to be in the family of God (a Jew inwardly), he must have been circumcised in the human spirit. The spirit is clearly located in the heart. The spirit has to be new. The circumcision was a physical type of the second birth.

Earlier we read in 1 Corinthians 7:37: "Nevertheless he that standeth stedfast in his heart, having no necessity, but hath power over his own will, and hath so decreed in his heart that he will keep his virgin, doeth well." Here we see that the heart and the will are interrelated. The Scripture speaks to the fact that not everyone has complete control over his will. The power over the will comes from the flow of spirit from the human spirit into the will. This power over the will also empowers the heart to stay steadfast. It serves to locate the will as probably within the heart. Thus, the spirit, if powerful in regard to an issue, can flow to the area of the will and allow the will be strong enough to make the heart steadfast.

Colossians 3:15 is a powerful key Scripture for being led by the Spirit of God: "And let the peace of God rule in your hearts, to the which also ye are called in one body; and be ye thankful." It tells us what we must do before making a decision about anything. The peace of God is a spirit with power, emotion, and purpose. The believer must learn to recognize this spirit with the spiritual senses of his human spirit. The believer in times of decision must wait on an action (flow of spirit) until this peace flows with it. If it does not, the action is not consistent with the purposes and will of God. A person cannot command God to release this peace. We have to wait patiently on it to fill our hearts with respect to any contemplated action before moving forward. This is the picture of waiting on the Lord with our human spirit. The Apostle John deals with this same concept in 1 John 3:20-21: "For if our heart condemn us, God is greater than our heart, and knoweth all things. Beloved, if our heart condemn us not, *then* have we confidence toward God." This Scripture uses the word *condemn* to indicate a lack of peace. If our heart has peace and does not condemn us about an issue, then we can move forward in confidence before God, knowing this to be His will for us on the particular issue about which we are praying.

In 1 Peter 3:4 we read: "But *let it be* the hidden man of the heart, in that which is not corruptible, *even the ornament* of a meek and quiet spirit, which is in the sight of God of great price." We have studied this text before. It serves to locate the spirit as the "hidden man" that is located within the heart.

SUMMARY OF THE SECTION ON THE HEART

In summary, then, we can look at what we have learned about the spirit of man and its interactions with the heart of man. We note that the spirit is located in the heart and that it is the hidden man. We learn that the heart is a true reflection to the Lord of who a person is. This also must involve an assessment of the human spirit, or inner man, as part of the assessment of the heart. The Lord will not condemn the human spirit of a person to whom He has given a new spirit. He may ask a person to cleanse his human spirit. We have seen how issues flow between the heart and the spirit. We have learned that the spirit is what gives life power to put into action the attitudes and beliefs of the heart. We have seen that the heart consists of a construction of attitudes, beliefs, memories, and thought patterns that must be shaped and molded by the Word of God in order for us to purify our heart. As spirit flows into the heart from the flesh and from the physical world, it shapes the heart. As spirit flows into the heart from the human spirit of man, it also shapes the heart. These spirits coming into the heart are able to change the heart, if they have enough power to overcome any resistance to change in particular areas. Conversely, these spiritual flows through the heart between the human spirit, the flesh, and the physical creation are changed by the structure of the heart. For example, a flow of love from the spirit of man initiated by the witness of the Holy Spirit may be damped down, and the resulting flow out of the heart toward another individual may be contaminated and mixed with a lot of other emotions and motives. The heart transmits spiritual flows based on its structure. The soul can examine the structure of the heart to some extent, but some of the heart is hidden from its owner. It is only by the help of God that an individual can have his heart tried for wicked ways (Psalm 139:24), and it is then only by yielding to God that an individual can change and purify his heart. Hearts are molded by internal and external spiritual flows. Only those from God are strong enough and directed accurately enough to tear down those strongholds and vain imaginations that have become entrenched in a diseased heart. We see that the heart itself is not a source of spiritual power; but it contains spiritual power and constrains spiritual power to flow in certain ways, depending on those strongholds and vain imaginations. This constraint of spiritual power also molds the spirit and affects the impact of external spirits on the spirit of man. The latter can be seen, if one has a heart that has trained the spirit to have power over fear. Then, when the enemy tries to force an individual to act out of a spirit of fear, the spirit can withstand this pressure and will eventually cause the devil to flee from this line of attack.

We note, from Scripture, that God looks at our heart in several dimensions. These include:

a) The degree of hardness or softness toward change as His light shines on it
b) Whether it is righteous, based on the acceptance of Jesus Christ as Lord and Savior
c) Whether it is pure or double minded in its functioning

We have seen that an evil spirit can place evil structures within the heart of man, just as God can place righteous structures within the heart of man. We must learn to recognize both. Of course, the structures of evil must be torn down, and the righteous structures must be maintained and built up. This is an ongoing cleansing process for all of us who have been through the second birth.

We see that the Lord will make changes to the structure of the heart without concurrent changes to the human spirit, when He is expecting a variety of spirits over time to be impacted by the structural changes He makes. The greatest change is the giving of a new heart at the second birth.

We have seen how an individual can learn how to wait on God by learning to recognize the spiritual force of God's peace.

We have seen in part; and we will learn more about the way God and the evil spirits fight for the heart of man, since the heart of man is an image of the man (Proverbs 27:19). The individual, if not aware of the war, has already lost it to the tyrannical control of the thought, attitude, and belief structures that the devil can build in his heart. We will learn that God gives an individual a lot of time to recognize and to repent of any backsliding into more and more evil ways. This is akin to the fall described in Romans 1:18ff. God is patient and tries to give the individual chances to reverse this slide; but at a certain point, known only to Him, He gives up striving with the soul of a particular individual. He leaves that heart in the evil state into which it has fallen, and that spirit is forever lost from being with God in eternity. We will look at more Scripture to support the contentions of this paragraph in the next chapter.

10
WORKINGS OF THE HUMAN SPIRITUAL HEART

When we study God's written Word, we should have an attitude of learning what He is telling us about Himself, about us, and about the creation; about how He wants us to relate to Him; and about how He wishes us to function in the creation. With this in mind we shall study the spiritual human heart. The key verse for the spiritual heart is found in Proverbs 27:19: "As in water face *answereth* to face, so the heart of man to man." God sees us as our heart is. Therefore, the condition, content, and state in which we maintain our heart are critically important in our relationship with God.

THE RELATIONSHIP OF THE HEART AND THE SOUL

The heart of the spiritual man is clearly not the soul, although it is a part of the soul. We read about Rehoboam in 2 Chronicles 12:14: "And he did evil, because he prepared not his heart to seek the LORD." The Scripture indicates that the soul can control the state of the heart and that God expects the soul to keep the heart in a condition of seeking Him. Anything short of this is evil. This is further shown in 2 Chronicles 25:2 where we read about Amaziah: "And he did *that which was* right in the sight of the LORD, but not with a perfect heart." We see from this example that the soul can overrule the intents of the heart. This Scripture reinforces the concept that the soul is responsible for the condition of its heart. This situation in which a soul acts in a manner to contradict the flow of spirit from his heart ("did right… but not with a perfect heart") is almost always the *modus operandi* of fallen mankind. It may deceive a person who is not spiritually perceptive, but it will not deceive God.

In Job 27:6 we read: "My righteousness I hold fast, and will not let it go: my heart shall not reproach *me* so long as I live." Here Job is stating that the condition of his heart may reproach his soul, if the condition is not right before God. Job has control over the condition of his heart, and he is determined not to let the condition of his heart be a reproach to his soul. Therefore, we see clearly that the spiritual heart is a part of the soul and that the condition of it is under the control of the soul. In Jeremiah 17:9-10 we read: "The heart *is* deceitful above all *things*, and desperately wicked: who can know it? I the LORD search the heart, *I* try the reins, even to give every man according to his ways, *and* according to the fruit of his doings." Here the Lord is talking about men before the second birth; but the same applies to people who have gone through the second birth, unless they have purified their heart to meet the standard by which God judges purity. Most people have not purified their heart. In Proverbs 28:26 we read: "He that trusteth in his own heart is a fool: but whoso walketh wisely, he shall be delivered." God is telling us here that He alone knows the depths of our hearts. He then tells us not to trust in our own heart but to walk wisely. Therefore we must be willing to examine everything that our heart would have us do and test it to walk wisely. We shall see how to do this later in this chapter. Finally, God instructs our soul to keep our heart with all diligence. In Proverbs 4:20-23 we read: "My son, attend to my words; incline thine ear unto my sayings. Let them not depart from thine eyes; keep them in the midst of thine heart. For they *are* life unto those that find them, and health to all their flesh. Keep thy heart with all diligence; for out of it *are* the issues of life." In using the term *diligence*, Solomon emphasizes remaining alert at all times and working hard to do it. It is a task always before us. We will see that our heart shapes our eternal spirit; thus, it is critical to keep the heart in the correct condition to shape our eternal future. Let us go on to try to understand more about what the heart is by looking at its structure, functions, conditions existing in it, and relationships with other parts of spiritual man.

THE HEART

THE STRUCTURE OF THE HEART

In 1 Peter 3:4 we read: "But *let it be* the hidden man of the heart, in that which is not corruptible, *even the ornament* of a meek and quiet spirit, which is in the sight of God of great price." Therefore, we can see that the heart contains a hidden man, and this hidden man is our spirit. We shall see that the heart is like a husk around a seed in some ways.

The heart shapes the human spirit, and God uses the human spirit to communicate with us and to give wisdom to us.

The great complexity of the structure of our heart is addressed in part by the following points:

1. Our heart has a midst to it (Proverbs 4:20-23).
2. Our heart has an intelligent mind. Our heart supplies the words that we speak; therefore, it has an intelligent mind (Matthew 15:18-20). This is supported by Proverbs 16:9, where we learn that a man's heart devises his ways.
3. In God's sight the heart is who the person is (Proverbs 27:19). This speaks to the great complexity of the spiritual heart. We (the soul) do not know the depth of our own heart, except as God reveals it to us (Jeremiah 17:9-10).
4. Hearts contain an area called a table (Proverbs 3:3 and 7:3).
5. Hearts can contain idols (Ezekiel 14:3).
6. Heart contain imaginations (Proverbs 6:18).
7. Hearts contain high places (2 Corinthians 10:5).
8. Hearts have the Law of God written in them (Psalm 37:31; Romans 2:15).
9. Hearts can be as fat as grease (Psalm 119:70).
10. Things can be hidden in hearts (Job 10:13).
11. Hearts can meditate (Psalm 49:3).
12. Hearts can contain evil spirits in those who hate [at least seven (Proverbs 26:25)].
13. Mercy and truth can be written on the table of the heart (Proverbs 3:3).
14. An epistle can be written in the heart (2 Corinthians 3:2).
15. Hearts can contain the Holy Spirit (Romans 5:5; 1 Corinthians 6:19) and the Lord Jesus (Ephesians 3:17).
16. Hearts can be large (1 Kings 4:29) and deep (Psalm 64:6).

The Scriptures tell us that there are many devices in a man's heart (Proverbs 19:21). Devices are like compartments for different issues, plans, schemes, desires, and emotions.

In Hebrews 10:22 we find that the heart contains the conscience. The wording suggests that it is on the outer or the inner surface of the heart. We see that to God our heart is who we are. The structure of the human spiritual heart is very complex, containing many devices, imaginations, high places, and even hidden things. Various spirits can be resident, depending on our spiritual well being; even the Lord Jesus can dwell there by faith. The conscience is associated with it. The major issue to realize for those who have been through the second birth is that God judges our heart and expects purity. We (soul) are responsible for the condition of our heart, and we can change the condition of it with God's help. God expects our heart to be wholly toward Him and to be pure.

THE FUNCTIONS OF THE HEART

To contain wisdom

In Job 38:36 we read: "Who hath put wisdom in the inward parts? or who hath given understanding to the heart?" Here we see that God puts wisdom into the inner parts (spirit) and that He then has the spirit interpret this wisdom to the heart so that the heart understands His desires. Therefore, to hear from God and understand His desires for us, we must look into what is happening to the heart and not what the thoughts of the mind are. We must learn how to do this if we are to be led by the Spirit of God. In Hebrews 4:12 we read: "For the word (*logos*) of God *is* quick, and powerful, and sharper than any twoedged sword, piercing even to the dividing asunder of soul and spirit, and of the joints and marrow, and *is* a discerner (judge) of the thoughts and intents of the heart." This tells us that our soul uses the written Word of God to discern what the thoughts and intents of our heart are. Thereby, the soul can tell from how the heart is reacting to the written word what the state of the heart is in regard to a particular issue. We must read the Word, watching our heart and ignoring our thoughts, or at least placing them in a secondary position.

The thoughts of the mind of the soul are like surface waves upon which many external circumstances play. It is the mind of the heart that determines our words and actions. This is like the deep that is not readily changed by the surface winds but can be changed by the right forces acting on it. We read more in Psalm 4:4: "Stand in awe, and sin not: commune with your own heart upon your bed, and be still. Selah." This tells us that we must commune with our own heart. We must observe the state of it and judge its thoughts and intents. This is frequently done best when the flesh is less active, such as at night when resting. At that time the eyes are closed, and the hearing is lessened. It is easier to focus attention internally. Note that this is not meditation, but observation and listening. It is observing how we feel inwardly about issues as they are lit up by the written Word. Needless to say, one's ability to do this is as wide as one's knowledge of the Word. This is amplified in Psalm 119:11: "Thy word have I hid in mine heart, that I might not sin against thee." This reinforces to us that we must have the *logos* hidden in our hearts as fully as possible in order not to sin, or at least to minimize our sin. If we have it to a lesser extent, we are going to fall into sin a lot more readily. In Proverbs 4:20-23 we read: "My son, attend to my words; incline thine ear unto my sayings. Let them not depart from thine eyes; keep them in the midst of thine heart. For they *are* life unto those that find them, and health to all their flesh. Keep thy heart with all diligence; for out of it *are* the issues of life." This summarizes that God wants us to keep His words in the midst of our heart and before our eyes constantly. This, incidentally, shows us that the heart has a structure; for there is a midst of it. We also see that our soul is required to keep diligently our heart in the correct condition. God is telling us that our heart puts out from it all of the issues of life.

To put forth the issues of life and words from the mouth

We see that our heart is that part of us from where all of the issues of life come. We know that the spirit is in the heart and that the spirit is that which gives life. It is the constant flows of spirit from our heart that are the issues of life. We see a metaphor: this spiritual flow from the spiritual heart into the surrounding spiritual universe is very similar to the physical heart's pumping blood to the individual cells, thereby carrying life to those cells. Our heart can impart issues of spiritual life or death to those beings that come under the influence of our spiritual heart. In Proverbs 16:1 we read: "The preparations of the heart in man, and the answer of the tongue, *is* from the LORD." This tells us what other

Scripture supports, that the soul must prepare diligently the condition of the heart. God has ordained that out of the heart will flow our words. Those words in their abundance will reflect the condition of our heart. Therefore, we are wise to observe our own words as a clue to the condition of our heart.

We read in Matthew 12:34-37: "O generation of vipers, how can ye, being evil, speak good things? for out of the abundance of the heart the mouth speaketh. A good man out of the good treasure of the heart bringeth forth good things: and an evil man out of the evil treasure bringeth forth evil things. But I say unto you, That every idle word that men shall speak, they shall give account thereof in the day of judgment. For by thy words thou shalt be justified, and by thy words thou shalt be condemned." Therefore, we see that our words are framed by the content of our heart. If we will ponder our words before speaking, we will be wise if we change our hearts based on what we find ourselves about to speak. Changing our heart is a process that takes time and spiritual effort. This is not deceit, for there is a change in the heart. To see what we are about to utter and to change our utterance but not our heart result in deceit in our heart. If we find ourselves changing our words to cloak our intent, then we know that there is deceit in our heart with which we must deal. To be sure, the motivation may seem good (Satan is an angel of light), but the use of deceit cannot ultimately bring forth good fruit. This issue of deceit is different from choosing our words carefully to reflect love, as in "speaking the truth in love" (Ephesians 4:15). However, if we speak loving thoughts when love is not in our heart, then we are practicing deceit. To be free of deceit, any communication must have the content and the emotion match. A person may express hatred if that is in his heart, and the words may be appropriate. Unless the issue is hatred of sin, then this is not a good thing to have in the heart; but the speaker is not also guilty of deceit.

In Matthew 15:18-20 we read: "But those things which proceed out of the mouth come forth from the heart; and they defile the man. For out of the heart proceed evil thoughts, murders, adulteries, fornications, thefts, false witness, blasphemies: These are *the things* which defile a man: but to eat with unwashen hands defileth not a man." Thus, it is the things that come out of the mouth that defile the man. It is a spiritual law that the mouth speaks out of the heart. It is immutable. The Lord was speaking in this passage of the old heart before the Lord gives a believer a new heart. We discussed deceit in which someone deliberately cloaks his inner thoughts and speaks, as it were, falsely. We saw this with Azamiah in the discussion above. When we try to deceive, God is not mocked; for the words coming out of the mouth are words of deceit; thus, the words are still from the abundance of the heart. In this situation the abundance of the heart is to deceive, and the words will be judged. It is not just the words themselves but the spirit that is associated with them. In Proverbs 16:2 we read: "All the ways of a man *are* clean in his own eyes; but the LORD weigheth the spirits." Therefore, there is not just an isolated "physical" word devoid of spirit, but all words are spirit and are issues of life. This is why the preparation of the heart is so important. God tells us in Matthew 15:8: "This people draweth nigh unto me with their mouth, and honoureth me with *their* lips; but their heart is far from me." Here the Lord was talking about people who had not been through the second birth. Here we see that the Lord sees within the heart the intent to deceive that is causing the mouth to utter deceitful words. The people in those times would not have realized that their religious leaders' hearts were in this condition. God sees, even when we do not.

To devise the way of a person

One of the chief functions of the heart is to plan what a man will attempt to do. This is the source of the soul's future plans. In Proverbs 16:9 we read: "A man's heart deviseth his way: but the LORD directeth his steps." This Scripture tells us that it is the heart of the man that devises what the soul will do. God looks at the purposing of the heart and directs the steps of a man to achieve what his heart devises. The Lord will arrange the circumstances in a person's life to fulfill His will for that individual. In Proverbs 20:9 we read: "Who can say, I have made my heart clean, I am pure from my sin?" This tells us that even if a man devises to be clean before the Lord, he cannot do it. The best that a man can do is to ask the Lord to cleanse his heart. In Proverbs 23:19 we read: "Hear thou, my son, and be wise, and guide thine heart in the way." God is telling us that our soul can guide the heart in the plans that it makes. The heart does the planning, but the soul can direct the nature of those plans. A soul has to learn as much as it can about the condition of its heart. The Lord tells us that the heart is desperately wicked and no one can know all of the thoughts and intents of it except God. However, God can teach us and lead us in purifying our heart. He expects us to purify our heart, as we saw above. Not to do it is sin. Even when we receive a new heart, that heart becomes polluted before it has a chance to be otherwise in our present age. Therefore, these Scriptures speak to those who have been through the second birth as much as those who have not.

To show God who a person is

We read in Proverbs 27:19: "As in water face *answereth* to face, so the heart of man to man." Here we see that there is an analogy to describe the function of the spiritual heart. The face reflected in water is an image of the face. The face sees itself and how it appears. In the same way the heart and its content are an image of who we (the soul) are. If we want to know ourselves, we must know our heart. To do this, we need to ask the Lord to show us and we must know His Word (Hebrews 4:12). As He does this, we must be quick to repent and to ask Him to cleanse areas that we have identified as being in need of cleansing.

In Proverbs 28:26 we read: "He that trusteth in his own heart is a fool: but whoso walketh wisely, he shall be delivered." This is parallel to the Scripture that tells us that only God knows (all of) the thoughts and intents of the heart (Jeremiah 17:9-10). To walk wisely is to walk after the spirit, which is within the heart. However, it is separate from the heart; and we must learn to distinguish between the leading of the spirit and the thoughts and intents of the heart. Re-read Hebrews 4:12 in order to understand this better. The heart is a part of the soul, but it is the human spirit that bears witness to the Holy Spirit. The heart has been greatly contaminated by the flesh. Even the spirit is polluted by the flesh. We see how God expects us to work with Him to purify our heart in Hebrews 4:12. It consists of letting the Word of God discern the thoughts and intents of the heart. You will wonder how this occurs until you practice it daily, and you will find that the written Word of God, as taught by the Holy Spirit, witnesses to our spirit. As it does this, new wisdom is released into our heart; and we can ask God to apply this new wisdom to cleaning out things that need to go. As you do this, you will find that the motivations are exposed behind your current choices; and you must always discard any choice that is even partly motivated by self. There will be times when God will want you to do a certain thing, but you must not attempt it until the motivation is right. God is as particular, or more so, about the way a thing is done, than the doing of it. We saw this in the example of Amaziah, who did right but with an impure heart.

In Jeremiah 7:24 we read what God has to say about those who do not listen to Him: "But they hearkened not, nor inclined their ear, but walked in the counsels *and* in the imagination of their evil heart, and went backward, and not forward." We have learned that the human spirit is in the heart, but a person may be quite deaf to the spirit and walk in the counsels and imaginations of his evil heart (the heart is hardened and will not hear the spirit, even if it is giving new revelation). This passage of Scripture applies to the Israelites' leaving Egypt, but it can apply equally to a new heart that has been polluted in a person who has the second birth but who has not learned how to be led by the Spirit. In Jeremiah 17:9-10 we read: "The heart *is* deceitful above all *things*, and desperately wicked: who can know it? I the LORD search the heart, *I* try the reins, even to give every man according to his ways, *and* according to the fruit of his doings." This is very serious for one who is not predisposed to do the work of God. God is saying that we do not even know the depths of our own heart. He alone does. As He searches the heart and the reins (kidneys, which were thought to be the seat of the emotions), He gives to every man a reward based on the individual's ways and the results of those ways. There can come a point after the heart has been purified that the Lord can lead one by the desires of his heart. We see this in Psalm 37:4, and the preconditions for this to occur are listed in Isaiah 58:1-14.

CONDITIONS THAT CAN EXIST IN THE SPIRITUAL HEART

There are 158 conditions of the heart listed below. The Scriptures speak of these in the relationship of the spiritual heart to God. As you review this list, you will note various groupings. A study of this list with prayerful meditation will help to understand the various conditions that can be found in hearts by God as He looks at them. References to Scriptures are included so that you can study them readily in context in order to understand more completely the issues surrounding each point.

i) Degree of wisdom

1. Hearts can be wise (Exodus 35:10).
2. Hearts can be understanding to judge (1 Kings 3:9).
3. Hearts can be wise and understanding (1 Kings 3:12).
4. Hearts can be applied to wisdom (Psalm 90:12).
5. Wisdom can enter the heart (Proverbs 2:10).
6. Hearts can be applied to understanding (Proverbs 2:2).
7. Hearts can be understanding (Proverbs 8:5).
8. People can be wise of heart (Proverbs 11:29).
9. One can reason in his heart (Mark 2:6).
10. A man can deceive his own heart (James 1:26).
11. People can muse in their hearts (Luke 3:15) and reason in their hearts (Luke 5:22).

ii) Attitude toward God

12. Hearts can be willing toward God (Exodus 35:22).
13. Hearts can work in part or in whole (seeking God with a whole heart [Deuteronomy 4:29]).
14. Hearts can fear God (Deuteronomy 5:29).
15. Hearts can be lifted up against God (Deuteronomy 8:14) and against other people (Deuteronomy 17:20).
16. Hearts can be upright before God (Deuteronomy 9:5).
17. Hearts can be circumcised before God (Deuteronomy 10:16).
18. Hearts can turn away from God (Deuteronomy 29:18; 1 Kings 11:4).
19. Hearts can be inclined toward God (Joshua 24:23).
20. Hearts can rejoice in the Lord (1 Samuel 2:1).
21. Hearts can be returned to the Lord. This can be in part or with all the heart (1 Samuel 7:3).
22. Hearts can serve the Lord wholly or in part (1 Samuel 12:24).
23. Hearts can be after God's own heart (1 Samuel 13:14).

24. Hearts can be perfect with the Lord (1 Kings 8:61) and not perfect (1 Kings 15:3).
25. People can walk before the Lord in integrity of heart (1 Kings 9:4).
26. Hearts can be tender toward God (2 Kings 22:19); this can lead to humility (2 Chronicles 34:27).
27. People can seek the Lord with all their heart (2 Chronicles 15:12).
28. A heart can be found faithful toward God (Nehemiah 9:8).
29. Hearts can carry someone away from God (Job 15:12).
30. Hearts can trust in the Lord (Psalm 28:7).
31. We can have the law of the Lord in our hearts (Psalm 37:31).
32. Hearts can be fixed on God (Psalm 57:7).
33. Hearts can be poured out before God (Psalm 62:8).
34. Hearts can live, if they seek God (Psalm 69:32).
35. God can create a clean heart (Psalm 51:10). Man cannot make his own heart clean (Psalm 73:13; Proverbs 20:9).
36. Hearts can tempt God (Psalm 78:18).
37. Hearts can be not right with God (Psalm 78:37).
38. Hearts can cry out for God (as can the flesh [Psalm 84:2]).
39. Hearts can praise God wholly (Psalm 86:12).
40. Hearts can be forward (and will be made to depart from God [Psalm 101:4]).
41. Hearts can stand in awe of God's Word (Psalm 119:161).
42. A foolish man's heart can fret against the Lord (Proverbs 19:3).
43. Hearts can do the will of God (Ephesians 6:6).
44. We can sanctify the Lord God in our hearts (1 Peter 3:15).

iii) Emotions within the heart

45. Hearts can hate (Leviticus 19:17).
46. Hearts can be grieved (Deuteronomy 15:10).
47. Hearts can be hot (Deuteronomy 19:6).
48. Hearts can be glad (Deuteronomy 28:47).
49. Hearts can be merry (Judges 16:25)—this seems often to refer to partying with alcohol.
50. People can be cut to the heart (Acts 5:33).

iv) Malleability of the heart

51. Hearts can be set (Deuteronomy 32:46; Psalm 62:10).
52. Hearts can melt (Joshua 2:11).
53. Hearts can fail (1 Samuel 17:32).
54. Hearts can be enticed (Job 31:27).
55. Hearts can be bowed (2 Samuel 19:14).
56. Hearts can be as firm as stone (Job 41:24).
57. Hearts can be like wax (Psalm 22:14).
58. Hearts can be broken (Psalm 34:16).
59. Hearts can be overwhelmed (Psalm 61:2).

v) Hearts can contain these items:

60. God's Word can be in the heart (Deuteronomy 30:14).
61. Mercy and truth can be written upon the table of the heart (Proverbs 3:3).
62. In a heart in one who hates there are seven abominations (evil spirits [Proverbs 26:25]).
63. One can lay up a thing in his heart (Luke 1:66).
64. A heart will be where its treasure is (Matthew 6:21).
65. Out of the abundance of the heart are the words of the mouth (Matthew 12:34).
66. Our heart can have idols set up in it (Ezekiel 14:3).

vi) Actions the heart can perform

67. Hearts can be wicked (Deuteronomy 15:9).
68. Hearts can be inclined toward a person or persons (Judges 5:9).
69. People can speak in their heart (1 Samuel 1:13).
70. Hearts can tremble (1 Samuel 4:13).
71. Words can be laid up in the heart (Job 22:22; 1 Samuel 21:12).
72. Hearts can stir up a person (Exodus 35:21).
73. Hearts can be smitten (1 Samuel 24:5).
74. Hearts can be offended (1 Samuel 25:31).
75. Hearts can be as the heart of a lion (2 Samuel 17:10).

76. A nation can be described as having a heart in a certain direction (1 Kings 12:27).
77. Hearts can be very troubled (2 Kings 6:11).
78. A heart can be lifted up after an accomplishment (2 Kings 14:10).
79. People can swear an oath with all their heart (2 Chronicles 15:15).
80. Hearts can be proud (2 Chronicles 32:26).
81. Words can be uttered out of the heart (Job 8:10).
82. Things can be hidden in the heart (Job 10:13).
83. Hearts can reproach the soul (Job 27:6).
84. Hearts can sing (Job 29:13).
85. People can be hypocrites in their heart (Job 36:13).
86. Hearts can be upright (Psalm 7:10; 94:15).
87. Hearts can be double (Psalm 12:2).
88. Hearts can have largeness (1 Kings 4:29).
89. Hearts can pant (Psalm 39:3).
90. Hearts can gather iniquity to themselves (Psalm 44:18).
91. Hearts can work wickedness (Psalm 58:2).
92. Hearts can err (Psalm 95:10).
93. Hearts can be forward (and will be made to depart from God [Psalm 101:4]).
94. Hearts of evil men are used to devise wicked things (Psalm 140:2).
95. Hearts can devise wicked imaginations (Proverbs 6:18).
96. Hearts can decline to the ways of another (Proverbs 7:25).
97. Hearts can utter perverse things (Proverbs 23:33).
98. Hearts can study destruction (Proverbs 24:2).
99. A heart can meditate terror (Isaiah 33:18).
100. Hearts can be set to do mischief (Daniel 11:27).
101. A person can commit adultery in his heart (Matthew 5:28).
102. Hearts can forgive (or not forgive [Matthew 18:35]).
103. We can doubt or not doubt in our heart (Mark 11:23).
104. People can purpose in their hearts (2 Corinthians 9:7).
105. One can make melody in his heart (Ephesians 5:19).
106. Our heart can condemn us (1 John 3:20).

vii) States of the heart

107. Hearts can have sorrow (Psalm 13:2).
108. Hearts have desires (Psalm 21:2; 37:4)
109. Hearts can be pure (Psalm 24:4).
110. Hearts can have disquietness (Psalm 38:8).
111. Hearts can meditate (Psalm 49:3).
112. Hearts can be broken and contrite (Psalm 51:17).
113. Hearts can be very pained (Psalm 55:4).
114. Hearts can have war within them (Psalm 55:21).
115. A heart can be exercised with covetous practices (2 Peter 2:14).
116. Hearts can be wounded within (Psalm 109:22).
117. Hearts can be as fat as grease (Psalm 119:70).
118. Hearts can be haughty (Psalm 131:1).
119. Hearts can be desolate and spirits overwhelmed (Psalm 143:4).
120. Hearts can despise reproof (Proverbs 5:12).
121. Hearts can be froward (Proverbs 6:14).
122. Hearts can lust (Proverbs 6:25).
123. Hearts can be subtle (Proverbs 7:10).
124. Hearts can be perverse (Proverbs 12:8).
125. Hearts can be deceitful (Proverbs 12:20).
126. A heart can be heavy (Proverbs 12:25).
127. A heart can be sickened by hope deferred (Proverbs 13:12).
128. A heart can be backslidden (Proverbs 14:14).
129. A heart can be sound (Proverbs 14:30).
130. A heart can be destroyed when a man is haughty (Proverbs 18:12).
131. Foolishness is bound in the heart of a child (Proverbs 22:15).
132. Hearts can be vexed (Ecclesiastes 2:22).
133. The hearts of a people can be made fat (Isaiah 6:10).
134. Hearts can be fearful (Isaiah 35:4).
135. Hearts can be pained and make a noise within (Jeremiah 4:19).
136. Hearts can be rebellious (Jeremiah 5:23).
137. Hearts can be faint within (Jeremiah 8:18).

138. Hearts can be uncircumcised (Ezekiel 44:7).
139. Hearts can be divided (Hosea 10:2).
140. Hearts can be exalted (Hosea 13:6).
141. Hearts can be torn (Joel 2:13).
142. Hearts can be pure (Matthew 5:8).
143. One can be meek and lowly in heart (Matthew 11:29).
144. Hearts can be overcharged with surfeiting and drunkenness (Luke 21:34).
145. People can be slow of heart (Luke 24:25).
146. Hearts can burn within (Luke 24:32).
147. Sorrow can fill our heart (John 16:6).
148. Hearts can be pricked (Acts 2:37).
149. Hearts can be impenitent (Romans 2:5).
150. A heart can have great heaviness and continual sorrow (Romans 9:2).
151. Hearts can have anguish (2 Corinthians 2:4).
152. Hearts can be blind (Ephesians 4:18).
153. Hearts can have singleness of purpose (Ephesians 6:5).
154. Hearts can be comforted (Ephesians 6:22).
155. Hearts can be evil from unbelief (Hebrews 3:12).
156. Hearts can be established (James 5:8).
157. Hearts can have a veil upon them (2 Corinthians 3:1).

viii) Miscellaneous

158. A person can tell another all his heart (Judges 16:17); and, if one is perceptive, this can be detected by the other (Sampson and Delilah [Judges 16:18]).

ix) Dimensions of the heart—largeness (1 Kings 4:29) and deepness (Psalm 64:6).

x) Hearts can contain the Holy Spirit (Romans 5:5; 1 Corinthians 6:19) and the Lord Jesus (Ephesians 3:17).

THE RELATIONSHIPS OF THE HEART TO OTHER AREAS OF SPIRITUAL MAN AND TO OTHER SPIRITS

SOUL

We have looked at some of the key issues in this interrelationship with the soul earlier in this chapter. The following points expand on our earlier understanding.

Ecclesiastes 5:2 states: "Be not rash with thy mouth, and let not thine heart be hasty to utter *any* thing before God: for God *is* in heaven, and thou upon earth: therefore let thy words be few." This Scripture commands the soul to control the heart, as it tries to utter words through the mouth. Words are spirit and, therefore, have power. We need to be guided by the spirit and not by the heart; therefore, we have to understand experientially and operate in the truth of Hebrews 4:12: "For the word of God *is* quick, and powerful, and sharper than any twoedged sword, piercing even to the dividing asunder of soul and spirit, and of the joints and marrow, and *is* a discerner of the thoughts and intents of the heart."

The soul is responsible for the condition of the heart before God. We learned at the beginning of this chapter that our heart defines who we are before God and, therefore, also defines who we are before men. We need to understand how our soul can change our heart.

What motivates the heart to change?

We can clearly see from the above passages of Scripture that God expects us not only to change our heart but to purify it and then to keep it with all diligence. We have also seen that we cannot change our own heart. Proverbs 20:9 tells us: "Who can say, I have made my heart clean, I am pure from my sin?" This is a rhetorical question. In Psalm 73:13 we read: "Verily I have cleansed my heart *in* vain, and washed my hands in innocency." The first question is answered by the assertion that one is free from sin. This is only achieved through faith in the atonement. Thus, only God could make the way available for a heart to be cleansed; then the individual has to grasp this by faith in order to have his heart cleansed. Psalm 51:10 tells us: "Create in me a clean heart, O God; and renew a right spirit within me." Here we see that only God can create a clean heart in a person. The Hebrew word for *create* here is the same word that is used in Genesis 1. In this setting we can understand it to mean that there is no way an individual can bring about cleanness of heart. Note that cleanness and purity are not the same thing. Cleanness is a state conferred by God as we accept His sacrifice for our sin. Purity is the result of following God's Spirit as we become sanctified. In order to purify our heart, we must see what motivates us to change our heart.

We read in Matthew 6:21: "For where your treasure is, there will your heart be also." This tells us that our heart is focused on achieving what we regard as treasure. We must replace mammon with the Lord Jesus, the pearl of great price. When we do that, our heart will be purified. We have to continually assess what we are truly treasuring (seeking after). When we really understand what we are seeking, then we will understand the condition of our heart. This understanding of what we seek after gradually matures as we seek after the Lord. We must put God first in all things and seek Him with all our mind, strength, and whole heart. When we learn to do this, we will become pure in heart.

How can we purify our heart?

We read in Acts 15:9: "And put no difference between us and them, purifying their hearts by faith." Therefore, as we are convicted by the Word, we begin to trust God and walk in faith before Him. As we do this, we will have our heart purified. This is God's criteria for purification. It is a heart that wholly trusts Him and is wholly obedient to Him. God refines our faith through trials and tribulations. We also recall that faith comes by hearing and hearing by the *rhema* of God. Therefore, we have to be able to learn how to hear reliably from God (*rhema*) and how to relate to Him as an individual in order to have our hearts purified.

Difference between soul and heart

In Matthew 12:23 we read: "And to love him with all the heart, and with all the understanding, and with all the soul, and with all the strength, and to love *his* neighbour as himself, is more than all whole burnt offerings and sacrifices." This indicates that the heart and the soul are not the same. Also, the heart and understanding are not the same. We need to keep this in mind as we study the interrelationship of all of these components of spiritual man.

An example is seen in 2 Corinthians 5:12: "For we commend not ourselves again unto you, but give you occasion to glory on our behalf, that ye may have somewhat to *answer* them which glory in appearance, and not in heart." This tells us that the soul can try to be glorified by others by the appearance of outward behavior and speech, but this is not a glory of the heart. The heart, not the soul, is the true reflection of the man. We must learn to be discerning, looking for evidence of the intent of the heart, not just hearing the words spoken and seeing how an individual appears, if we are to understand that person.

FLESH

In this section we will review some Scriptures that show physical events perceived by the flesh that impact the heart.

Genesis 18:5 shows that Jacob's heart failed on hearing news that Joseph was still alive. Joshua 2:11 shows the Israelites' hearts melted on receiving bad news.

In Psalm 107:12 we read: "Therefore he brought down their heart with labour; they fell down, and *there was* none to help." Here the Lord used hard labor to get the attention of the Israelites.

Proverbs 14:30 states: "A sound heart *is* the life of the flesh: but envy the rottenness of the bones." God's Word is health to all our flesh (Proverbs 4:22), but obviously this is mediated in part through developing a sound heart.

Proverbs 15:13 reads: "A merry heart maketh a cheerful countenance: but by sorrow of the heart the spirit is broken." Proverbs 15:30 adds: "The light of the eyes rejoiceth the heart: *and* a good report maketh the bones fat." These Scriptures show conditions of the heart that impact or are impacted by the flesh (and also in turn impact the spirit).

Proverbs 27:9 reads: "Ointment and perfume rejoice the heart: so *doth* the sweetness of a man's friend by hearty counsel." This shows that the senses of the flesh can cause emotion in the heart.

Romans 10:10 tells us: "For with the heart man believeth unto righteousness; and with the mouth confession is made unto salvation." This tells us that the heart must believe that the Lord Jesus is God's Son sent for salvation for a man to have righteousness imputed. It is not sufficient just to have a thought at the mind level that agrees when one hears or discusses the situation. It is the belief in the heart that causes the mouth to confess unto salvation. The mind of the soul is like waves on the surface of a deep body of water. Beliefs will come and go and barely affect the heart, if they are not ones that the heart apprehends. It is the mind of the soul, however, that, acting in conjunction with the will, brings change to the belief of the heart. We saw above that, where the treasure is, there will be the heart. We cannot serve both God and mammon. We can have only one treasure. Our words and actions will tell which our treasure is, and this will be that in which our heart has faith. It will be what our heart expresses as belief. We may say the right words from the mind about salvation and even deceive ourselves, but the heart is what must believe for salvation. Many people are trapped in this intellectual belief (just in the mind of the soul) that has never penetrated into belief in the heart. Heart belief will bring forth a desire to be led by the Spirit of God. It is not difficult to know when we are seeking to be led by the Spirit of God.

In Romans 16:18 we read: "For they that are such serve not our Lord Jesus Christ, but their own belly; and by good words and fair speeches deceive the hearts of the simple." This speaks of people who do not have a heart belief but portray an intellectual belief for whatever purposes they may have. The basic attitude is to deceive.

MIND

In Genesis 6:5 we read: "And GOD saw that the wickedness of man *was* great in the earth, and *that* every imagination of the thoughts of his heart *was* only evil continually." Here we see that the heart has its own thoughts.

1 Samuel 6:6 states: "Wherefore then do ye harden your hearts, as the Egyptians and Pharaoh hardened their hearts? when he had wrought wonderfully among them, did they not let the people go, and they departed? We see that our soul has a mind capable of discerning and altering the condition of the heart. The Lord would not otherwise hold us accountable for hardening our hearts. There are many similar Scriptures that show us that God expects us to understand and alter the condition of our heart.

Therefore, we see that spiritual man has two minds (actually there are more, as we will learn in Chapter 11) that interact together, the one in the heart and the one in the soul. It is out of the abundance of the mind of the heart that we speak our words. The beliefs in the heart are the ones that are important to God in terms of righteousness. Proverbs 23:7 tells us: "For as he thinketh in his heart, so *is* he: Eat and drink, saith he to thee; but his heart *is* not with thee." This emphasizes that what we think in our heart, as opposed to the mind of our soul, makes us who we are.

Proverbs 3:5-6 tells us: "Trust in the LORD with all thine heart; and lean not unto thine own understanding. In all thy ways acknowledge him, and he shall direct thy paths." This tells us that the heart can trust in all or in part. There is a complexity to the heart that allows it to trust partly or wholly. In addition, the Lord tells us to not lean on our own understanding. He is telling us to depend on revelation knowledge that He gives to us before we make a decision. He is telling us not to try to work out our solutions in our minds. He is saying to us that we should do this in all our ways. When we are doing this—depending on revelation knowledge being given into our spirit, discerning it with our heart and mind, and then acting on it—we shall be in a condition in which God is directing our paths. This is so reassuring. It is so good to learn that we can be a willing partner with God, as we learn to walk after His Spirit.

We can look at Psalm 77:6 and see: "I call to remembrance my song in the night: I commune with mine own heart: and my spirit made diligent search." Here the Scripture tells us that a good time to try to determine the thoughts of our own heart is in the night. We can also see that we must make a decision to commune with our heart. We do not know our heart without a conscious decision to interact (commune) with it. Our spirit is that part of us which communes with our heart. It is only the spirit that can see the depths of the heart. Therefore, to commune with and to understand our heart, we must use our spirit. Recall that our human spirit is in communication with and bears witness to the Holy Spirit. As our spirit searches our heart, enabling us to commune with it, we are getting information from the Holy Spirit about our heart's situation. Our spirit will speak to us informing us of truth. It is better to do this at night in order to shut out all the clamor of the flesh. This allows for more focus on the spirit.

The soul can tell what the condition of the heart motivating speech is. Look at Psalm 55:21: "*The words* of his mouth were smoother than butter, but war *was* in his heart: his words were softer than oil, yet *were* they drawn swords." David could certainly discern the deceit in this man's heart that was being expressed by the words of the mouth. The heart has many beliefs and attitudes in it continually until it is purified. Here we see two of them, war and deceit. We can also discern what is in our own heart as we look at what we say and what we feel. Are we angry inside and cloaking that with surface words? This is like the person of whom David spoke. Deceit is in the heart of anyone who imagines evil (in any small or large way). The Scripture tells us this in Proverbs 12:20: "Deceit *is* in the heart of them that imagine evil: but to the counselors of peace *is* joy." It also tells us that, when one is a counselor of peace, there is joy in the heart. Note that the deceit is toward God and the counseling of peace is toward God. If one imagines evil, then he will want to try to deceive God.

In a way, we can look at the mind of the heart as being like a gyroscope, propelling us on a course. This course can be changed by the soul as it observes the situation. The analogy is not complete but may be of help. The gyroscope is firmly set on a particular course, and it takes a force to change the direction. This has to be a spiritual force. God has to be the author; and we, the willing recipients. The heart is who we are before God. God judges us by the thoughts and intents of our heart. He holds us accountable for the condition of our heart.

One could ask why God uses these two minds in this interaction, and not just one. We need to recall that the spirit is contained in the heart. It is in the heart that God gives His revelation knowledge and implants directional desires to individuals. It is in the soul that the individual makes decisions as to what to allow his heart to be like. The heart itself is where spirit and flesh meet and mingle. It is in the heart that revelation knowledge is mixed with vanity and imaginations. In allowing man to be independent in his response to God, God has separated the mind into two parts with somewhat different functions. The heart mixes two types of knowledge, worldly and revelation. The mind of the soul decides what it will allow the mind of the heart to become. When man fell into sin, his fleshly mind in the soul was condemned to spiritual and physical death. The heart was also condemned to death with its mind. At the second birth, when God replaces the heart of stone with a heart of flesh, the new heart initially is in step with God's desires. However, we are told to renew the mind in our soul. When we do not do this in our soul, we allow all sorts of evil into our new heart and into our new spirit. If we allow it, our new heart can transmit revelation knowledge to our old mind; and then it can be renewed. As it is renewed, our soul is able to keep and guard the new heart from attacks from the lusts of the flesh and from evil spirits.

It is as though our soul after the second birth is placed in charge of nurturing and developing the new life that it has been given. It is up to the soul to make those highest level decisions and up to the heart to make us what we are. We must remember the Scripture in Proverbs 27:19, which tells us: "As in water face *answereth* to face, so the heart of man to man." The heart of man determines who we are before God and man. The soul controls what this will be. The soul requires spiritual power to make changes in the heart.

We should note here that the mind is never described in the Scriptures as generating an emotion. Emotions begin in the spirit as part of the tripartite structure that is spirit. The reasoning and remembering abilities of the mind are distinct from the emotions of the spirit. The mind may, however, remember and equate a particular emotion with a particular event.

The Scripture often refers to people speaking in their heart. Examples are Genesis 17:17, when Abraham was told he and Sarah would have a son, and Genesis 24:45, when the servant Abraham sent to find a wife for Isaac formulated his plan.

In Joshua 23:14 we read: "And, behold, this day I *am* going the way of all the earth: and ye know in all your hearts and in all your souls, that not one thing hath failed of all the good things which the LORD your God spake concerning you; all are come to pass unto you, *and* not one thing hath failed thereof." This Scripture tells us that both the mind of the soul and the mind of the heart have memory. In Psalm 19:14 we read: "Let the words of my mouth, and the meditation of my heart, be acceptable in thy sight, O LORD, my strength, and my redeemer." This indicates that the mind of the heart is capable of deep thought when pondering and deciding complex issues. In Psalm 64:6 we read: "They search out iniquities; they accomplish a diligent search: both the inward *thought* of every one *of them*, and the heart, *is* deep." This indicates that God sees the heart to have the inward thoughts; the mind of the soul, in contrast, would have outward thoughts. *Inward* means "in the midst, among, or inwards." The inward thoughts are guarded by the soul. We also note that the heart in its structure has great depth. In addition, the use of *diligent* implies that the mind of the heart is capable of intense and profound (deep) thought. We know, however, that the mind of the soul does not have complete understanding of the mind of the heart; for God tells us in Jeremiah 17:9: "The heart *is* deceitful above all *things*, and desperately wicked: who can know it?"

An area with which we shall deal at length in Chapter 11 is that of the imaginations. In Luke 1:51 we read: "He hath shewed strength with his arm; he hath scattered the proud in the imagination of their hearts." Note from this Scripture that our hearts have imaginations. Mary states that the proud have imaginations in their hearts. These imaginations are structures that are within the mind of the heart and which are frequently founded on false premises. It is these that Paul talks about in Ephesians 6 in the area of spiritual warfare. Any belief that is not anchored on revealed truth is an imagination. False visions and ruminations about one's future are also imaginations of a particular sub-category.

It is very important, if we are to be led by the Spirit of God, to understand how the mind of the soul perceives this leading. The Holy Spirit witnesses to our spirit in the heart. The heart accepts this information into its mind and mixes it with its current attitudes and beliefs. As we commune with our heart, we can determine what is going on and thereby know what God wants of us with respect to a particular decision. In John 14:27 we read: "Peace I leave with you, my peace I give unto you: not as the world giveth, give I unto you. Let not your heart be troubled, neither let it be afraid." We should read this in conjunction with Paul's admonition in Colossians 3:15: "And let the peace of God rule in your hearts, to the which also ye are called in one body; and be ye thankful." These two Scriptures reveal a fundamental spiritual law that God has ordained for being led by His Spirit. We can see the following:

a) There is a peace that God gives to the heart.
b) This peace is different to the false peace that comes from the world. Such a false peace may come after we make a wrong decision just because the evil spirits will then leave us alone.
c) One must learn how to differentiate these two types of peace.
d) The peace of God must rule in our heart by a choice of the will.
e) When the peace of God rules, we are being led by His Spirit.
f) We know that we are not in God's peace if trouble and fear are coming from our heart.

We must apply these rules to all of our decision making, if we are to be led by the Spirit of God.

OTHER SOULS

In Proverbs 22:11 we read: "He that loveth pureness of heart, *for* the grace of his lips the king *shall be* his friend." People can discern purity of heart, and they will instinctively trust it. It is not threatening, and it is not manipulative.

Ezekiel 13:22 tells us: "Because with lies ye have made the heart of the righteous sad, whom I have not made sad; and strengthened the hands of the wicked, that he should not return from his wicked way, by promising him life." Here we see the impact of the false prophets of Israel on the righteous but undiscerning heart. We must have God's wisdom to judge a situation, and we must not be led by the things that we hear with the ear.

EVIL SPIRITS

In Mark 4:15 we read: "And these are they by the way side, where the word is sown; but when they have heard, Satan cometh immediately, and taketh away the word that was sown in their hearts." Here we see quite clearly that Satan (and his demons) can see into the heart of a man and can remove content from it. We see in John 13:2: "And supper being ended, the devil having now put into the heart of Judas Iscariot, Simon's *son*, to betray him." Here we see that Satan and his minions can also place content into the heart of a man. These two processes are not rare, but they operate rather continuously throughout our lives. This is why we have to be so careful to determine what spirit leads us to think, act, or speak. God tells us to test the spirits always. This must be done on a continual basis.

In Acts 5:3 we read: "But Peter said, Ananias, why hath Satan filled thine heart to lie to the Holy Ghost, and to keep back *part* of the price of the land?" This again tells us that Satan can interfere within the heart and can fill it. It is important to note that the Holy Spirit would have already known Ananias' decision to lie, since He would have been presumably residing in Ananias' heart, since he was a believer.

It is of note that when Satan is banished to the pit for 1000 years, he is out of God's presence. At the same time the Holy Spirit is no longer given to men to indwell them. During this time evil spirits will not infiltrate the heart. There will be no overt following of Satan; most sin will be hidden in the heart. At the end of this time, when Satan and his demons are loosed for a short time, multitudes of men follow them. This shows that man's heart is evil. This paragraph is inserted just for interest and further meditation is needed to understand the issues.

WITH GOD

There are many Scriptures that address the interactions of God with the human spiritual heart. The remainder of this chapter takes those of special interest and discusses them. The order is based on their location in the Bible.

Things God does to the heart

1) God hardened Pharaoh's heart (Exodus—mentioned in many places).
2) God can send faintness of heart (Leviticus 26:36).
3) God can cause astonishment of heart (Deuteronomy 28:28).
4) God can give a heart to perceive (Deuteronomy 29:4) or not to perceive (Deuteronomy 29:4).
5) God can circumcise the heart (Deuteronomy 30:6).
6) God can give another heart ("And the Spirit of the LORD will come upon thee, and thou shalt prophesy with them, and shalt be turned into another man. And it was *so*, that when he had turned his back to go from Samuel, God gave him another heart" [1 Samuel 6:9]). This is instructive, because when one is given another heart, then he becomes another man. In this case it was not as complete as at the time of the second birth, but the people who saw Saul prophesy when the Spirit descended on him were amazed.
7) God can give a wise and understanding heart (1 Kings 3:12).
8) God can give largeness of heart (1 Kings 4:29) and can enlarge a heart (Psalm 119:32).
9) God can incline our hearts to walk in His ways (1 Kings 8:58).
10) God tries the heart (1 Chronicles 29:17).
11) God can give a group of people one heart for a particular purpose: "Also in Judah the hand of God was to give them one heart to do the commandment of the king and of the princes, by the word of the LORD" (2 Chronicles 30:12).
12) God can put a course of action into a person's heart. ("And my

God put into mine heart to gather together the nobles, and the rulers, and the people, that they might be reckoned by genealogy. And I found a register of the genealogy of them which came up at the first, and found written therein." [Nehemiah 7:5]). This was a complex revelation from the Spirit into Nehemiah's heart. It also was accompanied by a spirit to cause Nehemiah to act on the information.

13) God can take away the heart of the chief of the people of the earth (Job 12:24).
14) God can hide understanding from the heart of people (Job 17:4).
15) God can make a person's heart soft (Job 23:16).
16) God tries the hearts. Psalm 7:9 reads: "Oh let the wickedness of the wicked come to an end; but establish the just: for the righteous God trieth the hearts and reins."
17) God will prepare the heart of the humble (Psalm 10:17).
18) The Lord can prove the heart (Psalm 17:3).
19) In Psalm 27:14 we read: "Wait on the LORD: be of good courage, and he shall strengthen thine heart: wait, I say, on the LORD." This is very important in the walk of faith. The Lord does not usually give us instantaneous changes in our circumstances. He seems to wait and let us prove our hearts in faith. The Scripture is telling us that, if we ask anything according to God's will, He will strengthen our heart in faith in order that we might receive it. Many have had an experience in their own lives in which they can recall asking the Lord over a period of time for something and one day having faith to claim the request dwelling in the heart. God has strengthened the heart in faith in this area.
20) God will give the desires of the heart to a soul, if the individual is delighting himself in the Lord ("Delight thyself also in the LORD; and he shall give thee the desires of thine heart" [Psalm 37:4]).
21) God alone knows the secrets of the heart. In Psalm 44:21 we read: "Shall not God search this out? for he knoweth the secrets of the heart." In 1 Corinthians 14:25 we read: "And thus are the secrets of his heart made manifest; and so falling down on *his* face he will worship God, and report that God is in you of a truth."
22) God can create a clean heart in a person: "Create in me a clean

heart, O God; and renew a right spirit within me" (Psalm 51:10).

23) God is the strength of some people's heart: "My flesh and my heart faileth: *but* God *is* the strength of my heart, and my portion for ever" (Psalm 73:26).
24) God can unite a heart in a behavioral characteristic: "Teach me thy way, O LORD; I will walk in thy truth: unite my heart to fear thy name" (Psalm 86:11).
25) God can work in the heart at a national or at an individual level: "He turned their heart to hate his people, to deal subtilly with his servants." (Psalm 105:25). Here we read of God's turning the hearts of the Egyptians to hate His people.
26) God can change the inclination of a heart: "Incline my heart unto thy testimonies, and not to covetousness" (Psalm 119:36). Here we see the soul deciding that it does not have the spiritual power to prevent covetousness. It asks God to incline (gentle turn) the heart to assist in stopping this sin pattern. Essentially, we all have to do the same with all sin patterns that have power over us. If we did it ourselves, it would bring forth power in the flesh which is certainly not what we want. It may take God a while to make the change; but we must cooperate with Him, knowing that He will not allow us to be tempted beyond our strength.
27) God can know the whole heart, but people cannot know their own hearts completely: "Search me, O God, and know my heart: try me, and know my thoughts: And see if *there be any* wicked way in me, and lead me in the way everlasting" (Psalm 139:23-24). If people could know their hearts, there would be no need to ask God to reveal any wicked ways in their hearts to them. We also see that the thoughts cannot be known without the individual's being tested (tried) in areas. God can know the heart by searching it, since it has a resident structure and compartmentalization to it. The thoughts can originate inwardly in the heart or can come into it from the soul. The soul here is requesting God to try it to know whether it will respond correctly to challenges in the spirit, in the heart, and in the flesh. Therefore, wicked ways can be in both the heart and soul or in the heart only. The soul is responsible for sowing to the flesh or to the spirit, and it is responsible for the

structure of the heart. Only challenges will show the soul what it will choose to do.

28) God uses the flesh to interact with the heart to bring it down: "Therefore he brought down their heart with labour; they fell down, and *there was* none to help" (Psalm 107:12).

29) God will give understanding: "Give me understanding, and I shall keep thy law; yea, I shall observe it with *my* whole heart" (Psalm 119:34). Here the soul recognizes a need for understanding. If given it, the person is committing to God that he will keep His law with his whole heart (not just a part of it). He will apply God's law to every situation that his heart encounters. This tells us that hearts are compartmentalized into many different issues and concerns.

30) God refines the heart through testing and further testing: "The fining pot *is* for silver, and the furnace for gold: but the LORD trieth the hearts" (Proverbs 17:3).

31) God will make His counsel stand in a man's heart: "*There are* many devices in a man's heart; nevertheless the counsel of the LORD, that shall stand" (Proverbs 19:21). This is a very reassuring Scripture that will help us a lot if we desire to be led by the Spirit of God. The passage tells us that there are many devices (thoughts, schemes, plans) in a man's heart. If that man has sought the Lord, as in counsel, and has done so honestly, then the Lord will make His counsel to stand. This is echoed in James 1:5-8 where we read that if we ask the Lord for wisdom, He will give it to us if we ask with an unwavering heart. The Lord will make sure that we who are asking will be able to recognize His counsel in the midst of our own thoughts and schemes. We may have to wait on the Lord for it to clarify, but this need to wait is consistent with other Scriptures. This passage is echoed in Proverbs 20:5: "Counsel in the heart of man *is like* deep water; but a man of understanding will draw it out." Here we see that the Lord places His counsel deeply within the heart, and it comes as spiritual revelation. To fasten onto that counsel, a man of understanding will work on being still before the Lord and mediating upon His Word to see that the counsel measures up to the standards in James 3:17: "But the wisdom that is from above is first pure, then peaceable, gentle,

and easy to be intreated, full of mercy and good fruits, without partiality, and without hypocrisy." The the man of understanding has to bring the counsel of the Lord up from the depths of the heart. For a course of action to be counsel from God the advice needs to match all of the criteria in the passage from James 3:17. We have to remember that *peaceable* is the spiritual sensation. It is different from what one feels when he ceases to struggle after committing to a course of action in a situation. The Lord is writing, not a man, so the words have to be examined in the light of what God means when He speaks and writes them. Our human concept of peace is vastly different to that of God's.

32) God has the power to change the human spiritual heart as He will: "The king's heart *is* in the hand of the LORD, *as* the rivers of water: he turneth it whithersoever he will" (Proverbs 21:1). Here we read that the Lord will do as He will to the heart of the king. We look at the example of Nebuchadnezzar to see this. In Daniel 4:16 we read: "Let his heart be changed from man's, and let a beast's heart be given unto him; and let seven times pass over him." This shows the power of God to change the human heart as He will. In Nebuchadnezzar's case he went around eating grass on all fours for seven years. It is very important to note that the Lord gave King Nebuchadnezzar the heart of a beast, and this change in his heart led to changes in his physical appearance and behavior. This illustrates why it is so important to purify our heart in cooperation with the Lord. Parenthetically, we should note that the Lord gives us our leaders, and He uses them for His own purposes. We have to remember that He is the potter; but at the same time it is not His wish that any perish. In ways that are above our ways, God balances all of the impartiality that He has toward men to conform to the history that He has chosen for these times up to the end of the age. What can one say except that He is God? We must bow before Him.

33) God observes and ponders the hearts of men. In Proverbs 21:2 we read: "Every way of a man *is* right in his own eyes: but the LORD pondereth the hearts." Here we note that a man will always follow a way that seems right to him. It may be an evil way, but that man will think it right based on his life's frame of reference. If he

does not think there is a God, then he can justify almost anything. When a man is trying to decide what God's will is for him and is using the mind and not the spirit to discern this, then he will think it right to do what he decides. The Lord looks at every heart to see what the content is; and, as we have seen, He judges man based on the content of the heart. We see in Proverbs 23:6-7: "Eat thou not the bread of *him that hath* an evil eye, neither desire thou his dainty meats: for as he thinketh in his heart, so *is* he: Eat and drink, saith he to thee; but his heart *is* not with thee." This Scripture tells us that as a man thinks in his heart, he is that person.

34) God will let us observe His ways when we give Him our whole heart: "My son, give me thine heart, and let thine eyes observe my ways" (Proverbs 23:26). This is an excellent example for understanding how to be led by the Spirit of God. When we give God our whole heart, we just have to look around us at our circumstances and the situation of those about us to learn God's ways. The prerequisite is to give God our whole heart. This is not easy for most of us. When we do it, we gain spiritual insight and wisdom.

35) God will in the future cause Israel to return to Him with her whole heart: "And I will give them an heart to know me, that I *am* the LORD: and they shall be my people, and I will be their God: for they shall return unto me with their whole heart" (Jeremiah 24:7).

36) God has power over the spiritual heart: "And he shall turn the heart of the fathers to the children, and the heart of the children to their fathers, lest I come and smite the earth with a curse" (Malachi 4:6). Here we note that God will use a prophet to accomplish this before the final judgment.

37) God gives peace to our heart: "Peace I leave with you, my peace I give unto you: not as the world giveth, give I unto you. Let not your heart be troubled, neither let it be afraid" (John 14:27). Here we see that God can give a peace to our heart that is different from what the world gives. It is not peace related to one thought or a few thoughts about a small number of issues, but rather a peace over the whole heart that does away with all the turmoil,

trouble, and fear. We are asked to seek this peace in our heart (Colossians 3:15) in order to make decisions in the will that allow us to be led by the Spirit of God. In Philippians 4:7 we read: "And the peace of God, which passeth all understanding, shall keep your hearts and minds through Christ Jesus." This peace is beyond understanding; it is not reasoned; it is not saying, "Ah! Yes! I have peace." It is only experienced, and once experienced it cannot be counterfeited by the devil. It is also discernible to others spiritually. It is this peace that will keep our hearts and minds at rest in the midst of the spiritual wars to which we are exposed, as we walk after the Spirit of the Lord.

38) God sheds His love abroad in the heart of one who has gone through the second birth. This is an extremely important issue to grasp. In Romans 5:5 we read: "And hope maketh not ashamed; because the love of God is shed abroad in our hearts by the Holy Ghost which is given unto us." Here we see that the Holy Spirit, who resides in the new heart given at the second birth, sheds the love of God into the new heart. Unfortunately, God's love is released by very few hearts and then not continuously. Therefore, the new heart has structures erected within it and around it that block this love from being released. In letting the Lord cleanse our new heart and in our tearing down imaginations, we will be able to release a spirit that is carrying the love of God to the recipient. This is something for which to strive, and it comes as a result of being led by the Spirit of God.

39) God seals us after the second birth: "Who hath also sealed us, and given the earnest of the Spirit in our hearts" (2 Corinthians 1:22). This Scripture tells us definitely that the Holy Spirit is resident within our heart. The heart of man is complex—having tables, compartments, and a place of residence for the Holy Spirit. It contains imaginations and high places. In Galatians 4:6 we read: "And because ye are sons, God hath sent forth the Spirit of his Son into your hearts, crying, Abba, Father." Here God is telling us that he has given us that same Spirit that He gave to the Lord Jesus, which enabled Jesus to call Him "Abba, Father." By this same spirit we can also say, "Abba, Father." In reality, we will do this only when we come to the point of being able to recognize

the presence of this Spirit within us. This Spirit is given only to those who have experienced the second birth. Sometimes it may be difficult for a person to recognize the Spirit. It may not be recognized immediately after the second birth, while the new heart is still pure. Later, when the new heart needs cleansing, it may not be detected by the recipient until the new heart has been cleansed.

40) God the Son can dwell in our hearts by faith: "That Christ may dwell in your hearts by faith; that ye, being rooted and grounded in love" (Ephesians 3:17). We are introduced here to the concept that through faith the Lord Jesus, now a spiritual soul now, can dwell in our hearts. It is consistent with other passages of Scripture such as Revelation 3:20. It denotes in the context of the passage a mighty release of the Holy Spirit's power to strengthen our inner man (spirit). The continual abiding in our heart of the Lord Jesus comes only after time, with the maturing and strengthening of our spirit. When this occurs, the person will carry a permanent sense of being in the presence of the Lord Jesus. There will be no cheap subsidy or counterfeit to this occurrence. The love of God will flow continually out of that individual. Satan has no counterfeit to the love of God. Human lusts do not even begin to approach it, although the novice may be deceived by these.

41) God will eventually declare the condition of our heart: "Therefore judge nothing before the time, until the Lord come, who both will bring to light the hidden things of darkness, and will make manifest the counsels of the hearts: and then shall every man have praise of God" (1 Corinthians 4:5). God will reveal whose leading the soul has been following when the Lord Jesus returns. God will praise men according to whom they have followed—evil spirits, human spirits, or God's Spirit.

42) God has shined in our hearts: "For God, who commanded the light to shine out of darkness, hath shined in our hearts, to *give* the light of the knowledge of the glory of God in the face of Jesus Christ" (2 Corinthians 4:6). Here we see that God has shined in our hearts in a way similar to the light's being made at the creation. The purpose is to give His light to the fallen world. He does this by manifesting His glory in one who has been through

the second birth. This is more completely demonstrated as our heart is purified.

43) God's Word can work in a person to enable him to know whether the spirit released from his heart originates in the human spirit, soul, or flesh. In Hebrews 4:12 we read: "For the word of God *is* quick, and powerful, and sharper than any twoedged sword, piercing even to the dividing asunder of soul and spirit, and of the joints and marrow, and *is* a discerner of the thoughts and intents of the heart." Here we see that the Word of God is a discerner of the thoughts and intents of the heart. We remember that the Word of God is living (quick). It is kept in our heart of flesh. As our heart thinks and plans, the Word of God in our heart can understand what our heart is doing. As we ponder in our hearts for decision making, the Word of God will convict us regarding our thoughts and plans. These thoughts and plans have to pass through, as it were, a living filter formed by the Word before they can be acted on. This is part of how God's Word acts for us. It will be only as efficacious in helping us be led by the Spirit of God as we have been diligent enough to ponder and meditate upon it. We have to be able to internalize God's Word within our heart, if we are going to be led by the Spirit. Without it we are of very limited use to the Lord in fighting the spiritual wars for which we must be available.

44) God places His laws in our heart and mind: "For this *is* the covenant that I will make with the house of Israel after those days, saith the Lord; I will put my laws into their mind, and write them in their hearts: and I will be to them a God, and they shall be to me a people" (Hebrews 8:10). This passage is specifically addressed to the future house of Israel, but we have seen Scriptures to indicate that the same applies to an individual after the second birth.

45) God will put things into the hearts of unbelievers to fulfill His will. In Revelation 17:17 we read: "For God hath put in their hearts to fulfill his will, and to agree, and give their kingdom unto the beast, until the words of God shall be fulfilled." Here we see God placing something in the heart of the unbeliever to fulfill His purposes. He is all powerful.

What our heart can do to God

The following are a few Scriptures to show how our heart will influence God.

God can be tempted. In Psalm 78:18 we read: "And they tempted God in their heart by asking meat for their lust." God was able to control His response, but the people of Israel tempted Him by their heart attitudes.

God will stop working with our heart. In Psalm 81:12 we read: "So I gave them up unto their own hearts' lust: *and* they walked in their own counsels." Here we read that God stopped trying to work with the hearts of these people.

God will not listen to us. Psalm 66:18 reads: "If I regard iniquity in my heart, the Lord will not hear *me*." This principle is very important in being led by God's Spirit. If we regard iniquity, then God will not listen to us.

God is longsuffering but just. In Ecclesiastes 8:11 we read: "Because sentence against an evil work is not executed speedily, therefore the heart of the sons of men is fully set in them to do evil." God does not execute justice immediately. Our spiritual death did not occur instantaneously, otherwise we could never repent. We can get some idea of why by pondering what a world of instantaneous justice (as judged by God) would be like. There would not be many of us around to repent of very much. Man in his folly thinks that he has been able to get away with his actions because justice does not come. Man forgets the long suffering and the mercy of God. It is due to the long suffering, merciful character of God that the sentences are not executed speedily. They will surely be executed, however.

The wholehearted seeker will find God. In Jeremiah 29:13 we read: "And ye shall seek me, and find *me*, when ye shall search for me with all your heart." There are equivalent passages in the New Testament about seeking God with our whole heart.

God reads the condition of our heart. In Ezekiel 14:3 we read: "Son of man, these men have set up their idols in their heart, and put the stumblingblock of their iniquity before their face: should I be enquired of at all by them?" God is reading the condition of the hearts of certain elders of Israel who came to Ezekiel.

CONCLUSIONS

Our heart contains images which we use to guide our behavior. Our soul is responsible for determining whether it allows false images to remain instead of completing a purification process. We have discussed before the analogy between the deliverance of Israel from Egypt and the believer's deliverance from the world system. God told the Israelites that they must conquer the whole Promised Land. Numbers 33:55-56 tells us: "But if ye will not drive out the inhabitants of the land from before you; then it shall come to pass, that those which ye let remain of them *shall be* pricks in your eyes, and thorns in your sides, and shall vex you in the land wherein ye dwell. Moreover it shall come to pass, *that* I shall do unto you, as I thought to do unto them." In the same way, those areas of our heart that we leave impure will become problems for us that will continue to trouble us. We must systematically, as God helps us, tear down false images and build up images of truth so that the Lord Jesus will be formed in our hearts, as Galatians 4:19 describes: "My little children, of whom I travail in birth again until Christ be formed in you." In forming this image of the Lord, we must be very careful that it is true and not our own construction; for God warns of the severe penalties for having and worshipping a false image in many places in Scripture. One particularly sobering passage is in Romans 1:19-32. It is so easy, especially in this age of Biblical illiteracy, to form a false image of the Lord in our hearts. This will earn God's wrath (Deuteronomy 4:24-28).

We must with God's guidance (Deuteronomy 7:16-26) take back our heart from the enemy, tear down the false images, and build up true images. It will take a great work in our lives to do this; but, when we consider the consequences, there is no other choice. As we purify our heart, God will be pleased and will use us for His Kingdom work. Our hearts will conduct His communications to the creation within our sphere both in the natural and spiritual realms. Isaiah 40:3-5 is a passage that demonstrates the result of purifying one's heart. For the glory that is set before us must submit to our Lord in these changes.

11
WORKINGS OF THE MIND OF SPIRITUAL MAN

INTRODUCTION

The mind is, according to Scripture, located in four areas—the soul, the flesh, the heart, and the spirit. The mind can be renewed after the second birth, but is not able to be renewed if one has not been through the second birth. Indeed, after the second birth, God's Word gives a command that we renew our minds. The Scripture is not entirely clear on how the distinct areas of the mind interrelate but the model that we shall set forth seems to be a good fit. The functions of the mind are:

a) to remember including memories of all five senses (smell, taste, touch, hear, see) and position sense
b) to reason
c) to make decisions and plans
d) to communicate with other persons and spirits
e) to observe through the spiritual and through the physical senses

Topics for this chapter are:

1. Introduction
2. How the mind of man is co-ordinated and how it functions
3. What God expects of our mind
4. How the mind interacts with other parts of spiritual man
5. Building blocks of the processes of our mind
6. States of mind—wisdom, understanding, and knowledge
7. Detailed studies of wisdom, understanding, and knowledge
8. Special topics about the mind

It is important to note that the mind cannot function without a language. Linguistic experts tell us that our language constrains our decision-making abilities. If a problem cannot be framed in clear language, we cannot reason about it and resolve it. The structure of a language constrains thought in that language. That is why, for example, people who speak an Indo-European language fail to understand some ideas in Semitic (such as Hebrew) languages. We cannot communicate with other people or with spirits without a language.

At the time of the building of the tower of Babel, God disrupted the common language of the time and gave different languages to different groups of people. In the context of the story one purpose seems to have been to make communication between the different people groups more difficult (see above and cp. Genesis 1:1-9).

We can see how language constrains problem solving by noting how different people groups make quite different assumptions about an object that they are shown. For example, if one shows a bottle of water to various people groups and asks them what they are viewing, Jewish people will likely give a functional answer, describing a use of the water, while other groups will more likely give a descriptive answer, describing the container and the contents.

For the vast majority of people the original Bible was written in a language other than their own. The Old Testament, particularly, was written in a Semitic language which makes it more difficult for people who speak Indo-European languages. We must, therefore, try to understand the communication that God is making to us in the way that He intends. This involves seeking to know how He prefers to think. He tells us that His thoughts are above our thoughts. To understand the Scriptures fully, we have to let the Holy Spirit reveal the truth that He wishes to impart to us by revelation rather than by reason. This will be a difficult concept for an academic, or for anyone who is used to reasoning a lot, to understand and to embrace.

In Psalm 147:5 we read: "Great *is* our Lord, and of great power: his understanding *is* infinite." God also tells us that His thoughts are above our thoughts. We read in Isaiah 55:8-9: "For my thoughts *are* not your thoughts, neither *are* your ways my ways, saith the LORD. For *as* the heavens are higher than the earth, so are my ways higher than your ways, and my thoughts than your thoughts." God is infinitely more intelligent than we are. We need to realize that, in comparison to the intelligence of

God, the difference in intelligence between the greatest earthly genius and the feeblest of earthly intellects is minutely small. Pondering this will give us a more accurate understanding of our own comprehension of reality, of our understanding of the natural, of our memory, and of our ability to reason.

As we ponder this and take it into our heart as a *modus operandi*, we begin to gain humility, which is the utter reliance on God. Does this mean that God does not expect us to reason? Of course it does not. God is glorified by the creativity of man, who is made in His image. He watched Adam closely, as he named the animals. He delights in seeing us use those talents that He gave to us. He wants us to worship Him with our whole mind. We do not begin to understand this, if our definition of worship is confined to praise and music in formal settings. This limitation robs us of true worship, which consists of a deep heartfelt joy in the creation and the work of God's hands and of abiding in His presence. We need to live life to the fullest in awe of Him and what He can do. We must be children before Him. What does a child do with his parents? He looks up to them and reveres them until he is old enough to discern fallibility. In God there is no fallibility. Our whole being must worship God in His creation in all aspects of that creation. We will want to know more about it in order to behold His greatness. We will want to discover new things in research and bring them before the Father, thanking Him for making us in His image so that we can appreciate the magnificence of the subatomic to the astronomic ranges of our "playground." He will be pleased to help us in our pursuit of understanding, when we come to Him for revelation. Look at how God talked with Job in the final chapters of that book. God talked much about His impact on the natural world and universe. Read Job 38:1 – 41:34. God delights in describing His abilities and personality to Job in terms of the physical world and universe. Recall that among other things a very important theme in the book of Job concerns the personality of God. The three friends of Job have their varied, less than full, knowledge of God as a personal God. Job has a greater understanding but falls short of the expectations of God. God, therefore, reveals Himself more fully to Job; and the record is in these chapters. We must know how God wishes us to think about Him in order to know Him. Finally, after God's discourse to Job in these chapters Job responds in Chapter 42:1-3 : "Then

Job answered the LORD, and said, I know that thou canst do every *thing*, and *that* no thought can be withholden from thee. Who *is* he that hideth counsel without knowledge? therefore have I uttered that I understood not; things too wonderful for me, which I knew not." Dwell on the fact that God knows every single thought of every individual who has ever lived and who will ever live. Think of the implications of this for your daily life. We try to hide much from others, and to no avail, because God knows it all; and it is He who will judge us.

HOW THE MIND (HEART, INNER MAN, FLESH, AND SOUL) IS CO-ORDINATED AND HOW IT FUNCTIONS

We understand from Genesis that Adam was given the capacity to express language. He could communicate with God because he was made in the image of God. God uses language. It is part of Him. Therefore it is part of us. God reprogrammed us at the time of the Tower of Babel to have varied languages. God is intelligent and reasons. Therefore, so are we intelligent and able to reason. God remembers; and, therefore, we also can remember. Since God was able to make us in such a way that we also can oppose Him if we choose, He had to provide us with the means to do this. Therefore, we have all of our functions of the mind split into what we shall label as natural observation and reasoning and supernatural observation and reasoning. The mind of the heart and the mind of the inner man are not the ultimate decision makers of the soul; but they have their own thought processes, memories, and agendas. The mind of the soul is responsible for the content and for the thought processes of the minds of the heart and of the spirit. The mind of the soul does not have full access to the contents of the minds of these other parts; but as a soul depends on God, He is willing to reveal hidden things to the mind of the soul through the inner man, as they are needed for particular purposes. As we progress through this chapter, we shall look at Scriptures that support this model. It is important to note that, when Scripture uses the word *mind*, it is always referring to the mind of the soul unless it specifically states otherwise. As an example the word *meditate* appears in Scripture twenty times. The context will define where the soul is to meditate. In Psalm 19:14, Psalm 49:3, and Isaiah 33:18 the soul is instructed to meditate in the heart. The other seventeen times we are meant to meditate in the mind of the soul. In performing meditation in the mind of the soul, we will probably have to search the minds of the heart and the inner man. We shall now look at two Scriptures that show that the heart has a mind and that it is not completely accessible to the mind of the soul.

Romans 2:13-15 addresses this hierarchy of minds: "For not the hearers of the law *are* just before God, but the doers of the law shall be justified. For when the Gentiles, which have not the law, do by nature the things contained in the law, these, having not the law, are a law unto themselves: Which shew the work of the law written in their hearts, their conscience also bearing witness, and *their* thoughts the mean while accusing or else excusing one another." Here we see that an individual's thoughts are able judge another. Thought A can judge thought B. This shows that the mind of the soul can judge the mind of the heart and the mind of the inner man in terms of thought content and that it can decide which thoughts are righteous, depending on the conscience for guidance.

Psalm 119:59-60 also helps us in our understanding: "I thought on my ways, and turned my feet unto thy testimonies. I made haste, and delayed not to keep thy commandments." Here we see the correct attitude—to turn to follow the Lord's commandments without delay as soon as we perceive them in our thoughts or meditations. The soul here is reflecting on the heart and its leading.

Mind of the heart

In 1 Chronicles 29:18 we read: "O LORD God of Abraham, Isaac, and of Israel, our fathers, keep this for ever in the imagination of the thoughts of the heart of thy people, and prepare their heart unto thee." This shows that the heart has imaginations and thoughts and therefore has to have a mind.

In Proverbs 28:26 we read: "He that trusteth in his own heart is a fool: but whoso walketh wisely, he shall be delivered." This shows us that the heart has a set of recommendations that it makes to a soul; but

God recommends that the Israelites not trust the recommendations of their heart, but rather walk wisely. Thus, the mind of the soul and that of the heart can be in conflict so far as walking wisely before God. This situation can be reconciled by the renewing of the mind and the purifying of the heart, after one has gone through the second birth.

In Jeremiah 17:9-10 we read: "The heart *is* deceitful above all *things*, and desperately wicked: who can know it? I the LORD search the heart, *I* try the reins, even to give every man according to his ways, *and* according to the fruit of his doings." This shows that a soul cannot know the full content of the heart, but God knows it and judges it.

Therefore, we see that the heart has a separate mind to that of the soul, that the soul does not know all the content of it, and that the two minds are not necessarily thinking in the same direction. The story of King Amaziah doing the Lord's will, but not with a whole heart, pictures this separation in action (2 Chronicles 25:2).

Mind of the inner man

In Psalm 51:6 we read: "Behold, thou desirest truth in the inward parts: and in the hidden *part* thou shalt make me to know wisdom." The hidden part is the inner man. This Scripture tells us that God will give the inner man wisdom. In 1 Peter 3:4 we read: "But *let it be* the hidden man of the heart, in that which is not corruptible, *even the ornament* of a meek and quiet spirit, which is in the sight of God of great price." To be meek and quiet, the inner man must have a mind. In 1 Corinthians 2:11 we read: "For what man knoweth the things of a man, save the spirit of man which is in him? even so the things of God knoweth no man, but the Spirit of God." This shows that the inner man knows more about us than our soul does. Therefore, the mind of the inner man is superior to the mind of the soul.

Mind of the flesh

We learned in Chapter 7 that the flesh and the inner man are always at enmity. They are completely antagonistic and one hundred and eighty degrees apart in all aspects of the operations of their minds at all times. These include the flows of spirit from them. Therefore, we will study the mind of the inner man in this chapter and will understand that the mind of the flesh is at all times the exact opposite to the mind of our spirit. Thus, we will see from this study how the mind of the flesh works.

Mind of the soul

It is the mind of the soul that has to choose whether to sow to the flesh or to the inner man. It has to choose whether to purify the heart. It has to choose whether to let the inner man mature. It has to weigh the physical realm versus the spiritual realm as to where thoughts are originating and whether they represent wise thoughts or vain imaginations. It has to decide whether to live for this age or whether to prepare the inner man for eternity.

In Psalm 7:9 we read: "Oh let the wickedness of the wicked come to an end; but establish the just: for the righteous God trieth the hearts and reins." God is telling us here that He will hold us accountable for the condition of our mind and for the condition of our heart. It is no idle thing that God wants of us when He commands us to "renew" our mind. This has to be purposeful and continual. It is moment by moment without a break. It is the mind of the soul that God asks us to renew.

SUMMARY

We have now examined Scripture, and we see that there are four minds within the soul and that they are not necessarily synchronized. We have looked in a limited manner at the hierarchy of these four areas of mind and how they interact. We shall continue to examine the Scripture to get a detailed understanding of how these four areas of mind interact. Before beginning to do this, we will look at one Scripture in Proverbs 16:1: "The preparations of the heart in man, and the answer of the tongue, *is* from the LORD." God tells us that out of the mouth come the thoughts and intents of the heart. We have been designed in such a way that we can listen to our own words and discern the state of our preparations of the heart. We cannot speak without this connection to the tongue, since

God has created us this way. Therefore, if a person takes heed to listen to what he says, then he can learn what needs to be changed in his heart by the thoughts and words he does not express and by the thoughts and words he chooses to express. The mind of the soul is responsible for diagnosing the state of the heart and for purifying it. The mind of the soul is where the will interacts with decision making. The mind of the soul has to analyze the condition of the inner spiritual man and of the heart and then has to work with God to allow healthy maturation of the inner man and purification of the heart and the inner man. As we proceed through this chapter, we will see that the statements in this paragraph have Scriptural support.

WHAT GOD EXPECTS OF OUR MIND

Recall that the functions of the mind are:

a) to remember, including memories of information from all five senses and from position sense
b) to reason, which is the processing of information both from current content in the mind and from past information stored in memory
c) to make decisions—immediate, short-term, and long-term
d) to communicate with other persons and spirits, sending and receiving information (both natural and spiritual)
e) to observe our natural and spiritual environments (receiving information from both spiritual and natural sources)

After the second birth God expects us to renew our mind actively. This involves using the mind of the soul to analyze the present condition of the minds of the heart and of the inner man. The mind of the soul is responsible for knowing God and for knowing His desires. The mind of the soul then has to plan and work with God to bring about transition from the present state into the renewed state that God desires. We shall now look at these five areas of the functions of the renewed mind.

THE RENEWED MIND

God has given us the ability to have the mind of Christ, and He has asked us to be renewed in the spirit of our mind in order to accomplish this. The spirit of our mind must be transformed by renewing to be like the spirit of the mind of the Lord Jesus. We have to come to love God with our whole mind. This involves taking captive all thoughts. Thought is the fundamental mechanism by which our mind operates. All of the more complex processes are built up of many thoughts in varied sequences.

Receiving information

Information comes into the mind of the soul from two sources. The first source is from the physical environment through the physical senses, and from there it is sent to the heart and then to the spirit. This information we could call observed information. The second way that a soul acquires information is from God by impartation into the inner man, and this we can term revelation knowledge. From the inner man the revelation goes into the heart and then into the mind of the soul. We see this second method described in the construction of the tabernacle where God filled people with a spirit of wisdom. In Exodus 28:3 we read: "And thou shalt speak unto all *that are* wise hearted, whom I have filled with the spirit of wisdom, that they may make Aaron's garments to consecrate him, that he may minister unto me in the priest's office." In Exodus 31:3 we read: "And I have filled him with the spirit of God, in wisdom, and in understanding, and in knowledge, and in all manner of workmanship." In Exodus 35:35 we read: "Them hath he filled with wisdom of heart, to work all manner of work, of the engraver, and of the cunning workman, and of the embroiderer, in blue, and in purple, in scarlet, and in fine linen, and of the weaver, *even* of them that do any work, and of those that devise cunning work." These Scriptures talk about the revelation knowledge being given by impartation of spirit into the inner man and of the filling of the heart with the thought structures and processes to get the work done. They also mention something that we shall come back to in more detail: the filling of the spirit was in wisdom, in understanding, and in knowledge. These three terms will be defined later. God means something different by each of them. We shall now look at what God expects of us in the sources to which we turn for information from the natural world.

Revelation knowledge compared to learned (studied) knowledge

Revelation is an impartation into the inner man by the Spirit of God. It comes in package form as a whole and may consist of a vision; words; or occasionally taste, touch, and smell sensations. It is discerned quietly within and arises effortlessly to our conscious awareness. It is unobtrusive and all too easily overlooked. It does not have to be reasoned through; it just "is" in the same way that God is "I AM." In the communication there will be information given, and usually this is associated with understanding of what to do with this information. This understanding is present without one's having to go through a reasoning process. The information and understanding will be a novel thing for the recipient.

In one revelation from the Lord I saw a view of the creation as if it were all a symphony harmonizing throughout time. It was a symphony beyond earthly description other than by the analogy. Every movement was perfect, and all was orchestrated by the Lord of Lords and the King of Kings to perfection. At the time of this revelation I was not even thinking about music or the creation. It was revealed to me. This shows some features of revelation knowledge that differentiate it from learning acquired by inductive or deductive reasoning.

In another instance I had specifically asked the Lord to give me an olfactory revelation. He did within a few days. I was driving and suddenly smelled burning candles. I was puzzled, and then into my spirit came the awareness that God was answering my desire.

With learned knowledge the Scripture points out that the study is wearying (Ecclesiastes 12:12). We have to work at remembering details. An example is learning to fly an airplane. We have to study for a test, learning details and committing them to memory. It takes time and effort, and it has to be redone from time to time in order for one to be proficient.

God could certainly give us the same knowledge, if it were His will, in a much simpler manner which would stay with us. His revelation tends to become a subconscious part of our functioning since it dwells in our heart, whereas we have to work at learned knowledge to get it into our heart and to get it to become a part of who we are.

Reasoning and thought content

In Philippians 4:8 we read: "Finally, brethren, whatsoever things are true, whatsoever things *are* honest, whatsoever things *are* just, whatsoever things *are* pure, whatsoever things *are* lovely, whatsoever things *are* of good report; if *there be* any virtue, and if *there be* any praise, think on these things." These are the things with which God wants us to fill our attention and mind. If something does not get past all of these gates—true, honest, just, pure, lovely, of good report, virtuous, and praiseworthy—then we should not allow it to maintain our attention. We should apply these criteria to any conversations, to any reading, to any listening or watching, to any touching or feeling, and to any studies. If the thing under examination does not measure up to these criteria, then it should be ruthlessly cut off from our attention. Dwell on and ponder how differently you would think and be in your heart if you did this. How different would your spirit be? Remember that it is spirit that gives birth to spirit. If you want to influence people to enter the Kingdom of God through Christ Jesus, then ponder the impact of a person who has been obedient to what God commands in the content of what his thoughts should be.

The apostle Paul writes in 1 Corinthians 2:1-16:

> And I, brethren, when I came to you, came not with excellency of speech or of wisdom, declaring unto you the testimony of God. For I determined not to know any thing among you, save Jesus Christ, and him crucified. And I was with you in weakness, and in fear, and in much trembling. And my speech and my preaching *was* not with enticing words of man's wisdom, but in demonstration of the Spirit and of power: That your faith

> should not stand in the wisdom of men, but in the power of God. Howbeit we speak wisdom among them that are perfect: yet not the wisdom of this world, nor of the princes of this world, that come to nought: But we speak the wisdom of God in a mystery, *even* the hidden *wisdom*, which God ordained before the world unto our glory: Which none of the princes of this world knew: for had they known *it*, they would not have crucified the Lord of glory. But as it is written, Eye hath not seen, nor ear heard, neither have entered into the heart of man, the things which God hath prepared for them that love him. But God hath revealed *them* unto us by his Spirit: for the Spirit searcheth all things, yea, the deep things of God. For what man knoweth the things of a man, save the spirit of man which is in him? even so the things of God knoweth no man, but the Spirit of God. Now we have received, not the spirit of the world, but the spirit which is of God; that we might know the things that are freely given to us of God. Which things also we speak, not in the words which man's wisdom teacheth, but which the Holy Ghost teacheth; comparing spiritual things with spiritual. But the natural man receiveth not the things of the Spirit of God: for they are foolishness unto him: neither can he know *them*, because they are spiritually discerned. But he that is spiritual judgeth all things, yet he himself is judged of no man. For who hath known the mind of the Lord, that he may instruct him? But we have the mind of Christ.

This passage sets a tone for the use of the mind in preaching the gospel. It shows that man's wisdom is not sufficient for faith in the Lord. There is a false faith that can be imparted to an individual that rests on intellectual apprehension of facts. It is not sufficient for knowing God. It may or may not be sufficient for salvation, but it is a poor substitute for the demonstration of the gospel with a display of power.

This passage also sets forth that there is a great difference between the wisdom of man and the wisdom of God. The passage tells us that we learn this wisdom of God, because we have the spirit that God gave to us: "Now we have received, not the spirit of the world, but the spirit which is of God; that we might know the things that are freely given to us of

God. Which things also we speak, not in the words which man's wisdom teacheth, but which the Holy Ghost teacheth; comparing spiritual things with spiritual." The Scripture goes on to tell us about the natural man: "But the natural man receiveth not the things of the Spirit of God: for they are foolishness unto him: neither can he know *them*, because they are spiritually discerned." This makes it very clear that, because of the inner man's discerning the "things of God," we can receive them after the second birth. The Scripture goes on to tell us that the inner man has "the mind of Christ." This is probably because of the unity of the Spirit of God and the new inner man that is given at the second birth.

Therefore, the wisdom of God is perceived by the spiritual man and is vastly different to the "enticing words of man's wisdom," even to the words used that are taught by the Holy Spirit. The spiritual inner man then communicates this wisdom to the heart and to the soul.

God tells us to dwell only on those things that are pure, noble, and of good report. We must learn what God means by good, by pure, and by noble. Then, as we do not let our minds dwell on anything that does not measure up, we start to purify our mind by purifying the information that we are taking in through the senses. This is very important, obviously, in the physical realm with sight and hearing; but in the spiritual realm all are important. Demons and demonic works have a very evil odor. In the natural world the sensation of touch can be used to transmit spiritual information and even spirits. This is why the Word of God tells us to sin not in the accepting of the sudden laying on of hands (1 Timothy 5:22). I have known of people to whom a spirit of infirmity was transmitted by unknown people laying on hands in a group in church settings. We should be very careful to know the spiritual purity of anyone whom we permit to lay hands on us. We can see that we have to guard both the physical and the spiritual senses in order to renew our minds.

Exporting information to others

In our output of information, actions, words, attitudes, and beliefs God expects us to fulfill the first two commandments. This occurs only when the mind has been renewed and the inner man and heart have been purified. This defines God's expectations for all of our communications to Him, to His creation, to men, to fallen angels, and to God's angels (Jude 8).

Remembering

God wants our memories to be structured to memorialize our milestones in our walk with Him (Joshua 4). He wants our memories purged of any grievances against others, just as He forgets our sins. He wants our memories to be those things that are retained as we perform the command of Philippians 4:8 (above).

Making Decisions

God expects us to make decisions in the will that are based upon His desires and advice for us. This involves learning to know His voice and recognize the things that the inner man is telling us. It may involve asking for power in our inner man to be able to make and stick to a difficult decision.

HOW THE MIND INTERACTS WITH OTHER PARTS OF SPIRITUAL MAN

INTRODUCTION

Natural observations

We see that observations come into the mind of the soul both through the natural organs of the flesh and through God's revelation into our inner man.

Information coming into the mind of the soul from the natural organs of the flesh, as we have already learned, is spiritual. It is stored in memory in the mind of the soul and is also transmitted to the mind of the heart. In the heart it is mixed with our current belief and attitude structures. These structures consist of the imaginations, high things (2 Corinthians 2:5), and devices. It is then stored in the memory of the heart, where it may modify to some degree the existing content of the heart. A response is then transmitted into the inner man. The information coming to the inner man causes a response back to the heart. After this the combined response of the inner man and of the heart is transmitted to the mind of the soul, accompanied with an imagination from the heart. After receiving this output from the heart, the mind of the soul then coordinates a response from the flesh. This response from the flesh is transmitted into the spiritual and into the natural universes. The will becomes involved, if change in the soul is needed; and the conscience becomes involved in critiquing the information before or after the response from the flesh. The inner man also transmits a response into the spiritual universe, and the heart transmits a spiritual response from its mind.

Information from the inner man

Information comes to the inner man from God, from other spirit beings, and from the spirits of other men. The inner man deals with this information by committing it to memory and transmitting it to the heart. Some of it will come to the attention of the mind of the soul, depending on how well the heart has been purified to receive and transmit this information. It will be coupled with an imagination of the heart. This may contaminate it from its original purity, depending on the condition of the heart. The mind of the soul then forms a response that manifests both in the flesh and in the transmission back to the heart and to the inner man. The minds of the heart and the soul commit the issue to memory. Just as with natural observations (above) the will becomes involved, if change in the soul is needed; and the conscience becomes involved in critiquing the information before or after the response from the flesh.

THE SOUL

Proverbs 16:3 highlights some of these processes: "Commit[roll] thy works unto the LORD, and thy thoughts shall be established." Here we see an obvious connection between our thoughts and our work. Obviously, to perform a work, we need to think about it. God is telling us how our work can be performed meaningfully under His guidance and direction. If we will commit ourselves to being led by Him into our work, our thoughts will come from our inner man as He gives us wisdom for the work. From our inner man the wisdom that we receive from God will come into the mind of our soul, as we seek the leading of His Spirit. Because it is His work, it will be done; thus, our thoughts will be established. God has promised to bless the work of our hands when we are His children. This blessing is a general promise; but, as we seek God for His desire regarding what work He wants us to do, then we will have the even greater blessing of seeing our thoughts established. The word for *established* in the Hebrew indicates that our thoughts will be prepared or established. Think about how we spend a lot of time considering our work. This can be frustrating or enjoyable, depending on the degree of success that we have in our work. Here God promises to make our thoughts fruitful by speaking into our heart His thoughts about the work. As we listen to our spirit, the thoughts in our heart take up the same pattern that we are receiving from the Holy Spirit. There is much peace and joy in this, since there is no frustration. That is not to imply that there will be no hardship; in fact, there may be much opposition to our work from the demonic forces.

In a different direction regarding thoughts and the soul we read in Proverbs 23:6-7: "Eat thou not the bread of *him that hath* an evil eye, neither desire thou his dainty meats: For as he thinketh in his heart, so *is* he: Eat and drink, saith he to thee; but his heart *is* not with thee." Here we see that a person is what is in the thoughts of his heart. We have seen this even more so in Chapter 10. If the thoughts of the heart are righteous, then a man will be righteous. If the thoughts of the heart are evil, then a man will be evil. If the thoughts of the heart are proud, a man is proud. The heart is the root that supports the tree. One cannot have good fruit coming from a poor root. God has ordained the creation to work this way. That does not mean that a person cannot be deceived regarding the heart of another person when perceiving in the natural universe; but if one is using spiritual sight, he will not be deceived. This is a key point for diagnosing the content of and for understanding one's own heart; for out of the abundance of speech flow the thoughts and intents of the heart. Also, as we read above in Proverbs 16:1, the preparations of the heart are with man; but God has designed us to let the tongue express what is in the heart. We must listen to what we say and what others say very carefully. It is wise to listen and not talk much, for then discernment will be easier as one hears an abundance of speech from someone else. It is easy to deceive someone over a short time period, but not over a long period. This is, in part, why people in various parts of the world will not do business with someone before getting to know him well.

How the soul and heart interact in producing a response to natural observations

In Isaiah 65:2-6 we read: "I have spread out my hands all the day unto a rebellious people, which walketh in a way *that was* not good, after their own thoughts; A people that provoketh me to anger continually to my face; that sacrificeth in gardens, and burneth incense upon altars of brick; Which remain among the graves, and lodge in the monuments, which eat swine's flesh, and broth of abominable *things is in* their vessels; Which say, Stand by thyself, come not near to me; for I am holier than thou. These *are* a smoke in my nose, a fire that burneth all the day. Behold, *it is* written before me: I will not keep silence, but will recompense, even recompense into their bosom." Here we see that the thoughts behind the actions of these people who displeased God were not the thoughts of God. Hence, God can state that these people walk in a way that was not good, after their own thoughts. Whenever we walk after our own spirit or after an evil spirit, we are doing the same thing. Not all independent actions are as offensive to God as others, but all fall short of His command to us to follow His Spirit. It is quite evident from this passage that God wants us to be led by His Spirit. It is also very evident that we can be led by our own thoughts. When we are led by our own thoughts, it is from the thoughts of the heart and neither from the thoughts of the inner man nor from the thoughts of the soul. The reason for stating this is that, in respect to being led, the issue with which God was dealing related to worship and obedience. This is a core attribute of who the people in this Scripture were; and, as the Scripture states in Proverbs 27:9, the heart is who the man is.

In Luke 24:37-39 we read: "But they were terrified and affrighted, and supposed that they had seen a spirit. And he said unto them, Why are ye troubled? and why do thoughts arise in your hearts? Behold my hands and my feet, that it is I myself: handle me, and see; for a spirit hath not flesh and bones, as ye see me have." Here we see that the disciples saw a natural sight, and it terrified them. The Lord confirms that this natural vision was relayed by the natural senses to the heart, where it led to thoughts arising in the heart that caused terror and troubling. The terror was transmitted back into the soul, where visible manifestations in the flesh could be observed. Passages such as these confirm the manner in which we, as hybrid spiritual and soul beings, function. We also note that thoughts originate (rise) in the heart. There is a connotation that the thoughts come upward from the heart. Thus, it is the heart that responds to the severe stress the people experienced. This passage illustrates the environment impacting the mind of the soul *via* the physical senses. This information is carried to the heart from the mind of the soul. Here the information goes into the inner man and releases a spirit of fear into the heart. This spirit energizes the heart to invoke a physical response in the flesh of the soul.

Matthew 18:12 states: "How think ye? if a man have an hundred sheep, and one of them be gone astray, doth he not leave the ninety and nine, and goeth into the mountains, and seeketh that which is gone astray?" We see many different Greek and Hebrew words translated as "think," "thought," or similar words in the Scriptures. Many words such as *think* in "How think ye?" are present in the Scripture and do not carry any connotation of being performed in the heart. These are examples of the mind of the soul performing its usual processes to sift through information and to draw conclusions. When a conclusion is reached, it is passed through the mind of the heart before expression is given to it. The lips always answer from the heart. We can see that the mind of the soul does some initial observing and processing of data; but before a response can be elicited, the mind of the heart is involved. If something is morally neutral, such as answering what two plus two equals, then the heart will add an imagination to this. Such an imagination may present as sarcasm if the heart thought it was being "put down." A child answering this question may respond with evident pride in knowing the answer. The heart adds the spirit with which the answer is given. This is evident in the next Scripture that we shall look at in Mark 14:72 where we see the following: "And the second time the cock crew. And Peter called to mind the word that Jesus said unto him, Before the cock crow twice, thou shalt deny me thrice. And when he thought thereon, he wept." This is a good passage to show us how the mind perceives the information, sorts it against memory, and sends it to the heart for a response. Hearing the cock crow would not be an issue in most circumstances, but Peter remembered the word of the Lord, and thus the information led to a profound emotional response from the heart. Therefore, from this passage we see even more clearly how the incoming sensory information from the physical world is perceived in the mind of the soul, is cross matched to our memories, and then goes to the heart where it is linked to an imagination. This imagination is then paired to a spirit in the heart and expressed once more through the mind of the soul and the flesh.

THE HEART

In Isaiah 10:5-11 we read:

> O Assyrian, the rod of mine anger, and the staff in their hand is mine indignation. I will send him against an hypocritical nation, and against the people of my wrath will I give him a charge, to take the spoil, and to take the prey, and to tread them down like the mire of the streets. Howbeit he meaneth not so, neither doth his heart think so; but *it is* in his heart to destroy and cut off nations not a few. For he saith, *Are* not my princes altogether kings? *Is* not Calno as Carchemish? *is* not Hamath as Arpad? *is* not Samaria as Damascus? As my hand hath found the kingdoms of the idols, and whose graven images did excel them of Jerusalem and of Samaria; Shall I not, as I have done unto Samaria and her idols, so do to Jerusalem and her idols?

We see that the Assyrians do not *think* that they intend to cut off nations and destroy them. Their heart does not think this. However, because they have allowed other grandiose thoughts to dwell in their hearts, then their heart actually contains that which they do not see. Our hearts are too deep for our own understanding, and God alone can discern the full content. Of course, eventually this thing within the heart will bear fruit. How then can we protect against something unknown and evil arising in our own heart? Only by developing a perfect heart toward God, by meditating on His word, by hearing His voice, and then by capturing all of our thoughts and forsaking those which are not holy can we purify our hearts and, therefore, our thoughts. Note from the Scripture that we just studied that as the heart is, so will the thoughts be.

Matthew 15:18-19 tells us: "But those things which proceed out of the mouth come forth from the heart; and they defile the man. For out of the heart proceed evil thoughts, murders, adulteries, fornications, thefts, false witness, blasphemies." Here we see further confirmation that the lips speak the content of the heart. In the circumstances the Lord was addressing there would have been evil things in the heart; if the heart were pure, then pure things would come out. Note that it is from the heart and not from the mind from which these evil things proceed. The mind of the soul in a sense is more neutral in morality than the heart, although it can harbor evil thoughts; and it does have to be renewed. It is the mind of the heart that harbors all of the evil that a soul may have in him.

In Matthew 9:4-5 we read: "And Jesus knowing their thoughts said, Wherefore think ye evil in your hearts? For whether is easier, to say, *Thy* sins be forgiven thee; or to say, Arise, and walk?" Here we see that God knows our thoughts. He again attributed these evil thoughts to the hearts. Moral thoughts of all types arise in the heart. We read a similar thing in Luke 9:46-47: "Then there arose a reasoning among them, which of them should be greatest. And Jesus, perceiving the thought of their heart, took a child, and set him by him." Remember that God judges the heart and its content. He does not judge the soul directly. He tells us to renew the mind of our soul. In these Scriptures we see that God attributes the evil thoughts of a soul to evil thinking in the heart. It is the heart that sets our moral compass. The soul is responsible for knowing the condition of the heart and changing it to meet God's requirements.

Further Scripture that speaks to the seat of evil thoughts as arising from the thoughts (mind) of the heart occurs in Acts 8:20-23: "But Peter said unto him, Thy money perish with thee, because thou hast thought that the gift of God may be purchased with money. Thou hast neither part nor lot in this matter: for thy heart is not right in the sight of God. Repent therefore of this thy wickedness, and pray God, if perhaps the thought of thine heart may be forgiven thee. For I perceive that thou art in the gall of bitterness, and *in* the bond of iniquity." Here we see that Simon's heart had the wrong attitudes. Peter was able to discern that the problems in the heart were bitterness and a bond of iniquity. God attributes the evil thoughts to the heart.

INNER MAN

In Matthew 10:19 we read: "But when they deliver you up, take no thought how or what ye shall speak: for it shall be given you in that same hour what ye shall speak." We see here that God is able to speak into our heart *via* the inner man in order to give us a reply from the lips. In Mark 13:11 this is amplified: "But when they shall lead *you*, and deliver you up, take no thought beforehand what ye shall speak, neither do ye premeditate: but whatsoever shall be given you in that hour, that speak ye: for it is not ye that speak, but the Holy Ghost." Here Jesus specifically bids His disciples not to premeditate what they will say when they are brought before civil councils. It is further confirmation of the same things that we have already learned. The spirit receives information and transmits it to the heart; the heart, then, allows us to speak out what is filling our spirit. In this particular situation there may be a divine special power given for these specific circumstances.

Dreams coming from the spirit

Job 4:12-15 relates: "Now a thing was secretly brought to me, and mine ear received a little thereof. In thoughts from the visions of the night, when deep sleep falleth on men, Fear came upon me, and trembling, which made all my bones to shake. Then a spirit passed before my face; the hair of my flesh stood up." Here Eliphaz is recounting a dream or nighttime vision. He describes the process in part as resulting in thoughts that came as a result of the vision or dream. Thus, an impartation results in thoughts relating to the content and process.

In Daniel 2:29-30 we read: "As for thee, O king, thy thoughts came *into thy mind* upon thy bed, what should come to pass hereafter: and he that revealeth secrets maketh known to thee what shall come to pass. But as for me, this secret is not revealed to me for *any* wisdom that I have more than any living, but for *their* sakes that shall make known the interpretation to the king, and that thou mightest know the thoughts of thy heart." Here we see that dreams take place in the heart; therefore, Daniel is able to tell the king that he will make known the thoughts of his heart. We also see that God considers dreams to be thoughts. If a dream originates from the Spirit of God, then it will arise in the heart. All dreams probably originate in the heart. Certainly those from the Holy Spirit do.

CONSCIENCE

Romans 2:13-15 states: "(For not the hearers of the law *are* just before God, but the doers of the law shall be justified. For when the Gentiles, which have not the law, do by nature the things contained in the law, these, having not the law, are a law unto themselves: Which shew the work of the law written in their hearts, their conscience also bearing witness, and *their* thoughts the mean while accusing or else excusing one another.)" Here we see that an individual's thoughts are able to judge one another. Thought A can judge thought B. The mind of the soul can judge the mind of the heart and the mind of the inner man.

MISCELLANEOUS SCRIPTURE ON THESE TOPICS WORTH MEDITATION

In 1 Corinthians 8:1-3 we read: "Now as touching things offered unto idols, we know that we all have knowledge. Knowledge puffeth up, but charity edifieth. And if any man think that he knoweth any thing, he knoweth nothing yet as he ought to know. But if any man love God, the same is known of him." Here Paul is talking about the tendency of knowledge to lead to pride. Until a person has received revelation knowledge from God pertaining to all aspects of a topic, he really does not have true knowledge, but rather a rudimentary form of it. Knowledge and love are contrasted in their impact on one's heart. (The word translated "charity" in the KJV means love.) Paul is also telling us that we cannot ever have full knowledge of a topic because of our physical limitations. Therefore, when interpreting an issue on which others hold different viewpoints, we should consider love first. If we are guided by the Holy Spirit, we will do this since God does not hold our lack of knowledge against us but rather judges us by the thoughts and contents of the heart. One should be careful to get knowledge in the correct perspective. Our present world system places such a premium on learning and knowledge that we easily hold vain imaginations based on this. God is not as concerned about our knowledge, for true knowledge comes from Him. His purpose in training us for the future is not to enhance the intellect but rather to prepare the heart. As much as He asks us to learn His Word, even more so He wants our hearts to be right before Him.

2 Corinthians 10:3-6 expands this idea: "For though we walk in the flesh, we do not war after the flesh: (For the weapons of our warfare *are* not carnal, but mighty through God to the pulling down of strong holds;) Casting down imaginations, and every high thing that exalteth itself against the knowledge of God, and bringing into captivity every thought to the obedience of Christ; And having in a readiness to revenge all disobedience, when your obedience is fulfilled." This passage tells us that we must war against evil with the power of God. God's power (not our own) allows us to pull down strongholds of evil. These evil strongholds are spiritual, and they are embedded in our hearts. These strongholds exist in the spirit and heart as imaginations (images) and high things (philosophies, goals, education, worldly knowledge, and other things) that lift themselves up by opposing the knowledge of God. The spirits behind these images and forces can be opposed by the power of God's Spirit and can be overcome. They cannot be overcome by the inner man's power. Every thought in a person's heart has to be brought into captivity to the obedience of the Lord.

In Philippians 4:6-8 we read: "Be careful for nothing; but in every thing by prayer and supplication with thanksgiving let your requests be made known unto God. And the peace of God, which passeth all understanding, shall keep your hearts and minds through Christ Jesus. Finally, brethren, whatsoever things are true, whatsoever things *are* honest, whatsoever things *are* just, whatsoever things *are* pure, whatsoever things *are* lovely, whatsoever things *are* of good report; if *there be* any virtue, and if *there be* any praise, think on these things." Paul is telling us not to be anxious; rather, we should pray about every single thing in our lives with thanksgiving for our circumstances. When we do this, we have God's peace (which cannot be described—only experienced), which will guard our hearts and minds. Paul then gives us a command from God about what the content of our sensory input is to be. If something does not measure up to these criteria, then we should not keep it in our minds. We may have to deal with an issue, but then it must not be allowed to come back into active thought processing.

In Hebrews 4:12 we read: "For the word of God *is* quick [alive], and powerful, and sharper than any twoedged sword, piercing even to the dividing asunder of soul and spirit, and of the joints and marrow, and *is* a discerner of the thoughts and intents of the heart." Here we see that the Word of God discerns the thoughts and intents of the heart. We can use it to mirror our hearts and intents. Of course, to do this, we must know it well and also take advice of those more expert than ourselves in dividing the Word. Note that the thoughts of the soul are not at issue here.

BUILDING BLOCKS OF THE PROCESSES OF OUR MIND

God's word instructs us about the fundamental building blocks of the processes that go on in our minds. These building blocks link and aggregate to become (on the Godly side) true wisdom, true understanding, and true knowledge; but on the worldly side they become high things, devices, and false imaginations. These building blocks and their assembly become those things that govern our behavior and govern what spirits we release into the universe. The building blocks that we shall study below are: thinketh/thought, imaginations, visions, devices, conceits, and meditations. After studying these building blocks we shall learn how to acquire God's wisdom, understanding, and knowledge and compare them with vain wisdom, vain understanding, and vain knowledge. We will learn how God views the condition in an individual of being wise. At the end of the chapter we shall return to studying the mind in more detail having learned these new concepts as a prerequisite.

THINKETH/THOUGHT AND IMAGINATIONS

We will not try to define *thought* and *think*—these are understood by common usage. We need to understand imaginations from God's perspective, since it is not the definition that one would normally understand. Normally, we think of *imaginations* as being something like a daydream or a meditation on future plans. Indeed the Scriptures include this understanding, but they go beyond it.

In Genesis 6:5 we read: "And GOD saw that the wickedness of man *was* great in the earth, and *that* every imagination of the thoughts of his heart *was* only evil continually." We have to differentiate *imagination* from *knowledge*, and this will be done later. In this Scripture God is telling us that every imagination of the thoughts of the heart was always evil in those days. This Scripture tells us that imaginations are a part of the thoughts and that they are associated with the mind of the heart. Imagination is future-looking and is based on what a person sees for his future. Imagination is associated with every single thought, even a mundane one; and it amplifies it into a future plan of action. For example, when one thinks of driving to a store to pick up a grocery item, the mind imagines to some degree the trip, and one may have a fleeting impression of the store. This is, of course, future thought, for the store may have some disaster occur before one gets to it; thus, this thought is linked to an imagination. All thoughts carry an imagination, regardless of how fleeting it may be. An example of this is an image we form of the appearance of a person whom we have never met to whom we are talking on the telephone. An imagination is a picture image, word image, or other sensory image that goes with the thought. The language of the spirit is conducted a lot in images, which, of course, convey much more to us than many words. We see also from this Scripture that we can never have a thought from the heart that is not associated with an imagination. From this Scripture we also see that the heart has thoughts, and we can infer that it has very complex thoughts.

We read further of the complexity of thought processes in the heart in Psalm 64:6. In 1 Chronicles 28:9 we see God's requesting that His people serve Him both with a perfect heart and with a willing mind.

God tells us that He understands all of the imaginations of the thoughts of the heart. God knows all of our future scheming and planning, even if they are never verbally expressed. In Job 42:1-2 we read: "Then Job answered the LORD, and said, I know that thou canst do every *thing*, and *that* no thought can be withholden from thee." God is omnipotent, and in the spiritual universe all thoughts are remembered and weighed.

Imaginations can be for good or for evil. We read of this in 1 Chronicles 29:18-19. The imaginations are a necessary part of how we perform our future planning. Without imagination we could not plan independently for the future. We would be limited to a walk before God in a mechanistic, current-time manner. Imaginations feed on past memories, experiences, and goals.

In Psalm 10:4 we see that God expects to be in all of a person's thoughts. When He is, a person will seek after Him. He expects us to look at His hand in every aspect of our lives. If we are not doing this in even small details, then we are falling short of God's expectation of us. We live our lives in the presence of others. In the case of a spouse, that person's presence is always of influence in our actions. We may take on extra work to get that person a special gift. As we look at every single thing that we do, we can see the influence of the spouse on those actions. Pause and think about it. God is asking us to have Him in our thoughts in an even greater way, so that we will do nothing without having His concerns in mind.

Psalm 94:17-19 shows that the comforts promised by God in the thoughts of the Psalmist cause delight to his soul. It is not the rest of his many thoughts that do this. Here we see that our soul is comforted, as we reflect on how God has kept faith with us through His promises. It is a contrast to the vain thoughts of the unrighteous man. Our thoughts, which are based on God's Word and His past interactions with us, lead our soul to delight. Delight is such a vivid contrast to vanity or emptiness.

In Psalm 146:4 we read: "His breath goeth forth, he returneth to his earth; in that very day his thoughts perish." This is a very profound

Scripture; we should get it into our heart through meditation. It tells us that it does not matter what we sow to the mind in terms of eternity. The thoughts stop immediately after the first death. After death it is only the spirit, which has been shaped by the soul through the heart, that goes into eternal life. Therefore, do not concentrate on earthly wisdom and acquisition of earthly knowledge. It will not go with you into eternity. You may be rich in earthly knowledge; but if your heart has not been transformed so that it has transformed your inner spiritual man, then you will be poor in the spirit that you take into eternity. Dwell on this, until it takes you by force and transforms your entire focus and attitude. Your life of intellectual pride will mean nothing in eternity. Does that mean that we should not study in universities? Perhaps, but the answer to that is in Daniel 1:17. The key is being led by the Spirit of the Living God and doing His will as an obedient servant in all things. If God wants us to go to university, then we should do it in obedience to Him; and we should do all of our study before Him in such a way that He will be pleased.

In Isaiah 55:7-10 we read: "Let the wicked forsake his way, and the unrighteous man his thoughts: and let him return unto the LORD, and he will have mercy upon him; and to our God, for he will abundantly pardon. For my thoughts *are* not your thoughts, neither *are* your ways my ways, saith the LORD. For *as* the heavens are higher than the earth, so are my ways higher than your ways, and my thoughts than your thoughts." Here we see that if we are unrighteous in any area of our heart, we must forsake our thoughts in this matter in order to change our heart. There is no other way. This is the process whereby we renew our minds and take every thought captive for the Lord. It is hard, continuous, unrelenting crucifixion of the old man. It has to be done, and the power to do it comes only from the resurrection power of the Lord, as He gives us of His spirit. As we do this, we begin to have the mind of Christ arise within. Our thoughts gradually become His thoughts; and our ways His ways, as we walk after His Spirit. The ancient Israelites, walking after the pillar of fire and the cloud, are a picture of this process. They followed God's way for them, although since their hearts were unchanged, this is just a type (example) of what is seen fully in those who have been through the second birth.

VISIONS

The need for visions

Proverbs 29:18 tells us: "Where *there is* no vision, the people perish: but he that keepeth the law, happy *is* he." People will perish, if they do not have vision to see the things of God that He has planned for them. They are created in His image, and this is part of it. If a vision for the future is suppressed or denied, the people will perish.

In 1 Samuel 3:1 we read: "And the child Samuel ministered unto the LORD before Eli. And the word of the LORD was precious in those days; *there was* no open vision." Since there was no open vision all words from heaven were precious. They sustained the people. Man does not live by bread alone except by every word that proceeds from the mouth of God (Deuteronomy 8:3).

True visions can guide people

Matthew 17:9 states: "And as they came down from the mountain, Jesus charged them, saying, Tell the vision to no man, until the Son of man be risen again from the dead." Here the Lord Jesus is referring to the transfiguration as a vision for Peter, James, and John.

In Acts 16:9 we read: "And a vision appeared to Paul in the night; There stood a man of Macedonia, and prayed him, saying, Come over into Macedonia, and help us." We see God leading Paul through a vision. Peter was also led by a vision (trance) in taking salvation to the house of Cornelius (Acts 10:3 ff.).

False visions

In Isaiah 28:7 we read: "But they also have erred through wine, and through strong drink are out of the way; the priest and the prophet have erred through strong drink, they are swallowed up of wine, they are out of the way through strong drink; they err in vision, they stumble *in* judgment." Here we see that anyone who is in the habit of using alcohol, when under its influence, is going to err in vision and judgment. We do not know how much is too much or how often is too often. When one studies alcohol in the Scriptures, he can see very clearly that those in higher service to the Lord (such as the priest on duty in the tabernacle) cannot use it at all (Leviticus 10:9). This principle is also shown in the fact that deacons are expected to drink little wine, while elders are expected to drink even less (1 Timothy 3:2-12). We are priests for the Lord, when we have been through the second birth; and we are on active duty continually. Therefore, we should abstain from alcohol, if we want to be pleasing to the Lord and in the closest of communion with Him.

In Jeremiah 14:14 we read: "Then the LORD said unto me, The prophets prophesy lies in my name: I sent them not, neither have I commanded them, neither spake unto them: they prophesy unto you a false vision and divination, and a thing of nought, and the deceit of their heart." Jeremiah 23:16 adds: "Thus saith the LORD of hosts, Hearken not unto the words of the prophets that prophesy unto you: they make you vain: they speak a vision of their own heart, *and* not out of the mouth of the LORD." These passages show us clearly that one must examine all visions to determine their source. They can be from the Lord God, from the soul (which was the case with these prophets), or from the demonic. We should note that it is easy for us, if we are not experienced in the things of God and if we do not understand how to be led by Him, to fall into being led by soulish imaginations. There are many ways we can test this, but the true safety is to know the Lord well and to know His voice.

Ezekiel 13:7 speaks of these areas: "Have ye not seen a vain vision, and have ye not spoken a lying divination, whereas ye say, The LORD saith *it*; albeit I have not spoken?" The prophets and the people were so far from God that they believed vain (soulish) visions; and, even worse, they believed demonic visions through divination.

Effects of the lack of true visions

In Micah 3:6-7 we read: "Therefore night *shall be* unto you, that ye shall not have a vision; and it shall be dark unto you, that ye shall not divine; and the sun shall go down over the prophets, and the day shall be dark over them. Then shall the seers be ashamed, and the diviners confounded: yea, they shall all cover their lips; for *there is* no answer of God." Here God is, among other things, showing us that He will choose whether to give spiritual vision to His people. For various purposes He may choose to allow darkness in the spiritual realm so far as men are concerned.

Prophetic and future visions

In Habakkuk 2:2-3 we read: "And the LORD answered me, and said, Write the vision, and make *it* plain upon tables, that he may run that readeth it. For the vision *is* yet for an appointed time, but at the end it shall speak, and not lie: though it tarry, wait for it; because it will surely come, it will not tarry." Here we see vision as a prophetic device for a specific future time.

DEVICES

What is a device?

We see In Isaiah 32:7 that a device consists of a structure of words or ideas. Wicked devices have lying words. A false stock prospectus in this age could be considered a wicked device. In Ecclesiastes 9:10 we learn that a device is different to knowledge, work, and wisdom.

We see an example of a device in Jeremiah 18:18. "Then said they, Come, and let us devise devices against Jeremiah; for the law shall not perish from the priest, nor counsel from the wise, nor the word from the prophet. Come, and let us smite him with the tongue, and let us not give heed to any of his words." It seems that devices frequently consist of words of a plan, but not always; for in Acts 17:29 we read: "Forasmuch then as we are the offspring of God, we ought not to think that the Godhead is like unto gold, or silver, or stone, graven by art and man's device." Here a device is a plan for the construction of the figure. Essentially devices are plans for carrying out a task and are of varying complexity.

Where are devices located?

Devices are located in the heart. "*There are* many devices (thoughts, imaginations) in a man's heart; nevertheless the counsel of the LORD, that shall stand (Proverbs 19:21)."

Who uses devices?

The Lord uses devices.

In Jeremiah 18:11 we read: "Now therefore go to, speak to the men of Judah, and to the inhabitants of Jerusalem, saying, Thus saith the LORD; Behold, I frame evil against you, and devise a device against you: return ye now every one from his evil way, and make your ways and your doings good."

There are many devices in the heart of man, but if we ask the Lord for counsel (nothing wavering [James 1:6]), then His counsel will be able to stand against all other plans. "*There are* many devices in a man's heart; nevertheless the counsel of the LORD, that shall stand" (Proverbs 19:21). It will be recognizable as His advice.

People use devices.

Jeremiah 18 relates God's creating a device against the men of Judah. These men responded: "And they said, There is no hope: but we will walk after our own devices, and we will every one do the imagination of his evil heart" (v.18). Thus, the people used their own devices.

In Psalm 37:7 we read: "Rest in the LORD, and wait patiently for him: fret not thyself because of him who prospereth in his way, because of the man who bringeth wicked devices to pass." The devices (thoughts) can be wicked or good.

Satan uses devices.

2 Corinthians 2:11 tells us: "Lest Satan should get an advantage

of us: for we are not ignorant of his devices." Here the devices seem to represent structures for proceeding against the believers. They would be words leading to actions with a planned end. Such a device could involve stirring up one synagogue against Stephen with the eventual aim of taking his life. We read of this in Acts 6:9-7:60. The good thing is that we are not ignorant of his devices.

Other Scriptures on devices include: 2 Chronicles 2:14, Esther 8:3, Job 5:12, Job 21:27, Psalm 10:2, Psalm 37:7, Proverbs 19:21, Ecclesiastes 9:10, Isaiah 32:7, Jeremiah 18:11-12, Daniel 11:24-25, Acts 17:29, and 2 Corinthians 2:11. These Scriptures give us a good flavor for the use of the term. It indicates a complex scheme, or series of actions, that can be planned by God, men, or the devil. If God plans it, then it is for good. If man or Satan plans it, then it is wicked and for evil.

CONCEIT(S)

In Proverbs 18:11 we read: "The rich man's wealth *is* his strong city, and as an high wall in his own conceit." The word *conceit* is also translated "imagination." It is the wealth that is the strong city, but the reliance on this wealth for the future (building a high wall) is the imagination. "Answer a fool according to his folly, lest he be wise in his own conceit (Proverbs 26:5)." Here the word *conceit* can be replaced by eyes or imagination. Note that the fool is not wise, but in his imagination he is wise. The imagination is not accurate or true.

Romans 12:16 warns us to beware of thinking that our fleshly imaginations are wise. "*Be* of the same mind one toward another. Mind not high things, but condescend to men of low estate. Be not wise in your own conceits."

MEDITATIONS

Where do we meditate?

We meditate in the mind of the soul and in the mind of the heart.

In Psalm 19:14 we read: "Let the words of my mouth, and the

meditation of my heart, be acceptable in thy sight, O LORD, my strength and my redeemer." Here we see that meditation comes from the heart and that the mind of the soul decides after meditating on the words coming from the heart what should be spoken. The meditations of the heart, however, are primary to those of the soul; and they give rise to the spoken words. God has ordained it this way. The words from the heart may be angry. The mind of the soul reflects on these angry words and feels that it would be ill-advised to vent anger. This information goes back to the heart, and the heart supplies deceitful words that the mind of the soul determines to express.

In Psalm 49:3 we see that wisdom follows understanding of God's ways. "My mouth shall speak of wisdom; and the meditation of my heart *shall be* of understanding."

How do we meditate?

God tells Joshua in Joshua 1:8: "This book of the law shall not depart out of thy mouth; but thou shalt meditate therein day and night, that thou mayest observe to do according to all that is written therein: for then thou shalt make thy way prosperous, and then thou shalt have good success." Here God asks Joshua (but applicable for us) to mull over, pray about, and constantly think about His Word. We are also asked to pray without ceasing in 1 Thessalonians 5:17. Meditation and prayer are similar. Both involve sitting before God, talking to Him about His written Word, and discussing our needs and requests. We are interacting with His Word. Other Scriptures that are worth reviewing here include Psalm 1:2 and Psalm 63:6. In the night when the external senses diminish their input to the soul, the soul can focus on the Lord more readily. This is, in part, why God speaks in dreams and at unusual times. When our soul is quiet, we can hear the "still, small voice" more readily. We should meditate on all of God's work (Psalm 77:12). We see an example of this in 1 Timothy 4:11-15.

Results of meditation

Results vary, depending on the issue upon which one is meditating.

Good outcomes

David states in Psalm 5:1: “Give ear to my words, O LORD, consider my meditation.” Here he is asking God to consider his thoughts.

In Psalm 119:97-99 we read: “O how love I thy law! it *is* my meditation all the day. Thou through thy commandments hast made me wiser than mine enemies: for they *are* ever with me. I have more understanding than all my teachers: for thy testimonies *are* my meditation.” We see that understanding comes from meditation on God’s word.

Psalm 104:34 adds: “My meditation of him shall be sweet: I will be glad in the LORD.”

In Genesis 24:63 we read: “And Isaac went out to meditate in the field at the eventide: and he lifted up his eyes, and saw, and, behold, the camels *were* coming.” Here *meditate* could mean “pray.”

Bad outcomes

In Isaiah 33:18 we read: “Thine heart shall meditate [can be translated as “muse upon”] terror. Where *is* the scribe? where *is* the receiver? where *is* he that counted the towers?”

When do we not meditate?

In Luke 21:14 we read: “Settle *it* therefore in your hearts, not to meditate before what ye shall answer.” Here we see the Lord asking the disciples to settle something in their hearts in advance of an event so that they would not have to think about it at the time of crisis. Specifically, He was referring to the time when they would be arrested for their Christian testimony. A reason not to meditate is if God has asked us not to.

STATES OF MIND—WISDOM, UNDERSTANDING, AND KNOWLEDGE

Defining wisdom, understanding, and knowledge

A key Scripture to illustrate what God means by these three words is found in Proverbs 24:3-4: "Through wisdom is an house builded; and by understanding it is established: And by knowledge shall the chambers be filled with all precious and pleasant riches."

Taking this analogy that God has given to us allows us to get an idea of what He means when He uses these words. In order to build a house, one needs to be able to form plans and follow them. One needs construction techniques and knowledge of how to put materials together. Once a building is erected, a person may have a roof over his head; but in order for the reputation and importance of that house in the community to become permanent, one needs a broader set of skills. This broader set of skills to go beyond the mere mechanics of putting a building together is termed *understanding*. Once a house has acquired a reputation in the community by understanding, then knowledge is used to fill the areas of it with just the right things. Thus, knowledge is built on understanding, which in turn is built on wisdom.

Another key Scripture in looking at wisdom and knowledge is Proverbs 1:1-7: "The proverbs of Solomon the son of David, king of Israel; To know wisdom and instruction; to perceive the words of understanding; To receive the instruction of wisdom, justice, and judgment, and equity. To give subtilty to the simple, to the young man knowledge and discretion. A wise *man* will hear, and will increase learning; and a man of understanding shall attain unto wise counsels: To understand a proverb, and the interpretation; the words of the wise, and their dark sayings. The fear of the LORD *is* the beginning of knowledge: *but* fools despise wisdom and instruction."

Here we see again the transition from wisdom to understanding and on to knowledge. One can be wise and gain some understanding, but beyond this one cannot go without revering the Lord God.

An excellent example of the progression from wisdom to understanding and on to knowledge occurs in the vision that Peter received at Joppa. In the vision itself he obtained wisdom. Only when he arrived at Cornelius' home and saw the household receive the baptism of the Holy Spirit did he get some understanding of the vision. It was only as he pondered what to say to the Church council that he developed knowledge of God's heart toward the Gentiles and of what the Lord's atonement had done for mankind more completely.

Acquiring Wisdom, Understanding, and Knowledge

If we look at the life of a person before God, we note that He gives wisdom and also knowledge to those who fear Him. We cannot even begin to get wisdom or knowledge without fearing God. We see that, in order to get wisdom, we must also learn to hear God. After hearing, a wise man will increase his learning by meditation on God's *logos*.

God has ordained that a man cannot develop understanding without the counsel of other wise men (Proverbs 1:5; 11:14). As we work in the body of the Lord Jesus, we grow in reverence (fear) for God and develop understanding. As we continue intently on this path, we will begin to know God and His ways. Knowing God's ways goes beyond wisdom and understanding. We can gain some wisdom and understanding from God and still not know His ways. An example is that of Moses' being taught God's ways, whereas Aaron had wisdom and understanding in his priestly duties but did not understand God's ways as Moses did.

The Lord Jesus Christ as wisdom personified

A second key fact in the study of wisdom is to understand that the Lord Jesus Christ is wisdom personified (Proverbs 8). In Proverbs 2:10 we read: "When wisdom entereth into thine heart, and knowledge is pleasant unto thy soul." Here we see that wisdom must enter into the heart. Wisdom is the Lord Jesus. As He enters one's heart, then knowledge (true revelation knowledge) will become pleasant to the soul. The soul will no longer thirst after vain knowledge once it tastes true knowledge. It can be very hard for intellectually gifted people to understand the significance of this. People who depend on vain knowledge for power in the world system will find it very difficult to let go of their position; and yet that is what the Lord calls people to do. They will have to try to walk between two kingdoms or declare themselves for one or the other. An example of this is seen in the stance that a believer must take toward evolution. The secular scientist believes in the theory of evolution. A believing scientist, once he has worked through the issues, will believe the creation account in Genesis. In declaring this belief, the believing scientist will suffer at least some ridicule and may suffer more significant persecution. The believing scientist will suffer loss of secular power.

Wisdom, understanding, and knowledge—spirits of anointing that God gives to us

Isaiah 11:2-4 prophesies concerning the Lord Jesus: "And the spirit of the LORD shall rest upon him, the spirit of wisdom and understanding, the spirit of counsel and might, the spirit of knowledge and of the fear of the LORD; And shall make him of quick understanding in the fear of the LORD: and he shall not judge after the sight of his eyes, neither reprove after the hearing of his ears: But with righteousness shall he judge the poor, and reprove with equity for the meek of the earth: and he shall smite the earth with the rod of his mouth, and with the breath of his lips shall he slay the wicked."

Here we see that the Lord Jesus had several spirits resting on Him. Note the Lord needed the spirit of knowledge, the fear of the Lord, and the spirit of wisdom and understanding. If He needed these spirits resting on Him, then how much more do we need to ask God to give us an anointing of these spirits! Without such an anointing our wisdom, understanding, and knowledge are going to be relatively weak. We can ask for God to give us these spirits as an anointing or as an impartation. We see this in Ephesians 1:17-18 and Colossians 1:9-10.

Furthermore, we see clearly that there is a difference between a spirit of wisdom and a spirit of knowledge in 1 Corinthians 12:8: "For to one is given by the Spirit the word of wisdom; to another the word of knowledge by the same Spirit." Both are prophetic gifts.

Contrast between wisdom, understanding, and knowledge

We have looked at Proverbs 24:3-4: "Through wisdom is an house builded; and by understanding it is established: And by knowledge shall the chambers be filled with all precious and pleasant riches." This passage gives us the relationship between wisdom, understanding, and knowledge. Wisdom is the Lord Jesus Christ personified (Proverbs 8)—just as in truth. To build on the rock, we have to build on Him. Just so, in any endeavor, we have to have Him to give us revelation knowledge of what He wants in the future. We shall just note here that the words *imagination* and *wisdom* as used in the Scriptures are almost opposites. Wisdom is God's plan for the future; imagination is our wish or guess about the future. If we consider a man to be wise, it is because that man can extrapolate into the future. Therefore, if we have the Lord Jesus reveal wisdom to us, then we need to meditate on this and understand it. Wisdom is like a word of wisdom. After the plans, if it is wisdom from God, then we can rest assured that, if we apprehend the timing and the manner of the project, the house is as good as built. It becomes established as it is built, and then the work is carried on by words of knowledge. Thus, wisdom is like the gift of the word of wisdom, and knowledge is like the gift of the word of knowledge. An example of wisdom about the building of a literal house was King David's realizing that a temple needed to be built. This came from revelatory wisdom. He had to understand that, while he could gather the materials, the Lord wanted his son Solomon to build it. After having been built, the temple was operated by the word of knowledge of what the Lord wanted. Words of wisdom and knowledge are His desires. If we do not understand and act on them, they will not come to pass in His primary plans; and He will choose others to complete His plans (as exemplified in Mordecai's words in Esther 4:14).

WISDOM

Wisdom and *wise* are a noun and an adjective, respectively. There is so much Scripture for both that they are each discussed below under separate major headings. *Wisdom* and *wise*, while similar, are not quite the same thing in God's writings. We shall discuss wise first and then *wisdom*.

WISE

Definition of being wise

God's definition: In Genesis 41:39 we read: "And Pharaoh said unto Joseph, Forasmuch as God hath shewed thee all this, *there is* none so discreet and wise as thou *art*." This shows us the definition that God has for being wise, *i.e.*, the person sees things from God. The world has a vastly different view of being wise. "Choose this day which one you will follow," Joshua admonished the people of his day.

The world's definition: In Genesis 3:6 we read: "And when the woman saw that the tree *was* good for food, and that it *was* pleasant to the eyes, and a tree to be desired to make *one* wise, she took of the fruit thereof, and did eat, and gave also unto her husband with her; and he did eat." Here we see the human and Satanic definition of being wise, i.e., to know both good and evil and to be as gods. Both the human and Satanic versions of what it means to be wise have a spirit of the wrong power behind it. This spirit desires to be something that it should not be and to control that which it should not control.

Being wise involves being able to see something (not necessarily with sight).

Deuteronomy 16:19 commands: "Thou shalt not wrest judgment; thou shalt not respect persons, neither take a gift: for a gift doth blind the eyes of the wise, and pervert the words of the righteous." Taking bribes makes the wise unable to see and perverts the righteous person. Note that being wise is associated with being able to see. The essence of being wise is being able to see what is coming. Recall Jesus' address about reading the signs of the times to the Pharisees. Being wise is correlated with being able to discern the future correctly. A prophet is wise, if he is a true prophet.

When one reads through all of the Scriptures dealing with being wise and having wisdom, he sees the difference between God's view of wisdom and the world's view of wisdom. In the past wisdom often was thought to consist of being able to discern spiritual things such as dreams (as Pharaoh, Nebuchadnezzar, and other kings suggested). Men whom God viewed as wise were those who had listened to Him and who were able to give His message to others. He also viewed those as wise who received special impartations of spirits into their hearts, such as for building the Tabernacle. We have seen this in Chapters 9 and 10. Esther 1:13 indicates that discerning the times was a sign that leaders valued as wisdom.

Scriptures to read relating to this include 1 Samuel 18:14-15 and Matthew 7:24.

Those whom God views as unwise are described as puffed up in their own wisdom or conceit. False prophets are described as blind. It pleased God to confound the wisdom of the world by choosing those who were not thought of as wise from the world's viewpoint to be wise in true wisdom (see 1 Corinthians 1:19-27 below).

We see some of these things in the following Scriptures.

Who is considered wise?

In Matthew 11:25 we see that babes are considered wise, but people with worldly wisdom are not. A major Scripture on wise and wisdom is found in 1 Corinthians 1:19-27:

> For it is written, I will destroy the wisdom of the wise, and will bring to nothing the understanding of the prudent. Where *is* the wise? where *is* the scribe? where *is* the disputer of this world? hath not God made foolish the wisdom of this world? For after that in the wisdom of God the world by wisdom knew not God, it pleased God by the foolishness of preaching to save them that believe For the Jews require a sign, and the Greeks seek after wisdom: But we preach Christ crucified, unto the Jews a

> stumblingblock, and unto the Greeks foolishness; But unto them which are called, both Jews and Greeks, Christ the power of God, and the wisdom of God. Because the foolishness of God is wiser than men; and the weakness of God is stronger than men. For ye see your calling, brethren, how that not many wise men after the flesh, not many mighty, not many noble, *are called*: But God hath chosen the foolish things of the world to confound the wise; and God hath chosen the weak things of the world to confound the things which are mighty.

We see God's reasons for making the wisdom of the world foolish. We need to keep this firmly in mind when reasoning with an unsaved person.

True "wise" as opposed to "worldly wise"

Job 15:2 shows that a wise man should not answer with vain knowledge.

In Daniel 4:18 we read: "This dream I king Nebuchadnezzar have seen. Now thou, O Belteshazzar, declare the interpretation thereof, forasmuch as all the wise *men* of my kingdom are not able to make known unto me the interpretation: but thou *art* able; for the spirit of the holy gods *is* in thee." Here we see the king's attributing the presence of the "holy gods" as being in Daniel, because Daniel was able to discern the dream when the other wise men could not. Daniel, of course, had the presence of the true God.

In Matthew 2:1 we read about the wise men. They were wise because they listened to God, were led by Him, and avoided Herod's request.

In Matthew 10:16 we read: "Behold, I send you forth as sheep in the midst of wolves: be ye therefore wise as serpents, and harmless as doves." God evidently feels that serpents are wise.

The Lord gives a parable to show who is wise in Matthew 25:7-9: "Then all those virgins arose, and trimmed their lamps. And the foolish said unto the wise, Give us of your oil; for our lamps are gone out. But the wise answered, saying, *Not so*; lest there be not enough for us and you: but go ye rather to them that sell, and buy for yourselves." We see the wise as those who listened to the Lord and did as He said, in contrast to the foolish who did not. The folly of the foolish had eternal consequences.

In Romans 11:25 we read: "For I would not, brethren, that ye should be ignorant of this mystery, lest ye should be wise in your own conceits; that blindness in part is happened to Israel, until the fulness of the Gentiles be come in." We are told not to be wise in our own conceits. The Greek word for *conceits* is correctly translated as "self."

For further reference, read Exodus 28:3, Deuteronomy 1:13, Deuteronomy 4:5-6, 1 Samuel 18:5, 1 Kings 3:12, and Hosea 14:9.

False "wise" Scriptures

Exodus 7:11 shows false wisdom: "Then Pharaoh also called the wise men and the sorcerers: now the magicians of Egypt, they also did in like manner with their enchantments." Note that these wise men had some power but not as great as that of Jehovah (see Exodus 7:11 and 8:7, cp. 8:18-19).

Esther 1:13 tells us: "Then the king said to the wise men, which knew the times, (for so *was* the king's manner toward all that knew law and judgment." Here we see that the king valued wisdom in knowing the times. This is still so today among leaders.

In Esther 6:13 we read: "And Haman told Zeresh his wife and all his friends every *thing* that had befallen him. Then said his wise men and Zeresh his wife unto him, If Mordecai *be* of the seed of the Jews, before whom thou hast begun to fall, thou shalt not prevail against him, but shalt surely fall before him." These wise men were correct. They answered Haman well. False prophets often are true prophets who have gone astray from truth because of their own lusts. We do not know specifically in the case of these wise men what the power behind this statement was.

In Isaiah 5:21 we read: "Woe unto *them that are* wise in their own eyes, and prudent in their own sight." We see that one can be wise in God's eyes or in his own eyes. We know the difference is based on hearing accurately from the Lord either through the natural signs of the creation or through direct supernatural revelation.

Isaiah 19:12 instructs: "Where *are* they? where *are* thy wise *men*? and let them tell thee now, and let them know what the LORD of hosts hath purposed upon Egypt." God tells Isaiah to see if the wise men really know what the future is for Egypt. This will tell whether these men are really wise. Of course they do not know; therefore, they are not wise.

In Jeremiah 8:9 we read: "The wise *men* are ashamed, they are dismayed and taken: lo, they have rejected the word of the LORD; and what wisdom *is* in them?" The wise men are ashamed, since they have been found lacking after rejecting the Word of the Lord.

Jeremiah 51:57 states: "And I will make drunk her princes, and her wise *men*, her captains, and her rulers, and her mighty men: and they shall sleep a perpetual sleep, and not wake, saith the King, whose name *is* the LORD of hosts." God tells us that He will specifically prevent the wise men of Babylon from seeing.

In Romans 1:21-22 we read: "Because that, when they knew God, they glorified *him* not as God, neither were thankful; but became vain in their imaginations, and their foolish heart was darkened. Professing themselves to be wise, they became fools." Vanity in the imaginations led to a false concept of wisdom with eternal consequences.

How does one become wise?

In Psalm 19:7 we read: "The law of the LORD *is* perfect, converting the soul: the testimony of the LORD *is* sure, making wise the simple." This is how one becomes wise, *i.e.*, through the testimony of the Lord. Meditate on His Word. Talk with Him. Commune with the Lord. You will then become wise.

God hides things from the wise and prudent of the world but reveals them to babes. In Matthew 11:25 we read: “At that time Jesus answered and said, I thank thee, O Father, Lord of heaven and earth, because thou hast hid these things from the wise and prudent, and hast revealed them unto babes.” We must be a “babe” so far as believing the world system. Similarly in Luke 10:21 we read: “In that hour Jesus rejoiced in spirit, and said, I thank thee, O Father, Lord of heaven and earth, that thou hast hid these things from the wise and prudent, and hast revealed them unto babes: even so, Father; for so it seemed good in thy sight.”

1 Corinthians 3:18-20 tells us: “Let no man deceive himself. If any man among you seemeth to be wise in this world, let him become a fool, that he may be wise. For the wisdom of this world is foolishness with God. For it is written, He taketh the wise in their own craftiness. And again, The Lord knoweth the thoughts of the wise, that they are vain.” This is similar to the passage in 1 Corinthians 1. It is the advice to those who are esteemed to be wise in the world. If you have much education, you need to be very careful about how your mind functions. You have to become foolish deliberately, in the sense that spiritual truth must be revealed by the Lord and not by the intellect. This is part of the crucifixion of the old man. It is essential.

What is the result of being wise?

There is great strength in wisdom (Ecclesiastes 7:19). Wisdom is evident in a shining face and a bold face—the countenance is altered (Ecclesiastes 8:1). We will walk circumspectly in the world, not as a fool (Ephesians 5:5). We will win souls (Proverbs 11:30).

In Luke 16:8 we read: “And the lord commended the unjust steward, because he had done wisely: for the children of this world are in their generation wiser than the children of light.” This is wisdom for daily operations. It does not mean that God condoned it, but it shows that God expects us to use the intellectual capacity that He gave to us in our dealings with the world. We must use it in subjection to His authority. He is really condoning the thinking process that leads to goal-driven results. The steward was goal-driven to make his life easier after losing his position. The Lord will set our goals, but we are expected to use wisdom to achieve them.

In James 3:13 we read: “Who *is* a wise man and endued with knowledge among you? let him shew out of a good conversation his works with meekness of wisdom.” If we are wise, we will have good works. If there are no good works, then we are not wise.

Other Scripture on being wise

There is much in Proverbs about wisdom and being wise. A selection of these Scriptures includes: Proverbs 1:5, 3:7, 3:35, 6:6, 8:33, 9:8, 9:9, 9:12, 10:5, 10:8, 10:14, 10:19, 12:15, 12:18, 13:20, 14:16, 14:35, 15:2, 15:7, 16:14, 16:21, 17:10, 17:28, 18:15, 20:1, 21:22, 24:6, 26:12, 28:7, 28:11, 28:26, 29:8, and 29:11.

Proverbs 20:1 is of interest in that it discusses another aspect of alcohol that has to be taken into account by all who wish to come to God’s view (true wisdom) on this topic. It reads: “Wine *is* a mocker, strong drink *is* raging: and whosoever is deceived thereby is not wise.” Note that quantity is not specified in this Scripture, so it has to be taken in context with all other Scripture. Be very careful with alcohol, since it can lead to lack of wisdom.

WISDOM

What is wisdom?

In Job 28:28 Job defined *wisdom* and *understanding*: “And unto man he said, Behold, the fear of the Lord, that *is* wisdom; and to depart from evil *is* understanding.” *Wisdom* is the revering of the Lord. *Understanding* is to depart from evil. Departing from evil follows revering the Lord, as understanding builds on wisdom. Psalm 111:10 tells us that the fear of the Lord is just the beginning of wisdom. Wisdom leads to understanding when it is translated into action—doing all His commandments. In Proverbs 9:10 we read: “The fear of the LORD *is* the beginning of wisdom: and the knowledge of the holy *is* understanding." Here we see wisdom and understanding explained even better. Reverence of the Lord is the beginning of wisdom but as we know God better and better, closer and closer, then we develop understanding.

Wisdom is a spirit.

Isaiah 11:2 tells us, speaking of the Lord Jesus: "And the spirit of the LORD shall rest upon him, the spirit of wisdom and understanding, the spirit of counsel and might, the spirit of knowledge and of the fear of the LORD."

Wisdom is the Lord Jesus personified.

In Proverbs 8, especially, the Lord Jesus is portrayed as wisdom personified. This is a key passage. Proverbs says much about wisdom.

Where does God place wisdom?

Psalm 51:6 explains: "Behold, thou desirest truth in the inward parts: and in the hidden *part* thou shalt make me to know wisdom." God desires truth to reside in our hearts, and David states that God will make the hidden man of the heart to know wisdom. This wisdom is available to us as we listen to our spirit.

How does a person acquire wisdom?

1. In Proverbs 2:2 we read: "So that thou incline thine ear unto wisdom, *and* apply thine heart to understanding." We take in wisdom through the senses; and by meditating on wisdom in the heart, we gain understanding. The natural and the spiritual senses can receive wisdom. Understanding, then, is processed or digested wisdom. Proverbs 2:6 states: "For the LORD giveth wisdom: out of his mouth *cometh* knowledge and understanding." It is the Lord who is the source of all wisdom and understanding and knowledge.

2. We can acquire wisdom by receiving an anointing. In Deuteronomy 34:9 we read: "And Joshua the son of Nun was full of the spirit of wisdom; for Moses had laid his hands upon him: and the children of Israel hearkened unto him, and did as the LORD commanded Moses." Here we see that there is a spirit of wisdom that is transmitted by the laying on of hands. This is a supernatural mantle of wisdom similar to what Solomon received. This is more than just being wise. It is an anointing in the inner man. Other examples of a specific anointing for wisdom are found in 1 Kings 4:29-30 and 4:34, Ezra 7:25, Luke 21:14-15, Ephesians 1:17, and Colossians 1:9.
3. We can request God to give it to us for a specific purpose. In James 1:5-8 we read: "If any of you lack wisdom, let him ask of God, that giveth to all *men* liberally, and upbraideth not; and it shall be given him. But let him ask in faith, nothing wavering. For he that wavereth is like a wave of the sea driven with the wind and tossed. For let not that man think that he shall receive any thing of the Lord. A double minded man *is* unstable in all his ways." This is the means for asking wisdom from God for making personal and corporate decisions. We must ask in faith with a willingness to accept and act on the answer.
4. We gain wisdom in the acts of daily life by observing God in action. In Proverbs 1:20-22 we see that it is easy to hear and see wisdom. "Wisdom crieth without; she uttereth her voice in the streets: She crieth in the chief place of concourse, in the openings of the gates: in the city she uttereth her words, *saying*, How long, ye simple ones, will ye love simplicity? and the scorners delight in their scorning, and fools hate knowledge?"

What do we do with wisdom?

1. Psalm 90:12 indicates that we should number our days. We should value our time, knowing that we are preparing for eternity. If, for example, we knew that we would live 5003 more days (or five), it would make a difference in our approach to those days. It brings sobriety. God is telling us to approach others with this perspective in order to help them to acquire wisdom in the heart.

2. Proverbs 14:8 shows that a wise person wants to know truth. A fool wants to be deceived.
3. In Proverbs 18:4 we read: "The words of a man's mouth *are as* deep waters, *and* the wellspring of wisdom *as* a flowing brook." Words come from the depths of our heart. When wisdom is present, it flows in a stream. It has a musical quality of symphony to it—hence the comparison to a brook.
4. Fruits develop in our soul as a result of having wisdom (Matthew 11:29).
5. A spirit of wisdom is irresistible as we speak it out (Acts 6:10).
6. The Holy Spirit gives words of wisdom to the perfect man for him to speak. This does not mean his using a prayer language, but rather using the *logos* instead of his own words whenever he possibly can. We read about this in 1 Corinthians 2:1, 2:4-7, and 2:13:

> And I, brethren, when I came to you, came not with excellency of speech or of wisdom, declaring unto you the testimony of God. For I determined not to know any thing among you, save Jesus Christ, and him crucified. And I was with you in weakness, and in fear, and in much trembling. And my speech and my preaching *was* not with enticing words of man's wisdom, but in demonstration of the Spirit and of power: That your faith should not stand in the wisdom of men, but in the power of God. Howbeit we speak wisdom among them that are perfect: yet not the wisdom of this world, nor of the princes of this world, that come to nought: But we speak the wisdom of God in a mystery, even the hidden wisdom, which God ordained before the world unto our glory: Which things also we speak, not in the words which man's wisdom teacheth, but which the Holy Ghost teacheth; comparing spiritual things with spiritual.

In this passage Paul is contrasting worldly wisdom (man's wisdom) with power and the presence of the Holy Spirit. They are very different. Much of our preaching and teaching today is intellectual discourse; and, therefore, the faith of many rests in this and not the true gospel, which is always associated with power. If there is no power, then there is earthly wisdom only present in most cases. 1 Corinthians 4:20 states: "For the kingdom of God *is* not in word, but in power." If there is no power, the kingdom is likely not present.

True Wisdom

We see a detailed description of true wisdom that God gives in answer to our request for situational wisdom. In James 3:15-17 we read: "This wisdom descendeth not from above, but *is* earthly, sensual, devilish. For where envying and strife *is*, there *is* confusion and every evil work. But the wisdom that is from above is first pure, then peaceable, gentle, *and* easy to be intreated, full of mercy and good fruits, without partiality, and without hypocrisy." This is written to provide guidance for us to discern the wisdom that comes from God. It will be bring peace to the hearts of all involved in the decision.

Fools and false wisdom

In Proverbs 1:7 we read: "The fear of the LORD *is* the beginning of knowledge: *but* fools despise wisdom and instruction."

Proverbs 10:23 contrasts fools and men of wisdom: "*It is* as sport to a fool to do mischief: but a man of understanding hath wisdom."

Proverbs 14:8 states: "The wisdom of the prudent *is* to understand his way: but the folly of fools *is* deceit." This is so true. The wise want to know truth. Fools want to be deceived.

Proverbs 14:33 tells us: "Wisdom resteth in the heart of him that hath understanding: but *that which is* in the midst of fools is made known." A wise person does not have his heart revealed readily—he is careful with his words. A fool's heart is revealed readily—it is not difficult to see it.

In Colossians 2:23 we read: "Which things have indeed a shew of wisdom in will worship, and humility, and neglecting of the body; not in any honour to the satisfying of the flesh." This passage gives a list of some of the results of vain wisdom.

UNDERSTANDING

What does God mean by understanding?

Proverbs 9:10 explains wisdom and understanding well: "The fear of the LORD *is* the beginning of wisdom: and the knowledge of the holy *is* understanding." Reverence of the Lord is the beginning of wisdom; but, as we know God better and better, closer and closer, then we develop understanding.

In Daniel 8:16 we read: "And I heard a man's voice between *the banks of* Ulai, which called, and said, Gabriel, make this *man* to understand the vision." This is perhaps the clearest passage of Scripture showing the relationship between wisdom and understanding. Wisdom is the vision. Having seen the vision, Daniel needs God's help to understand it. So it is with us.

Understanding can be an anointing with a spirit.

In Isaiah 11:2 we read: "And the spirit of the LORD shall rest upon him, the spirit of wisdom and understanding, the spirit of counsel and might, the spirit of knowledge and of the fear of the LORD." Isaiah is speaking of the Lord Jesus. *Understanding* is a spirit of anointing in this case.

In Exodus 31:3 we read: "And I have filled him with the spirit of God, in wisdom, and in understanding, and in knowledge, and in all manner of workmanship." These are all spirits imparted by God for a specific purpose.

In 1 Kings 3:9 we read: "Give therefore thy servant an understanding [also hearing] heart to judge thy people, that I may discern between good and bad: for who is able to judge this thy so great a people?"

Understanding can refer to using the mind.

In 1 Corinthians 14:14-15 we read: "For if I pray in an *unknown* tongue, my spirit prayeth, but my understanding is unfruitful. What is it then? I will pray with the spirit, and I will pray with the understanding also: I will sing with the spirit, and I will sing with the understanding also." *Understanding* is much more frequently translated as "mind" from this Greek word (21 out of 24 times). It does help to see what is meant by *understanding*.

Understanding, therefore, can refer to natural observation or spiritual impartation. We see this in Colossians 1:9: "For this cause we also, since the day we heard *it*, do not cease to pray for you, and to desire that ye might be filled with the knowledge of his will in all wisdom and spiritual understanding."

Where does understanding reside?

Understanding resides in the minds of the heart, soul, and inner man. The following Scriptures help us to see this.

In Job 38:36 we read: "Who hath put wisdom in the inward parts? or who hath given understanding to the heart?" God puts wisdom into the inner man (spirit), and then He gives understanding to the heart (mind of the heart). The word is not the usual one for the heart and may be translated as the mind. Wisdom is placed into the inner man from seeing and hearing. The inner man conveys this to the heart, where it is meditated upon; and God gives the heart understanding again by revelation to the inner man. Understanding in the heart is like digested wisdom.

In Proverbs 14:33 we read: "Wisdom resteth in the heart of him that hath understanding: but *that which is* in the midst of fools is made known." This is telling us that a person with understanding does not have his heart revealed readily. He is careful with his words. A fool's heart is revealed readily.

In Matthew 13:13-15 we read: "Therefore speak I to them in parables: because they seeing see not; and hearing they hear not, neither do they understand. And in them is fulfilled the prophecy of Esaias, which saith, By hearing ye shall hear, and shall not understand; and seeing ye shall see, and shall not perceive: For this people's heart is waxed gross, and *their* ears are dull of hearing, and their eyes they have closed; lest at any time they should see with *their* eyes, and hear with *their* ears, and should understand with *their* heart, and should be converted, and I should heal them." We see that it is the heart that has to understand. Understanding is a function of the heart. Wisdom is perceived in the spirit (as is understanding). The people did not want to be converted; and, therefore, they chose to be dull of hearing and not to see.

In Mark 12:33 we read: "And to love him with all the heart, and with all the understanding, and with all the soul, and with all the strength, and to love *his* neighbour as himself, is more than all whole burnt offerings and sacrifices." One can love with all of the understanding.

Where do we obtain understanding?

Ultimately, understanding is given to us either by hearing from God directly in the inner man by impartation or by observation in the natural realm. This natural observation can be through wise counselors. We are to seek God for it. Scriptures that show these things include: Luke 24:45, Proverbs 8:1, Job 34:34, Proverbs 1:2, Proverbs 5:1, and Proverbs 28:5.

We read of a special case in Daniel 1:17: "As for these four children, God gave them knowledge and skill in all learning and wisdom: and Daniel had understanding in all visions and dreams." Here we see that the Lord gave Daniel understanding of what he had seen—it is like an interpretation of a vision.

In Daniel 8:16 we read: "And I heard a man's voice between *the banks of* Ulai, which called, and said, Gabriel, make this *man* to understand the vision." We again see that wisdom was given as a vision, but now God is asking an angel to give Daniel understanding of this imparted wisdom.

Therefore, all understanding comes from God, but it may come through intermediary wise counselors or even through an angel. We see angels giving the apostle John understanding in the book of Revelation.

Result of understanding

We see that we can speak wisdom when our heart has understanding (Psalm 49:3). We can carry out complex tasks for the Lord when we have understanding (Exodus 36:1). We can judge complex situations with understanding residing in our heart (1 Kings 3:9).

Another look at the link between wisdom, understanding, and knowledge

In Proverbs 3:19-20 we read: "The LORD by wisdom hath founded the earth; by understanding hath he established the heavens. By his knowledge the depths are broken up, and the clouds drop down the dew." Compare this with Proverbs 24:3-4 that we looked at above under the heading "contrast between wisdom, understanding, and knowledge." There is in both analogies a progression in the depth of detail in the situation, and there is in both a transition from structure to function. Both begin with a vision of the end product (wisdom). Next is an intermediate step of how the structure will exist in a wider context (understanding). Finally, the detailed working of the structure in context is realized (knowledge). These Scriptures tell us how God schematically works out solutions for His plans. Since we are made in His image, we should expect to be successful in His view when we do the same. We must get His vision for any new project. We must understand the place of that project in the broadest context. When we have both of these things fixed, then we can build and place the vision into proper operation. Remember that we must get the vision from God in our spirit within our heart. We must meditate on this before God, and in His timing He will give us an understanding of the context. Until we get this greater context from the Lord as understanding, we should not try to build the vision (Isaiah 40:31). It is as we gain understanding of the broader context for the work that God can then impart knowledge for the operation of the work. We must wait on this three-fold revelation of information from God for the work to be His work in His timing. Luke 14:28-30 refers to the need to plan our resources and understanding before starting to build. It is relevant to accumulate spiritual knowledge and to have everything ready before beginning a new work that God is authoring. While we are waiting on God, the principle from Scripture is to continue doing our current work to which we have been called before making a transition (1 Corinthians 7:20).

In Daniel 2:21-22 we read: "And he changeth the times and the seasons: he removeth kings, and setteth up kings: he giveth wisdom unto the wise, and knowledge to them that know understanding: He revealeth the deep and secret things: he knoweth what *is* in the darkness, and the light dwelleth with him." Knowledge follows understanding. One must have understanding to be given knowledge. Recall that to the pure, all things are pure. To a man of understanding, God will reveal the deep things of darkness; but it will not overcome the light that is in him (the man). In order to understand and operate in God's will, we must understand the role of evil now that it is present in the world.

Understanding and the interactions of the parts of spiritual man

We shall now examine how understanding interacts with the various components of spiritual man.

Soul

1. Understanding allows a soul to discern the things of God coming from the inner man. Without understanding we cannot do this. In Proverbs 20:5 we read: "Counsel in the heart of man *is like* deep water; but a man of understanding will draw it out." This is a very profound statement. God's counsel is deep in the heart, where the inner man has placed it. A man who has understanding of the things of God will be able to draw this counsel out and identify it for what it is. However, until we have experienced (have understanding of) the separation of spirit, soul, and flesh (Hebrews 4:12), we can be easily misled in determining what is from self, Satan, and God.

2. In Proverbs 20:24 we read: "Man's goings [also steps] *are* of the LORD; how can a man then understand his own way?" This is by the understanding of the process identified just above.

3. A soul can acquire prophecy and see the natural fulfillment of the prophecy. If the man has understanding, he will draw the right conclusion from the natural observation. In Matthew 24:15 we read: "When ye therefore shall see the abomination of desolation, spoken of by Daniel the prophet, stand in the holy place, (whoso readeth, let him understand:)." An example in which understanding was lacking was after the feedings of the multitudes. The disciples still did not understand the miraculous workings of the Lord. They were chided for this because their hearts were still hard (Mark 8:14-21).

4. People who have not trained their inner man to hear God's words cannot understand what He is saying: "Why do ye not understand my speech? *even* because ye cannot hear my word. Ye are of *your* father the devil, and the lusts of your father ye will do. He was a murderer from the beginning, and abode not in the truth, because there is no truth in him. When he speaketh a lie, he speaketh of his own for he is a liar, and the father of it" (John 8:43-44). We see that, when we cannot hear God's word, then we cannot understand His speech. We hear the noise, but we do not perceive. It is like the Israelites in the wilderness, who heard noise (when God spoke) but had no understanding. We have to learn to listen to how God speaks. It is easy to be confused if we do not learn the variations of God's voice. The hard hearts of the disciples stopped the word from entering.

5. 1 Corinthians 13:2 is a profound statement: "And though I have *the gift of* prophecy, and understand all mysteries, and all knowledge; and though I have all faith, so that I could remove mountains, and have not charity, I am nothing." Even if a soul understands everything, he is nothing without charity (love).

6. In 1 Corinthians 14:19-20 we read: "Yet in the church I had rather speak five words with my understanding [usually translated "mind"], that *by my voice* I might teach others also, than ten thousand

words in an *unknown* tongue. Brethren, be not children in understanding [only used twice and once for understanding of the heart]: howbeit in malice be ye children, but in understanding [second occurrence mind] be men." The soul has to control the understanding of the heart. Also of interest is the emphasis on teaching "*by my voice.*" This would be consistent with other ways of teaching that the apostle used, including demonstrations of spiritual power.

7. In Hebrews 11:3 we read: "Through faith we understand [mental] that the worlds were framed by the word of God, so that things which are seen were not made of things which do appear." It is by choosing to act in faith that we see things differently.

Understanding and the heart

When our hearts are hard or "waxed gross," we cannot receive understanding (Mark 8:17-19); and when our hearts are blind, we cannot understand (Ephesians 4:18). We are asked to be men in understanding but children in malice (1 Corinthians 14:19-20).

Understanding and the mind of the soul

Understanding may refer to a natural observation and its implications. In Mark 14:68 we read: "But he denied, saying, I know not, neither understand I what thou sayest. And he went out into the porch; and the cock crew." This is another use of understand applied to the natural observations from the senses. One can understand with the mind of the soul and with the mind of the heart. Peter had deceit in his heart because of fear of suffering. He claimed not to understand; but really he did understand the charge. He also knew that he would be in danger.

God decides whether we can understand. In John 12:40 we read: "He hath blinded their eyes, and hardened their heart; that they should not see with *their* eyes, nor understand with *their* heart, and be converted, and I should heal them." The hardness of the heart stops us hearing from God. We can be soft in some areas and hard in others. God does this, presumably based on past behavior. Note that spiritual understanding occurs in the heart and that the mind of the soul is not where spiritual understanding occurs. Also the Lord blinded the eyes (in other passages "made them not to hear") in case they did understand in the mind and change their hearts. We read above in Matthew 13:13-15, where the inability to hear and the inability to see were ascribed to the people. I do not have an adequate understanding of how to explain these seemingly divergent responsibilities. This issue is framed within the greater issue of where a person's free will is bounded by God' pre-determined plans. We could conceive of the fact that God hardens our heart, and we also harden our heart, as being similar in the spiritual realm to that of a force field in which moving an object causes an equal and opposite reaction. As we choose to do something, God also does it in response. Those who know the laws of physics will understand this analogy. Scripture tells us that man and God are linked spiritually and that everything that the spirit of man does causes a response from God, and vice versa (see discussion under the heading "Spiritual Comprehension" on page 321). Ultimately, in these issues of free will versus God's predetermined plans, one has to accept both to be equally true. A person then has to operate in his daily walk before God, believing both free will and predetermined plans to be true in any decision that he makes. Since we can take responsibility for our decision, then it is best to make decisions based on our perceived responsibility to God as if we will be held accountable for all that we do and say. The apostle Paul used similar arguments to the churches in his letters in which he discussed such issues as continuing to sin in order to magnify grace (Romans 6:1).

Understanding and the interaction with other spiritual beings

Understanding and God

In Jeremiah 51:15 we read: "He hath made the earth by his power, he hath established the world by his wisdom, and hath stretched out the heaven by his understanding." In Psalm 147:5 we read: "Great *is* our Lord, and of great power: his understanding *is* infinite."

1. God wants us to love Him with all of our understanding (Mark 12:33). Here we see that one can love with all of the understanding. God

wants us to process our observations and impartations of wisdom that He has given us, so that in understanding we can love Him. If we love Him just out of our imparted and observed wisdom, we will not have as deep a relationship with Him.

2. God tells us that he will destroy the wisdom of the wise and understanding of the prudent in 1 Corinthians 1:19. The wisdom of the wise is based on the natural and on the understanding of how something works in the natural. The natural world does not work the way people reason. An example of this is the fact that the creation is held together by God's utterances (*rhema*), not by the laws of physics (Hebrew 1:1-3).

3. God enlightens our understanding in response to prayerful requests. In Ephesians 1:18 we read: "The eyes of your understanding [more frequently translated as mind] being enlightened; that ye may know what is the hope of his calling, and what the riches of the glory of his inheritance in the saints." Similarly in Colossians 1:9 we read: "For this cause we also, since the day we heard *it*, do not cease to pray for you, and to desire that ye might be filled with the knowledge of his will in all wisdom and spiritual understanding." There is both a spiritual understanding and, by implication, a natural understanding.

4. We have to ask God for understanding in all things. We cannot come to it without His revelation to us. In 2 Timothy 2:7 we read: "Consider what I say; and the Lord give thee understanding in all things." We are given impartations of wisdom into the inner man constantly and further impartations to understand those we already have been given. We may not be able to go back and recall those from our past; but any true knowledge of God was imparted into our inner man in times past, and it continues. We have to learn to hear and see it.

5. Ultimately, God has given us understanding in the advent of the Lord Jesus Christ (1 John 5:20). "And we know that the Son of God is come, and hath given us an understanding [often translated "mind"—probably "understanding" is better here], that we may know him that is true, and we are in him that is true, *even* in his Son Jesus Christ. This is the true God, and eternal life."

Beyond understanding

Philippians 4:7 tells us: "And the peace of God, which passeth all understanding, shall keep your hearts and minds through Christ Jesus." The understanding here is in the capacity of spiritual understanding. The receipt in our inner man of a spiritual force can be described in most cases, but that of the peace of God is not able to be described since there is little in the natural world to correlate with it. When we rest after making a difficult decision, we experience peace as an absence of frustration; but this is not the same peace that comes into our spirit from God.

Miscellaneous Scriptures about understanding

In Colossians 2:2 we read: "That their hearts might be comforted, being knit together in love, and unto all riches of the full assurance of understanding (mind), to the acknowledgement of the mystery of God, and of the Father, and of Christ."

"Go to, let us go down, and there confound their language, that they may not understand one another's speech" (Genesis 11:17).

In Revelation 13:18 we read: "Here is wisdom. Let him that hath understanding [translated "mind" 21 out of 24 times] count the number of the beast: for it is the number of a man; and his number *is* six hundred threescore *and* six."

KNOWLEDGE

True Knowledge

True knowledge can come from observations in the natural realm that are accurate. It can also come from the witness of the Holy Spirit to our inner man.

Acts 4:13 illustrates this: "Now when they saw the boldness of Peter and John, and perceived that they were unlearned and ignorant men, they marvelled; and they took knowledge of them, that they had been with

Jesus." Here we see non-vain knowledge. The knowledge came from accurate observation. Therefore, knowledge could be described as that information which is learned by observation or revelation. If something is falsely observed, then it will be vain (empty) knowledge. Knowledge, to be such, has to be remembered. We see this in Romans 3:20 where we read: "Therefore by the deeds of the law there shall no flesh be justified in his sight: for by the law *is* the knowledge of sin." We see that the law brings observational awareness of sin; and, thus, we have the knowledge of sin.

Knowledge that is true comes ultimately from God. God defines the word *knowledge* as "something that He has taught to men." Knowledge that does not come from God is called "vain knowledge." See Psalm 94:10.

Perhaps the best definition of true knowledge occurs in Colossians 3:9-10 where we read: "Lie not one to another, seeing that ye have put off the old man with his deeds; And have put on the new *man*, which is renewed in knowledge after the image of him that created him." Here we see that true knowledge is after the image of God. Anything that is consistent with God and His person is true knowledge. Anything that is not is vain knowledge.

How do we qualify to be given true knowledge from God?

We have to be weaned from milk and drawn from the breasts (Isaiah 28:9). There has to be a degree of maturation in the inner man for God to impart knowledge. Knowledge is a spiritual impartation, and it will not work to attempt to transfer intellectual understanding into this arena without the right spirit. It does not work. We have to have growth in the inner man. There has to be demonstrable development that God can see, and we cannot "fake it" by last minute "cramming." Unfortunately, living in an era where intellect is considered supreme makes us think that growth in the spirit is the same as learning for an exam. It is not so, and it will not work with God. We must go through the experiences with God, as He trains and teaches us. We must grow in our faith in order to advance.

In Psalm 119:6 we read: "Teach me good judgment and knowledge: for I have believed thy commandments." This is an interesting Scripture. The Psalmist realizes that just learning the commandments of God, which is wisdom, does not guarantee that he will have good judgment and knowledge. Knowledge is more than facts. Good judgment is more than facts. Knowledge is God's revelation of how things fit together into a whole. He breathes life into facts. Good judgment comes from His blessing us with it. It does not come from learning sentences and words. To get these two things, we must have an impartation of a spirit. This is so critical for us to understand. We will never get it just from reading the Scriptures without interacting personally with God as we read, meditate on the *logos*, and ask for knowledge.

God wants us to apply our heart to gaining knowledge (not vain knowledge). That means that we have to be taught by Him. We have to be spiritual children, and we have to allow our Father to instruct us. Proverbs 22:17 illustrates this process: "Bow down thine ear, and hear the words of the wise, and apply thine heart unto my knowledge." God is commanding us to apply our heart to the gaining of His knowledge. We note that God wants this knowledge in our mind of the heart and not just in the mind of the soul. When it is in the heart, it is a part of who we are before Him.

In 2 Chronicles 1:10 we read: "Give me now wisdom and knowledge, that I may go out and come in before this people: for who can judge this thy people, *that is so* great?" Solomon is asking for both wisdom (skilled use of the mind) and knowledge (understanding of God). In this passage we see a contrast between wisdom (also good judgment) and knowledge. We also see that knowledge is more than just learning a list of facts. God has to give it to us. It is not part of the world system or of the natural education process. We also see that we can ask God to give us these spirits. We may not manifest them or be given them until we have grown within the inner man, but God wants to be able to give good gifts to His children. We see below how we must ask God for knowledge.

We must highly esteem and avidly seek knowledge to be given it.

In Proverbs 2:3-7 we read: "Yea, if thou criest after knowledge, *and* liftest up thy voice for understanding; If thou seekest her as silver, and searchest for her as *for* hid treasures; Then shalt thou understand the fear of the LORD, and find the knowledge of God. For the LORD giveth wisdom: out of his mouth *cometh* knowledge and understanding. He layeth up sound wisdom for the righteous: *he is* a buckler to them that walk uprightly." Here we are told how to seek knowledge from God. We must cry out for it long and loudly, and we must seek as if after silver and hidden treasure. It is the Lord who gives wisdom, understanding, and knowledge. He keeps sound wisdom for the righteous. We are not going to have it fall into our laps; we must invest considerable time and energy. In Proverbs 8:10 we read: "Receive my instruction, and not silver; and knowledge rather than choice gold." Here God is telling us how we must value knowledge that He gives to us. We can do this only when we are living following the Spirit and when we are intensely involved in the new walk.

The Apostle Paul sought after knowledge in Philippians 3:8: "Yea doubtless, and I count all things *but* loss for the excellency of the knowledge of Christ Jesus my Lord: for whom I have suffered the loss of all things, and do count them *but* dung, that I may win Christ." The apostle Paul is talking about the worth of knowing the Lord Jesus.

Vain knowledge

Vain knowledge is knowledge that is not from God. It is called worldly knowledge. The Hebrew word translated "vain" means "empty." Scriptural examples are abundant. Some that are worth considering are: Isaiah 45:20, Job 15:2, 2 and 2 Timothy 3:7-8.

We see the disastrous effects of vain knowledge in Isaiah 5:13, where we read: "Therefore my people are gone into captivity, because *they have* no knowledge: and their honourable men *are* famished, and their multitude dried up with thirst." Here we see the impact on a people of the lack of true knowledge. It is disastrous. The people thirst for knowledge but do not have it; as a result, God gives a physical counterpart to illustrate the spiritual lack. It is very important to look at the physical realm, because it highlights what is happening in the spiritual realm. It must be this way, for otherwise one would have things in the natural that are not in the spiritual. There must be this similarity in the natural to what is happening in the spiritual realm in order for us to learn about the spiritual. God points out in Romans 1 that we should be able to see Him and to understand some aspects about His character by looking at the stars and constellations in the heavens.

In Romans 10:2 we read: "For I bear them record that they have a zeal of God, but not according to knowledge." This refers to the non-believing Israelites who try to establish a works approach to God. They do have zeal for God but do not look at the truth.

True knowledge can include acquisition of vain knowledge.

Knowledge in one's career mixes vain and true knowledge. God wants us to understand vain knowledge in order to live in the world and interact with those who live by it. In this sense we learn vain knowledge bounded by truth—knowing what is vain and what is true.

We see this with Daniel and his friends. In Daniel 1:4 we read: "Children in whom *was* no blemish, but well favoured, and skilful in all wisdom, and cunning in knowledge, and understanding science, and such as *had* ability in them to stand in the king's palace, and whom they might teach the learning and the tongue of the Chaldeans." These types of children were sought out by the king. In Daniel 1:17 we read: "As for these four children, God gave them knowledge and skill in all learning and wisdom: and Daniel had understanding in all visions and dreams." It is important to note that God wanted these children in the king's service; and, therefore, He equipped them for the work by giving them knowledge and skill in all learning (both vain and non-vain) and in all wisdom (non-vain). Thus, we can see that for His purposes God will encourage wisdom in worldly disciplines. The true study of science, if left only at the observational realm, would be consistent with non-vain knowledge. The key here is that God wanted these young men for a purpose. We all have a purpose before God, and we need to come to an understanding of what our purpose is. As we fulfill His purpose, we will feel more completed within our spirit. Life will be much more meaningful and can be lived more fully. This Scripture about how God gave Daniel and his friends wisdom in vain knowledge is a good example of and is consistent with Titus 1:15.

We can look again at the way this works out in a scientist who does not adhere to the theory of evolution, still understanding his colleagues who may believe it. This scientist is able to see the whole situation with the world system and, thus, can help his colleagues by gently nudging them into being confronted with truth. Such occurs with debates between creationists and evolutionists. To get into the debate at all, the creationist must be credible within the relevant science.

How do we learn from wise men?

In 1 Corinthians 14:6 we read: “Now, brethren, if I come unto you speaking with tongues, what shall I profit you, except I shall speak to you either by revelation, or by knowledge, or by prophesying, or by doctrine?” Here we see that there are four ways that Paul could impart information to another person. These are:

a) revelation, which is current illumination in the spirit
b) knowledge, which is observed truth either by past revelation or accurate observation of the natural or spiritual realms as taught by God
c) prophecy, which is the revealing to the prophet of the heart of the Lord Jesus
d) doctrine, which is learned and synthesized understanding based on true wisdom and knowledge

Paul makes it clear that all of these methods of instruction or impartation are profitable. We then need to meditate on the things that wise men tell us in order that our heart and inner man can be changed.

Some benefits of knowledge

In 2 Peter 1:2 we read: "Grace and peace be multiplied unto you through the knowledge of God, and of Jesus our Lord." Here we see that knowing God gives us grace and peace. We cannot have peace without some knowledge of God. The greater our knowledge, the more likely peace will reside in our heart.

In 2 Peter 1:5-10 we read: "And beside this, giving all diligence, add to your faith virtue; and to virtue knowledge; And to knowledge temperance; and to temperance patience; and to patience godliness; And to godliness brotherly kindness; and to brotherly kindness charity. For if these things be in you, and abound, they make *you that ye shall* neither *be* barren nor unfruitful in the knowledge of our Lord Jesus Christ. But he that lacketh these things is blind, and cannot see afar off, and hath forgotten that he was purged from his old sins. Wherefore the rather, brethren, give diligence to make your calling and election sure: for if ye do these things, ye shall never fall." Here we see that (true) knowledge is a step in the path to fruitfulness in our walk with the Lord.

Where does knowledge reside?

Wisdom and knowledge reside in the heart (Ecclesiastes 1:16).

After knowledge, what?

In 1 Corinthians 13:8 we read: "Charity never faileth: but whether *there be* prophecies, they shall fail; whether *there be* tongues, they shall cease; whether *there be* knowledge, it shall vanish away." Here we are told that revelatory knowledge will not be necessary when the Lord reigns on the earth (v. 10). At that point perfect knowledge will be available by observation.

Ephesians 3:19 tells us that the love of God is beyond knowledge: "And to know the love of Christ, which passeth knowledge, that ye might be filled with all the fulness of God." This love has to be experienced; it cannot be described. Language cannot encompass it. This is a good example of how the natural world is subject to and less than the spiritual world. We must carefully note that this is a prayer that the apostle Paul prayed for all believers. Note that to know the love of Christ is a prerequisite to being filled with all the fullness of God. In Philippians 1:9-10 we read: "And this I pray, that your love may abound yet more and more in knowledge and *in* all judgment; That ye may approve things that are excellent; that ye may be sincere and without offence till the day of Christ." In this passage we see that love should govern the use of knowledge and judgment. This is consistent with 1 Corinthians 13.

What is the age of accountability regarding knowledge?

In Leviticus 4:27-28 we read: "And if any one of the common people sin through ignorance, while he doeth *somewhat against* any of the commandments of the LORD *concerning things* which ought not to be done, and be guilty; Or if his sin, which he hath sinned, come to his knowledge: then he shall bring his offering, a kid of the goats, a female without blemish, for his sin which he hath sinned." God tells us that (under the Old Covenant system) if someone sins out of ignorance, he is still guilty; and, when the issue comes to mind, then a sacrifice is necessary. 1 John 1:9 gives us the instructions for the New Covenant: "If we confess our sins, he is faithful and just to forgive us *our* sins, and to cleanse us from all unrighteousness." God tells us to confess those sins of which we are aware; when we do, He will cleanse us from all of our sins that we have not remembered.

Deuteronomy 1:39 instructs: "Moreover your little ones, which ye said should be a prey, and your children, which in that day had no knowledge between good and evil, they shall go in thither, and unto them will I give it, and they shall possess it." Here God is telling us that there is an age at which He begins to hold people accountable. These children had no knowledge of good and evil when an earlier decision was made. These children at some age will have this knowledge and be accountable. We see David telling us that, when he died, he would go to be with the child Bathsheba bore (2 Samuel 12:23). This baby was in Paradise, because God did not hold him accountable at that age. We do not know exactly at what age God starts to hold a child accountable, but we should always err on the side of safety. The age may be different for each individual, according to his circumstances.

Miscellaneous Scriptures about knowledge

It is useful to study the following Scriptures on knowledge:

Job 33:2-3 shows us that the heart is able to express knowledge which means that memory flows out of the heart to the mind of the soul to give rise to speech.

In 2 Corinthians 4:6 we see that when we get the Holy Spirit in our hearts at the second birth, we have the light of the knowledge of the glory of God in the face of Jesus Christ shining in our hearts.

2 Corinthians 10:5 was reviewed above when we discussed thought. It also speaks about knowledge.

In Proverbs 12:23 we read: "A prudent man concealeth knowledge: but the heart of fools proclaimeth foolishness." A prudent man will be one of few words; he will be observing spiritually and discerning. He will wait until God's timing to initiate a conversation in which he imparts knowledge. A foolish man knows none of these things and will prattle. We see this also in Proverbs 17:27 where we read: "He that hath knowledge spareth his words: *and* a man of understanding is of an excellent spirit."

In Romans 11:33 we read: "O the depth of the riches both of the wisdom and knowledge of God! how unsearchable *are* his judgments, and his ways past finding out!" Paul says it all here. We can find out His ways only by asking Him to reveal them to us.

SPECIAL TOPICS ABOUT THE MIND

We have now seen that the mind of man is comprised of four separate areas which communicate with each other—the mind of the soul, the mind of the heart, the mind of the flesh, and the mind of the inner man. In this section we will explore more about the mind of man and how it works. We will not go into any detail about the mind of the flesh, since it always opposes the mind of the spirit. Therefore, to understand the one automatically gives us understanding of the other (Galatians 5:17).

Connections between the mind and spiritual man

We see connections between the mind and the various components of the spiritual man as we study the following passages.

In Deuteronomy 28:65 and Daniel 5:20 we see the heart and mind linked in an emotional state.

Numbers 24:13 links the will and the mind.

1 Samuel 9:20 and Jeremiah 51:50 show the link between the mind and the soul.

In 1 Chronicles 28:9 we read: "And thou, Solomon my son, know thou the God of thy father, and serve him with a perfect heart and with a willing mind: for the LORD searcheth all hearts, and understandeth all the imaginations of the thoughts: if thou seek him, he will be found of thee; but if thou forsake him, he will cast thee off for ever." Here we note several concepts that God is revealing to us in this conversation between King David and his son Solomon. We note that minds can be controlled by our soul to be willing toward God. We again see the connection between the imaginations and the thoughts of the heart.

Isaiah 26:3 shows that a mind can be stayed on the Lord, resulting in perfect peace.

In Matthew 22:37 we read: "Jesus said unto him, Thou shalt love the Lord thy God with all thy heart, and with all thy soul, and with all thy mind." God commands us to love Him with all our mind. It is important to know what the phrase "all of the mind" means. We need to meditate on what this translates to in everyday activity and apply it as God gives understanding to us.

Romans 8:5 tells us: "For they that are after the flesh do mind the things of the flesh; but they that are after the Spirit the things of the Spirit." This tells us that our minds are focused on what we are following, the Spirit or the flesh. There is no other choice.

God controls what comes into our minds.

In Isaiah 65:17 we read: "For, behold, I create new heavens and a new earth: and the former shall not be remembered, nor come into mind." God controls what He allows to come into the minds of men. This includes what He allows from the environment and from the Spirit. We are responsible for how we process these things internally.

Hebrews 8:10 states: "For this *is* the covenant that I will make with the house of Israel after those days, saith the Lord; I will put my laws into their mind, and write them in their hearts: and I will be to them a God, and they shall be to me a people." The Lord places His laws in the believer's mind and on his heart. The heart and mind then can work together. It is important that the law be in both places. God obviously thinks this is necessary.

States of mind mentioned in Scripture

In Nehemiah 4:6 we read about the people having a mind to work.

In Proverbs 21:27 we read that minds can be wicked.

Luke 8:35 states that a man can be in his right mind. This is in comparison with behavior patterns. It reads: "Then they went out to see what was done; and came to Jesus, and found the man, out of whom the devils were departed, sitting at the feet of Jesus, clothed, and in his right mind: and they were afraid."

In Luke 12:29 we see that a person can be in a state of doubtful mind.

Acts 17:11 discusses readiness of mind.

In Acts 20:19 we read of humility of mind.

In Romans 1:28 we see that God gives some people over to a reprobate mind.

Romans 7:23 mentions a law of the mind.

God describes some minds as carnal. These minds are at enmity with God and cannot be subject to the law of God. “Because the carnal mind *is* enmity against God: for it is not subject to the law of God, neither indeed can be” (Romans 8:7).

Minds can be fervent (2 Corinthians 7:7), can be willing (2 Corinthians 8:12), can be ready (2 Corinthians 8:19), and can be forward (ready [2 Corinthians 9:2]).

In Philippians 2:2 we read that we should be likeminded and of one mind with the body. We see in Philippians 2:3 that we should have lowliness of mind. We learn in Philippians 2:5 that we can “let this mind be in you, which was also in Christ Jesus.”

Colossians 2:18 shows that minds can be fleshly.

2 Thessalonians 2:2 is an interesting passage: “That ye be not soon shaken in mind, or be troubled, neither by spirit, nor by word, nor by letter as from us, as that the day of Christ is at hand.” The Apostle Paul is illustrating for us that we can be shaken in mind by a spirit, by a word, or by a letter. All of these entities can shake our minds. We must grow in spirit, of course, so that we are not shaken by any of these things. This is what God is expressing to us here.

Titus 1:15 states: “Unto the pure all things *are* pure: but unto them that are defiled and unbelieving *is* nothing pure; but even their mind and conscience is defiled.” In the unbeliever the mind and the conscience are defiled. This is why both have to be renewed and cleansed after the second birth. The pure have a pure mind.

In Revelation 17:9 we read: "And here *is* the mind which hath wisdom. The seven heads are seven mountains, on which the woman sitteth." This passage defines one aspect of the wise mind, or of having wisdom. It is to be able to understand the Lord's prophetic utterances (be they words, visions, dreams, or other form of revelation). This leads us now to review the Scriptures relating to being wise and having wisdom.

Spiritual Comprehension

"And he that searcheth the hearts knoweth what *is* the mind of the Spirit, because he maketh intercession for the saints according to *the will of* God" (Romans 8:27). God searches our hearts and knows (note that He does not hear, but that he just knows) the mind of the spirit. Spiritual comprehension is like that. It does not come by puzzlement or reasoning, but it is just there and can be explored. The Spirit knows our individual needs and intercedes for us as God has willed.

Hebrews 8:10, that we looked at above under the heading "God controls what comes into our minds," is also relevant to consider under this heading.

Renewing the mind

In Romans 12:2 we read a key passage: "And be not conformed to this world: but be ye transformed by the renewing of your mind, that ye may prove what *is* that good, and acceptable, and perfect, will of God." We cannot do the will of God in any form—good, acceptable, or perfect—if we have not had our mind renewed. The renewal of the mind allows us to begin to perform God's will, which is based on discerning the will of the Holy Spirit and following His will (and not our own). Renewing of our mind transforms us and stops us being conformed to the world, including the knowledge structure of the world. 1 Corinthians 2 is very relevant for the renewing of the mind. We have to learn a new language and a new method for communicating and for receiving knowledge. We have to begin to grow in the spirit for this to occur. We must emphasize that this learning cannot occur on our timetable. We are no longer in control. This is a part of the renewing of the mind. It is exponentially greater (more in the sense of grandeur) than reading and learning different material in a traditional college or high school sense. Meditate on this before the Lord. Renewing of the mind is fundamental to following after the Lord. If we do not do it, we cannot walk after the Spirit. Renewing the mind is a conscious and planned act of submission and obedience to the Scripture that tells us how to do it. We already know that a large part of it is the constant battle to take every thought captive and to test every spirit before releasing it.

In Ephesians 4:23-24 we read: "And be renewed in the spirit of your mind; And that ye put on the new man, which after God is created in righteousness and truth holiness." Here we see that the mind has an overall spirit (power, emotion, and knowledge). It is this spirit that has to be renewed for the mind to be renewed. Therefore, we have to tackle all issues deliberately and concurrently. We need to submit to the power of the Holy Spirit in using our minds; we have to use our mind to make sure we are working toward always transmitting a spirit of love; and we have to reorganize the knowledge base we have—how we acquire it and how we impart it. This is the key to renewing the mind. It can be done only with the power of God. We have to work co-operatively with Him in the process. He will show us things to change; and, as we honestly ask, He will give us the power to implement His changes.

In 1 Peter 1:13 we read: "Wherefore gird up the loins of your mind, be sober, and hope to the end for the grace that is to be brought unto you at the revelation of Jesus Christ." The use of the phrase "loins of the mind" indicates that we have to make sure that we protect and, therefore, strengthen the mind.

Unity of mind in the believer

In Romans 12:16 we read: "*Be* of the same mind one toward another. Mind not high things, but condescend to men of low estate. Be not wise in your own conceits." Here we see that the body of the Lord Jesus (the Church) has an overall mind (also immediately below in 1 Corinthians 1:10). When one is evaluating whether a particular thought is from the Lord, this evaluation can be used as part of the testing of the spirit of that thought. If one's thought is from the Lord, then it will produce harmony in those persons in the body of believers with whom he has contact (this is similar to the test given in James 3:17-18). Do not proceed with plans that do not meet this standard. Be careful about falling into the trap that you are in an elevated spiritual mode and that the advice of others is not going to be relevant—God's Word does not tell you to seek out mature believers only. He is able to influence those around you to give the advice that He wants you to get. Consider, before being high minded, that God is able to make stones cry out and is certainly able to bring those of less spiritual maturity into feeling harmony with you on any desire He has given to you. The being "of the same mind one toward another" is a work of God and not of man (also see Romans 15:6). We need each other in the body. Disregard the earthly status of a believer when evaluating their advice. It is of no consequence in determining the spiritual insight and authority he may have.

In 1 Corinthians 1:10 we read: "Now I beseech you, brethren, by the name of our Lord Jesus Christ, that ye all speak the same thing, and *that* there be no divisions among you; but *that* ye be perfectly joined together in the same mind and in the same judgment." This further speaks of being of one mind in the body. This is a very important check for anyone before proceeding with significant change in his life. The Spirit will never lead one into controversy and conflict with others. If there is disagreement, then he may need to go before elders to sort it out; but this must be done in love. In this verse Paul was writing about contentions regarding whom to follow in doctrine. The passage in James 3:17 shows the same issues for personal decisions. The "go-it-alone" believer is very immature, not discerning the need for the body. As we know the Lord better, we cannot do other than hold the body in great respect.

In Philippians 1:27 we read: "Only let your conversation be as it becometh the gospel of Christ: that whether I come and see you, or else be absent, I may hear of your affairs, that ye stand fast in one spirit, with one mind striving together for the faith of the gospel." The body has to have one spirit and one mind. We can have one mind and independent spirits or one spirit with different minds. We need both one spirit and one mind in the body of Christ to keep the faith of the gospel.

Paul instructs in Philippians 4:2: "I beseech Euodias, and beseech Syntyche, that they be of the same mind in the Lord." It is enough to beseech people that they need to be in the same mind in the Lord. In some issue, such as choice of color for a drape in the home, there may not have to be agreement; but in anything (and this is virtually everything) that pertains to the things of the Lord, we need to be in one mind. Even in the choice of color for a drape the Lord will give you His opinion, if you seek it without wavering, as in James 1.

Minds are to be fully persauded for faith.

In Romans 14:5 we read: "One man esteemeth one day above another: another esteemeth every day *alike*. Let every man be fully persuaded in his own mind." In terms of our following the Spirit, we need to be fully (fully, completely, beyond doubt) persuaded in our own mind that a certain action is God's will for us. He has His body to be all things to all people. Therefore, expect great diversity of behavior and thought about things that are not central to the faith. Sometimes this is also because of differences in spiritual insight (Romans 14 and 15:1-4). Sometimes it is because God calls everyone to a particular work at a particular time. Every tree will bear fruit in its season. The point is that we should never act without faith. Faith is being **fully** persuaded of some future occurrence based on what God has said. It is the substance of things hoped for (Hebrews 11:1). Without faith we can never please God (Hebrews 11:6).

The mind of Christ

In 1 Corinthians 2:16 we read: "For who hath known the mind of the Lord, that he may instruct him? But we have the mind of Christ."

We have the ability to go to the Lord when we lack wisdom and ask Him for advice and for His desire. This will give us His mind on a particular issue. As we grow in the spirit, we understand the deep things of the Lord better; and from this point of view we can begin to think as He does. This is limited in that we are far inferior to Him in ability and His thoughts are far above ours, but to a degree we can grow closer.

1 Peter 4:1 tells us: "Forasmuch then as Christ hath suffered for us in the flesh, arm yourselves likewise with the same mind: for he that hath suffered in the flesh hath ceased from sin." We see that we can choose to make the same decisions that the Lord made. In this respect we are like-minded with Him.

Fallen minds

In Ephesians 2:3 we read: "Among whom also we all had our conversation in times past in the lusts of our flesh, fulfilling the desires of the flesh and of the mind; and were by nature the children of wrath, even as others." God has set up a law that we will fulfill the desires of our mind and of our flesh before salvation and before the renewing of our minds after the second birth. After we renew our mind and meet the conditions in Isaiah 58 and Psalm 37:4, then we are led by the desires of our heart but not our mind. We have a lot of changing to do before this occurs. Prior to that we may like something and misapply that as a desire of the heart, when really it is a desire of the "fleshly" mind. This passage also shows that our mind can have desires independent of the heart, until the mind is renewed and the heart is purified. Gentiles, prior to salvation and prior to renewing the mind, walk in the vanity of their mind (not their heart [Ephesians 4:17]).

Colossians 1:21 tells us the state of the mind in the unbeliever: "And you, that were sometime alienated and enemies in *your* mind by wicked works, yet now hath he reconciled." Note that the works lead the mind. The flesh. heart, and spirit set the pace; and the mind follows in the unbeliever.

We discussed Titus 1:15 on page 320. This passage also shows the condition of the mind and conscience of the unregenerate man.

SUMMARY

We have reviewed the mind as presented in the Scriptures. We have done this in great detail; and, in doing so, we need to make sure that we do not lose the overall view. The mind, as used in those who have been through the second birth, has the main purpose of preparing the inner man for eternity with the Lord God.

Therefore, the mind must learn to communicate with God through the inner man and through the environment. The major way is through the inner man. We want to plant good seed into the Kingdom of God. Our mind has to be renewed; it has to worship God in its entirety; and it must increase in the wisdom, understanding, and knowledge of God. As the mind controls this process and fulfills it, the inner man is enabled to grow and mature. The mind has to work with the soul to be "in the spirit" as much as possible. In this way the inner man will develop his senses.

As we make decisions that allow all of this to occur, our heart is purified; and our inner man is cleansed. We are able to develop a very close relationship with the Lord, and He will occupy all of our senses. We will lose ourselves in Him. Indeed, the mind has a wonderful task.

It also has to relate to the world and spiritual universe under the authority of the Lord Jesus, as it learns to follow the Spirit of God. In this way we can be in the world and yet not be of it.

12
WORKINGS OF THE FLESH OF SPIRITUAL MAN

DEFINITION

When flesh is first mentioned in the Scripture in Genesis 2:21-23, it represents the physical component of our body that we can contact with our physical senses. We will use this model in this book for what *flesh* means. It contains our skeleton, our muscles, and our internal and external organs. It is encased by and includes our skin. The heart and blood vessels are also flesh, as is our anatomical brain. (There is a spiritual heart, mentioned in the Scriptures and which we have already studied extensively in Chapter 10, which is not the heart of the flesh.) Our mind is not of the flesh but is based in the brain and nervous system. The flesh can influence the mind to be "fleshly," as we will see. In this chapter we shall now examine the interactions of the flesh with the other spiritual components of man, with other spiritual beings, and with other men. It is important to note 1 Corinthians 15:39: "All flesh *is* not the same flesh: but *there is* one *kind of* flesh of men, another flesh of beasts, another of fishes, *and* another of birds."

WORKS OF THE FLESH

Galatians 5:19-21 explains the works of the flesh: "Now the works of the flesh are manifest, which are *these*; [a]dultery, fornication, uncleanness, lasciviousness, [i]dolatry, witchcraft, hatred, variance, emulations, wrath, strife, seditions, heresies, [e]nvyings, murders, drunkenness, revellings, and such like: of the which I tell you before, as I have also told *you* in time past, that they which do such things shall not inherit the kingdom of God." When we examine the power, emotion (including motivation), and intellectual structure behind any thought, belief, attitude, or work and find even a small amount of one of these characteristic fruits in it, we must not perform it. A little bad mixed with a lot of good is not acceptable to God. Paul shows this clearly in 1 Corinthians 5:6-8. Leaven in the Scriptures always represents sin. We must be pure and holy, even as He is. Galatians 5:19-21 is a key Scripture to use when learning to walk after the Spirit. The Spirit will never initiate anything that has any of these characteristics. We must recall the Lord Jesus' definition of adultery, idolatry, murder, witchcraft, and so on; for His standards are a lot higher than ours. We must walk by His standards, not those of men. The Lord Jesus says that if we lust even in our heart—God considers this as adultery (Matthew 5:28). Therefore, we must examine our planned release of all spirit to prevent releasing any work of the flesh inadvertently.

THE THREE SOURCES OF SIN

John tells us that sin is due to three different entities—lust of the flesh, lust of the eyes, and pride of life in 1 John 2:16-17: "For all that *is* in the world, the lust of the flesh, and the lust of the eyes, and the pride of life, is not of the Father, but is of the world. And the world passeth away, and the lust thereof: but he that doeth the will of God abideth for ever." Pride of life and lust of the eyes are different from lusts of the flesh. Pride arises in the soul in response to a success (or desire for a future success) of the flesh. It is, in that regard, closely linked to the flesh. "Lust of the eyes" refers to desires that originate from our seeing something that is attractive to our flesh. Frequently, all three sources combine together, as we see in the Garden of Eden in Genesis 3:4-7: "And the serpent said unto the woman, Ye shall not surely die: For God doth know that in the day ye eat thereof, then your eyes shall be opened, and ye shall be as gods, knowing good and evil. And when the woman saw that the tree *was* good for food, and that it *was* pleasant to the eyes, and a tree to be desired to make *one* wise, she took of the fruit thereof, and did eat, and gave also unto her husband with her; and he did eat." We see that the devil appealed to pride (ye shall be as gods). Eve saw that the tree was good for food (lust of the flesh), was pleasant to the eyes (lust of the eyes), and that it would make one wise (pride). The things that the eyes see are not necessarily evil, but our thoughts after seeing them can be evil. The will of the flesh is always evil in its will.

INTERACTIONS WITH OTHER COMPONENTS OF SPIRITUAL MAN

SPIRIT

We have examined the interaction between the flesh and the spirit in Chapter 9. In this chapter we shall just review key concepts. We shall look at one passage that serves to place in context the relationship between flesh and spirit: "To deliver such an one unto Satan for the destruction of the flesh, that the spirit may be saved in the day of the Lord Jesus" (1 Corinthians 5:5). We see how powerful the flesh is to pollute even the new spirit that God gives at the second birth. This man was a believer who had been through the second birth and had received a new spirit and a new heart. He was in a bad sin pattern due to his giving way to the will of the flesh. The flesh and the spirit are always at war, even after the second birth (Galatians 5:17). The flesh is so powerful that it could even bring down this new spirit to lose eternal security, if God did not choose to deliver the spirit before this could occur. There were many at Corinth who died before their time (1 Corinthians 11:27-30), because they did not approach the communion table properly. This again shows God's mercy toward a child of His caught in a sin pattern. It also implies the doctrine of eternal security; that is, God would remove a person from the earth before letting him lose his salvation.

In 2 Corinthians 1:17 we read: "When I therefore was thus minded, did I use lightness? or the things that I purpose, do I purpose according to the flesh, that with me there should be yea yea, and nay nay?" The apostle Paul tells us that he has a choice between the will of the flesh and the will of the soul (that is influenced by the spirit and the flesh).

We are again reminded in Galatians 5:17 that, in terms of leading a soul, the spirit and the flesh are always (without exception) contrary (diametrically opposed): "For the flesh lusteth against the Spirit, and the Spirit against the flesh: and these are contrary the one to the other: so that ye cannot do the things that ye would." Therefore, we should look to see whether any planned act, thought, or word portrays any of the fruit of the flesh, as described in Galatians 5:19-21, or any characteristics discussed in 1 John 2:16-17—pride, lust of the flesh, or lust of the eyes. If it does, it will not be acceptable to God. We have to look for evidence of wisdom from above as discussed in James 3:17. If we find wisdom from above regarding the planned act, no hint of the three sin areas, and none of the lusts of the flesh, then it is safe to walk in this plan.

SOUL

Location of the soul

Note that the soul is contained within the flesh. Job 14:22 states: "But his flesh upon him shall have pain, and his soul within him shall mourn." The soul is formed by the spirit's being breathed into flesh (Genesis 2:7). The soul may or may not completely take up all the physical volume of the flesh. However, this would indicate to us that the soul does not exceed the boundary of the physical flesh. This does not mean the inner man is confined within the flesh.

God expects the soul to rule the flesh.

In Romans 6:19 we read: "I speak after the manner of men because of the infirmity of your flesh: for as ye have yielded your members servants to uncleanness and to iniquity unto iniquity; even so now yield your members servants to righteousness unto holiness." We see that God expects us to choose what we want (or allow) our flesh to do. The will may need to be strengthened by God's releasing power to us in the inner man. We need to ask Him for this.

Galatians 6:7-8 amplifies this: "Be not deceived; God is not mocked: for whatsoever a man soweth, that shall he also reap. For he that soweth to his flesh shall of the flesh reap corruption; but he that soweth to the Spirit shall of the Spirit reap life everlasting." The soul must choose either to do a work in obedience to the Holy Spirit or to do a work that builds up the flesh. There is no in-between ground. We are moment by moment sowing either to the flesh to build it up or to the inner man to build him up.

Actions in the soul cause reactions in the flesh, and vice versa.

In Proverbs 11:17 we read: "The merciful man doeth good to his own soul: but *he that is* cruel troubleth his own flesh." We see the impact on the flesh of a soul that allows himself to be cruel. Likewise, in Proverbs 14:30 we read that envy in a soul leads to rottenness in the bones.

Ecclesiastes 12:12 speaks of a secular form of gaining knowledge: "And further, by these, my son, be admonished: of making many books *there is* no end; and much study *is* a weariness of the flesh." God, when He teaches by impartation of revelation, does not cause fatigue.

The Lord tells us that we judge after the leading of the flesh in John 8:15: "Ye judge after the flesh; I judge no man." We, as people, are almost constantly evaluating and judging others; and, as we do, it is according to our physical perceptions. On the other hand, Jesus contrasts Himself with us in that He does not judge, since the Father reveals things to Him and since He always follows the Father's will. Since He is always obedient, He does not need to judge, since God the Father does the judging and reveals truth to the Lord Jesus. In following revealed truth, we do not need to make any judgment. It is only when we rely on imperfect information from natural sources with natural perception of natural events that we need to be evaluative and form a judgment.

In Romans 7:5, 7:18, and 7:25 we read: "For when we were in the flesh, the motions of sins, which were by the law, did work in our members to bring forth fruit unto death.... For I know that in me (that is, in my flesh,) dwelleth no good thing: for to will is present with me; but *how* to perform that which is good I find not.... I thank God through Jesus Christ our Lord. So then with the mind I myself serve the law of God; but with the flesh the law of sin." These passages show that there is nothing good in the flesh in that it always, left to itself, serves the law of sin and brings forth fruit unto death. However, after the second birth the new spirit is able to war against and overcome the flesh. The flesh can be made to serve righteousness, as we saw above in Romans 6:19. This does not make the flesh righteous.

We must take care that we are not giving way to the flesh in these areas, as 2 Peter 2:10 admonishes: "But chiefly them that walk after the flesh in the lust of uncleanness, and despise government. Presumptuous *are they*, selfwilled, they are not afraid to speak evil of dignities."

Discerning whether we are following the Spirit of God or the flesh

After the second birth we have only two choices in any planned action—to follow the Spirit of God or to follow the flesh. Romans 8:3-5 explains this: "For what the law could not do, in that it was weak through the flesh, God sending his own Son in the likeness of sinful flesh, and for sin, condemned sin in the flesh: That the righteousness of the law might be fulfilled in us, who walk not after the flesh, but after the Spirit. For they that are after the flesh do mind the things of the flesh; but they that are after the Spirit the things of the Spirit."

It is the weakness of the flesh that causes men not to be able to keep God's law. God is able to enable us to fulfill the righteousness of the law, when we accept Jesus as our Lord and Savior. He then gives us a new spirit and a new heart that allow us to walk after His Spirit and not after the flesh. We do not do it perfectly; but if we yield to His Lordship, we will search for and wait on His will. As we practice doing these things and putting to death the lusts of the flesh on a moment-by-moment basis with His help, then we can be of value to His causes. This word again shows that our soul has to make choices moment by moment. We can determine which way we are walking by looking to see where our gaze is. Are we looking at and contemplating fleshly things, or are we contemplating spiritual things? When we are focusing our attention on the spirit (not just thinking about it in the mind but discerning it for information), then we are in the spirit.

How do we walk after the Spirit of God and not after the flesh?

In Galatians 5:16 Paul reminds us to walk in the Spirit and then we will not fulfill the lust of the flesh. He adds in Romans 13:14 we read: "But put ye on the Lord Jesus Christ, and make not provision for the flesh, to *fulfil* the lusts *thereof*." Our soul is commanded to clothe ourselves with the Lord Jesus in order not to make any provision for the flesh. It is, therefore, very important, if we are to walk after the Spirit of God, to do this. Therefore, we must learn how to do it and then ask God to give us power to do it. "Put ye on" in the original language is "sink into a garment." We must be so emptied of self and "sunk" into Jesus that He is showing through us in mind, attitude, emotion, and belief. Only He can transition us to this state as we yield ourselves to Him in utter and complete obedience.

Results of walking in the Spirit of God and not in the flesh

Galatians 4:29 tells us to expect persecution: "But as then he that was born after the flesh persecuted him *that was born* after the Spirit, even so *it is* now." The people who have not been through the second birth will persecute those who have. This follows, since the flesh is always at enmity with the spirit. The persecution may not be overt; but powers of darkness will act on bad thoughts (prayers) entertained by people. Persecution may also result from the powers of darkness stirring up the flesh of people who have not been through the second birth. The person who has not been through the second birth is governed by the lusts and will of the flesh. The flesh in that soul will war against the perception of a different spirit in someone who has been through the second birth.

Colossians 1:24 also addresses afflictions: "Who now rejoice in my sufferings for you, and fill up that which is behind of the afflictions of Christ in my flesh for his body's sake, which is the church." The meaning of this is unclear, but it probably means that we can expect to suffer in our flesh for the sake of the Church.

Galatians 5:24 states: "And they that are Christ's have crucified the flesh with the affections and lusts." After we have gone through the second birth (Romans 6:1-13), then we have a position in the Lord that renders our flesh dead. This is a legal position that the Lord Jesus obtained for us. Therefore, those who are in the Lord have crucified the affections and lusts of the flesh legally, but experientially they need to continue to do it on a moment-by-moment basis. We are symbolically baptized into the likeness of His death (Romans 6:1-13).

Paul affirms no soul ever hated his flesh in Ephesians 5:28-29: "So ought men to love their wives as their own bodies. He that loveth his wife loveth himself. For no man ever yet hated his own flesh; but nourisheth and cherisheth it, even as the Lord the church." We have to put it to death moment by moment, but we do not hate it. If we did, then by definition we would hate our spouse because the two become one flesh. We do have to cooperate with our spouse to put to death the will of the combined flesh.

In Philippians 3:3 we see an important truth: "For we are the circumcision, which worship God in the spirit, and rejoice in Christ Jesus, and have no confidence in the flesh." Our attitude toward the flesh must be to have no confidence in it—**never, ever**.

We have to come to an experiential understanding deep in our heart and spirit that we no longer have sin in our spirit. This is what being saved is. Hebrews 10:16-20 explains: "This *is* the covenant that I will make with them after those days, saith the Lord, I will put my laws into their hearts, and in their minds will I write them; And their sins and iniquities will I remember no more. Now where remission of these *is, there is* no more offering for sin. Having therefore, brethren, boldness to enter into the holiest by the blood of Jesus, By a new and living way, which he hath consecrated for us, through the veil, that is to say, his flesh." We have been given a new spirit at the second birth. Our flesh will continue to sin, but our spirit will not. This is the profound truth of the second birth. Our spirit is holy. We are told that God will put His laws into our hearts and minds. His laws supersede and exceed the laws of the Old Covenant. Praise God that we are no longer in need of this Old Covenant law! His law under the New Covenant is that to which Paul refers in Romans 7:22-25. It exceeds the Old Covenant law. It is the law of love. We have to focus on learning a whole new set of laws of the Spirit under the New Covenant. God at the time of Jesus' death stopped remembering the sins and iniquities of all who were the elect at that time and for all future time. The difference in the forgiveness of sins before and after the cross is seen clearly by looking at two verses, Romans 3:25 and Hebrews 9:15. In Hebrews 9:15 the author refers to the "redemption of the transgressions that were under the first testament." The Greek word for redemption is *apolutrosis*, which means "to put aside." In Romans 3:25 Paul refers to "the remission of sins" for the present age. The Greek word for remission is *aphesis*, which means "put away." The concept is that Old Testament saints had their sins put down, but they could not be permanently removed until the Lord Jesus actually died on the cross. After this the sins could be put away totally. This also explains why the animal sacrifice of the Old Covenant did not remove the awareness of a sin state within the spirit; but now a soul can have freedom from such awareness, when he receives a new spirit.

False Spirituality

In Colossians 2:20-23 we read: "Wherefore if ye be dead with Christ from the rudiments of the world, why, as though living in the world, are ye subject to ordinances, (Touch not; taste not; handle not; Which all are to perish with the using;) after the commandments and doctrines of men? Which things have indeed a shew of wisdom in will worship, and humility, and neglecting of the body; not in any honour to the satisfying of the flesh." These are the kind of things that are really a work of the flesh in trying to put to death the flesh. It is false and produces only pride as the fruit. Paul calls it "will" worship. We must remember that we are to follow the Spirit and we cannot **ever, ever, ever** have a rule about anything. The issue is that we are supposed to be walking after the leading of the Spirit of God. The Spirit of God will never lead us into sin. The problem is that most of the time we are led by our mind. It has a stored set of rules, and it is easier for us to use these rules than to consult the Lord on each issue. We have to learn to discern how to follow His Spirit. It does not come automatically or as easily as following a rule. The problem is that most situations to which we are exposed could have a number of alternative behaviors that would be defensible by various Scriptures, but only the Spirit of the Lord can guide us to the desired behavior. It is a little akin to being in the "good, acceptable, and perfect will" of God (Romans 12:2). Each is all right, but God looks on some more favorably than others. A test is whether we are free to do something or whether we feel that we should not because of a rule. The Lord came to fulfill the requirements of the law and also told us that none of it would pass away. He told us that our righteousness had to exceed it. It does in the Lord, when we follow His Spirit by sensing His leading as opposed to using our mind to interpret something written in the Scriptures. He will never violate His written Word; but we may be prone through lack of understanding, not to comprehend properly the hierarchy of the Word (2 Timothy 2:15) as it applies to a given situation which requires a decision. An example of particular situations in which the Scriptures cannot lead us would be the issue of which new car to buy or whom we should visit when we have some free time. If we are going to perform the perfect will of God in these issues (as opposed to the good or acceptable will), then we must learn to follow the Spirit. When learning to follow the Spirit, we must make sure that our actions will not violate the New Covenant, since we are now under it. We have to remember that the purpose of the law was to show us that we could not keep it. Therefore, we should not try to keep it now, when the Lord has replaced it with something far superior, His Spirit in us. Will worship only strengthens the flesh. When we do will worship, we are serving an Old Covenant that had a law that we could not fulfill. Why would we want to go back partially under this law? The reason is that it is a sacrifice, and this is easier for our flesh than obedience is. Remember that God is not pleased with sacrifice of this nature, but He is pleased by our obedience. There are some sacrifices with which God is pleased in the New Covenant such as praise and a humble and contrite spirit (inner man). These New Covenant sacrifices result only from obedience to the Spirit of God.

HEART

We have examined the interaction between the heart and the flesh in Chapter 10. In this chapter we shall just review key concepts. The most important is that the flesh is always influencing the heart. The lusts of the flesh, if not opposed by the spirit, mold and form the attitudes of the heart. The flesh, if we sow to it, forms its fruit within the heart. It is out of the heart that the fruits of the flesh (Galatians 5:19-21 and Matthew 15:18-19) proceed. Thus, the flesh, if not opposed, would form all of the molding and shaping of the content of the heart. It causes high things and imaginations to be built up. These are the things that we have to destroy later in order to purify the heart. These things that the soul allows the flesh to form within the heart join together with what the soul allows the spirit to form within the heart to become what our heart is before the Lord (which is who we are to the Lord [Proverbs 27:19]). All of the impact of the flesh on the heart is mediated by the soul's allowing things to be sown to the heart from the flesh, rather than from the Spirit of God, as witnessed to by the inner man.

MIND

In Ephesians 2:3 we read: "Among whom also we all had our conversation in times past in the lusts of our flesh, fulfilling the desires of the flesh and of the mind; and were by nature the children of wrath, even as others." We see that the mind is not considered to be a part of the flesh (although a mind can be described as fleshly if it is led by the flesh). The flesh and the mind have separate desires. It is because the mind is not part of the flesh that it can be renewed. The flesh cannot be renewed; after the second birth it is dead.

One of the major principles for people who are trying to be led by the Spirit of God to learn is that the mind and the inner man are entirely different. Many try to be led by their thoughts, and these people will end up shipwrecked. Daniel 7:15 clearly shows this. If we are to be led by the Spirit of God, we have to learn to listen to our inner man and to stop following our thoughts. This takes time and much practice, but it leads to the result described in Hebrews 4:12.

CONSCIENCE

There are no Scriptures that demonstrate a direct link between conscience and flesh. All of the impact of the flesh on the conscience is mediated through the soul. We shall study this in Chapter 14.

WILL

John 1:12-13 is an incredible passage: "But as many as received him, to them gave he power to become the sons of God, *even* to them that believe on his name: Which were born, not of blood, nor of the will of the flesh, nor of the will of man, but of God." God gives power (note that it requires an investment of spiritual energy) to sinful men to become sons of His. We can infer that He does it because of His love for us (John 3:16). This means that God gives His spirit to those who believe on the name of Jesus. The passage then tells us that these individuals are born not of blood, nor the will of the flesh, nor the will of man. These three entities can give birth to spirit (not the new spirit or the Holy Spirit). The flesh can regenerate spirit through giving birth to children which can be due to the will (lust) of the flesh or a decision of the soul (will of man). The interesting part of the passage to note is that blood can transfer spirit. This is probably the best argument that spirit circulates in the blood. We have discussed this in Chapter 10 and review it later in this chapter. In addition, the Scripture teaches that the flesh and the soul have separate wills. Therefore, there are a will in the flesh and a will in the soul.

INTERACTIONS WITH OTHER PEOPLE, WITH OTHER SPIRITS, AND WITH GOD

INTERACTIONS WITH OTHER MEN

Our flesh constantly interacts with other people (flesh) both through the physical senses (sight, sound, touch, taste, pain, position, and smell) and through the inner man's sensing the emanation of spirit from another person. There is a dual communication between people—the natural and the supernatural. Both are operating constantly, as we interact with another person. We will accept as a given that natural interaction occurs. 1 Corinthians 5:3 shows that there is always a supernatural aspect to communications. In 1 Corinthians 2:15 we read: "But he that is spiritual judgeth all things, yet he himself is judged of no man." This is referring to the inner man. When our soul discerns the mind of the inner man, we can discern all things. 1 Corinthians 2:14-16 amplifies this in context. Thus, the Scripture witnesses to a constant spiritual communication that allows us to interact at this level with the inner man of other people. We have to learn to discern spiritually, and it is possible to perform this discernment only after our heart has been purified and our soul has been separated (Hebrews 4:12) following the second birth.

This dual natural and spiritual communication causes many of our interpersonal relationship problems. When we do not understand this dualistic process, we still intuitively receive what we may term "subliminal messages" (or other similar terminology) in all of our interpersonal communications. This is the spirit sensing the spirit of the message. Some people are more skilled in receiving these communications from the spirit than others. Communication problems result when the spoken words do not match the spirit in the message—such as when deceit is intended. In general, the more one uses the mind to analyze issues, the less skilled he will be at receiving and dealing with the whole spirit in the communication. It will still be received by his spirit, but it may be suppressed from the mind. Modern psychological studies support this dualism in communications—identifying an agenda and a hidden agenda.

INTERACTIONS WITH EVIL AND ANGELIC SPIRITS

In Job 4:15 we read: "Then a spirit passed before my face; the hair of my flesh stood up." This shows the impact of an angel on Eliphaz's flesh. Of course, there had to be a chain of spiritual communication within Eliphaz from the physical perception leading to the mind of the flesh and then into the heart and spirit. This inward flow produced a response back from the heart to the flesh with the physical manifestation of hair standing up.

A very important Scripture is Ephesians 6:12: "For we wrestle not against flesh and blood, but against principalities, against powers, against the rulers of the darkness of this world, against spiritual wickedness in high *places*." We must keep this in mind when we are confronted with evil actions by another soul. We have to use the spiritual weapons that God has provided and not weapons of the flesh.

INTERACTIONS WITH GOD

The following Scriptures, showing various interactions with God, are set forth in the order in which they are found in the Scriptures.

Genesis 2:24 shows that God has ordained for marriage to join the flesh of two individuals together to become one flesh. This is a spiritual concept that is very important for us to recall and to understand. It is very important in terms of what sin patterns and demonic influence each flesh brings to the union in marriage. Those things that have not been dealt with and cleansed by God will be transmitted to offspring.

In Genesis 6:12 we see that God tells us that all flesh had corrupted His way on the earth; and, as a result, the earth was corrupted. This led God to destroy almost all people and animals in the great world-wide flood.

Genesis 9:4 states that God regards the blood as the life of the flesh. In Leviticus 17:11 we read: "For the life of the flesh *is* in the blood: and I have given it to you upon the altar to make an atonement for your souls: for it *is* the blood *that* maketh an atonement for the soul." Blood is a very important concern for God in the atoning for sin; this is why the Lord Jesus Christ had to be made a blood sacrifice. It is certainly true that life ceases when the circulation of the blood stops and that Adam became alive as the spirit was breathed into him. The spirit is the life; therefore, one can safely assume that spirit circulates in the blood within the flesh. Moreover, Scripture tells us the life of all flesh—animals, fish, birds, and man—is in the blood (Leviticus 17:14).

In Psalm 38:3 we read: "*There is* no soundness in my flesh because of thine anger; neither *is there any* rest in my bones because of my sin." Here we see that God's anger leads to illness and disease being allowed to occupy the flesh. We see in the initial part of the book of Job that God puts limits on what the devil is allowed to do to a person. God first would not allow Satan to touch Job's body; then He allowed Satan to inflict Job with illness, but He would not allow Satan to kill him. God watches very carefully over our flesh and uses it to discipline us and to form patience in us. He used Job's sufferings in the flesh for His glory.

Our soul and our flesh (although it is fallen and has no good in it so far as God is concerned) can thirst and long for God, respectively, as seen in Psalm 63:1: "O God, thou *art* my God; early will I seek thee: my soul thirsteth for thee, my flesh longeth for thee in a dry and thirsty land, where no water is."

Psalm 119:120 shows the impact of God on a soul's flesh: "My flesh trembleth for fear of Thee."

The Scriptures are health to all a soul's flesh, as we see in Proverbs 4:22: "For they [God's Words] *are* life unto those that find them, and health to all their flesh." The outward working of this is through faith and obedience. It also is subject to God's purposes for an individual at a point in time, such as with Job who knew well and kept God's Word. God is King and Lord, and His will never violates His word; but there are layers of hierarchical application of the Word that have to be understood.

All flesh will come to worship before the Lord, according to a prophecy in Isaiah 66:23. He is well able to bring this about.

In Jeremiah 32:27 we read: "Behold, I *am* the LORD, the God of all flesh: is there any thing too hard for me?" This accentuates the point made about prophecy and the ability of God to bring His word to pass. He is the God of all flesh and reigns over us, regardless of whether a soul wishes to acknowledge Him as His God.

We read of God's plans for Israel in the future in Ezekiel 11:19: "And I will give them one heart, and I will put a new spirit within you; and I will take the stony heart out of their flesh, and will give them an heart of flesh." The stony heart before the second birth will be replaced by a heart of flesh. This is used in the sense of hardness and softness toward God.

Joel 2:28 shows the impact of the Spirit of God being poured out onto all flesh (*flesh* here means "people" or "souls"): "And it shall come to pass afterward, *that* I will pour out my spirit upon all flesh; and your sons and your daughters shall prophesy, your old men shall dream dreams, your young men shall see visions."

In Matthew 16:17 we read: "And Jesus answered and said unto him, Blessed art thou, Simon Barjona: for flesh and blood hath not revealed *it* unto thee, but my Father which is in heaven." It is interesting to note that the Lord indicates that there are two sources of knowledge—"flesh and blood" or the Father in Heaven. This is in regard to a question relating to who Peter thought Jesus is. This does not limit the revelation of who Jesus is to a direct revelation from the Father with spoken voice. The Father could communicate this revelation to Peter in any number of ways. The use of the term "flesh and blood" as opposed to just "flesh" has significance since it further supports the esteem that the Lord has for blood. In our naturalistic thinking we would consider blood as tissue that is liquid in that there are living cells in it and in that it has varied and many physiological functions. However, it seems that the Lord sees us as a combination of flesh and of blood. As we have seen above, God considers that our life is in the blood. Man through the ages has regarded the life to be associated with the heart. More recently, we have focused on the brain and its role in providing "meaningful life" while it continues to function. Men certainly think differently from God, as the Scripture clearly tells us. It seems that the spirit is carried by the blood to give life to the cells.

Matthew 19:5-6 states: "And [He] said, For this cause shall a man leave father and mother, and shall cleave to his wife: and they twain shall be one flesh? Wherefore they are no more twain, but one flesh." We see that God joins two individuals together as one flesh in marriage. Both play a role in the enmity toward the individual spirits of the two individuals. This is probably, in part, why God does not want His people unequally yoked. There is no indication that the spirits merge. They do not.

In Matthew 24:22 Jesus states: "And except those days should be shortened, there should no flesh be saved: but for the elect's sake those days shall be shortened." Here Jesus is referring to God's preventing physical death of all flesh during the Great Tribulation.

Jesus admonished the disciples, as described in Matthew 26:41: "Watch and pray, that ye enter not into temptation: the spirit indeed *is* willing, but the flesh *is* weak." Here we see God telling us that the spirit can be willing but that it has to struggle against the weakness of the flesh to avoid succumbing to temptation. We know that the spirit and the flesh are always at war with each other from other Scripture (Galatians 5:17).

The resurrected Lord Jesus appears to His disciples and says: "Behold my hands and my feet, that it is I myself: handle me, and see; for a spirit hath not flesh and bones, as ye see me have" (Luke 24:39). The Lord was showing that He was physically resurrected, and had flesh and bones. He was also teaching that spirits (angels) do not have flesh and bones.

In John 1:14 we read: "And the Word was made flesh, and dwelt among us, (and we beheld his glory, the glory as of the only begotten of the Father,) full of grace and truth." Jesus was made flesh after He was already Spirit. It was the opposite in the creation of Adam. Flesh was created, and then the spirit was breathed into it. The result was a living soul and a complete human being. When we have our spirit released at death from the body of flesh, it will be placed into a new "spiritual" body and will become a soul again. We know that God knew all of us before the foundation of the world (Ephesians 1:4). God gave us life in the flesh. That was by His breathing spirit into Adam, but not the Holy Spirit. In the case of Jesus he was also born in the flesh and had His spirit transmitted from God, not from an earthly father. God subsequently gave Him His Spirit without measure (John 3:34}. A visible manifestation of the giving of the Spirit of God occurred at the baptism of Jesus by John. Note that Jesus at birth did not inherit a sinful flesh, because He was conceived by the Spirit of God, and born of a woman. It is the male that carries the sin and transmits it genetically to all offspring. The Lord in His formative years did not sin and stayed in communication with God the Father, just as Adam would have if he had not sinned. Adam talked with God in the garden and had a very close personal relationship with Him. Jesus had this close personal relationship with the Father also. Jesus was the second Adam in that they are the only two men who had sinless spirits at the time of their birth and creation respectively. Because the Lord Jesus successfully led a sinless life, the spirit in Him was approved by God to be a life-giving spirit (1 Corinthians 15:45).

Jesus explains to Nicodemus about the need for the second birth in John 3:6: “That which is born of the flesh is flesh; and that which is born of the Spirit is spirit.” He expresses a profound principle of God in His answer. This principle is also seen in the natural world. A kind reproduces itself. All philosophies are inherently spiritual in that there are a power, an emotion, and a logical structure to them. If a work is initiated by the Holy Spirit, then it will carry the emotions, power, and mind of God within it. It will produce fruit that only the Holy Spirit can produce, since a kind can reproduce only itself. On the contrary, if a work is formed within the heart of man (and not his spirit), then that work will bear fruit consistent with the origin within the flesh. If man is used by the Holy Spirit perfectly, then that work that is created will be the pure work of the Holy Spirit and will produce His fruit. Work initiated by God, but imperfectly followed by a believer, will produce rather mixed fruits that will demonstrate the mixed spiritual input into the work (impure spirit of man mixed with the Holy Spirit’s pure influence on the man).

John 6:63 explains: “It is the spirit that quickeneth; the flesh profiteth nothing: the words that I speak unto you, *they* are spirit, and *they* are life.” God is telling us we need to concentrate on following the input from the inner man, as witnessed to by the Holy Spirit, and not follow the desires (lusts) of the flesh. He is telling us that the flesh cannot save us and that the spirit of man is what will remain alive after the physical death.

In Romans 8:3-4 we read: “For what the law could not do, in that it was weak through the flesh, God sending his own Son in the likeness of sinful flesh, and for sin, condemned sin in the flesh: That the righteousness of the law might be fulfilled in us, who walk not after the flesh, but after the Spirit. For they that are after the flesh do mind the things of the flesh; but they that are after the Spirit the things of the Spirit.” It was the weakness of the flesh that caused men not to be able to keep God’s law. God empowers us to fulfill the righteousness of the law, when we accept Jesus as our Lord and Savior. At that time He gives us a new spirit and a new heart that allow us to walk after His Spirit and not after the flesh. We do not always do it perfectly; but, if we yield to His Lordship, we will search for and wait on His will. As we practice doing these things and put to death the lusts of the flesh on a moment-by-moment basis with His help, then we can be of value to His causes. This word again shows us that our soul has to make choices moment by moment.

1 Corinthians 1:26 states: "For ye see your calling, brethren, how that not many wise men after the flesh, not many mighty, not many noble, *are called.*" God chooses to call people according to the power of the flesh in an inverse manner.

2 Corinthians 12:7 tells us: "And lest I should be exalted above measure through the abundance of the revelations, there was given to me a thorn in the flesh, the messenger of Satan to buffet me, lest I should be exalted above measure." We see that God uses the flesh to constrain the soul from glorifying itself in a form of spiritual pride. This helps the soul to keep on a correct path in his relationship with God.

CONCLUSION

The critical things to retain from this study of the flesh are:

1. God uses it to discipline the soul and to work patience into the heart.

2. The flesh is always at enmity with the inner man at all times and on all issues.

3. It can never be redeemed, but it can be used to glorify God when subjected to the will of the inner man after the second birth.

4. It is the source of all three forms of sin—the lust of the flesh, the lust of the eyes, and the pride of life

5. The demons use it as a battleground to keep the soul focused on issues pertaining to it and to distract the soul from concentrating on listening to the inner man. The flesh can make a lot of noise and pollute the heart greatly when not reigned in by the soul.

6. The soul, when given a new spirit, has the power to control the flesh but will frequently need help from God's giving His power into the inner man to win the victory. It will always need His power to win victory when the flesh is being strengthened by an evil spirit. Prior to the second birth the old spirit is controlled by the flesh. God still empowers the old spirit to victory for His purposes, such as giving anointing for special works—prophets, builders of the tabernacle.

7. The soul chooses moment by moment, thought by thought, action by action, belief by belief, and attitude by attitude whether to sow to the spirit or to the flesh. The one to which we sow grows stronger, and the other grows weaker. Sowing to the spirit reaps eternal benefit. Sowing to the flesh reaps eternal loss. It is our choice to make continually throughout our days of living in this age. Galatians 6:8-9 states this principle: "For he that soweth to his flesh shall of the flesh reap corruption; but he that soweth to the Spirit shall of the Spirit reap life everlasting. And let us not be weary in well doing: for in due season we shall reap, if we faint not."

13
WORKINGS OF THE SOUL OF SPIRITUAL MAN

When we speak of a person as an individual and when we use a pronoun in regard to an individual, we are speaking of or referring to the soul. We have seen previously that the soul has two components—the flesh and the spirit. Genesis 2:7 gives us the basis for this understanding: "And the LORD God formed man *of* the dust of the ground, and breathed into his nostrils the breath of life; and man became a living soul." The breath of life is the spirit that God placed into the flesh that He formed from the dust. The same word in Hebrew Scripture, *ruach,* is used for "breath," "wind," and "spirit." The same is true in the Greek with *pnuema*. The term *soul* represents the combination of spirit in flesh; *i.e.*, body + spirit = soul. The soul is the whole individual.

The Scriptures talk of several components which are spiritual in nature that make up man, as opposed to natural components such as the heart, lungs, liver, brain, and kidneys. These spiritual components could be said to form spiritual man, and it is very helpful in our relationship with God for us to understand how He has made us and how we function in the spiritual realm. We function in the natural realm with our natural components, and we function in the spiritual realm with our spiritual components. The soul is a hybrid that is composed of spiritual and natural components, as we saw above. We will study in this section of the book our spiritual components—the heart (not the same as the physical organ which pumps our blood), the mind, the will, the flesh, the conscience, the spirit (inner man), and the soul. We shall review these components in this chapter and learn how they are structurally arranged and how they interrelate in the functioning of spiritual man. For detailed Scripture references to support the statements in this chapter, we must look at the chapters about each component. Some key Scriptures will be repeated in this chapter for convenience.

THE STRUCTURE OF SPIRITUAL MAN

HEART

The soul contains a spiritual heart that we will refer to as the heart. It is not clear from Scripture just where this is located in regard to the natural organs. In the chapter on the heart we learned that it is quite complex and contains many thoughts and devices. In addition, it contains the spirit (inner man [1 Peter 3:4]). God writes His laws in the heart of an individual who has gone through the second (spiritual) birth, and the Holy Spirit is resident within that heart. If a soul has gone through the second birth, then after death of the natural body the spirit will dwell with God for eternity and will be given a new spiritual body after the resurrection from death. Hearts contain imaginations, high places, and devices. They have a mind that is separate from that of the soul. They have things hidden in them that the mind of the soul does not know. They are in need of being purified after being contaminated by the world system, even after the second birth. The conscience is on the surface of the heart (Hebrews 10:22). It is not clear whether it is the inner or outer surface, but it seems to be the outer surface. God looks upon the heart as representing who the man is (Proverbs 27:19). God holds the soul responsible for the contents and condition of the heart. The soul has the ability to decide what it wants the heart to be like, and with God's help the soul can change that condition. It will need an infusion of God's power for change to occur in the direction that He wants—purification.

MIND

The Scriptures describe four minds within the soul—that of the soul, which is associated with the anatomical brain; that of the heart; that of the inner man; and that of the flesh. The mind of the soul is the one that controls decision making for the soul. After the fall of man the mind of the flesh became set against the spirit and is always at enmity with it. If we understand the mind of the inner man, we know that the mind of the flesh will be absolutely set against it in every single desire, thought, behavior, and belief. Therefore, we do not need to study the mind of the flesh separately. Before the second birth the mind of the spirit (inner man) is dulled, decaying, and dying. The mind of the flesh, which rules over it, overwhelms it. The soul has little ability to hear from it, since the flesh overwhelms it. After the second birth the inner man has the ability to rule over the flesh. The soul can draw upon power from the new spirit to crucify daily the flesh. Many times the soul may call upon an infusion of power from God to defeat the flesh, when it is being strengthened by an evil spirit. Man was made a little lower than the angels; thus, a soul has less power than angels. Therefore, when a demonic attack comes through the flesh, the soul will need to call upon God for additional power in the spirit to rebuff it. The flesh, when battling the new spirit without demonic support, will lose. That is why God tells us in 2 Timothy 1:7: "For God hath not given us the spirit of fear; but of power, and of love, and of a sound mind." The power with the sound mind (recall from Chapter 6 that the Greek for *sound mind* has an aspect of being able to control) is sufficient to defeat the flesh. The mind of the inner man is in communication with God directly. It bears witness to the Holy Spirit. The inner man can be contaminated and can require cleansing; but the mind of the inner man probably does not require any renewing, or surely Scripture would mention it. The mind of the soul requires renewing after the second birth.

WILL

The will is like the mind in that the flesh, heart, mind, and soul all have a will. That of the soul is the pre-eminent one in deciding the course the soul will pursue through life. It is located somewhere separate from the mind (the location is not clear in Scripture); it may be contiguous. The inner man also has a will by implication, since he has a mind and desires. One will need strength in order for the will of the soul to overcome demonic attacks. This power will be supplied by God, as the soul submits to Him and asks for power in the inner man and in the will. The will is the part of spiritual man that gives the energy and ability to stay the course that the soul has decided to pursue. The mind of the soul in a given situation contemplates a behavioral decision based on the information coming to it. It takes into account the attitudes and beliefs of the heart and the imagination supplied by the heart about the situation. The conscience also supplies input into the decision making. When no change is required, then the will is not involved; but when change is required, the soul sets the will to power the change. In situations in which the soul is battling a demonic influence he will need to ask God for additional power in the will in order for the soul (1 Corinthians 7:37) to be able to effect the change. After the second birth the will of the soul is preeminent to the wills of the other components, but it is not powerful enough to stand against demonic attack. In this case it requires the Lord to join the battle. The soul can then make the choice to set the will with sufficient power to hold his choice.

FLESH

The flesh is the physical body made up of chemicals and formed into the various organ systems. When Adam and Eve sinned, God judged the flesh; and, in doing that, He determined that man should suffer physical death (corruption) of the body. God declared that there is no good thing in the flesh. He also deemed that man would undergo spiritual death, but He provided a means of rescue from this if an individual would accept His plan for this. The plan involves acceptance of the Lord Jesus Christ as a substitute for our spiritual death. When this acceptance becomes a part of the structure of our heart, then God gives us a new spirit and a new heart.

CONSCIENCE

Conscience is located on a surface of the spiritual heart and needs to be strengthened and matured after the second birth. It is a moral guide that convicts a soul when he plans to violate or has violated his present understanding of God's laws.

SPIRIT (INNER MAN)

The spirit is the gift of life energy from God. After the second birth we are given a new spirit. The spirit resides in the spiritual heart and has its own mind, which is far more intelligent than the mind of the soul. The new spirit is of God and communicates with Him directly.

SOUL

The soul is the individual and contains all of these individual components. It is responsible for all final decision making and carries the responsibility of preparing the spirit for eternity and purifying the heart in co-operation with God.

THE FUNCTIONING OF THE SPIRITUAL MAN

We shall list several points to keep in mind as we study how the components of spiritual man interrelate:

1. God made man to relate to Him as a family member and to let him rule and reign with the Lord Jesus.
2. God made man in such a manner that he (the soul) has a free choice to relate to God or to reject God. The flesh can no longer choose, since it was judged at the fall and was crucified with the Lord Jesus. The new spirit after the second birth is of God and will not be judged. The heart is judged by its contents.
3. The demonic powers wish to see God lose His relationship with mankind.
4. Man is a hybrid being with the same sensing and communicating abilities in both the natural and the spiritual universes (the senses of sight, hearing, touching, smelling, tasting, and position sense).
5. Man after the fall lost the rule of the earth and now lives in a hostile environment in a state of continual war. The demonic powers have set up a world system by which they ensnare the hearts and minds of men and try to prevent them from coming to know God and accepting the salvation that He offers from the spiritual death into which they are born. If a man is reborn, these powers attempt to prevent growth and maturation of the new man and attempt to block his ability to assist others in receiving the second birth.
6. In every word and action that man makes after the second birth he sows either to the flesh or to the spirit. After the second birth if a man sows to the flesh, then he will face judgment, but not

eternal condemnation (1 Corinthians 3:11-15). If he sows to the spirit, then the spirit is strengthened; and the man begins to hear and see more through the spiritual senses. He begins to mature in the spiritual universe.

THE HEART

The heart is a large repository of spiritual structures (thoughts, imaginations, high places, the laws of God, the Holy Spirit, and the inner man). Into and out of it there are continuing flows of spirit to the components of spiritual man and to other spiritual beings. In this sense it is like the physical heart. It can be thought of as a spiritual pump. Out of the heart come the issues of life and the words of the mouth.

Models for understanding the heart

The heart can also be viewed as like a gyroscope, set on a particular course by the soul, or like the depths of the ocean that are little stirred by a wind on the surface. Both of these models indicate that the heart keeps us going in the same stable direction, but it can change that with energy and effort. It is out of the heart that all of our behavior and all of our words stem. The soul can decide to change the heart, but it requires considerable spiritual power to do this. God can provide such power to those who wish to serve Him. The soul, with God's help, can identify those areas of the heart that need to be purified. The soul can set its will in a particular direction, but it will require power from God to hold to this in battles against the flesh and in any demonic confrontation. A soul knows that the heart needs to be purified. In Chapter 16 we shall learn more about this. After the second birth the soul needs to work co-operatively with God to purify his heart in order to begin a path of spiritual maturation.

It is helpful to model the structures, devices, lofty thoughts, and high places that the demonic powers have duped the soul into building in the heart. Think of these as barriers to God's light being shed abroad in our heart by the Holy Spirit's witnessing to our spirit. These structures, devices, lofty thoughts, and high places are built upon the foundations of philosophies that we have embraced, assumptions we have made, and learning that we have accepted that come from the world system and which are not true. These building blocks become linked into high places, towers, imaginations, and idols that we worship without even knowing that we are doing this or without questioning it. These are the things which make it hard for our soul to receive information from God. It is hard to hear His voice, to receive His love, and to relate to Him. We hold these various structures strongly in our hearts, and it takes considerable spiritual force and effort to tear them down. Much of the reason for the difficulty in taking them down is that we view our fleshly social power bases, our work, and our economic well-being to be dependent on our "fitting into the correct expectations held by society." One current philosophy that many accept is that of Darwin's theory of the origin of the species (evolution). When we hold to this, it blocks our ability to see light and understand that it is a lie from the enemy. There are countless other presuppositions from which one has to be delivered. Only as these structures begin to tumble, do we clear the path for communication between the mind of the soul and the inner man. These imaginations and devices are very deeply rooted, and we need to examine the root cause for our various behaviors and actions in order to tear out the root. If we leave roots of deception in our heart, then God will allow these to cause us problems. It is similar to the problems that the Israelites had when they left enemies in their land (Joshua). These enemies with their philosophies and idols seduced the Israelites. We need to analyze the words of our mouth as a guide to the content of our heart and then take every thought captive. As we take a thought captive, we are analyzing it as to why we have it, the source of it, and whom it is glorifying. Then we must decide whether we should continue to allow this type of thought. The Word of God must be the judge of our thoughts. The better we know the Word of God, the more power we will have to work with God to purify our hearts.

THE INNER MAN (SPIRIT)

The new spirit one gets at the second birth will go on to be with God in eternity. The spirit matures through our earthly life, as the soul feeds it. The soul can choose with every behavior, every belief, and every attitude whether it will serve the demands of the flesh or the needs of the spirit. The soul, with God's help, can then learn to change all of the beliefs, attitudes, and behaviors he holds that are not consistent with truth. The spirit is contained in the heart and is influenced by the content of the heart. It can be polluted or clean.

Interactions of the soul and spirit

The soul determines what level of maturity the spirit will have reached, when it is released from the flesh in death (1 Corinthians 3:11-15). It does this moment by moment by choosing which beliefs, attitudes, and behaviors to express and which to eliminate. Behaviors include choosing our words. The soul enforces its choice by using available spiritual power to set the will, which brings about planned change within the heart. This change in the heart, in turn, molds the spirit. Oftentimes, we can make our planned changes only by availing ourselves of the power of God to bring them about. The flesh is extremely powerful in its own right; furthermore, demonic forces try to battle the soul to prevent spiritual rebirth in the first place; and if this occurs, they try to prevent spiritual growth and maturity.

The spirit is the life that God has given to us. Without it our flesh dies. If we keep in mind the formula, body + spirit = soul, we can see this. Body + nothing = body, and that body returns to the dust. The spirit (inner man) has a structure that is identifiable with spiritual vision. The soul is responsible for molding and maturing the inner man (Proverbs 25:28). The spirit supplies the energy for all of our actions. This includes everything from maintaining all of the functioning of the biochemistry and physiology of countless millions of individual cells throughout our body up to evaluating and functioning within large-scale complex societies. Our spirit empowers our thoughts, our speech, our beliefs, and our attitudes. It supplies power for maintaining and changing the structures within our heart. We need power from it for defense of our soul against spiritual attacks by the flesh and by evil spirits. To defend against demonic attacks, we must have additional power given to our spirit by God (Ephesians 3:16). We need this additional power to be successful when we set our will against the flesh. The inner man is always opposed to the flesh after the second birth (Galatians 5:17). This is opposition in every single thought, word, deed, attitude, will, and belief. **It is total.** The consequences of this for our soul are worthy of intensive and recurring meditations.

After the second birth the new spirit lives in a new heart that is given at the second birth. These quickly become polluted again by the world system, because the mind of the soul is not renewed at the second birth; and, of course, the flesh is not renewed. There is very little support (and frequently none) for spiritual neonates. They are not nurtured as well as they should be. Consequently, within a short timespan the new heart regains many of the old structures, high places, idols, philosophies, devices, and imaginations that the un-renewed mind has transmitted to the heart. The new spirit is of God and is never judged. The new spirit lives in the new heart, which is progressively polluted by spiritual filth. The soul requires it to support behaviors based on vain imaginations. After months and years of this it needs cleansing (2 Corinthians 7:1). Ephesians 5:26 tells us that the Word of God performs this cleansing as we immerse ourselves in it. *Immerse* is not merely to dabble, such as reading occasionally from the Scripture. The Word must be our source for decision making in all things, and we must approach it for wisdom in all decisions. This is the beginning of immersion.

Communications between the soul and spirit

We shall now examine the various ways that the inner man and the soul communicate. The inner man receives communication from the Holy Spirit, who also is resident in our heart after the second birth. The inner man also receives information from the Spirit of God. God intends these communications to be passed on to our soul. Our inner man does this, although the barriers that we have allowed to be erected in our heart interfere with the communication and although evil spirits will try to interfere with it. All of our communications between the components of the spiritual man consist of flows of spirit, which we have defined in Chapter 6. As we begin to take every thought captive that occurs in the mind of our soul (2 Corinthians 10:5), we need to determine the origin. We need to learn how to know when our spirit speaks and when our flesh is speaking, in order to fulfill Hebrews 4:12. This is a prerequisite to beginning to walk after the Spirit of God. We must be able to hear reliably His voice to hear His instructions.

God speaks to our inner man in various ways:

1. By the Holy Spirit bearing witness to our spirit (Romans 8:16)
2. By our conscience (Romans 2:15 and 9:1)
3. By His Spirit interacting with our spirit (1 Corinthians 2:10-13)
4. By the creation (Romans 1:19-25, Mark 11:13-14, and Mark 9:5)
5. By sending angels (Daniel 10:13)

God speaks to our soul in various ways:

1. By communicating with the inner man as described above—this is the most usual way
2. By speaking audibly to us—this is quite rare (Exodus 20:19)
3. By giving an external vision while we are in a conscious state (Acts 9:3-7)
4. By speaking to us while we are in a trance-like state (Acts 10:10, 22:17)
5. By giving us an out-of-the-body (death) state (very rare [2 Corinthians 12:2])

We can learn to recognize His communications to us, as we examine the spirit that is interacting with our spirit. We must learn to sense the whole spirit rather than just the informational part of the spiritual flow. Recall that all spiritual flows have three components—power, emotion, and information (2 Timothy 1:7). As we learn the Word, we will be able to test more reliably the origin of all of the spiritual flows coming into our mind. (2 Corinthians 7:5 is a good example of how Paul describes the difference between internal and external spiritual flows—he considers them as different "sides.") When we overdevelop our intellect in comparison to our emotions, we become used to dealing with information only. If we over-exercise our emotions, we become seekers of emotions only. We ignore the information coming to our mind of the soul regarding the power in both these situations. Both are unbalanced. When we receive any communication from another spiritual being, it will come to the mind of our soul either from our heart or from the natural environment (including our flesh). As we practice being in the spirit, we will sense how our spirit is reacting to the information it is receiving. We can gain sensitivity for this over time. In this manner we can discern quickly if our spirit is getting witness of approval from the Holy Spirit, in which case God is giving His approval to the communication. God will give His assent to a spirit of truth in any communication, regardless of who initiates it. We need to be adept at discerning when a person is speaking with a spirit of fear or deceit (or with any of the other many types of spirits that can be present in a communication). After our inner man has received a communication, he will send his opinion to the mind of the soul. This transmission is passed through the heart where our flesh, and sometimes an evil spirit, will try to influence the content by adding to it or removing from it. The communications from the spirit to the soul are distorted by this transit through the heart, until the heart is purified. The soul can learn to focus on the information coming from the spirit, and the ability to receive from the spirit increases with practice over time.

When God speaks to us, there is authority that is unmistakable (the power); there is an intuitive knowledge that it is for good (if we have been through the second birth [Romans 8:28]); and there is information that fits well (James 3:17) with the circumstances. We have to reach beyond the immediate reaction of our heart, unless it is pure, to note how our inner man receives all communications. When we fail to learn the difference between the reaction from the heart and that from the spirit, we have not completed the separation of Hebrews 4:12. Until our hearts are pure, we will have dual reactions to inflows of spirit. The heart will oppose the Word of God, while our inner man will embrace the Word of God. Until we have allowed our inner man to develop and the flesh to weaken, we can be easily confused by these reactions. Careful testing of the inflowing spirit is needed; and in important decisions the counsel of trusted and proven leaders should be sought. When God speaks, the fleshly heart will react in fear and will want to hide (Genesis 3:8). The inner man will embrace His words. The environment also speaks to our heart and spirit. God uses it to speak to us, and He expects us to listen to it (Romans 1). When we observe our heart filling with the true peace of God as we test information coming to us, then we have discerned that the spirit in the communication is from God.

The character of the spirit in a communication can help with discernment of the origin. God always leads communications with creative power, and the whole creation reacts (Psalm 114:4 *et al.*). He knows His desires and is not apologetic for them. He wants to build toward eternity and wants the best for His children in that regard. The enemy spirits always oppose God by reacting and trying to incite our fleshly desires or by bringing fear into our heart. God initiates, and evil spirits react (this is a spiritual universe law).

When we initiate an action, we have to learn to recognize the spirit of the reaction to it. Since man is made in God's image, then a soul, when acting, will experience a reaction from the spiritual universe. We have to learn to distinguish between two particular reactions—that from the conscience convicting us of error and that from the enemy trying to confuse us with a false guilt. The two are similar; and until a soul learns the difference, that soul can be confused and led onto the wrong path.

Learning to understand the various states of the heart and the inner man takes time and experience, but it is essential if we are to be led by the Spirit of God. Only God can teach us these things. As we work with God to learn these things, He is glorified, because we are truly seeking and knocking and He will open the door of spiritual growth to us. We are deepening our relationship with Him. We need to realize that the heart and the inner man become very similar in their emotional state, and we cannot really sense any difference until we deliberately begin a process of purifying our heart. There are many Scriptures that illustrate this point. Review the list in Chapter 9 on conditions in the human spirit and in Chapter 10 on the states of the heart. Read the source Scriptures in context, and you will see that the same or a similar state exists in both the heart and the spirit for various circumstances in which the soul exists.

Our goal for the state in our spirit should be for it to be aware constantly of the presence of God and to have peace and joy always

(Romans 14:17). This should be our normal, everyday state; and when we perceive that something is coming against that state, we must war against it. Praising the Lord and calling upon the Lord for protection are very important in this fight.

Contrasting spiritual flows from people to those from God

When people speak with earthly, reasoned wisdom, there will be less power (compared with power from God) in the spiritual flow because it does not meet the criteria for truth; thus, the Holy Spirit will not witness to it. Those people may speak loudly or gesture wildly to emphasize a point; but, if we look inward to our inner man and not to the outward appearance, we can test the spirit. We must see how our inner man is reacting to it. For example, if a person has plans for a venture, he may give many reasons to support his choice; but if the plans are not of God, then his spirit will lack God's power as he releases his own words. We shall look at some examples to illustrate why it is so important to receive the spirit in any communication and not just the information or the emotion.

1. Consider a child about to place his hand on a hot stove. The mother may raise her voice and say "No" in order to prevent the child from being harmed. This word *no* may be spoken in irritation, in concern, in fear, and in various other states. The child's spirit will recognize the power from his mother's spirit and will also detect the emotion and the information. The child will not be capable of analyzing the spirit but will place the experience into his memory in the heart. This builds good structures in the heart when "No" is spoken in love; but when it is spoken in anger, it builds bad foundations. A childhood spent in building up bad foundations takes a lot of work to set right in adulthood.
2. Consider a scientist grappling with research findings. There have been examples of deliberate fraud in published research. If the scientist is able to sense with his spirit, rather than just parse information with his mind, the Holy Spirit will keep him from accepting something that is not true. There will be an ever so gentle restraint he will experience in the spirit. This same scientist

may be trying to observe natural phenomena. God can lead him to the correct observations and interpretation, as he interacts prayerfully with the data.

3. Consider a person who is used to allowing his emotions to dominate his decision making. When listening to a politician, he will detect the emotional component of the spirit being radiated and will form his decision for action based on this and will ignore the principles for which the individual stands that will govern future decisions.
4. Read Acts 9:10-18. Consider what Ananias would have done if he had been governed only by his own understanding. He might not have gone to lay hands on Paul. We see that we should detect the spirit behind the communication. In this case Ananias knew that God was telling him to do this (because through experience he could test the spirit). He could, therefore, trust God with the future that he could not know himself. In similar situations in our society one must know which spirit may be urging him to communicate with an individual who is in a position of power.

It is by reason of use that we can begin to listen to our spirit and to hear more reliably. As our inner man is able to influence us and as our soul follows him, he will grow stronger; and the flesh will grow weaker, since the two are absolutely polarized.

We must learn to distinguish the movements of our conscience, as we try to discern what is from God and what is not. Our conscience matures and convicts us according to our faith and our level of comprehension of God's Word. The enemy will try to confuse us by moving against our spirit with a spirit of false guilt. It takes practice to discern this; and it can trip us up frequently, as we begin to learn to listen to our inner man.

God likes to communicate intimately with us (Matthew 6:6). One knows when a loved one is suffering internally or when there is joy inside without words being spoken. We could be blindfolded and have our hearing blocked and still sense these things, because we pick up these issues in our inner man without the need for any natural observations of expressions or body posture. We can improve and mature these spiritual senses by use (Hebrews 5:14). As we develop them, we are able to communicate with God in our spirit much more intimately. We can sense His presence and spend time in it. God likes this; He is pleased by it. Hebrews 5:14 teaches about distinguishing between good and evil with our senses. Any communication is good, part good and part evil, or evil. Only God is good (Matthew 19:17). Therefore, any spirit that we receive must be tested for the good in it. If we cannot do this in the spirit because we have not learned to do this, then we will follow many false spirits because we lack discernment (Mark 13:22).

We must stop operating in the mind of our soul, just on the informational or the emotional aspect of a spiritual flow, without any attempt to discern the complete spirit behind the information. If we do not begin to test all of the spirits (1 John 4:1-2), then we will be deceived time and again by the devil, who only too readily appears as an angel of light. When we look at naturally-reasoned solutions or plans that are built up in our mind, we may develop enthusiasm for them that originates from the flesh's having perverted the heart. 1 Corinthians 1:17–2:5 speaks at length about natural wisdom and Godly wisdom. We have to know how to operate in the inner man to understand the difference in a particular situation. Our natural reason will lead us astray. The lusts of our flesh, the lusts of our eyes, and the pride of life will operate to deceive us into thinking that God is in something that is really nothing but our flesh, perhaps assisted with a little confusion from the enemy. We must be careful while still spiritual babes to seek counsel from those with greater spiritual authority and maturity when making important decisions.

We can see that any communication between the inner man and the mind of our soul or any other spiritual being must traverse the heart. God, the Holy Spirit, exists in our heart after the second birth; thus, communications are very close between God and our spirit. The devil and demons can place content into our hearts as we give them authority by our attitudes, beliefs, and behaviors (John 13:2, Acts 5:3). The demons can also remove content from our heart (Matthew 13:19). Spiritual communication is direct spirit to spirit within the spiritual universe, but it can be hampered when it is being translated into the natural realm (such as when the answer to Daniel's prayer was delayed (Daniel 10:10-15).

When our hearts are not right before God, we do not perceive spiritual truth correctly. All the evil devices and false imaginations in the heart have to be torn down for us to see God as clearly as we are able and to hear from Him as clearly as we need to. The devices, false idols, imaginations, and the efforts of demonic beings disrupt the purity and clarity of communications between God and our inner man and between our inner man and our soul.

Spiritual flows from the soul to the spirit

We have looked at communications between the inner man and the soul largely from the viewpoint of those initiated by the inner man. We must also examine the situation of the soul's speaking to the inner man. The soul can speak to the inner man audibly by putting voice to thoughts. The inner man is also aware of the thoughts of the mind of the soul. We have studied this in detail in Chapters 9-11. We can strengthen the inner man by speaking audible words of encouragement to him. The thoughts of the mind of the soul communicate with the mind of the heart, and the inner man is aware of all of these thoughts (1 Corinthians 2:11). We have examined in Chapters 9-11 the way information from the natural realm traverses the flesh, the mind of the soul, and the heart and how it elicits a response from the heart, powered by the inner man and coupled with an imagination. This response then goes back into both the spiritual and the natural realms.

When we speak truth into the natural and spiritual realm, God releases His power. This we see in Mark 16:15-18. When we speak God's truth, we are bringing the Lord Jesus to those hearing (John 1:17). We cannot speak the truth without this, since the two are one (truth and the Lord Jesus [John 8:32 and14:6]). In fact, God is truth (John 14:17). As we speak and preach the truth, and only to the extent that we do this out of purified hearts in faith, then God will release great spiritual power; and great signs and wonders will follow. If we want to see our society transformed—the blind to see, the deaf to hear, and the lame to walk—then we must allow God to purify our hearts so that we can worship Him in spirit and in truth, since we then will see Him more clearly. We must allow the Lord Jesus to be formed in our hearts (Galatians 4:19). Until we yield fully, we resist God in a full release of His desires for us and those with whom we are in contact. We should be His salt and light. It prevents those around us being able to see God clearly when our hearts are not pure. The transformation from our present state of the soul to the state desired by God can be accomplished only as we yield to God and consent to His working change in our heart. When we are changed to carry His image in our heart, we can truly speak and teach the truth. We see so little power following most speaking and preaching about the Lord, because it is done with poorly transformed hearts that have incomplete images of Him formed in them. Transforming the heart is an arduous process that must be done in partnership with God, as He gives us insight about what needs changing and supplies our spirit with power to make the change. The changes are made belief by belief, attitude by attitude, behavior by behavior, moment by moment, and thought by thought. We must take every thought captive (2 Corinthians 10:5). This is a process of demolishing philosophies and world views that we have unwittingly and passively accepted. Each brick in these high places, towers, strongholds, and false imaginations must be taken out; and these huge structures must be taken down. We should expect it to be a process that is powered by God, as we accept His viewpoint and walk in it by faith that governs ever-widening areas of our behavior.

WHAT IS GOD'S EXPECTATION FOR OUR SOUL?

Luke 1:46-47 tells us: "And Mary said, My soul doth magnify the Lord, And my spirit hath rejoiced in God my Saviour." God wants our soul to magnify Him. We are to lift up the Lord Jesus for others to see (as we yield our will to God more and more this will occur, as God releases His Spirit through us). Our soul can magnify God in a way that our spirit and flesh cannot. Since the flesh has been judged, the will of the flesh is always antagonistic to the will of the inner man. When we allow our inner man to rule over the flesh, it glorifies God (2 Corinthians 4:11); but, since it is of God, it is not going to be judged. Our original spirit is from Adam (Genesis 5:3). This spirit was judged in the past by God to be worthy of death and was condemned. We receive a new spirit from God when we go through the second birth. This spirit comes from the Lord Jesus and has been tried and found to be true (1 Corinthians

6:17). It will never suffer death (Romans 8:10-16; 1 Corinthians 2:12, 6:17, 6:20, 15:45; Galatians 4:6; and Philemon 25). The new spirit does not, therefore, make a choice. It is our soul which is always allowed to make a free choice. When we know God and as we know Him better, the choice always remains. As our soul agrees to be conformed to the image of Jesus because we see Him as He is (with full knowledge and truth of the situation in the spiritual universe set before us) and value Him beyond all else, then we can be like Mary and say, "My soul doth magnify the Lord."

We can look at the elements in Mary's speech which allowed her to state that her soul magnified the Lord. Read Luke 1:46-55. The obvious components for magnifying the Lord with our soul consist of the following:

1. Let our spirit rejoice in God.
2. Acknowledge God as our Savior.
3. Praise Him for His personal dealings with us.
4. Acknowledge God as mighty.
5. Acknowledge God as holy.
6. Fear God.
7. Give thanks for His mercy to us.
8. Acknowledge specific acts He has performed on our behalf.
9. Acknowledge His provision for our daily needs.

God will be magnified by these items only when all are present in the heart. It takes a long work for the soul to bring the heart to the purity with which the Lord is pleased. When it is complete, the above elements will come forth from it; and the Lord will be magnified. That does not mean that we have to wait until all are present and correct. Our soul can make the decision to begin to do these things before the heart is pure, and God will bless the intent of our heart and will work with us to bring our hearts to purity. It is important to speak out these things, because our speech is living and creative. As we speak, the world system will attempt to counter our creativity. As we persevere in faith, our words will change our hearts; for God will bless any truth in our words (Luke 9:50) and will respond with power to bring them about (1 John 5:14-15). It is His will that our hearts be purified. It is very important to commune with our heart, determine what plans and issues we have faith for (as opposed to hope for), and then test the spirit of the faith to see if this faith is from God. If the faith is from God as we walk in it, committing actions based on it, we will build a foundation to extend our faith in God into further places. As we do this, we begin to work with God in our daily life; and we can begin to give Him thanks for the specific acts that He performs for us and for the provision of our daily needs for sustenance and protection from the evil one. One cannot perform these things, until he is living in a dynamic relationship with God.

INTERACTIONS OF THE SOUL WITH THE COMPONENTS

We shall now go on to look at some further Scripture that will amplify what we have just studied about the soul.

INTERACTIONS OF THE SOUL WITH THE FLESH

1. The soul is responsible for the food choices, the clothing, and all of the other needs of the flesh. 1 Kings 21:27-29 shows that Ahab's soul recognized sin and, as a result, that he humbled himself before the Lord. As part of the humbling process his soul determined the need to dress the flesh in clothing suitable to the situation. Thus the clothing of the flesh was an outward sign, taken by God as appropriate, that showed humbling. There is much emphasis in Scripture about the clothing of the flesh that is a responsibility of the soul. God made the first choice of clothing for Adam and Eve. We must be very careful in this age how we choose to clothe the flesh, lest we offend Almighty God.

2. God frequently uses the soul's flesh to perform His work. In 2 Kings 4:34 we read of Elisha's being used of God to restore life to a dead child. God wanted to make a point for eternity for the use of this technique in this situation. He could quite well have asked Elisha to call forth life. The methodology used in restoration of dead people varies, but the common theme is that the flesh is always involved. God has determined that man has to partner

with Him in all aspects of the bringing of the Kingdom to the earth. God does not act without telling His prophets in advance (Amos 3:7). He discusses it with them on occasion and is willing to be entreated by them. An example showing this is Abraham's discussing the destruction of Sodom and Gomorrah with God (Genesis 18). The collective flesh of mankind is used extensively by God in bringing about His purposes for the earth.

3. The interactions of the soul and flesh in suffering and illness are frequently linked in the purposes of God. He uses illness and suffering in the flesh to get the attention of the soul. His purposes in this always include restoration of the troubled soul to Himself (2 Kings 5:10). Since the fall of the flesh in the Garden of Eden it seems that God has determined to use fallen flesh to gain the attention of lost souls. He does this through various devices such as hunger, illness, and other needs—in order to bring those souls into a relationship with Him. After the relationship of a soul with God begins, God continues to allow the fallen flesh to serve His needs to sanctify and purify the soul through further sufferings. We read in Job 2:5: "But put forth thine hand now, and touch his bone and his flesh, and he will curse thee to thy face." Here is a very important illustration in the spiritual realm of the expectation of the devil, Satan, that Job would curse God, if God allowed sufferings in his flesh. The flesh is a key battleground for the soul and the devil. Satan uses illness and pain to focus our attention away from spiritual issues; he tries to make us focus on our flesh. We should note that God sets limits on what He allows Satan to do to every person. God sometimes brings illness about through the environment. There is no record of God using an angel, other than a fallen angel, to cause illness. He certainly allows His angels to cause death in war. To gain a spiritual perspective on the relationship of the soul and the flesh, we have to see the flesh in its role in the war between the Lord, with His angelic host, and the devil, with his princes, for the souls of men. The flesh is used by the devil to take attention away from the spirit by causing the soul to dwell on the satisfying of fleshly needs. God uses the

flesh as a means of attracting the attention of lost men to Him and of the purifying and sanctifying of the believers. The book of Job dwells a lot on this relationship of suffering and whether Job will focus on the spiritual realm or the natural realm of the flesh. In Job 14:22 we read: "But his flesh upon him shall have pain, and his soul within him shall mourn." Here we see the physical suffering of Job impacting his soul with mourning. At this point he has not been able to understand the Lord's purpose for his sufferings. We have the advantage of knowing God's purposes in suffering in the flesh; therefore, we should be able to work co-operatively with God in our physical sufferings.

4. In Psalm 16:8-10 we see the impact on the flesh of a sinless life. The Lord Jesus was without sin, and as a result David is confident that the Father will not allow Jesus' soul to stay in hell, and His flesh will rest in hope. Few of us will achieve this (Enoch and Elijah possibly did), but our spirit will get a new "spiritual" body after the rapture of the Church.

5. In Psalm 38:3-8 David states a profound truth, that his sin caused the anger of the Lord and that this has resulted in disease. Sin is the root cause of disease. God uses physical suffering and illness to discipline and to perfect His children. We have seen that Satan is often the agent that God uses in this process of disciplining and perfecting. We have also seen that God places limits on what Satan can do to an individual. We always have to look at God's purpose for illness and suffering in our lives. Sometimes it is because our soul has chosen to sin, and we need discipline. Sometimes it is to perfect us in sanctification through the teaching of patience, and sometimes it is for purification from unrecognized sin patterns during our sanctification. We must always ask God to reveal to us what His purpose is for our situation so that we can co-operate with Him. In recognizing the intentions of God to be good to us, we can truly be joyful in our inner man in even the most adverse of physical circumstances in the flesh. This is part of the result of the separation spoken of in Hebrews 4:12.

6. Even the flesh of a soul can cry out for God (Psalm 84:2).

7. God will give health to our flesh, when we have faith to accept His word as discussed in Proverbs 4:20-22. God asks His child to attend to His words (this means to walk by all of them) and to incline his ear (meaning to be strongly desiring with a consuming passion) to hear God's words. When we fulfill both of these commands, our flesh will have health. This is indeed a high and lofty standard, but with God's power we can achieve it and expect to walk in physical health (one seldom sees an individual who fulfills these two commands). Since it is impossible for us to know when God deems that we have met this standard, we should be very careful not to be critical of others or of ourselves when we continue to have illnesses. There are so many other areas of God's Word that have a bearing on the issue of physical health that it is difficult, if not impossible, for us to place them in the correct hierarchy and know when one area of the Word takes precedence over another. Also, God is the one who grants us the faith to believe His Scripture in our heart. It is He, then, who allows us to fulfill this Scripture when He is ready to give us the faith for it.

8. Our soul's attitudes and behaviors shape what happens to our flesh (Proverbs 11:17).

9. In John 8:15 we see the impact of years of the flesh being allowed to lead the soul. The souls of fallen men judge after the issues of the flesh. Therefore, we see the flesh's leading the soul due to the spirit's being in a state of death. In souls that have not been through the second birth the flesh is the dominant input to the soul. Through years of the flesh leading the soul the heart has become polluted, the mind in need of renewal, and the spirit further polluted.

10. Romans 6:19 speaks about the responsibility of the soul for how we allow our flesh to act.

11. The soul after the second birth must choose which it will follow, fallen lustful flesh with a polluted spirit or the new spirit (Romans 7:18, Galatians 5:17). The Lord's death delivered us from slavery to the flesh, because our former spirit was dead. After His resurrection He gave us a new spirit at the second birth. This gives our soul a choice—following the new spirit or the fallen flesh. In Romans 8:4 we read: "That the righteousness of the law might be fulfilled in us, who walk not after the flesh, but after the Spirit." Here we see that the law still must be fulfilled after we have been through the second birth. We keep that righteousness by faith in the Lord as our substitute; and we are sanctified as we walk after the Spirit, not letting our soul walk after the flesh. We see again that it is a decision of the soul as to which is the leadership to which it will submit, flesh or Spirit. In Romans 8:5 we see a good test that we can give to our soul in choosing which way to go on any specific issue—that is, whether the issue is elevating or succumbing to a flesh desire or whether it is a desire of the Spirit. There are other tests, but using this in combination with them will help a soul to mature in choosing correctly in those difficult situations to which God will allow us to be exposed in order for us to mature. Other tests include looking at which choice involves faith and observing who is being glorified. There are many others that we will discuss in later chapters. Romans 8:13 states: "For if ye live after the flesh, ye shall die: but if ye through the Spirit do mortify the deeds of the body, ye shall live." If we have been through the second birth, we have the ability **only** through the spirit (not the flesh) to mortify the deeds of the body (flesh). This emphasizes what we said above concerning Romans 8:4. Our soul has to make the choice of whether to be ruled by the flesh or to submit to the Holy Spirit (Galatians 5:17). 2 Corinthians 4:11 shows that when we mortify the flesh, the life of the Lord Jesus can manifest in our mortal flesh.

12. Our soul must make a decision to cleanse our inner man and our flesh in order to perfect holiness in the fear of God. In 2 Corinthians 7:1 we read: "Having therefore these promises, dearly beloved, let us cleanse ourselves from all filthiness of the flesh

and spirit, perfecting holiness in the fear of God." The promises refer to God's dwelling in us. With this in mind the Apostle Paul is telling us to let our soul choose to touch not the unclean things and to be separated from the world. This is a command, but we have to make a choice to follow it. Whenever our soul submits to a command of God, then it is serving God and not the flesh. We may frequently need to ask God to strengthen our will to walk after His Spirit in a particular area, until our spirit grows strong enough to resist the devil in that area. Obedience by the soul to God's Word is the way we work with God to follow His spirit and not the flesh. The Word that we follow can be the *logos* (Scripture) or the *rhema* (word of knowledge, prophetic word, or word of wisdom). Note that the spirit must be cleansed from filthiness that has crept into it since our second birth.

INTERACTIONS OF THE SOUL WITH THE MIND

We will discuss the interactions of the soul with the mind in the order that Scripture introduces them.

1. The mind of the soul discerns and experiences the emotions of the soul (Genesis 26:35; Deuteronomy 18:6, 28:65). In Deuteronomy 28:65 we see that the soul has an integrated response to calamity—the flesh cannot rest, the heart trembles, vision fails, and the emotion of the mind is sorrow. In the same circumstance the soul could have responded differently from the flesh but the Lord intervened in the spirit to cause the heart of the people to tremble. God was acting on the soul through the spirit and also through the physical circumstances.

2. The mind of the soul chooses which way the soul will take, as we see with Moses in Numbers 16:28.

3. In 1 Chronicles 28:9 we observe that the soul's mind has, in addition to desire and emotion, a dimension of will. We also see that there are imaginations of thought. We saw in Chapter 11 that the soul's mind can have both imaginations and knowledge as the

basis of thought.

4. Proverbs 21:27 shows that a soul that is not submitted to God can offer a sacrifice. This can be done in two ways—one, a way of habit; the other, with willful scheming in the mind to achieve some goal. The second way is much more abhorrent to God.

5. Isaiah 26:3 declares that a soul can choose to focus its mind on God. "Thou wilt keep *him* in perfect peace, *whose* mind *is* stayed *on thee*: because he trusteth in thee." The result of this choice is that God keeps that soul in perfect peace. This is a good test as to how focused our mind is on God. Are our souls always in perfect peace, or are there areas of anxiety with which we have not dealt? We have to identify these areas of anxiety and work with God to deal with them.

6. God wants souls to keep Jerusalem in their memories (Jeremiah 51:50, Psalm 137:5-6).

7. A soul can harden its mind through a sin pattern of pride (Daniel 5:20).

8. The mind of the soul can be changed by a series of external events (Habakkuk 1:11).

9. The Scriptures clearly distinguish between the soul and the mind of the soul (Matthew 22:37). We have seen in Chapter 11 that the soul, the heart, the inner man, and the flesh all have a mind. The minds of the latter three are all subservient to the decisions of the soul. The mind of the soul is basically distributed into other areas which are able to function with a high degree of autonomy in the spiritual realm. There is a natural model of how this works in the human nervous system. In the flesh the nervous system has many parts with specialized functions such as the cerebellum, the autonomic nervous system, and the spinal cord. These three are subject to the cerebral hemispheres for higher level commands. I do not suggest that the model is complete or perfect but rather

offer it as a help for conceptualizing the spiritual components and their various minds.

10. Souls can be in their right mind (or a wrong mind). Luke 8:35 speaks about this. The state of the mind is associated with behavioral differences.

11. The Lord expects us (soul's) to control the state of mind that we have with respect to our faith (Luke 12:29).

12. God compares states of mind between two people groups (groups of souls). He expects us to control the state of our mind that governs our acceptance of His Word (Acts 17:11). Those who accept His Word with a readiness of mind are deemed to be nobler than those who do not.

13. A soul can maintain its mind to have humility of mind toward God (Acts 20:19).

14. God holds a soul responsible for choosing not to retain Him in his knowledge. As a result He gives that soul over to having a reprobate mind (Romans 1:28).

15. God tells us that there are several laws that govern the behavior of a soul (Romans 7:23). There are laws for the flesh (members); there is a law for the mind; there are laws for sin (which is in the flesh). The key point to note here is that the law governing the mind is distinct from the flesh; and, therefore, the mind is not regarded as part of the flesh (the brain is part of the flesh). The mind has to be renewed after the second birth. In Romans 8:7 we read that the carnal (fleshly) mind is at enmity with God. We read here that there is a law of God. The carnal mind is not subject to this law, but after the second birth the carnal mind can be renewed through subjection of the soul to the Spirit of God. We read about this in Romans 7:25 below.

16. "I thank God through Jesus Christ our Lord. So then with the mind I myself serve the law of God; but with the flesh the law of sin" (Romans 7:25). This passage shows how the mind works with the soul and the flesh. It is a key passage to understand. When we have been through the second birth, our mind is able to serve God (it will need to be renewed continually [Ephesians 2:3] and will need to apprehend the desires of the spirit). Our flesh will never voluntarily serve God. The flesh will always pull us down, but our soul can learn to stop listening to it. We have to ask God to develop us in this; otherwise we will fall into initiating a reform of the flesh in the flesh. We see this from John 3:6: "That which is born of the flesh is flesh; and that which is born of the Spirit is spirit." If something is initiated as a fleshly desire, it remains a deed of the flesh. Even the desire to clean up our soul from listening to the flesh can be an act of the flesh (Colossians 2:23). If we are not careful to ask the Lord to make the changes in us that are needed and then look toward working with Him as He does it, we will use the flesh to heal the flesh. This results in a fleshly fruit rather than a spiritual fruit. Usually, the net fruit that results is a form of pride.

17. The soul is responsible for being conformed to the world or for being transformed through the renewing of the mind (Romans 12:12). The transformation has to be very thorough. There has to be a complete restructuring of the way we perceive issues and how we decide among choices. We have to decide to what we will pay attention in both the spiritual and natural realms. We have to decide on what to meditate and in what to believe. We have to decide what to remember. We have to decide which behaviors to permit. We have to change all the uses of our mind and the way it is used in order for renewal to be complete. We have to renew our mind by submitting to and following the Holy Spirit. If we try to renew it ourselves, we will fall into a work of the flesh; and the net fruit will be pride. The fruit of the renewal under the Holy Spirit will be humility toward God. If you have never chosen to undergo this renewal, you will probably find that you

still think the way the world does, act the way the world does, and desire what the world desires. This can be a good mirror for your soul in self examination. Self examination should be no more than an observation of speech and behavior; to stay in a state of self examination usually results in one's being focused on self, not the Lord. Once you have made an observation, you should make a decision to be obedient to the command of God to renew your mind in respect to the problem speech or behavior. Without undergoing a revolutionary renewing of your mind, you will never be able to demonstrate in your life that good, acceptable, and perfect will of God. This failure really harms the cause of God greatly.

18. Romans 12:16 indicates that God asks a soul in the body of Christ to be of the same mind toward another and to not be wise in himself (conceit). God wants us to be wise in Him and in His wisdom. When we are, we will be of the same mind one to another. 1 Corinthians 1:10 and 2 Corinthians 13:11 speak about similar issues. Only when we all follow the Spirit of God, will this unity occur. This unity is very important to God. It must be our priority also. In Philippians 2:2-3 we read: "Fulfil ye my joy, that ye be likeminded, having the same love, *being* of one accord, of one mind. *Let* nothing *be done* through strife or vainglory; but in lowliness of mind let each esteem other better than themselves." Again we see God's commanding the soul to be likeminded with the brethren and to be in lowliness of mind toward each other, esteeming others better than himself. God would rather us show this humility than to be in a spirit of pride toward others. Having this spirit of humility in the mind does not mean that one cannot disagree over a point; but, if one does, that soul should resolve the problem according to the rules God has given for this process and only after meditating deeply before God about the problem. There is no place for sudden answers and quick retorts. We do not fight against people but rather the powers of darkness.

19. God requires of souls that everything they do must be done as the result of faith (Romans 12:23 and an application in Romans

14:5, Hebrews 11:6). If something is done that is not as a result of faith in Him, He counts it as sin. We must never proceed on a course when we have doubt. If we do, then that is sin. God allows different people to have divergent views about many issues, but each person must be fully persuaded in his own mind that the course he chooses is God's will for him (Romans 14:5). We are not to judge others based on our calling (or in any other issue [Romans 14:13]).

20. Our soul has the mind of Christ (1 Corinthians 2:14-16), but we must be completely yielded to Him with renewed minds and emptied of self for this to manifest. Philippians 2:5-8 shows His mind. When this occurs in our mind, we shall see clearly in spiritual issues, the planks having been removed from our eyes. We shall then be able to discern spiritual states in other people.

21. 2 Corinthians 7:7 states that a soul can have a fervent mind.

22. God wants our soul to have a willing mind (2 Corinthians 8:12). God wants us not to worry about our lack of resources (what a man has not) but instead to focus on what He has given us (what a man has) and to give out of our current situation. God looks to see if we have a willing mind in terms of giving resources.

23. The flesh and the mind have carnal desires before the second birth (Ephesians 2:3). We can renew the mind but not the flesh. The flesh can be presented as a living sacrifice when ruled by the inner man.

24. God commands our soul not to walk in the vanity of its mind (Ephesians 4:17-18). Having a renewed mind consists, in part, of not walking in vanity of the mind (our own thoughts that are not anchored on God's revelation). We may think various thoughts, as we walk after the Spirit in our learning years. We may not be sure whether something is revelation or vanity. In this case we have to wait and ask the Lord to clarify whether it is of Him or if it is vain. He will tell us, if we ask according to the guidelines in

James 1. We cannot proceed, that is walk, until we can do so in faith (see our discussion above). God will cause us to understand at the right time. It will be important to Him that we wait until we are certain in a particular issue—this is one way we can stay on God's schedule for a work that He has ordained for us.

25. God commands the soul to be renewed in the spirit of the mind (Ephesians 4:22-24). We have examined the meaning of this in Chapter 11. It means to be renewed in the spiritual power, emotions, and reasoning that operate the mind of the soul (the three components of any spirit). A mind may express many spirits, but they should all be within the scope of the work of the Holy Spirit. At the same time we are commanded to put on the new man, our new spirit, and to live by it rather than from the old fleshly lusts. We can both put on the new man and renew the spirit of the mind, but only as we are led by the Holy Spirit.

26. God wants us to put on a humble mind toward Him and our neighbors (Colossians 3:12-13).

27. The soul must strengthen the mind for it to survive trials and tribulations (1 Peter 1:13).

28. God tells us that unbelievers have defiled minds and defiled consciences (Titus 1:15).

29. The soul must have a ready mind toward the things of God (1 Peter 5:2).

30. It is the command of God that our soul choose to have the same mind that was in Christ Jesus, as described in Philippians 2:5-8. The characteristics of this mind are:

    i) Recognizing our high position as a child of the King of Kings
    ii) Seeking and allowing no reputation before men
    iii) Being a servant to all

iv) Being obedient to the Lord God, even to death
v) Being willing to suffer in the flesh (1 Peter 4:1) —implies ceasing from sin

INTERACTIONS OF THE SOUL WITH THE WILL

God's will must be done.

The Lord tells souls that they must be obedient to Him in order to enter the Kingdom of Heaven. Matthew 7:21 states this principle: "Not every one that saith unto me, Lord, Lord, shall enter into the kingdom of heaven; but he that doeth the will of my Father which is in heaven." This does not mean total obedience in every area, since flesh is too strong for saints to achieve this; but our spirit must be focused on learning and submitting to God's will out of love for Him. The one area of obedience that is necessary for entering the kingdom of heaven is, of course, accepting the Lord Jesus Christ as Lord and Savior.

In Mark 3:35 we read: "For whosoever shall do the will of God, the same is my brother, and my sister, and mother." God commands a soul to do His will. His will for us includes learning to be led by the Holy Spirit.

The model for man's will

The Lord Jesus states in John 5:30: "I can of mine own self do nothing: as I hear, I judge: and my judgment is just; because I seek not mine own will, but the will of the Father which hath sent me." We see a difference between the will of God and the will of man. Submission to God's will allows one to judge justly. The Lord Jesus perfectly submitted His will to that of the Father. We should perfectly submit our will to God.

1 Corinthians 7:37 shows that a soul can choose to have power over his own will: "Nevertheless he that standeth stedfast in his heart, having no necessity, but hath power over his own will, and hath so decreed in his heart that he will keep his virgin, doeth well." This is a key passage for showing the need for a soul to control and to have power

enough to control its will. It is, therefore, possible to submit the soul's will to that of God.

God commands the soul to will to do the will of God from the heart (Ephesians 6:6-7): "Not with eyeservice, as menpleasers; but as the servants of Christ, doing the will of God from the heart; With good will doing service, as to the Lord, and not to men." We have seen that it is possible to do the will of God, but not from the heart. King Amaziah (2 Chronicles 25:2) did this, and God was not pleased. Therefore, we need to ask God to change our heart, when we do something that we perceive correctly to be God's will but without a purity of heart regarding it. When we do not do it from the heart, we have other motivations that are wrong in God's judgment.

Miscellaneous

In Ephesians 2:3 we read: "Among whom also we all had our conversation in times past in the lusts of our flesh, fulfilling the desires of the flesh and of the mind; and were by nature the children of wrath, even as others." The word translated "desires" is actually the Greek word for *will*. Souls can be led by their spirit, by their flesh, or by a mixture. This is the same in both the Old Testament and the New Testament times. Both God and Satan influence with power the flesh and the spirit. God does this in order to get the attention of the individual, while Satan does this to control the individual. When a person has been through the second birth, that soul has the spiritual power in his inner man to will to subdue the flesh and to succeed. The soul who has not been through the second birth cannot subdue his flesh without the power of God assisting. After the second birth one needs the power of God to overcome demonic attacks in the realm of the flesh, since the new spirit does not have as much power as an evil spirit.

2 Peter 1:21 gives an important statement about prophets: "For the prophecy came not in old time by the will of man: but holy men of God spake *as they were* moved by the Holy Ghost." This passage shows that men can will to deliver prophecy; but, as we see in Ezekiel and other

books, these people prophesy out of their own soul, not in obedience to Him. They are termed false prophets.

INTERACTIONS OF THE SOUL WITH THE CONSCIENCE

The desired state for the conscience

A soul should maintain the conscience void of any offence toward God or man (Acts 24:16). In order to know that the conscience is operating correctly, we must purge it of dead works.

Purging and restoration of the conscience

This purging and restoration must be done to serve God; they occur through the blood of the Lord Jesus, as we accept His salvation and go through the second birth (Hebrews 9:14). Before the second birth our conscience was busy with dead works from which it needs to be purged. This purging and restoration is something that the Lord will need to work in a soul. These dead works that we once offered to God to merit His favor could never accomplish the goal. In like manner Hebrews 9:9 tells us: "Which *was* a figure for the time then present, in which were offered both gifts and sacrifices, that could not make him that did the service perfect, as pertaining to the conscience." Even in the Old Covenant the work of offering a gift or a sacrifice could not perfect the conscience.

Titus 1:15 states: "Unto the pure all things *are* pure: but unto them that are defiled and unbelieving *is* nothing pure; but even their mind and conscience is defiled." Before the second birth, our conscience was defiled. The conscience has to be restored by God after the second birth.

To restore the conscience to proper functioning after the second birth, we must let God purge it from dead works and areas in which it has been defiled. God has to do this work. For the Old Covenant Jewish people the dead work of sacrifices purged the conscience, and in both the Jew and Gentile it had to be cleared of defilement. Romans 2:15 speaks of the defilement in the Gentiles' conscience. The Gentiles still had operating consciences which witnessed to the law written in their hearts. The Pharisees had defiled consciences (John 8:9). When a soul passes a boundary in his relationship with God, then God will allow that soul's conscience to be seared, rendering it inoperable (1 Timothy 4:1-2).

Restoration of the conscience after the second birth

During the restoration process of the conscience after the second birth, the conscience may be weak. 1 Corinthians 8 and 10 discuss this regarding meat sacrificed to idols. If we wound the conscience of a brethren with a weaker conscience, we sin against Christ (1 Corinthians 8:12).

In Hebrews 10:22 we read: "Let us draw near with a true heart in full assurance of faith, having our hearts sprinkled from an evil conscience, and our bodies washed with pure water." At the second birth our hearts are sprinkled from an evil conscience (showing that the conscience is probably on the inner or outer surface of the heart). However, the conscience must be strengthened after the second birth. This occurs through having a pure heart and from maintaining a strong faith, as we shall see.

Paul charges Timothy to edify people through Godly faith (1 Timothy 1:4). He adds this commandment: "Now the end of the commandment is charity out of a pure heart, and *of* a good conscience, and *of* faith unfeigned" (v 5). In keeping the faith, people will develop a good conscience and a pure heart.

1 Timothy 1:19 states: "Holding faith, and a good conscience; which some having put away concerning faith have made shipwreck." The putting away of faith shipwrecks the soul, since the conscience becomes unreliable. We saw that what is not done in faith is done in sin.

1 Timothy 3:9 shows the link between a pure conscience and faith: "Holding the mystery of the faith in a pure conscience." Paul adds: "Unto the pure all things are pure" (Titus 1:15). This means that the pure in heart have a pure conscience.

Therefore, the way to strengthen the conscience is to strengthen the faith and to purify the heart. If a soul does these things, then the conscience will grow progressively stronger toward the things of God. If a soul is purged from sin, then there is no more awareness of sin (Hebrews 10:2). Therefore, as the conscience grows stronger, it becomes an increasingly reliable guide as to when sin needs to be confessed to God. Hebrews 13:18 tells us: "Pray for us: for we trust we have a good conscience, in all things willing to live honestly." A soul can trust in faith that he has a good conscience when he can live honestly and with a pure heart before God and man.

INTERACTIONS WITH OTHER SPIRITS

In Ezekiel 38:10 we read: "Thus saith the Lord GOD; It shall also come to pass, *that* at the same time shall things come into thy mind, and thou shalt think an evil thought." Ezekiel is prophesying to the soul of Gog. Evil spirits have inserted a thought into the heart of Gog, and his mind perceives it. God is revealing the consequences for the soul of Gog, if he acts on the thought.

INTERACTIONS WITH GOD

The Lord performs acts to souls, using both the natural and spiritual senses. Some examples have been chosen to highlight how God interacts with souls.

1. Deuteronomy 28:59-68 gives an example of the soul showing an integrated response to calamity—the flesh cannot rest, the heart trembles, vision fails, and the emotion of the mind is sorrow. If God had allowed just the physical circumstances to speak to the people, they might have had a different spiritual response to the physical adversity of lack of ease. However, the Lord intervened in the spirit of the people to cause the heart to tremble. Here we see God acting on the soul through the spirit and also through the physical circumstances to produce the response of the soul.

2. The Lord tells us that He knows every thought that the soul has (Ezekiel 11:5). He is also able to cause thoughts to enter the mind of the soul (Daniel 2:29).

3. Romans 1:28 tells us that God holds a soul responsible for choosing not to retain Him in his knowledge. As a result He gives that soul over to having a reprobate mind.

CONCLUSIONS

It is the soul that decides the spiritual destiny and maturity of the inner man (spirit). If the soul is willing to accept God as sovereign and the Lord Jesus Christ as Savior and Lord, then it is given a new heart and a new spirit at that time of acceptance by God. When the soul chooses to let the Lord Jesus be Lord, it agrees to be subject to His leading. The soul has to be taught how to do this by God.

THE WRONG WAY

The Scriptures tell us: "There is a way which seemeth right unto a man, but the end thereof *are* the ways of death" (Proverbs 14:12). The New Testament depicts the wrong way as one's attempting God's work in the power of the flesh instead of obedience to the Spirit of God.

> Let no man beguile you of your reward in a voluntary humility and worshipping of angels, intruding into those things which he hath not seen, vainly puffed up by his fleshly mind, And not holding the Head, from which all the body by joints and bands having nourishment ministered, and knit together, increaseth with the increase of God. Wherefore if ye be dead with Christ from the rudiments of the world, why, as though living in the world, are ye subject to ordinances, (Touch not; taste not; handle not; Which all are to perish with the using;) after the commandments and doctrines of men? Which things have indeed a shew of wisdom in will worship, and humility, and neglecting of the body; not in any honour to the satisfying of the flesh.
>
> Colossians 2:18-23

In this Scripture God discusses the situation of a soul's trying to purify itself instead of having the Lord do it with the co-operation of the soul. It is a 180 degree difference; and in order to walk after the Holy Spirit, we must learn how to identify this false humility, or else we will find ourselves trapped in it. Following are some observations about this passage.

1. God begins by asking us to let no man beguile us. This tells us that the false is a work of man. It will be at variance with His Word in at least one area.
2. The humility is always voluntary; it is not an area that the Holy Spirit has identified to us for change. We hear it first from man, and we are falsely convicted.
3. The man who leads us into it will have pride in his knowledge, if we observe him closely (puffed up by his fleshly mind [note the mind is fleshly, but the pride is in the soul]). The area to observe in this man is in his relationship to the head, *i.e.*, the Lord. He will not accept the rest of the Word of God that reveals his work to be in error.
4. The areas of false will into which we will fall have to do with a fleshly lust and, therefore, frequently will involve food or material possessions. In the vision that Peter had (Acts 11) God clearly revealed that all food is now clean. If we are not led by the Holy Spirit into abstinence toward a specific food, then we should freely eat according to our tastes, providing we do not offend another. The reason for this is that God places us in various parts of society to minister to the lost in those areas. If we place food barriers that He has not required, then we will have a spirit of pride rising in this area that will be detected by the spirits of those to whom we are trying to minister.

Therefore, we must learn how to be obedient to God's Spirit and walk after it in order to avoid the trap of being led by man in these areas. We have to examine the roots of our attitudes toward the material world, including food, to see what our soul is gaining from these attitudes. What is the fruit of this attitude? Is it obedience, or is it a false humility? True humility is found only in obedience to the Holy Spirit in all things.

In order to help us to discern the spirit at the root of our beliefs, attitudes, and behaviors in all areas of our heart, God will bring testing. In order to discern the roots of the flows of our spirits which come out of our hearts, we should examine our response to correction in an area. Is there a pang if another corrects us, or is there a submission to the correction? The answers to these questions can indicate the roots. In addition, there are many other ways of discerning the spirit behind our behaviors.

One particularly bad behavior pattern is discussed in Philemon 14. Paul says that we should not coerce a person to do anything. He has to have a willing mind. There are many Scriptures that talk about the spirit behind manipulation and control as being that of witchcraft. We must avoid this spirit at all costs. We must not try to induce a guilt feeling in another, for it will be false guilt if the Holy Spirit has not convicted him. We frequently see manipulation in the raising of money for various purposes. God will not bless any behavior where the root is evil. A soul must be very careful to test the spirits behind all contemplated behaviors, including speaking, to stop the release of a spirit of manipulation and control. When one identifies such a spirit a soul must repent and ask the Lord for cleansing of his heart and inner man.

THE CORRECT WAY

Almost always the new heart and spirit become polluted by the world system, and the soul has to then work cooperatively with God to take back lost ground. It needs power from God to purify the heart, to quell the flesh into service for God, and to battle demonic efforts to thwart spiritual growth. The soul does not have the power to do it without working collaboratively with God. Even the disciples showed little change in their thoughts, attitudes, beliefs, and behavior after three years of being close to the Lord Jesus on a daily basis. This should be a strong warning to us. One even betrayed Him for financial gain. It was not until they saw the resurrected Lord that they started to change; and then they had to wait until given power, despite having already had the new spirit given to them by the Lord (John 20:22).

Those chosen to minister did not start until they had undergone intense training and internal change. The internal change in the disciples was vast and deep in its proportions. The apostle Paul spent possibly fourteen years in preparation, and during this time he had a complete inward renewal. It is most important to have the internal change to purity of heart for the Lord to have a powerful tool. Many people want to start a work before this process of purification is sufficiently advanced. The root of this desire is usually in the flesh, although the Lord is free to do what He will with His servants.

The process of spiritual maturation may seem long, because we are used to quick results in our society. Spiritual change comes through trials and suffering. 2 Peter 1 5-9 talks about the process of maturation: "And beside this, giving all diligence, add to your faith virtue; and to virtue knowledge; And to knowledge temperance; and to temperance patience; and to patience godliness; And to godliness brotherly kindness; and to brotherly kindness charity. For if these things be in you, and abound, they make *you that ye shall* neither *be* barren nor unfruitful in the knowledge of our Lord Jesus Christ. But he that lacketh these things is blind, and cannot see afar off, and hath forgotten that he was purged from his old sins."

Note that there is a stepwise progression, and that one step is patience. You cannot learn this and carry it in your heart without going through lengthy times of testing (Philippians 1:29 and 1 Peter 2:19-21). There are no short cuts. Notice also that patience is by no means the last step. Also note that, until you have completed this process (not just part of it), you are still blind in the spirit realm and cannot see far; and you have not been purged (completely) from sins. Thus, spiritual vision comes only through maturation; and this comes through adverse circumstances that we must embrace in joy, looking for the tutoring hand of the Lord as He prepares us to handle true riches.

As one progresses in the path of spiritual maturing, he must begin to learn how to hear reliably God speaking to him in all of the ways that

He does. This is like a baby's having to learn the same in the natural world so that he can be obedient to his parents. Once a soul can reliably hear from God, then the flesh has to be put to death daily; and the process outlined by Peter is underway. One learns to treasure small changes internally. One has to focus on discerning the condition of one's inner man and heart, constantly being aware of this state so that he can fulfill the command to pray without ceasing. He has to war aggressively against any state of the heart and the inner man that is not one of joy, peace, and the awareness of the closeness of God. The soul is responsible for maintaining this state before the Lord. There is no room for depression, anxiety, fear, or doubt. This is a place of faith (trust). It is the normal state for the heart, but in our age few achieve this. The demonic powers will try to oppose the spirit of such a person, but with the help of God and others joining in prayer the enemy will flee. We hear talk of spiritual mountains and valleys in the life of a soul, but this should be a transition stage, until the soul lives the Kingdom life (Romans 14:17). Certainly an aggressive attack from the demonic forces may besiege a soul's inner man and force him from the ideal place for a period of several hours or even days and weeks, but that soul should be battling with all of the resources that God has given him to get his inner man back into the correct position before God. When the enemy attacks is not a time to be passive, but the soul must stand at the very least. One should not give ground (Ephesians 6:11).

The Lord desires that His children purify their hearts, renew their minds, and follow His Spirit. He wants to see growth to the point where He can call us His friend, just as He did with Moses and Abraham. This involves a huge internal change with resulting external behavior. It is all accomplished by progressing in faith, as we trust Him in more and more issues. We have to be delivered from responding to anything in fear, and we must be perfected in love toward all of the creation. The Lord wants us to know His ways and to understand that we have the freedom to commit to them voluntarily, as we see that they are the better choice. This attitude glorifies Him more than one in which we submit to Him, believing that we can change nothing because we view Him as having all power and as having predetermined our path through life. The Lord wants us to progress beyond walking after any of the world system and to walk continually in truth. When we do, we are constantly showing Him to the world. He wants us to know the creative power that He has placed in us for bringing about change in the world around us by speaking truth. He wants us to follow His model of addressing spiritual issues and not temporal worldly issues, unless directed by Him. Our ministry is one of reconciliation (2 Corinthians 5). God wants us to be bold, speaking out present-day truth under His guidance and letting the world react, rather then have us cowered by a spirit of fear in any area. He wants us to have our spirits perpetually before Him in a state of prayerful listening, ready to detect the faintest expectation from Him. He expects our spirits to be continually full of joy and peace and the knowledge of His presence.

Our souls are responsible for choosing the changes that need to be made in our hearts to bring all of these things, and even more, to fruition. It is a great thing to be blessed with the freedom and the power to make these changes. When we fulfill God's desires in purifying our hearts, we will certainly be useful to God for His work (Ephesians 2:10) in our generation.

14
WORKINGS OF THE CONSCIENCE OF SPIRITUAL MAN

INTRODUCTION

The human conscience is mentioned by this name only in the New Testament. It is mentioned thirty-two times, and each time it comes from the same Greek word, *syneidesis*. There is no equivalent word in the Septuagint (The Greek Old Testament). The reason for this is not apparent, but it may well reflect the fact that the Israelites (to whom the Old Testament was written) were to be guided by the Law. They were not required to follow their conscience, although the fact that God still required obedience from a perfect heart would indicate that they needed an active and healthy conscience. Passages such as John 8:9, Acts 23:1, and Romans 2:15 indicate that people under the Law were still expected and were able to use their conscience.

LOCATION OF THE CONSCIENCE

Hebrews 10:22 indicates that the heart can be sprinkled from an evil conscience and that our bodies can be washed with pure water. This tells us that the conscience is delicate and that it is attached to the heart. It is probably on the outer or inner surface. The analogy to washing the body suggests that it is on the outer surface, through which possibly all of the thoughts and intents of the heart pass on the way to the mind of the soul. It is not the same as God's laws, which He intends to write in the minds and in the hearts of the Israelites at a future time (Hebrews 8:10, 10:16).

ACTIONS OF THE CONSCIENCE

The first work of the conscience is to alert us that an intended action is sinful. If we do not heed the reminder, then our conscience will alert us to the need to repent (Romans 2:15). The conscience bears witness to the law written in the heart. Thus, it is an interpreter of the law to a soul. In Romans 9:1-5 we see that Paul's conscience witnesses to him, jointly with the Holy Spirit, that he is telling the truth. Thus, the conscience is to be a witness to a person about what they say and about their attitudes and beliefs. It witnesses as to the truth of their words and feelings in comparison with divine truth. In Romans 9 Paul states that he knows that what he writes is true. His conscience did not accuse him of exaggerating. His conscience let him know that the writing is true and not a lie. Paul expresses such a radical statement here that he wants his reader to know that it is true; hence, he accentuates it by stating that his conscience did not challenge him.

Therefore, one work of the conscience is to bear witness to anything that we may try to say or do that is false or sinful. In this regard it helps the mind to know about the intents and thoughts of the heart. If something false is sent to the mind from the heart and the soul is tempted to express it, the conscience will give a warning to the mind of the soul that it is false. If we, as people who have been through the second birth, express the false issue, then we will grieve the Spirit of God and experience a spirit of recrimination (provided our conscience has not been seared or become impure [1 Timothy 4:2, Titus 1:15]). We must learn to distinguish this state in our heart from a state of false guilt with which an enemy spirit may try to burden us.

A second work of the conscience is to maintain a list of offences (sins) that we have committed to God and to men (Acts 23:1, 24:16).

A third function is to make sure that we do not violate the conscience of another individual. Our own conscience must be attuned to this requirement of God's: "But have renounced the hidden things of dishonesty, not walking in craftiness, nor handling the word of God deceitfully; but by manifestation of the truth commending ourselves to every man's conscience in the sight of God" (2 Corinthians 4:2).

A fourth function is to be pure, such as when we hold the mystery of the faith in a pure conscience (1 Timothy 3:9). One's conscience had to be pure in order to be eligible to serve as a deacon. Paul served God with a pure conscience (2 Timothy 1:3).

HOW THE CONSCIENCE OPERATES

INTRODUCTION

The conscience works by sending information (spirit) to the mind of the soul in conjunction with spiritual flows from the heart to the mind of the soul. These two thoughts (spirits) excuse or accuse each other depending on how the spirit from the conscience interacts with that from the heart. The spirit from the conscience presumably attaches itself to the flow from the heart. The mind of the soul is trained to recognize the "voice" of conscience (Romans 2:15).

The conscience remembers sin until the Lord cleanses our conscience of it.

The conscience also remembers the Law of God.

The conscience has to be cleansed and pure before God—He requires this, and it is how He made us. Therefore, when there was a memory of sin, the individual in the Old Covenant had to sacrifice. In the New Covenant he has to confess and repent.

BEFORE THE SECOND BIRTH

In Hebrews 9:8-10 we read: "The Holy Ghost this signifying, that the way into the holiest of all was not yet made manifest, while as the first tabernacle was yet standing: Which *was* a figure for the time then present, in which were offered both gifts and sacrifices, that could not make him that did the service perfect, as pertaining to the conscience; *Which stood* only in meats and drinks, and divers washings, and carnal ordinances, imposed *on them* until the time of reformation." This passage tells us a lot about the functioning of the conscience in Old Covenant times. (Since an unbeliever is basically depending on his works for salvation [whether or not he understands this], these principles from the Old Covenant apply to him.) Gifts and sacrifices were to thank God and to take away one's sins, if performed in faith. They fulfilled the requirements of God's Law but were not able to wash the conscience clean (see also the discussion about remission of sin in Chapter 12). These gifts and sacrifices were carnal ordinances of the Law. Thus, one could keep the Law, but he retained the memory of his sins. If the individual had not retained memory of sin, there would not have been a need for further sacrifice (Hebrews 10:2).

Hebrews 10:1-4 states: "For the law having a shadow of good things to come, *and* not the very image of the things, can never with those sacrifices which they offered year by year continually make the comers thereunto perfect. For then would they not have ceased to be offered? because that the worshippers once purged should have had no more conscience of sins. But in those *sacrifices there is* a remembrance again *made* of sins every year. For *it is* not possible that the blood of bulls and of goats should take away sins." Therefore, since the blood of bulls and goats could not take away sin, the very act of having to sacrifice continually year by year kept the awareness of sin in the minds and in the consciences of the people.

We see that those who brought the woman caught in the act of adultery to the Lord Jesus were all convicted by their own conscience of prior sin. None would cast the first stone (John 8:9). These people were living under the Old Covenant.

AFTER THE SECOND BIRTH

Hebrews 9:13-14 tells us: "For if the blood of bulls and of goats, and the ashes of an heifer sprinkling the unclean, sanctifieth to the purifying of the flesh: How much more shall the blood of Christ, who through the eternal Spirit offered himself without spot to God, purge your conscience from dead works to serve the living God?" Here we see that in the New Covenant the conscience is purged from dead works by the blood of the Lord Jesus Christ. Sin is no longer held in the memory of the conscience. We are freed from the Law and from memory of past sin in the conscience (not the memory of the mind of the soul). Thus, God sees a cleansed conscience when we abide in Him through receiving the Lord Jesus as our Lord and Savior and accepting that His blood has taken away our sin once and for all—past, present, and future personal sins.

In Hebrews 10:19-22 we read: "Having therefore, brethren, boldness to enter into the holiest by the blood of Jesus, By a new and living way, which he hath consecrated for us, through the veil, that is to say, his flesh; And *having* an high priest over the house of God; Let us draw near with a true heart in full assurance of faith, having our hearts sprinkled from an evil conscience, and our bodies washed with pure water." Therefore, because of the blood of Jesus we can enter into the holiest place by faith, since our hearts are sprinkled from an evil conscience and our bodies are washed with pure water. The memory of our conscience is washed clean.

No individual lives one hundred percent of the time under the New Covenant after the second birth. To the extent that we continue to have a "mixed walk," partly in the flesh under the Law and partly after the Spirit of God, we will have weakened consciences that will retain a memory of sin. That is because the part of our walk under the Law makes us feel a sense of sin in the conscience, when we violate any part of the Law. God can cleanse this, when we confess our sins to Him and repent: "If we confess our sins, he is faithful and just to forgive us *our* sins, and to cleanse us from all unrighteousness" (1 John 1:9).

STATES OF THE CONSCIENCE

WEAK CONSCIENCES

We read about *weak* consciences in 1 Corinthians 8:7-12 and 10:25-29. Consciences are said to be weak in relationship to knowledge. Those people with weak consciences are spiritual babes, who have not yet come to understand their freedom from the Law in the Lord Jesus. Thus a conscience works in relationship to the current level of knowledge that an individual has of God's laws. God's laws are written in the mind and in the heart of an individual who has been through the second birth. The conscience will always protest, if a soul violates God's laws, provided the conscience is pure. The conscience is maintained in a pure state as we walk in faith (Hebrews 10:19-22). A spiritual babe will tend to look for rules to follow rather than to learn to be led by the Spirit of God. God holds the individual responsible for violating these additional rules that he believes are God's rules. The conscience is reset automatically, as one increases in his understanding of God's laws and walks more after the Spirit of God.

Examples of people adding rules to God's law are the Pharisees, who were frequently upset by the Lord when they thought that He had broken the Law. However, their laws of tradition had added to God's law and in many cases had changed it. They had failed to recognize the hierarchy of God's law in such things as doing good work on the Sabbath. In the same way a babe in the Lord has failed to transition completely into the freedom from the Law that the Lord gives.

Those who have a greater understanding of the changes in the New Covenant, particularly in relation to dietary issues and sacrifices to idols (the Lord is the one who gives everything to us), have to be careful not to cause a person of less knowledge to infringe his conscience. This is a sin against the brethren and the Lord (1 Corinthians 8:12).

MATURING CONSCIENCES

Thus, the issues that cause one to violate his conscience are changed through maturation, as one learns and understands spiritual issues more comprehensively. The Lord has allowed the conscience to be a changing thing so that people at different levels of purification in heart and maturation in the inner man have different issues which cause them to sin before Him. Thus the Lord is able to deal with us all at our own level without deviating from His standards. He holds us all accountable for how we perceive His Law. This is not to say that the basic law can be violated, because there are bedrock principles that are not subject to change. It is these bedrock principles that are written on all people's hearts (as in Romans 2:15).

THE NORMAL STATE OF THE CONSCIENCE

The conscience should be kept void of offence toward God and toward men (Acts 24:16) by repentance of sin and avoidance of sin.

One must have a "good" conscience (1 Timothy 1:5). This "good" is toward God.

Peter says that water baptism is a picture of a good conscience toward God (*i.e.*, a conscience that has been cleaned [1 Peter 3:21]).

MALFUNCTIONING OF THE CONSCIENCE

We read that the conscience can be seared with a hot iron, when a person departs from the faith, gives heed to seducing spirits and the doctrine of devils, and speaks lies in hypocrisy (1 Timothy 4:2). The issues in context were related to food and marriage. These form the basis for vain philosophies, and they prevent a person from seeing the provision of God.

Minds and consciences are defiled in those who are unbelieving, and they are defiled by sin (Titus 1:15).

CONCLUSIONS

The conscience is associated with the heart. It remembers and identifies sinful thoughts and behaviors and presents these to the mind of the soul. It compares our intended or past actions to the Law of God and to those things that we add to the Law thinking they are of God (which people can add under either the Old or the New Covenant). The purpose is to witness to us about our intended or past actions when they violate (sin against) our current understanding and knowledge of God's laws. We can then avoid an intended action or repent of a past action (sacrifice for a past action under the Old Covenant).

The conscience is purged of the remembrance of sin under the New Covenant only to the extent that we are living under it. When we live under the Law and follow the Spirit of God in a mixed walk, we will have a weak conscience that has to be repeatedly cleansed of sin. Because all are not at the same level of maturity, those who are more mature must in love refrain from causing another to have an awareness of sin in his conscience. If one has a weak conscience, due to his ignorance of his freedom in the Spirit, when he violates a law in his conscience, he will have a memory of sin; he is, therefore, separated from God until he repents. It is a sin for a brother with a stronger conscience in respect to freedom in the Lord to violate the weaker brother by causing him to act against his conscience. 1 Corinthians 8:7-12 and 10:25-29 explain the mechanics of this.

The conscience is strengthened through growth toward maturity in the Lord. It has to be maintained in a state of purity and a state of being "good" toward God. When one goes against the faith and follows the doctrines of demons and seducing spirits, he will begin to tell lies hypocritically; and he will end up with a conscience that has been seared by a hot iron. He will no longer have an awareness of the conscience trying to work to prevent him from sinning; he will stay in a state of sin.

15
WORKINGS OF THE WILL OF SPIRITUAL MAN

INTRODUCTION

WORDS STUDIED IN THIS CHAPTER

We shall study four words that the Scriptures use for the noun form of the English word *will.*

Two words are Hebrew words.

Rsaba has the sense of "summoning one's wishes."

Ratsown has the sense of "pleasure, delight, favor, goodwill, acceptance, and will."

The other two are Greek words.

Boulomai has the sense of "to will deliberately, to have a purpose, and to be minded."

Thelema has a sense of "what one wishes or has determined shall be done, will, choice, inclination, desire, and pleasure."

The latter word, *thelema,* is the most useful in understanding the human will.

WHAT IS THE WILL?

The mind of the soul deals with a lot of inflows of spirit from the heart (and thus the inner man and evil spirits) and from the natural environment (other people, the world system, and the creation). People have various desires at any one time that they would like to see fulfilled. The mind assesses the pros and cons of transitioning these desires into implementing the means to bring them to fruition. The factors involved in this include, but may not be limited to, understanding from prior experience; non-specific fear; input from friends, colleagues, and family; hope; faith that this is what God wants one to do; conscience; fleshly restraints, and possibly a spiritual resistance, due to the effort that will need to be put forth; and restraining evil spirits. With each of these desires is an image of the future expectations that a person has, if the desire is fulfilled. The content of these images is extremely important to consider for determining if a desire is from God.

At some point in any such deliberation a soul may become satisfied with the evidence that indicates he should fulfill a particular desire. If he proceeds with implementing this desire, the soul then places the decision making into the category of saying, "I will do this." This center that we call the *will* is closely linked to the mind. Indeed, a mind has to have a highest decision-making area; and this is what we term the *will*. Ephesians 1:11 states: "In whom also we have obtained an inheritance, being predestinated according to the purpose of him who worketh all things after the counsel of his own will." This portrays God's will as giving counsel to Him. Therefore, it is separate from the mind of God to some degree, since He makes the distinction. We are made in His image; therefore, the same applies to souls. A mind has to have a will, since it has desires. Thus, a soul has an area of will in the flesh, heart, inner man, and the soul itself. The question of whether there is a separate will in the mind of the soul and another for the soul itself is probably a moot point so far as function goes. My impression is that there is a separate will for the soul, since the mind makes a decision that something needs to be changed in the soul's state. Also, we shall see below that the soul does not control its own will, since the soul has to pray for God to fill him with power to accomplish that will.

IMPORTANT ISSUES ABOUT THE WILL

An important point about the will is that a soul does not necessarily have control over it in order to perform God's desires (will). We have to obtain the power to control the will by fervent prayer made by ourselves and by others (Epaphras labored in prayer for the Colossians to stand perfect and complete in all the will of God [Colossians 4:12]). We shall see other Scriptural evidence for this below. We shall also look at how the will interacts with God, with angelic spirits, with other people, and with the other components of spiritual man.

There is a will in the flesh; there is a will in the soul; there is a will in the heart; and there is a will in the mind (mind of the soul). John 1:13 states: "Which were born, not of blood, nor of the will of the flesh, nor of the will of man [will of the soul], but of God." Paul adds: "Among whom also we all had our conversation in times past in the lusts of our flesh, fulfilling the desires [usually translated will] of the flesh and of the mind; and were by nature the children of wrath, even as others" (Ephesians 2:3). There is also a separate will for the heart (Ephesians 6:6). These three Scripture passages indicate separate wills for the flesh, for the soul, for the mind, and for the heart. The passages in Ephesians 1:11 and in Colossians 4:12 suggest that the highest will in the soul is not the same as the will of the mind of the soul.

The location of the primary decision-making will for the soul is in the soul separate to, but in close communication with, the mind of the soul. It can offer counsel to the soul (Ephesians 1:11), in that the mind of the soul can observe its inclination. This tells us that it must be in a location other than the mind of the soul. The will of the heart is a function of the heart. It determines which of all of our beliefs and attitudes are channeled into potential behaviors which are presented to the mind of the soul for a decision. The soul can will to control and change this will of the heart in order to express behaviors that follow after the desires (will) of God.

As we study the passages of Scripture with this word *will*, we learn that it is frequently used to indicate the "will or desire" of God. It describes what God wants in particular situations. When God wants something, He has the spiritual power to bring it about. We have seen in the chapters on spirit (9) and on heart (10) that we can "will or desire" something, but we do not always have the spiritual power to implement our will. Therefore, in man the "will of the soul" is an area that marshals our desires. There are separate centers for the flesh, the heart, the soul, and the mind. These may be in conflict, and hence they would lessen our power to implement a desire or purpose that the mind of the soul chooses. In previous chapters we have learned that, in order to implement the will of the Holy Spirit (that we have perceived in our soul's mind) in our lives, we will need the assistance of His power to overcome the opposing wills in our own heart and flesh. This infusion of God's power can change the old behavior patterns that are set in the heart.

GOD IN RELATION TO HIS WILL AND OUR WILL

A very important concept in walking after the Spirit of God is seen in 1 Thessalonians 5:18 where we read that it is God's will for us to give thanks in all things. We can do this as we focus on eternity and not on the present times. We have to know that all of the adversity that comes our way is designed by and allowed by God to help us to mature for eternity. As we embrace this, we can truly give thanks in all things.

God hears those who both worship Him and do His will (John 9:31). David was deemed to be a man after God's own heart, "who shall fulfill all my will" (Acts 13:22). Paul was an apostle by the will of God (2 Corinthians 1:1). God's will is related to His good pleasure (Ephesians 1:5 and 1:9). God works all things after the counsel of His own will (Ephesians 1:11). In order to perform God's will, we must align our soul's will with His will and then fervently pray for power to implement the will of our soul.

God has various desires for us—good, perfect, and acceptable

Romans 12:2 states: "And be not conformed to this world: but be ye transformed by the renewing of your mind, that ye may prove what *is* that good, and acceptable, and perfect, will of God." We see that a mind has to be renewed and a soul transformed in order to fulfill that good, perfect, and acceptable will of God. Note there are three levels of desires God has for us:

a) Good
b) Acceptable
c) Perfect

These are layers of closeness to the entire will of God. An example would be a teacher's talking to a student about faith at exactly the right moment when God has prepared the heart of that student to accept the thing being taught. The levels of will are:

a) Being a teacher and talking to students about faith is "good."
b) Talking to this particular student about faith is "acceptable."
c) Talking to this student at this time about faith completes God's will in its entirety and hence is deemed "perfect."

God's will for us

It is God's will that none should perish but rather that all should come to repentance (2 Peter 3:9). It is God's will for us that we should be sanctified (1 Thessalonians 4:3) and abstain from fornication.

A very important part of being led by the Spirit of God is found in 1 Thessalonians 5:18 where God asks us to give Him thanks in every thing (even in every minute detail of our life our heart attitude must be one of thankfulness—Ephesians 6:6). This is a test for whether we are operating in the spirit or in the flesh. If our "thank you" is reflexive, heartfelt, and genuine, then we are in the spirit. If we have to stop and think, "Oh yes, I should give thanks," then we are partly in the will of God, but not completely. In the latter case we are obedient, but not with a perfect heart (just like King Amaziah [2 Chronicles 25:2]).

After we have done God's will, we receive the promise; but we need to be patient in waiting for it (Hebrews 10:36).

God wants us to be perfect in every good work to do His will (Hebrews 13:21). We see that we have to pray for Him to make us perfect (Hebrews 13:20). We cannot make ourselves perfect; otherwise, it is a fleshly work. We have to let God prepare His own sacrifice of our flesh even as He prepared the sacrifice of His only begotten Son, the Lord Jesus. This passage shows us that it requires the Lord Jesus' working in us to be able to perfect us in doing the will of God. We need His power in us to be able to be perfect in this regard.

God's will is for us to silence the ignorance of foolish men with well doing (1 Peter 2:15). In like kind He may want us to suffer for well doing rather than to do evil (1 Peter 3:17, 1 Peter 4:19).

If we ask anything according to God's will, we can be confident of His hearing us (1 John 5:14). This is to be contrasted with asking from our own lusts (James 4:2-3). If our will is to ask Him anything according to His will, then He will hear. We need to know our Lord well enough to know those things that He will hear. We can then in faith receive these things.

Attitudes toward God's will

1. We can will to delight to do God's will, because His law is written within our heart (Psalm 40:8).
2. We can ask God to teach us His will (Psalm 143:10).
3. We should maintain good works (Titus 3:8).
4. We can will to be a friend of the world (this is enmity with God) or a friend of God—there is no middle ground (James 4:4).
5. We should no longer live (after the second birth) in the flesh to the lusts of men but rather to the will of God (1 Peter 4:2-3).
6. Consider Matthew 26:39 where the Lord Jesus was talking with His Father. His will (one of His many desires) did not coincide entirely with the Father's will. This is not sin, since we know that The Lord Jesus led a sinless life. The important point is that when we know God's will, then we must be obedient and submit to it even unto death. This was at the end of the Lord's life, so we can see that having a perfect heart does not preclude having a different set of desires. However, the hierarchical ultimate desire of the will must be to submit to the will of God in all things. This was the case with the Lord Jesus. If this is not the case in our will, then we may readily fall into sin patterns.

In Matthew 6:10 we read: "Thy kingdom come. Thy will be done in earth, as *it is* in heaven." Jesus is teaching man to pray in agreement with God for His will to be carried out on earth as it is in heaven. This is a profound Scripture. It teaches us that the will of God is declared in heaven, but it may not be carried out on earth due to the interference of evil spirits and sinful men. Our prayers can allow God to act in the earth to fulfill His purposes. Since our spirit is seated with the Lord, we may, when in the spirit, know God's will prophetically; but that does not mean it will be fulfilled. That is why we must be very careful to work with God to allow the words He speaks over us to come to pass.

Matthew adds in 7:21: "Not every one that saith unto me, Lord, Lord, shall enter into the kingdom of heaven; but he that doeth the will of my Father which is in heaven." God expects us to will to be in obedience to His will. We are expected to talk with Him and come to understand His will for us in all situations. Sometimes the written Word is sufficient; *e.g.*, we are not to covet. However, in choosing between two automobiles or two jobs, we need to seek the desires of God for us.

Our tongue turns our course as our soul wills (James 3:4). By always speaking the truth in love, we follow God's will (Ephesians 4:15). When we deviate from this standard, even in a minor issue, we are not following God's perfect will for us.

Differences between God's will and ours

Even the Lord Jesus' will differed from the Father's will, but the issue is that He submitted to the Father's will (Luke 22:42). We often may have desires that are different from God, the Father; but the issue is whether we will be obedient and submit to His will. He will not manipulate us to perform His will (for that would be akin to witchcraft). He wants us to make a freewill offering (Psalm 119:108). In John 6:38 and Hebrews 10:7 Jesus tells us that he came down from heaven, not to do His own will, but the will of Him who sent Him. We cannot do less.

ANGELIC SPIRITS

In 2 Timothy 2:20, 26 we read that Satan can, at his will, take captive those vessels in God's house that are wooden and of the earth, made to dishonor. These people can escape the snare of the devil, if they grow in the Lord to repentance and to the acknowledging of the truth.

OTHER PEOPLE

We have many interactions of the will with other people. We will not document any Scripture here. Needless to say, we must be obedient to God's will and seek it first above any desires other people may have for us. We should never make prior commitments to other people that are absolute commitments without knowing that this is the will of God for us. No person should be allowed to be a stumbling block to our seeking and fulfilling the acceptable will of God.

OTHER COMPONENTS OF SPIRITUAL MAN

Soul's interacting with the will

The soul must seek God's will, not its own.

In John 5:30 we read: "I can of mine own self do nothing: as I hear, I judge: and my judgment is just; because I seek not mine own will, but the will of the Father which hath sent me." Doing God's will and not one's own will allows accurate discernment in all situations. Jesus said that He could do nothing of His own self. He relied on hearing from God in all situations. We certainly have to do the same. Jesus is saying he discerns as he hears (from the Father).

Power over the will

1 Corinthians 7:37 shows that a soul can have (but does not necessarily have) power over his own will: "Nevertheless he that standeth stedfast in his heart, having no necessity, but hath power over his own will, and hath so decreed in his heart that he will keep his virgin, doeth well." We have to ask God to fill us with power in order to have power over our will. Our will gives the soul counsel (Ephesians 1:11—since we are made in God's image, this is so).

How to get power over our will

In order to stand perfect and complete in all the will of God, we have to pray fervently for it and also have others praying fervently for it (Colossians 1:9, 4:12).

In 2 Corinthians 1:1 we read: "Paul, an apostle of Jesus Christ by the will of God, and Timothy *our* brother, unto the church of God which is at Corinth, with all the saints which are in all Achaia." Paul begins most of his epistles with a similar statement. We see that it may be possible for a person to become what appears to be an apostle by his own will. He would not be an apostle of God.

Wise souls understand the will of God (Ephesians 5:17).

Heart interacting with will

Ephesians 6:6 tells us that we can do the will of God from the soul and from the heart. Men pleasers do it just from the soul and not the heart. This tells us that God expects the will of our heart and our soul to be the same and that they submit to His will. He does not want just the will of the mind of the soul, but He wants the heart to will (desire) to do His work (compare this with King Amaziah, mentioned above [2 Chronicles 25:2]).

Flesh interacting with will

John 1:12-13 states: "But as many as received him, to them gave he power to become the sons of God, *even* to them that believe on his name: Which were born, not of blood, nor of the will of the flesh, nor of the will of man, but of God." It is of note here that John's description highlights that the will of the flesh and the will of man (the will of the soul) can be different. If we allow our soul to be led by the Spirit of God, then the will of the flesh will be diametrically opposite to that of the soul (Chapter 9).

The apostle Paul states in Romans 7:18: "For I know that in me (that is, in my flesh) dwelleth no good thing: for to will is present with me; but *how* to perform that which is good I find not." In Romans 7:25

he states: "I thank God through Jesus Christ our Lord. So then with the mind I myself serve the law of God; but with the flesh the law of sin." These passages show how appositional the flesh is to the will of the soul that has a new spirit and who is *willing* to serve God.

Ephesians 2:3 also shows us that the flesh has a will of its own.

Mind interacting with will

Colossians 1:9 tells us to desire and to pray to be filled in the knowledge of God's will in all wisdom and spiritual understanding. We saw in the chapter on the mind that there is a hierarchy of wisdom, understanding, and knowledge. We have to pray and cry out fervently for this filling of the knowledge of God's will. We saw in Chapter 11 on the mind the conditions that are needed to have this prayer answered. Also note that we do not reason out His will; rather, we are filled with it as an impartation into our spirit from the Holy Spirit (or by a more direct utterance, vision, or dream).

Other components of the soul

We have dealt with these interactions among other components of spiritual man within the respective chapters of those components.

CONCLUSION

We have separate wills in our soul, in the mind of the soul, in the heart, in the flesh, and (while not explicitly stated) in our inner man. The will of the soul is the area that has to have power within it for the soul to accomplish transition from one condition (set of beliefs, attitudes, and behaviors) to another. This power can be obtained from God as the soul chooses to walk in His will. The soul cannot do this without God's power. He will give it, when we pray fervently for it. God expects the will of the soul to be set to follow His will; He also expects the soul to will to purify both the heart and the will of the heart. When we accomplish this, the wills of the heart and of the soul are aligned to follow His will.

Note that making a mental decision to follow a particular course does not give anyone the power to accomplish this. This is quite evident in the area of following God's will, since the flesh and evil spirits will oppose the soul. The flesh and evil spirits have power enough to prevent a soul from following God successfully, unless God gives power into the inner man, who can then empower the will of the soul to be set irresolutely to follow Him. With God's power the soul can succeed.

We see this same problem in many souls who make a new commitment (*e.g.*, New Year's resolutions) to accomplish behavioral changes in such areas as diet and exercise. They do not have the power to make the change. This is particularly evident in those who are prone to "procrastination." Procrastination is actually a spiritual malady that must be overcome through the strengthening of the spirit by the soul.

Degrees of power in the will

It is important to understand why people vary in what is commonly termed "will power." These apparent power differences result from one's past circumstances. Both before and after the second birth the inner man has power that varies among individuals. We see this from Scriptures such as Proverbs 25:28: "He that *hath* no rule over his own spirit *is like* a city *that is* broken down, *and* without walls." This speaks of a difference in degree of power among individuals. This Scripture is in the context of people's not having received a new spirit, since it is in the Old Covenant period. In the New Covenant we read Scriptures such as Ephesians 3:16: "That he would grant you, according to the riches of his glory, to be strengthened with might by his Spirit in the inner man." This Scripture also speaks of a variation in power within the spirit, in this case a new spirit.

The power that is spoken of is not that which sustains life but is rather that which is directed toward particular goals. This is implied in the contextual settings of these two Scriptures. In the first Scripture the context is related to withstanding external evil forces. In the second Scripture the power is necessary to survive the tests that the evil spirits and the flesh bring against a person's faith. Both passages contain the implication that the individual could do something different. The essential point to see is that we all have a similar amount of spiritual power given to us by God as our "life energy." In the old man before the second birth this spirit is dying and has lost much capacity to operate in the spiritual realm. In John 3 we see the spiritual deficits in Nicodemus and, thus, in the soul that has not had the "new birth." It is still able to operate in the natural realm and is subject to control by the soul (Malachi 2:14-16). The new spirit given at the second birth is also subject to control by the soul (Romans 12:11).

We see that the soul is responsible for the state of the spirit (Chapter 9 reviews this in detail). Recall that every single action that we make sows either to the flesh or to the spirit. When people do not take steps to sow to the spirit, they may be said to be procrastinating. What they are actually doing is refusing to sow to the spirit. They have allowed their flesh to build up too much strength, and they may be allowing evil spirits to oppose them without offering any resistance. They can be delivered by God, if they examine the facts, repent as necessary, and ask God to increase the power in their spirit to break the particular sin patterns in which they are bound. They must break any subtle lies they have believed that have allowed evil forces to bind them. They can entreat God under both the Old and the New Covenants to give power to the inner man to help them break out of sin patterns.

Natural Talents

We all receive the same or similar "life energy" in our inner man at birth. The expression and molding of this into what people deem to be naturally successful people—such as those who become great athletes, scientists, statesmen, and businessmen—are really functions of the diversity that God has built into the creation. A person who does not achieve great worldly stature has just as much life energy potentially available as another person, but he may not have the natural endowments of intellectual capability or physical health that allow him to be successful in the world's eyes. People can have a lot of natural gifting and not use it for worldly success, because they are not willing to go through much self denial of fleshly desires in order to succeed. This is a choice they make.

Spiritual Talents

All of us are able to be successful in the spiritual realm regardless of our natural gifting. Success in the spiritual realm is all that will matter when our spirit separates from the flesh at the first death. This success comes by learning to relate to God and to talk with Him about what His will is for us moment by moment and task by task. He will then power our success as we become obedient to Him. Worldly successes are short-lived and involve more the use of natural talents. God will certainly for His purposes have some of His children to be more successful in the natural things of the world. Provided they achieve this in obedience to Him, they are walking in His will.

Part V

16
HOW THE INNER MAN AND THE SOUL INTERACT

We have learned all of the details of the relationship between the inner man and the soul in the preceding chapters contained in Part IV. This will be a brief review in order to remind us of the essential highlights. It will help us to see how the task of the soul is to prepare the inner man as a seed that he will sow into eternity. In turn, this will highlight just how important it is to do all we can as a soul to bring about maturation in the inner man. In this chapter only a few key scriptures will be referenced, since much more detail has already been referenced.

BACKGROUND

HISTORY

God formed Adam and Eve in His image. God created man as a living soul, when He breathed His Spirit into the first Adam. He gave Adam and Eve the ability to reproduce. After the fall of Adam and Eve all offspring were formed in the image of Adam (Genesis 5:3). This meant that we are all born with a spirit (inner man) that is dying. We are all born in a state of sin where our flesh is stronger than our inner man. We are condemned to spend eternity in a state of spiritual death, forever separated from the love of God and continually subjected to torment.

The trust in the relationship between God and Adam had been destroyed by the presence of sin. In order to restore this situation and at the same time preserve our ability to choose our own destiny independently, God sent His only begotten Son, the Lord Jesus Christ, to become the Second Adam. By acting as a sinless sacrificial lamb and being slain on the cross by His own willing choice, the Lord Jesus Christ obtained the legal right to give us a new inner man. We obtain this new inner man through trusting the Lord Jesus as both our Lord and Savior. After trusting Him with this, we then have to confess Him as such before men with our mouth (Romans 10:9-10). When we do this, the Lord God performs a transaction within our soul whereby the following occurs:

1) He gives us a new heart.
2) He gives us a new inner man (spirit).
3) He writes His laws on our heart and in our mind.
4) The Holy Spirit begins to dwell within our heart.
5) As we mature in the inner man, the Lord Jesus will also begin to dwell in our heart.

Following this we have a spirit (inner man) that can rule the flesh successfully and that will live with God in eternity. The Lord Jesus after His resurrection became a life-giving spirit.

STRUCTURE OF THE INNER MAN

Our inner man residing within our flesh forms our soul. We have a spiritual heart that contains the inner man. It also contains all of our structured beliefs and attitudes. These are based on our world view, including all of the philosophies that we have embraced. Our heart is who we are before God. After the second birth He does not judge the inner man, since He gave the new inner man to us and since it is a part of Him. He does judge our heart and holds our soul responsible for the condition of our heart. The Holy Spirit becomes resident in our heart after the second birth, when we are given a new inner man.

Our heart, flesh, soul, and inner man have separate minds, and all four of these are in constant communication.

PRIOR TO THE SECOND BIRTH

Prior to our second birth we lived in a world system that we accepted in large part. We rejected aspects of it as we pondered the message of the gospel of the Lord Jesus Christ. However, the majority of it we retained. Our memory in the mind of the soul and in the mind of our old heart and old inner man has retained it. We are basically steeped in world-system viewpoints, beliefs, attitudes, and behaviors. Our old inner man had little knowledge of God, having failing senses, as it declined toward spiritual death. Our flesh defined our beliefs, attitudes, and behaviors. Our inner man was too weak to overcome the lusts of the flesh, the lusts of the eyes, and the pride of life.

AT THE SECOND BIRTH

After being sought by God, yielding to His Lordship, and confessing Him as Lord and Savior before men, a person is given a new inner man and a new heart. These are new and pure. The inner man knows the voice of God and can relay God's desires to the mind of the soul. Once one takes this step, the demons see what has happened and immediately begin a war against the new believer, who is a new creation in Christ Jesus. The war may have been going on for years, depending on one's spiritual birth date. They have gradually destroyed any nurturing environment to which this new creation, this new inner man, was exposed. Through the preceding centuries of spiritual warfare the spiritual milieu of our age has been reduced to a spiritual desert. Little food and water are available for most of those being born a second time. The spiritual neonate, our inner man, has very little nourishment and very little chance to grow.

AFTER OUR SECOND BIRTH

Our inner man is exposed to a mind of the soul which was not renewed at the second birth. God instructs us to renew the mind of the soul. The problem is that in almost every believer this does not happen because of the spiritual desert in our age (*e.g.*, almost invariably no one mentions or teaches the new believer these truths). As a result, over time, the new inner man is increasingly polluted and does not grow. The mind of the soul contaminates the new heart and inner man. The inner man is polluted through this process. Our new heart continues to deteriorate toward the state of the old heart in attitudes, beliefs, and behaviors. The flesh dominates the new heart and inner man, and we have a very stunted spiritual development.

The demons have set up legalistic philosophies to prevent our growing in faith, spiritual wisdom, understanding, and knowledge. The new creation the Lord planted is side-tracked from New Covenant freedom and a vital relationship to God (in which we speak to Him and listen to Him regularly). There is a resulting lack of spiritual maturity and power. These legalistic philosophies trap souls into an Old Covenant mode of living. The New Covenant is superior to the old (Hebrews 13:20). The Lord God wants us to be a New Covenant church and people. In the Old Covenant we were slaves to sin, and in the New Covenant we are freed from the consciousness of sin. It is the awareness of the law that brings knowledge of sin. We have to learn to follow the Spirit of God, rather than live by a set of rules. This is what God desires for us, and in obedience we must learn to do this.

LEARNING HOW TO FOLLOW THE SPIRIT OF GOD

We have learned the principle issues involved in learning how to follow the Spirit of God in the chapters of Section IV. We will now summarize this. Recall that all flows of spirit involve three things—power, emotional state, and information. This is the basis of all communication between individual spiritual beings (of which man is one) and within the thought flows of an individual spiritual being. Imaginations are attached to flows from the heart to the mind of the soul.

The Holy Spirit became resident in our heart at the time of the second birth. Our inner man hears from the Holy Spirit and communicates what he hears to the mind of the heart and to the mind of the soul. The mind of the soul is in constant communication with the mind of the heart and with the mind of the inner man. The mind of the soul constantly gets spiritual information from the environment and from other people *via* the sensory perceptions of the flesh (see, touch, taste, hear, smell, and position sense). The mind of the soul is the ultimate decision making mind for the soul. Information from external sources is sent from the mind of the soul to the mind of the heart.

The heart is the image of who we are in God's view. The heart mixes all of the information coming from the inner man and from the external environment *via* the mind of the soul. It then decides what response to suggest to the mind of the soul for all spiritual inflows that require a response. In the carnal Christian and in the person who has not been through the second birth the external issues, including those of the flesh, are far more easily discerned and are much more likely to get the attention of the mind of the soul. After the second birth the mind of the soul, even before it is renewed, can recognize the new spiritual flows coming to it from the new inner man. The Holy Spirit and the voice of the inner man are peaceful (quiet and still), give new revelatory (in the sense of interpreting the Scriptures but never ever adding to them or taking from them) information about God (which is always glorifying the Lord Jesus since this is the ministry of the Holy Spirit), and fit well in the soul (fulfilling James 3:17). Due to these characteristics of God's communications the noisy flesh and an evil spirit will tend to get our attention until we train our mind of the soul to hear and recognize the new language and communication patterns of the Holy Spirit. The heart will relay them to our mind for a decision about which behavioral response to select as a response to the incoming information.

Until a believer is adept at hearing from the inner man, then all of his "spirituality" will consist of learned behavior from observations of what other believers are doing. It is, basically, a Christianity of the flesh with occasional gleanings from the Spirit of God. It is, therefore, imperative for a new believer to be trained in how to follow the Spirit of God. Mentors of new believers in our age train them in a largely flesh-driven interpretation of Christianity. This fleshly interpretation of the faith requires learning, just as a soul has to learn how to follow the Spirit of God. The flesh-driven interpretation is so much easier, since one's mind prior to renewal knows this kind of behavior. To follow the Spirit of God, one must learn new communication patterns. These include dreams; visions; words of knowledge and of wisdom; changes in the emotional state of the inner man; testing of all spirits; learning how revelatory knowledge is discerned; and, above all, patience, since the timing of communications is at God's discretion and since the soul is not in control. The soul must become an observer and must learn to discern spiritual matters from the senses of the inner man. All of this is new, and it takes time and effort to develop one's new spiritual sensing abilities. In the spiritual realm one should never try to force God to a timetable. The soul must wait on the Lord, or else an evil spirit mimicking the voice of the Spirit of God or the voice of our spirit might give a counterfeit. This counterfeit is more difficult to detect when one is trying to get God to respond on his timetable. A soul must learn a lot of new laws (these are all found in the Book of Romans—faith, sin, God's, sin and death, Spirit of life, righteousness) for determining behavior. All of the prior rules no longer apply. Spiritual growth is a process that must take place on God's time. Maturity comes from faith, as one is obedient to do as God requests of him over many issues of varying complexity over a space of time. Changes have to come in the heart, so that one's spirit and one's mind of the soul are acting in one seamless accord. Only then can one worship God in spirit and in truth.

SOME CLARIFICATION—WHAT DOES THIS MEAN?

After the second birth a believer must be assisted in transitioning from paying attention to the flesh and the external environment to paying attention to the inner man. People have known this through the ages, and those who have attempted to do this have been dismissed as mystics. It always brings a confrontation with persons who are influenced by demonic control spirits. Once a believer starts actually talking with and hearing from God without needing an intermediary individual to interpret for him, he is freed from the law. There is, however, nothing "mystic" about this. God is certainly not irrational, and anything that a person who is following the Spirit of God says and does has to measure up to the interpretation of Scripture that is supplied by the Holy Spirit (as opposed to interpretion by men). **Be very careful to understand what I am saying.** The unrenewed mind is not capable of seeing the layers of meaning in God's Word. Studying the Word of God merely as an academic exercise will not reveal the depths in it. It is only as one lives out the Word in faith that the Spirit of God is willing to reveal more to that soul. It is like the situation with Moses with whom God spoke face to face, because Moses had been faithful in many tests. God spoke clearly to Him. In Moses' day no one else was able to hear from God as clearly. Many in the wilderness thought they knew better than Moses but were killed by God for their sin. The only way to make sure something is from God and not from an evil spirit is to test every spirit that would influence one's behavior. Other Spirit of God-led believers will readily discern whether an individual is truly following the Spirit of God or whether he is following some other strange spirit. When seeking advice from elders in the faith, never look at academic credentials or speaking ability. Look at their character. Look at the lives, and see what areas of their lives have been refined by testing of their faith. Look to see if the person has suffered trials for the faith. If one looks at worldly credentials, he will have a very high probability of getting very flesh-oriented advice. One has to test the spirits of the persons from whom he seeks advice.

Many people, when they hear that to follow the Spirit of God they must attempt to discern what the inner man is saying, will be concerned that the process is a form of meditation. Many religions teach mediation as a means of contacting the spirit world. Listening to the Spirit of God is different from meditation, since the person doing this will also be practicing the admonition of the Lord to test the spirits always. The problem with meditation in many religions is that it gets people to be in a passive state of awareness. They accept without discernment any spirit they may contact. With the believer it is a quite active listening and testing process to make sure what is heard is truly from the Spirit of God. The believer never gives over his mind to a passive state. Demons are great mimics, and without great care a spiritual babe in Christ could be misled easily. We as natural parents teach our children to know our voices. We teach them to avoid listening to those who may try to prey on them. This is teaching them situational awareness. It is similar in the spiritual realm. Babes in Christ need to be taught situational awareness. The Lord's sheep will know His voice (John 10). We also need to understand that our own voice sounds different with various moods and emotions. It is the same with the Lord's voice. A baby does not know all of the nuances in our voices. A baby must learn these things over time. It is the same with hearing from the Spirit of God.

We must also take account of language differences. God wrote the Scriptures that we use in Hebrew and Greek (with a very few passages in Aramaic). In order to gain optimal insight into Scripture, we should study these original languages, although the Holy Spirit can lead us into all truth without our having to do this. This is in part due to the fact that the spiritual language God uses is quite different from any of our languages. Recall that spiritual communication is much more comprehensive than our verbal communication. In verbal communication the person tends to focus on the words spoken; but even if the same words are used, the tone (emotion and power) can set apart the meanings of two different communications using the same word. Consider the words "Don't do that." In different tones this can be a friendly concern or a belligerent threat. With spiritual communications from God and from the enemy a whole concept can be conveyed without a spoken word. It is delivered to the inner man (by the Holy Spirit) or into the heart (by an evil spirit). We may just start to become aware, in our midst as opposed to our mind, that there is an issue to which we need to attend. Many would describe it as an intuition. One becomes aware of it and watches as the process unfolds. Spiritual communications can come as words, pictures, visions, dreams, and other sensory infillings. We do not need necessarily to be told what the issue is, if the communication is from God, since with the communication will come the knowledge of what we should do. Consider the filling with wisdom and understanding that the workers who had to build the tabernacle received. Prior to the impartation of this anointing they would have had no concept of what to do because there was no model. Moses gave them plans that he received from God; but he did not provide them with understanding of how to shape and work with the wood, cloth, metals, and other materials. God imparted this knowledge to them. These men would have found a new desire coming into their mind that they had not experienced before.

People in our age have elevated acquisition of worldly knowledge to a higher level than it should be. They think that science is pure because it is free of emotional persuasion and consists of accurate observation. The implication, then, is that ideas stemming from accurate observation are at a higher level than anything with emotion attached to it. Indeed these people look down upon emotion as being "unscientific." To receive God's truth, one must accept the three components of it—power, emotion, and knowledge. Together they form the entire communication. The knowledge needs the other two components to place it into a working concept. Examples of this are readily available if we look at the impact of fear versus love associated with the "Don't do that," discussed above. A person will react differently under fear than he will in an environment of love. A scientist making measurements in an environment of fear will make different observations to those in a situation of care and concern. The physiology of our body systems responds differently in different emotional states. Scientific observation is never free of the emotional milieu in which it is made.

SOME THINGS TO KEEP IN MIND

In learning to communicate directly with God through the inner man, we must keep in mind some of the following things:

1) The flesh is always at enmity with the inner man (even before the second birth and much more so, in a sense, after it). This means that, if we keep in mind the lusts of the flesh (Galatians 5), we can readily learn to discern the desires of our flesh. We know something is not of God, if it has any of these lusts associated with it. It always has to be crucified moment by moment.
2) The soul has to decide in every circumstance and thought that arise in its mind whether to allow a response from the inner man or from the flesh. By sowing to the inner man, he will grow in power and authority over the flesh. He will be able to perceive more readily in the spiritual realm, and his soul will benefit from this. We always, moment by moment, have to make a choice whether the flesh will grow and become stronger or whether the inner man will grow and become stronger.
3) The soul is responsible for the state of the heart and of the inner man. Our soul has to work with God to purify our heart and cleanse it from all iniquity. Our soul has to cleanse our inner man from all impurity.
4) Our heart gives rise to the words of our mouth and to all of our "imaginations." These imaginations are our way of being future-oriented. Our soul is responsible for making sure that our imaginations are consistent with God's purposes for us and that they are not evil. These imaginations should be analyzed to see who is being elevated in them. Examine them to see who is exalted—God or self. Maturity in the inner man associated with purity in the heart will lead to the imaginations' being concerned with the care for and advancement of the people of God. The

imaginations will demonstrate concern for God and the way the world has treated Him. They will focus on His work. Self will be diminished.

5) The Lord can speak to us through external circumstances as well as by His Spirit's leading us through the witness to our inner man. When we are attentive to the voice of God and mature enough to test and discern the spirits influencing our heart, then God can reliably speak to us through our inner man. This is where the kingdom is on earth at present. It is residing in the hearts of believers. God does not like leading us through external events as much as through our spirit in our intimate walk with Him, since the devil has authority in the external sphere and, therefore, since he could very easily lead us astray. We are expected to discern macro-events such as the signs of the times by looking at what is going on around us, and we have to look to see what God is doing with us in every single event that occurs to us. However, the fellowship with God in the inner man helps us to know how to respond to these events.

THE EXPECTED STATE OF THE INNER MAN

When we are to be led by the Spirit of God, we have to know what God expects the spiritual state of the inner man to be. If we do not know this, we cannot be led by the Spirit of God witnessing to the inner man. Scripture will give us this information. A short list follows:

Romans 14:17: "For the kingdom of God is not meat and drink; but righteousness, and peace, and joy in the Holy Ghost."

Romans 15:13: "Now the God of hope fill you with all joy and peace in believing, that ye may abound in hope, through the power of the Holy Ghost."

Galatians 5:22-23: "But the fruit of the Spirit is love, joy, peace, longsuffering, gentleness, goodness, faith, meekness, temperance: against such there is no law."

Ephesians 3:16: "That he would grant you, according to the riches of his glory, to be strengthened with might by his Spirit in the inner man."

Colossians 1:11: "Strengthened with all might, according to his glorious power, unto all patience and longsuffering with joyfulness."

Colossians 3:15: "And let the peace of God rule in your hearts, to the which also ye are called in one body; and be ye thankful."

James 3:13-17: "Who *is* a wise man and endued with knowledge among you? let him shew out of a good conversation his works with meekness of wisdom. But if ye have bitter envying and strife in your hearts, glory not, and lie not against the truth. This wisdom descendeth not from above, but *is* earthly, sensual, devilish. For where envying and strife *is*, there *is* confusion and every evil work. But the wisdom that is from above is first pure, then peaceable, gentle, *and* easy to be intreated, full of mercy and good fruits, without partiality, and without hypocrisy."

1 Peter 3:4: "But *let it be* the hidden man of the heart, in that which is not corruptible, *even the ornament* of a meek and quiet spirit, which is in the sight of God of great price."

2 Peter 1:5-7: "And beside this, giving all diligence, add to your faith virtue; and to virtue knowledge; And to knowledge temperance; and to temperance patience; and to patience godliness; And to godliness brotherly kindness; and to brotherly kindness charity."

These form a solid groundwork for learning how to be led by the inner man. These Scriptures reveal to us that our inner man should always display the fruits of the Holy Spirit. Remember that a spirit always has three components—power, emotional state, and wisdom. The above Scriptures show what God expects of us in these three categories.

a) **Power**: Any spirit that is coming from the Holy Spirit will carry authoritative power. As we walk in a manner of discerning the spirits that are coming from our heart, we will learn over time how to recognize God's power, our own power, and an evil power. A good example of this is in respect to healing. One may receive a word of wisdom that he can call forth healing for a particular problem. When we know from experience that this is God speaking, then we know that we can confidently declare healing. As we sense our inner man being filled with power for a particular task, then we will be confident that the task can be completed. We learn through experience to know the source of power behind a spirit coming to the mind of the soul from the heart. The power component is often discerned in retrospect with passage of time (Acts 5:34-39).

b) **Emotion**: As our soul tests the spirits coming to it from our heart, then we know that, if we are detecting anything inconsistent with Galatians 5:22-23, that spirit should not be followed. Remember that it is all right to be angry and not to sin when the Lord prompts us to be angry. We should be angry with sin and with Satan but not with the sinner, for our war is not against flesh and blood. As our mind of the soul is thinking about an issue, then the Spirit of God will be responding to us about that issue. If we are not sure, then we wait, since God is not pleased by anything that we do that is not of faith. We can continue to talk to the Lord about that issue. Emotion includes states such as meekness which may not be defined as an emotion but is a state of the heart and inner man toward another being. There is a hierarchy in the emotions that we must observe. This is given to us in 2 Peter 1:5-7 to some degree. We are not necessarily capable of expressing these things perfectly, even when our inner man is more mature; but we should strive for these things. Note that in the garden of Gethsemane the Lord Jesus did not have joy and peace initially. As He travailed in prayer, He submitted to the will of the Father in love. We may be momentarily dislodged from our heavenly position by the enemy, but we have to know what our baseline is and quickly, with God's help, get back to it. Frequently, beginning to praise and worship God will get us (our soul) back to baseline in the heart and the inner man because, we are then in the spirit when our eyes are fixed on God. Note that in Colossians 3:15 we are commanded to let peace rule in our heart. This means always. War comes about in our heart, when the inner man and the flesh (perhaps assisted by an evil spirit) oppose each other in a battle for supremacy in a particular issue. When a soul chooses a behavior that is not of God and which resolves a particular skirmish, there is a relative quiet (coming from the cessation of the struggle), which is really a false peace. We have to learn to distinguish this from true peace that comes from the Spirit of God, which can fill our inner man and heart when the soul decides to promote the agenda of the Lord. Any decision always causes a false or a true peace. We have to learn experientially how to distinguish these. It is reasonable for those who have questions about the validity of this inward observing by the soul to ask themselves how they can fulfill this command of God other than by looking inward. One cannot ignore a command of God. Our inner man's natural baseline state is righteousness, peace, and joy (Romans 14:17). When this is the steady state of our heart, then we are in fellowship and in proximity to the Lord. When we observe this state to be displaced, we must war against the flesh and any evil spirit that may be involved, asking God to fight for us and to fill us with His power. When righteousness, peace, and joy are not our current state in the heart, we have stopped praying without ceasing and have fallen into error. We have to return to this state as soon as we can by identifying the cause for the change and correcting it. If it is an attack from an evil spirit, then we will need God's power to defeat it. If it is a lust from the flesh or some other sin, then we must quickly repent; and our fellowship with the Lord will be restored immediately.

c) **Wisdom**: The major passage on God's wisdom is James 3:17: "But the wisdom that is from above is first pure, then peaceable, gentle, *and* easy to be intreated, full of mercy and good fruits, without partiality, and without hypocrisy." This shows us the characteristics of wisdom from God. Any spirit that would prompt us to action based on anything that cannot pass all eight points in this verse is not from the Spirit of God.

We must examine and test every spirit that is coming from our heart to the mind of the soul before following it. We must analyze these three components to make sure none of them is false. When we first start doing this, it will be difficult; but soon one acquires knowledge from prior experience. This makes the process much more spontaneous. It will then be novel situations that we need to contemplate before responding.

We should closely examine the ***imaginations*** *that come to the mind of the soul with every flow of spirit from the heart. The content and focus of these can be of great assistance in determining the source of a spiritual flow. The focus should always be on the Lord and not one's self.*

FEAR

One of the major attacking points for evil powers is through fear. This is why God distinguishes it so emphatically in 2 Timothy 1:7: "For God hath not given us the spirit of fear; but of power, and of love, and of a sound mind." We must always examine spirits coming from our heart to the mind of the soul for any facet of fear. The fear to which a spirit appeals may be quite subtle and hidden from all but the most discerning of examinations. If we detect a component of fear when contemplating an attitude, belief, or behavior, then we know that it is not of God. There can be attacks through fear of insufficiency, inadequacy, loss of respect, and all sorts of other concerns.

God expects us to walk in faith based on what He tells us directly by His spoken *rhema* (utterance) to us personally and on what we read in the Scriptures (*logos*). This is exactly what Adam and Eve did not do. We read in Romans 10:17: "So then faith *cometh* by hearing, and hearing by the word of God." The Greek word for *word* in this verse is *rhema*. *Rhema* means the continual utterance of God. *Logos* is the word for written Scripture. Therefore we can see that God expects us to talk with Him and to listen to Him speaking to us.

SUMMARY

To follow the Spirit of God, an individual must learn through experience to hear from God and trust God in faith. God uses different spiritual communications to talk or communicate with us. Remember that all communications within the soul of man are spiritual, and all communications between a person and another spiritual being are spirit. These always have the three components—power, emotion or state (*e.g.*, meekness), and wisdom or information. A particular communication may be 99% non verbal, but it still has all three components. In order to hear most clearly from God, we must be "in the spirit." This means that we are listening through the inner man and seeing through the inner man. Our focus is on God. John 5:30 quotes the Lord Jesus as saying: "I can of mine own self do nothing: as I hear, I judge: and my judgment is just; because I seek not mine own will, but the will of the Father which hath sent me." If the Lord Jesus could of His own self do nothing, then we even more so should of our own selves attempt nothing.

We must remain in the spirit and not listen to evil spirits or to our own heart until it is pure. As we do this, our inner man must be kept in an environment in the heart where he is not subject to the power of the flesh or to an evil spirit. We know that our inner man is in such a state when we are constantly in the kingdom of God. At these times our inner man will be radiating joy and peace to our mind of the soul. We will radiate the same spirit to those with whom we are in contact, and this will bring those persons into contact with God. We are not able to attend fully to the inner man when there are fruit other than those of the Holy Spirit in our heart. When our heart is filled with joy and peace, our inner man is able to relay to the mind of the soul more clearly the things he hears from God. We are able to be in a state of constant prayer to God by keeping our spirit (inner man) in such a state. Our inner man is in a position of waiting before God and is not being distracted by agendas from the flesh or from evil spirits. Waiting patiently and quietly before God in order to attend to His needs is the fulfilling of 1 Thessalonians 5:17: "Pray without ceasing." Note that our soul can be busy with the needs of everyday work or other requirements, while we have our inner man in this state. We can practice this successfully only when we have experientially gone through the separation of soul, spirit, and flesh described in Hebrews 4:12. After this separation the mind of the soul can reliably distinguish the spirits coming to it from our flesh, from our inner man, and from the soul itself. The process of learning this requires a very good knowledge of the Scriptures, for it is the *logos* that effects this separation (Hebrews 4:12). After undergoing this separation one can be led by the Spirit of God and can war against the flesh and evil spirits to keep his inner man in a state of righteousness, peace, and joy. Of course the state needs to be maintained and guarded. This takes effort.

It is, therefore, very important to learn all of the emotions and states of the heart that various spirits can cause. It is frequently easier to discern which spirit is present by focusing on this than on the components of wisdom and of power. Learning these things comes through practice and actively working with God. As we seek to understand these inner emotions and states, He will be only too pleased to teach us by providing circumstances in which we can experience them in a setting that makes it obvious from where the spirit is coming. This focusing on the inner man is not a form of mysticism. The mind is very actively involved in learning, and it will not result in any course of action that would violate any principles laid down in the Scripture. That is why a soul walking in this manner must know Scripture well.

We should not judge another individual about the content of his heart at any time, but we must discern what spirit he is radiating at any point in time in order to respond properly to him. All souls are accountable to an elder for the spirit they are transmitting, as they are for verbal expressions and overt behavior.

Finally, one may wonder how the Lord answers a specific question or concern. As we are thinking and meditating in the mind of the soul, the mind of our heart is also involved. Our inner man is immediately aware of these thoughts. The inner man knows even our deepest thoughts. He talks with the Holy Spirit about the situation. God may give an immediate answer, or He may delay it for a period of time—briefly or for a long time while He works with us to prepare us for the answer—in order to accomplish His purpose in us. Remember that He is always working for our eternal good. If we do not hear an answer, it will not be that God has not given it. It will be that we did not focus on it, or that we did not want to hear it. James 1:5 tells us: “If any of you lack wisdom, let him ask of God, that giveth to all *men* liberally, and upbraideth not; and it shall be given him.”

This is a brief outline of how the soul and inner man interact in order for the soul to be led by the Spirit of God. Chapter 20 will elaborate on further issues that we need to understand in order to be led by the Spirit of God.

17
IMMEDIATELY AFTER THE SECOND BIRTH AND FIVE YEARS LATER

IMMEDIATELY AFTER THE SECOND BIRTH

At the time of the second birth God gives us a new spirit and a new heart. He also writes His laws on our heart and in our mind. If we were immediately nurtured in a spiritual environment in which we learned to listen to God's voice, in which we learned how to follow the Holy Spirit, and in which we were constantly taught sound doctrine, then we would develop very differently in our inner man from what actually occurs in all but extremely rare exceptions. The Apostle Paul is a good example of maturing in the inner man. He placed himself alone with God for many years (Galatians 1 and 2:1). He learned how to communicate with God. God is not a respecter of persons. He has an ordained work for all of us to perform (Ephesians 2:10). We can fulfill this only as we learn to relate to Him in a vital and dynamic two-way communication. The Lord Jesus said that those who come after Him would do greater works that He did. We note that He did nothing of Himself but rather always looked to see what the Father was doing. We must turn our gaze off the world and into the spirit in order to do the same, albeit without the perfection that the Lord Jesus had.

In this condition of being a spiritual neonate we should feed our inner man on the Word of God and learn how to relate to God in just the same manner as we have learned to relate to others in the natural world. We had to learn how to listen to our earthly parents and how to relate to them; subsequently, we expanded our relations to a wider range of people. If this were to occur in the spiritual universe, our inner man would grow in strength and sensing ability. Our inner man would be able to rule the flesh readily and subject it to the glory of God. Living in the world, but being not of it, would be the norm for the soul. The soul would feel itself a sojourner in the things of the world system.

Instead of this situation occurring, a person who has been through the second birth is usually not taught doctrine, is usually not taught how to follow the Holy Spirit, and certainly is not taught how to relate to God personally. Instead, the individual stays in the world system mode of operating. The soul is overwhelmed by the flesh, which continues to exert control through a mind that is never deliberately and actively renewed. The soul never learns how to relate to the new inner man. As a result the inner man and the new heart become polluted by the world system. Evil spirits then control the soul most of the time (through world system philosophies), and the soul rarely follows the Holy Spirit. The soul may learn a lot *about* God, but it rarely enters into intimacy *with* God. There is frequently little expectation of hearing God during prayer. The worship of God is frequently *via* a religious spirit.

To see examples of these problems, all we have to do is read through the letters of the apostle Paul and note what problems plagued the churches that He had established. Individuals who have been through the second birth have various options on which to draw for deciding how they will behave. If the individual does not make a conscious informed decision, then he will default into another choice. The choices are:

a) To seek the leading of the Spirit of God—the desirable choice and the one which God expects of us if we are to be His sons (Romans 8:14)

The rest of the choices are default choices in that they will occur without active intervention by the soul.

b) To be led by fleshly desires

   i) To follow the law of God that was for the Old Covenant
   ii) To walk in a lawless manner
   iii) To walk in some mixture of these two options

c) To follow the Law within one's heart (Romans 1 [this is conscience-driven])

d) To be led by evil spirits

i) By direct leading
ii) By following philosophies
iii) By following the world system

e) To be led by some mixture of a), b), c) and d)

The individual who has not been through the second birth still has all of these options open to him, but he does not have the Holy Spirit indwelling him. Therefore, if he follows the Spirit of God, he will perceive the lesding in a less intimate manner; and the motivation for following will be different.

THE STATE FIVE YEARS AFTER THE SECOND BIRTH

As we look at the letters Paul wrote to the churches, we see the impact of these different ways of being led. In Romans 6-8 Paul relates how, after his second birth, he went back, as we all do, into following entities other than the Spirit of God. In these chapters he describes growth from following the flesh and the Law to following the Spirit of God. It is an active choice that we all should make. We will not make a similar transition, if we do not actively choose to make it. Then we must invest the effort and time and accept the trials that will follow. The Scriptures tell us that we must ask, seek, and knock (Luke 11:9). We do not gain true riches without great effort (the pearl of great price). Consider that the Lord Jesus said that we will not be trusted with Kingdom (or Church) responsibilities without proving ourselves with unrighteous mammon (Luke 16:11). We have to be responsible and hard working with what we have in the world, before God will give us true spiritual responsibility. Gifts, bestowed without repentance—apparently at the point of salvation (Romans 11:29), are to encourage us to go on to deeper spiritual growth. Notice that the Lord Jesus did not receive spiritual gifts but rather spiritual anointing (Isaiah 11:1-3). We, also, must move beyond the gifts to be anointed by God for greater works. Consider how we give our children gifts that will encourage them to learn concepts and principles that will aid them as they mature. They go beyond using the gift, as they grow into acquiring resident skills.

REVERTING TO THE LAW

In the regression from the moment of the second birth to a less-than-mature spiritual state for the soul, we will face the major issue of going back under the Law. We see this in the Galatian church, where the people lost their direction and started to fall back on legalism. There is a stronghold that the world system encourages ("there is a way that seems right to a man but the end thereof is the way of death"). It is independence from God. It may involve keeping God's law, but it does not require interacting with God. With respect to the legalism, look at Galatians 2 and follow Paul's argument about the circumcision. People who go back to legalism have never been taught, or have chosen not to receive, doctrine adequately and have never learned to relate to God personally, in order to understand how they can follow the Holy Spirit. If one follows the Holy Spirit, then one cannot follow the Law (his righteousness will have to exceed the standards in the Law). As much as a person learns how to follow the Holy Spirit, that will be the extent to which he has been freed from the Law. Look at what it cost Paul to do this. After an encounter with the living resurrected Lord Jesus, Paul went into isolation for at least three years, and maybe as many as fourteen years (Galatians, 1:1-2:1), learning to relate to the Lord so that he learned all that he learned from the Lord directly. This is possible, since the Lord Jesus himself taught us that the Holy Spirit would lead us into all truth. Indeed this is the expectation of the Lord, that we would learn directly from Him. That does not preclude studying from past and present writers. The Holy Spirit will lead a person to the writers that the Lord wishes him to read.

In Galatians 3:8-9 Paul points out that the Galatians really did not know God as they once did but rather are now known of God. This losing the ability to know God results from observing legalism. Follow Paul's argument through Chapters 2 and 3. When we are following anything but the Holy Spirit, then we will no longer know God as we once did immediately after our second birth. Furthermore, since we are not following God, we are following other spirits of the world system. Frequently, these are religious spirits. Oftentimes, it is a spirit of witchcraft that seeks to have us under its control by following the law. Following the law is so easy to do and involves less effort on our part than fighting an evil world system and hierarchy of evil powers in order to be set free in Christ Jesus our Lord and Savior. Note that Paul had taught the Galatians to follow the Spirit of God (3:3) initially, but they had been subverted by evil powers. It is a huge battle to be set free in Christ Jesus. It is along the proportions of the Exodus at a personal level. We are delivered from bondage to a world system and taken to our promised land where, with the Lord's leading, we are to battle the enemy for control of our soul. When the Israelites did not root out all the enemies according to God's directions, then those enemies remained to be a thorn to them. It is just so with us: if we do not co-operate with the Lord, then we will leave devices and imaginations in our heart that will continue to pollute and weaken our heart and inner man.

We will look at issues in some of the other letters written by the apostle Paul in summary fashion in order to see how quickly the initial state after the second birth degenerates. We will see examples in which all the above entities lead souls.

MORE LEGALISM AND WILL WORSHIP (PRIDE)

In Romans 14 God tells us not to judge in terms of foods and times of worship. He has His servants at all levels of maturation and can make them to stand. Therefore, judging people is a snare into which the individual not led by the Spirit of God can readily fall. When we start judging others, we know that we are far away from being led by the Holy Spirit.

FOLLOWING THE FLESH AND EVIL SPIRITS

In the letters to the Corinthians we see the following problems that indicate the falling away from being led by the Spirit of God in this group of believers. In 1 Corinthians 3 Paul refers to the believers as carnal and as being led by their fleshly lusts. They had never grown in the inner man. They had attached themselves to their teachers rather than to the living Lord Jesus. In 1 Corinthians 4 we see the people were judgmental. In 1 Corinthians 5 we see the people tolerated fornication and were not dealing with it. They were taking each other to court (1 Corinthians 6). 1 Corinthians 8 says that some had weak consciences. In 1 Corinthians 11 we find Paul telling the people that they had divisions and heresies amongst their church members and that they failed to take communion worthily. All of these errors result from being led by one of the wrong entities discussed in the first section of this chapter. If we are led by the Spirit of God, who leads us into all truth, then we shall not walk in these errors. Remember that the Corinthians had never matured sufficiently in the inner man for Paul to give them spiritual meat, since they were still spiritual babes in Christ (1 Corinthians 3:1-2).

FOLLOWING EVIL SPIRITS THROUGH THE WORLD SYSTEM

Another way to go astray is by following evil spirits through the world system. An example of believers going astray in this manner (very soon after their second birth) is in the Colossian church, in which we find the following problems:

a) Colossians 3:18-19 deals with false philosophy. The believers were worshipping angels and not holding to the uniqueness of the Lord Jesus Christ.
b) Colossians 3:20-23 discusses asceticism. This was a major reversion to legalistic living.

HOW DO WE FOLLOW THE SPIRIT OF GOD?

At this point it is worthwhile to answer a question that many may have. Why do we need the written Word of God, if we can effect a more perfect walk merely by following the Spirit of God? We need both to mature, since the Spirit of God uses the written Word to teach us. The written Word is spiritually discernible only when the Spirit of

God is teaching us (John 16:13). We need to come to know God, as He is revealed by the Holy Spirit who teaches us all truth. In the growing stages of our inner man it is very easy to fall into error, and it is still all too easy even as one matures. The devil actively comes against a person trying to mature in the inner man. The Lord will make us successful in our growth, if that is our heart's desire, despite the efforts of the devil. There is a qualitative aspect to learning intimacy with God, and the written Word of God acts as a boundary beyond which we are out of line. We should never move in a direction that is contrary to the written Word. The Pharisees show that it is possible to know all of the words of Scripture and still miss the main thrust of God's teaching; they actually missed God incarnate! They knew all of the jots and titles of the written Word, but they missed the whole emphasis of the Old Testament teaching. It is only with the qualitative inner feeling that we can know if we are being led into truth. We need both the written Word and the Spirit to open the Scriptures to us in order to be led into all truth.

SUMMARY

We have reviewed a few examples in the New Testament churches of believers' regressing from their pristine spiritual state immediately after the second birth. This continues to occur and is no different for almost every believer in this day. Our present-day churches demonstrate all of the errors of the New Testament churches and of the seven churches discussed in Revelation 2 and 3. Individual believers demonstrate many of the errors mentioned above. Legalism is a fundamental problem for many people.

We have to recognize the root cause for all of these problems. The root cause is an inadequate relationship on the personal level with the Lord God. As a result our inner man is subject to the flesh and becomes polluted. We remain spiritual babes. Our inner man lacks vision and hearing. He is not able to mature.

We are in great need of restoration and reclamation. We walk by our own will, never having learned to subject our will to that of the Spirit of God. We fall subject to the pride of life, lust of the eyes, and lust of the flesh. Consumerism and the pursuit of world-system knowledge are particular issues for many of the Western hemisphere churches and their people.

Pastors are not trained in teaching and do not study how to be led by the Spirit of God; as a result, they frequently do not walk much differently from their flock. The local church, while looking to the head, the Lord Jesus, fails to be led consistently by the Lord.

The church people are frequently caught up with the worship of mammon. It is not a direct worship, but by default it becomes so. The pursuit of mammon and career become idols, since the Lord Jesus is not held in sufficiently high esteem. We see this resulting in many problems within the church body. The natural spiritual order has been lost; and, as a result, false spirits often rule in our churches.

Certainly in some churches the Spirit of God is present in the service. However, there is a spiritual dryness in the land, and revival begins in pockets but seems to be quenched quickly. There was a time that I did not know God as I know Him now. I give thanks to the Lord that He opened my eyes to the spiritual universe. Prior to 1995 I would have been quite content to believe that there were little if any manifestations of miracles in the Church. After the Lord dealt with me, I became aware that many of the spiritual gifts were being restored to the church, including prophecy. Prior to 1995 I was closed to this as many readers may still be. Ask God to show you His truth and open yourself to new things. There is a strong spirit of control present in our modern churches that wrestles against the Spirit of God in the heart of individuals. Any spirit of control is a spirit of witchcraft. Until people in the church reject this spirit of control and open their hearts to God in large numbers, this world will remain spiritually dry and thirsty. God's Word in the Scriptures will speak for itself under the guidance of the Holy Spirit. The problem is that many in the church are not doing what the Lord says regarding keeping His word as a frontlet and meditating on it day and night. When the individual does this, then he will be immune to the false doctrines that controlling spirits have built up. He will begin to form a deepening relationship with the Lord Jesus at a personal level.

Without this personal relationship we worship the facts about God, but we do not worship God.

In the following chapters we will examine how we can restore our inner man to the position that he occupied five seconds after the second birth. Then we will see how we can begin to mature in the inner man.

18
SIGNS OF MATURATION IN THE INNER MAN

INTRODUCTION

We are living in a very results-oriented period of history, and people are inclined to want some estimate of their growth and maturity in the inner man. In many respects this desire can be very flesh driven; this will only be discernible to someone as he matures in the inner man. We need encouragement; this is a Godly desire, since the Scripture tells us that prophecy is for edification, exhortation, and comfort (encouragement [1 Corinthians 14:3]). It is therefore reasonable for a believer to expect the Lord to comfort and encourage him. The devil tries constantly to tear us down, and this can become very wearying. Whether we are looking for a measure of our progress for comfort or for fleshly enhancement depends on our motivation for seeking it. We mention this to show that, even in apparently "Godly" issues, one may be motivated with a spirit of error. Therefore, as you read the following, keep in mind that it is a guide and that you must keep in mind the motivation for actually using it.

THE DESTINATION

It will be of help in understanding our progress, if we look at the beginning of our sanctification and the end of it. At the time of our second birth we came from a state of sin and had been separated from God, because our spirit could not see or hear Him properly. This resulted in our minds not being open to Him. In Chapter 17 we looked at our neonatal spiritual state immediately after the second birth. God at that time gave us a new inner man that is a part of Him. After the second birth our spirit is in fellowship with God and can see and hear Him clearly. So far as knowledge, understanding, and wisdom are concerned we are babes immediately after the second birth (Hebrews 5:13 and 1 Peter 2:2). We have to go through a process of spiritual growth just as we had to go through physical growth. As an aside, we should recall that our physical growth occurred without our closely observing it; but we did need the correct nutrition, exercise, and environment for it to happen. We also needed to be free of illnesses which might have prevented it, such as lack of thyroid hormone or growth hormone. These physical issues are analogies for the spiritual issues that prevent spiritual growth.

Scripture describes the process of growth in the inner man as sanctification. The end result of this is that we are conformed to the image of the Lord Jesus Christ (Romans 8:29). God is looking for this image in us so that He (the Lord Jesus) may be the firstborn of many brethren (Romans 8:29). To understand what the end point of maturation is, we need to understand that God will be looking at the content and working of our heart (review Chapter 10). He judges the heart and not what is in the current thought patterns of our mind of the soul. He looks at our heart to see if the image of the Lord Jesus is formed in the beliefs, attitudes, and behaviors that lie there. What is in our heart and what is in our soul's mind can be very different (at least over a short period of time). God will be looking for key beliefs, attitudes, and behaviors of the Lord Jesus. These are seen in the following Scriptures:

Philippians 2:5-8: "Let this mind be in you, which was also in Christ Jesus: Who, being in the form of God, thought it not robbery to be equal with God: But made himself of no reputation, and took upon him the form of a servant, and was made in the likeness of men: And being found in fashion as a man, he humbled himself, and became obedient unto death, even the death of the cross."

Luke 22:26: "But ye *shall* not *be* so: but he that is greatest among you, let him be as the younger; and he that is chief, as he that doth serve." This is the complete reverse to the world order. It is diametrically opposed to it. It is easy to understand this in the mind but understanding it in the heart is a much more deep process.

John 5:30: "I can of mine own self do nothing: as I hear, I judge: and my judgment is just; because I seek not mine own will, but the will of the Father which hath sent me."

John 8:29: "And he that sent me is with me: the Father hath not left me alone; for I do always those things that please him."

John 14:12-14: "Verily, verily, I say unto you, He that believeth on me, the works that I do shall he do also; and greater *works* than these shall he do; because I go unto my Father. And whatsoever ye shall ask in my name, that will I do, that the Father may be glorified in the Son. If ye shall ask any thing in my name, I will do *it*."

John 15:5: "I am the vine, ye *are* the branches: He that abideth in me, and I in him, the same bringeth forth much fruit: for without me ye can do nothing."

Romans 1:9: "For God is my witness, whom I serve with my spirit in the gospel of his Son, that without ceasing I make mention of you always in my prayers." Service for God has to be done through the inner man. The soul cannot use the flesh to serve God. We have to be in the spirit (inner man) in order to accomplish service for God.

Romans 12:21: "Be not overcome of evil, but overcome evil with good."

Titus 2:14: "Who gave himself for us, that he might redeem us from all iniquity, and purify unto himself a peculiar people, zealous of good works."

1 John 3:8: "He that committeth sin is of the devil; for the devil sinneth from the beginning. For this purpose the Son of God was manifested, that he might destroy the works of the devil."

1 John 4:9: "In this was manifested the love of God toward us, because that God sent his only begotten Son into the world, that we might live through him."

Revelation 3:20-21: "Behold, I stand at the door, and knock: if any man hear my voice, and open the door, I will come in to him, and will sup with him, and he with me. To him that overcometh will I grant to sit with me in my throne, even as I also overcame, and am set down with my Father in his throne."

These Scriptures are just a few which attest to the character of the Lord Jesus and His works. To put it quite simply: our maturing in the inner man will make us appear to God as He did. We are to overcome the evil one; we are to have His (the Lord Jesus') character formed in our heart such that we will be a servant to all; and we will exhibit in our works for God greater power than the Lord exhibited Himself, because we will do them as He empowers us in His name (John 14:12). We need much more than just an intellectual assent to these as truths; we must walk in them continually. They must be in the heart so they are the basis for all of our daily and moment-by-moment decisions and behaviors. Our faith in God must have no upper limit.

A DEEPER LOOK AT THE CHARACTER OF THE LORD JESUS

Read Philippians 2:5-8 again. It sums up the character of the Lord. Before the foundation of the world He had agreed with the Father that He would completely empty Himself of all of His own desires and would forever throughout all eternity limit Himself of His expression of the powers of the Godhead. He did all of this for us as lost sinners who reviled Him and were enemies until we accepted Him as our Lord and Savior and confessed Him as such. We have to go through a complete emptying of self will and self determination in all areas to be like Him in this respect. Try doing this for twenty four hours and see what happens. You do not get to decide if you eat a certain item; you do not get to decide if you spend that quarter in your pocket. The Lord Jesus always looked to see what the Father was doing and could do nothing of Himself (John 5:30). He always pleased the Father (John 8:29).

When we are like this, then we will have His power. We will be doing things for Him in His name, and He will give each of us the power to fulfill those works (John 14:12-14). The original Greek in these verses indicates it is not that the Church as a whole who will do this but rather that each individual believer will do this. We have to be fulfilling the Lord's Great Commission (Mark 16:15-18: "And he said unto them, Go ye into all the world, and preach the gospel to every creature. He that believeth and is baptized shall be saved; but he that believeth not shall be damned. And these signs shall follow them that believe; In my name shall they cast out devils; they shall speak with new tongues; They shall take up serpents; and if they drink any deadly thing, it shall not hurt them; they shall lay hands on the sick, and they shall recover."). When we are preaching in the Spirit (Romans 1:9, John 15:5), then the power signs will be manifest and will follow the preaching. The Apostle Paul was bitten by the serpent and was unharmed (Acts 28:3-6). Paul healed the sick. Paul cast out demons. It is quite possible for an individual today to have the same commitment to the Lord that the Apostle Paul had. I have personally known people who have preached the gospel and have had the dead come to life. Some have experienced lesser miracles occurring. We should be seeing more of these things. Too often the gospel is preached in the flesh, and then the works will not follow. It has to be our serving God in the inner man (Romans 1:9) for miracles to occur.

We shall see the motivation of the Lord in emptying Himself as He did, if we look at Hebrews 12:2: "Looking unto Jesus the author and finisher of *our* faith; who for the joy that was set before him endured the cross, despising the shame, and is set down at the right hand of the throne of God." In Luke 15:7, 10 we see that this joy was due to lost sinners' repenting. We shall experience this same joy in our inner man, as under the guidance of the Lord Jesus we lead others to repentance. As we mature in our inner man, we will be able to serve the Lord in these areas.

THE END PRODUCT OF SANCTIFICATION

We can look at the Lord Jesus and at the Apostle Paul as role models in terms of their attitudes, works, and manifestations of power. Our sanctification is not a work that we can perform ourselves. It is a process that must be committed to the Lord's oversight. Flesh led desires and hands should not touch it. That is why it is so important to be led by the Spirit of God. We cannot grow, unless we are attached to the true vine (John 15:4-5). There is a pattern of training that must take place for the Lord to set us forth into ministry. That also has to be initiated by Him. Paul spent perhaps 14 years in training before beginning his ministry work. The Lord Jesus spent considerable training time—we do not know just how long. The Apostles spent three years training with the Lord and then had to be baptized with power.

These days we want to shorten all of this time. That is of the flesh. We clamor for experiences of baptism of the Holy Spirit and may receive it, but we are not mature enough for the Lord to commit His power to us. He cannot have us running around independently of Him and not looking to Him in everything that we do. The level of commitment has to be there. The training time must be served, and during this time of training the Lord will gradually change a person's circumstances and commitments so that he can be set forth to minister with power. We are all called to a ministry with power, but we have to see the vision that God has for our ministry and not invent our own. He will accept us as living sacrifices (Romans 12:1). Remember that a sacrifice is dead to itself. The Lord has to prepare us to the point that we can really understand the implications of this in the heart and then are willing to do it.

ON THE PATH TO THE END

We will know that we are maturing in the inner man, when we are able to discern readily what is of the flesh, soul, and spirit. Hebrews 4:12 instucts us: "For the word of God *is* quick, and powerful, and sharper than any twoedged sword, piercing even to the dividing asunder of soul and spirit, and of the joints and marrow, and *is* a discerner of the thoughts and intents of the heart.." We must be obedient to the Lord in order to get to this point of maturity. After reaching this place we can then know more surely when we are in the spirit (inner man) and when we are in the flesh or soul. After this we are able to be as led by the Spirit of God as we are willing to be. We can then know in the mind of the soul whether it is the inner man, the flesh, or an evil spirit that is presenting a situation to us. Before this point we have a very mixed walk—sometimes in the spirit, oftentimes in the flesh. This was somewhat the position of the Corinthian believers.

After this the Lord will present to us a series of choices that enable us to choose whether we will grow more. Further growth in the inner man involves a turning over of the will. This is a gradual process by which we empty ourselves. We can at any point in time choose to do this, "God being our helper." He will then work with us to perfect us for the work for which He has chosen us: "For we are his workmanship, created in Christ Jesus unto good works, which God hath before ordained that we should walk in them" (Ephesians 2:10). God asks us to let Him make all of the changes, since, if we mix in our own desires, His work is contaminated. This results in something that is unacceptable to Him. This contamination is the basis of Proverbs 14:12: "There is a way which seemeth right unto a man, but the end thereof *are* the ways of death." As we lose our own will, God will be able to trust us with more of His power and authority; and our inner man will grow, as we have a deeper and a broader experience in the spiritual realm.

RESULTS OF MATURING IN THE INNER MAN

a) As our inner man matures and as we stay in the inner man more and more, we will sense more often in the spiritual universe—seeing, hearing, and using our other senses. Again this is always at God's discretion. It can be quite disconcerting to walk about in the natural universe, continually seeing spiritual and natural bodies. The Lord limits our exposure to these bodies to suit His purposes.

b) There is increasing ability to know what is from the flesh, the soul, and the inner man (Hebrews 12:4).

c) We will spend more time in the spirit and less in the flesh.

d) Our soul will emanate the fruit of the Holy Spirit more and more.

e) We will be in a place of rest for the inner man.

f) We undergo our own loss of will.

g) We see God's purpose more readily in all of the events of our lives.

h) We protect our inner man from exposure to the flesh to avoid contamination.

i) We seek after things that will help our inner man to grow.

j) We experience more hatred from the world system, even to outright persecution.

k) We see God high and lifted up.

l) We are more aware, like the Apostle Paul, of our own spiritual poverty.

m) We become very reliant on the Lord, not trusting ourselves; for we have seen into the spiritual realm and know the terrible powers that are arrayed against us. We cannot defeat them outside the Lord Jesus. Under His wings we are covered, and we are hidden in the rock.

n) The world system can trouble our flesh, but not our inner man.

o) We see the flesh in a new way.

p) We are poured out as a drink offering, as the Apostle Paul was.

q) We see the spiritual gifts as just that. They are not a part of character, and many who use them fall into allowing the flesh to be built up. As our inner man matures, we see the working out of 1 Corinthians 2:15: "But he that is spiritual judgeth all things, yet he himself is judged of no man." Discernment becomes a part of us. We develop that meek and quiet spirit that the Lord finds so pleasing (1 Peter 3:4).

r) We walk beyond the gifts with increasing anointing of power and spiritual authority as we take down strongholds in our own lives.

s) We do all things for the Lord and do not look to man for praise.

t) In every thing we give thanks, for this is the will of God in Christ Jesus concerning us (1 Thessalonians 5:18).

u) At times we may sense our inner man seated in the heavenly places: "And hath raised *us* up together, and made *us* sit together in heavenly *places* in Christ Jesus" (Ephesians 2:6).

v) We receive the spirit by which we may cry, "Abba Father" (Romans 8:15).

These points are not in any order of progression. They are just some of the things that we will experience as our inner man matures. They are all supportable by the experiences of the Apostle Paul, recorded in the Scriptures that he wrote.

We shall define in Chapter 20 what it means to be "in the spirit" as opposed to being "in the flesh." We have alluded to this above, but it is important to understand this experientially. It will help if we can describe it, so that you may have a better idea of when you are in this state. It is very critical for spiritual growth of the inner man to be in this state as much as possible.

19
THE ROLE OF FAITH IN FOLLOWING THE SPIRIT OF GOD

"Now faith is the substance of things hoped for, the evidence of things not seen" (Hebrews 11.1).

HOW SCRIPTURE DEFINES FAITH AND SOME ATTRIBUTES OF FAITH

Faith in the New Testament is always the word *pistis* or a derivative. Strong's *Concordance* lists the following meanings, among others:

1. An absolute conviction of the truth of anything
2. A strong and welcome conviction or belief that Jesus is the Messiah, through whom we obtain eternal salvation in the kingdom of God
3. Belief, with the predominate idea of trust (or confidence), whether in God or in Christ, springing from faith in the same

Faith is the "substance of things hoped for, the evidence of things not seen" (Hebrews 11:1). Faith allows hoped-for outcomes to occur. It is trust in the certainty of the outcome of an event that has not yet occurred. In respect to issues of the Lord God, it is a complete trust in His Word, both spoken *rhema* and *logos*. Included in this statement is an underlying assumption that the thing or person that one trusts will be able to deliver on the things entrusted. In other words, if there is no ability to be one hundred percent certain that a thing can occur, then there is no evidence for it; hence, there can be no faith for it. Faith can exist only in a situation where one can absolutely expect reliable results. If one can only expect a better-than-even chance of something happening, then it is not faith that is involved but hope. God tells us in this Scripture that when we have certainty in our heart about an issue, this becomes the evidence that things not seen will occur.

2 Corinthians 5:7 tells us that God emphasizes that walking by faith involves walking not by sight: “For we walk by faith, not by sight”. The two are mutually exclusive. When we see an endpoint, then there is no room left for trust (faith).

We see the same concept in Mark 11:23-24: “For verily I say unto you, That whosoever shall say unto this mountain, Be thou removed, and be thou cast into the sea; and shall not doubt in his heart, but shall believe that those things which he saith shall come to pass; he shall have whatsoever he saith. Therefore I say unto you, What things soever ye desire, when ye pray, believe that ye receive *them*, and ye shall have *them*.” It is very important to notice in this passage that the Lord is not restricting this ability of faith to act only in accordance with His will. Note that the individual trying to perform something in faith has to have no doubt in his heart. Faith has to be one hundred percent; and this in the heart, not just the mind. This represents a problem, for we saw in Chapter 10 that the mind of the soul cannot completely understand our heart.

Therefore, there are two conditions for a person to be able to exercise mountain-moving faith:

1) The need to know the heart completely, which really occurs only when it is purified

2) The knowledge that one has the power delegated to him to perform an act that is beyond his own ability

The important point is that the Lord has designed this world to operate on the faith principle. Events occur only as an individual spirit entity exercises one hundred per cent trust in the outcome. The devil frequently attempts to diminish or kill this faith. He has authority in this world to exercise power, and he and his demons are formidable foes and can expect to influence outcomes of issues within their sphere of delegated power.

WHERE DOES FAITH ORIGINATE?

Hebrews 12:2 tells us: "Looking unto Jesus the author and finisher of *our* faith; who for the joy that was set before him endured the cross, despising the shame, and is set down at the right hand of the throne of God." This tells us that our faith is a result of the Lord Jesus' actions and that He is also the one who initiates and finishes our faith. Ephesians 2:8-9 also emphasizes that faith is a gift from God. It is important to consider that both of these Scriptures are addressed just to believers. The Lord is not the author of the faith of an unbeliever. In a general sense, as part of the functioning of the creation, the Lord ordained that faith would be the key to creating and sustaining this universe. Note that the creation came about as the Lord spoke and commanded it. By His continuous utterance the Lord sustains the continued functioning of this universe: "Who being the brightness of *his* glory, and the express image of his person, and **upholding all things by the word of his power**, when he had by himself purged our sins, sat down on the right hand of the Majesty on high" (emphasis added [Hebrews 1:3]). In this Scripture the Greek for *word* is *rhema*.

HOW DO WE GET FAITH?

Romans 10:17 states: "So then faith *cometh* by hearing, and hearing by the word of God." In this Scripture *word* in Greek is *rhema*, not *logos*. It tells us that for faith to arise we have to hear reliably from God; and eventually, as we mature, we must recognize and understand all of the ways that He talks with us. The Lord Jesus said that His sheep will hear His voice and will know His voice (John 10:2-4). One of the most frightening issues is how much people assume they know what God thinks and desires without ever really knowing from Scripture what God really thinks and desires. We have to be able to hear the *rhema* for faith to occur. If we do not have a growing faith, then we are not going to do works for God, because we cannot hear Him leading us into the works He wants us to accomplish. We may do work that we offer to God, but He does not want our sacrifices; rather, He commands our obedience. Cain and Abel illustrate this difference (Genesis 4:1-8). Psalm 51:16-17 shows King David understands this issue regarding sacrifice and obedience. Hebrews 13:15-16, by implication, shows the same.

Once we have gone through the second birth, having heard the voice of God drawing us, then the Lord may bless us with a spiritual gift or gifts. One such gift is that of faith which gives an individual a supernatural impartation of faith that goes beyond his level of maturity in the inner man (1 Corinthians 12:9).

AMOUNTS OF FAITH

Faith can vary in amount. The Lord Jesus was critical of many people, saying, "O ye of little faith" on several occasions. He also told the disciples why they were powerless in Matthew 17:20: "And Jesus said unto them, Because of your unbelief: for verily I say unto you, If ye have faith as a grain of mustard seed, ye shall say unto this mountain, Remove hence to yonder place; and it shall remove; and nothing shall be impossible unto you." Therefore, even a very small amount of faith allows great results. However, as we noted above, for a particular event to occur, one hundred per cent faith is needed. Therefore, the Lord, when He tells people that they have little faith, must be talking about something other than faith for that particular event. We frequently assume that the Lord is addressing faith just for this issue. Actually, He is often addressing the overall quality of the relationship that the individual in question has with Him, as God. We see several examples in Hebrews 11 of differing issues that required faith. Luke 18:8 is an example of the Lord's talking in general of the issue of faith as a relationship as opposed to faith for a particular event. Luke 17:5 is another example of a request for a deeper trust in God.

In Acts 14:9 we read: "The same heard Paul speak: who stedfastly beholding him, and perceiving that he had faith to be healed." Thus a man of faith (Paul), and by default the Lord, can look at a heart and see whether faith is sufficient for healing. For the Lord to heal there has to be faith present. God has ordained that healing is not a one-sided event. We also see this clearly in the passage in Mark 6:4-6: "But Jesus said unto them, A prophet is not without honour, but in his own country, and among his own kin, and in his own house. And he could there do no mighty work, save that he laid his hands upon a few sick folk, and healed *them*. And he marvelled because of their unbelief. And he went round about the villages, teaching."

HOW CAN WE INCREASE OUR FAITH?

The Lord speaks to us, and we can learn to know His voice. He will reveal His desires for us; and, of course, these are conditional on our response and on other individuals' responses. For example, the Lord desired to protect Jerusalem, but the leaders refused to allow Him to do that: "O Jerusalem, Jerusalem, *thou* that killest the prophets, and stonest them which are sent unto thee, how often would I have gathered thy children together, even as a hen gathereth her chickens under *her* wings, and ye would not!" (Matthew 23:37). A spoken word is considered a *rhema* to us personally. This personal word is a powerful mechanism for our faith to be increased (Romans 10:17). This is discussed below. The *rhema*, according to Scripture, is the means of acquiring faith; without it there is no other way of obtaining faith. God may announce that His desire is to perform something for us, but there are almost certainly conditions to be met on our part. Very rarely in Scripture does God assume responsibility for both sides of a covenant. It is almost certainly God's desire to heal those who approach Him for healing, since that is His nature. We saw that in Chapter 2. Many things can hinder this occurring; not the least is the overall response in our heart. As we shall see below, He is willing even to meet us somewhere on the one hundred-percent issue, but many other factors may influence the outcome. We can ask the Lord to enumerate the things that we must do in order to have our desire met, but then we must know Him well enough to hear His response. One issue that frequently is a stumbling block is lack of repentance over attitudes of not forgiving others. The Lord's Prayer states that we are asking for our trespasses to be forgiven as we forgive those who trespass against us. When we do not forgive, we are not forgiven (Matthew 6:12-15, Mark 11:25-26). In Psalm 66:18 we read: "If I regard iniquity in my heart, the Lord will not hear *me*." Therefore, the Lord cannot answer our prayer when we continue to keep known iniquity in our heart. Thus, we need to repent of all known iniquity, especially unforgiving attitudes.

We shall now look at an example of the Lord meeting someone halfway in the issue of faith. One could ask how a person could trust a little and still have complete faith that an event may occur. The answer is obviously that one either believes something, or he does not. However, there are many circumstances where one would like to believe an event could occur, but he just does not have complete trust. He may trust the ability of the Lord to perform a healing; but he does not have trust that He will, because he has not discerned from the *logos* that He will. This is where the *rhema* comes into the situation. A good example is in Mark 9:20-24 in which a father asks the Lord to heal his child from seizures. The man told the Lord that he believed but asked for help with his unbelief. The Lord healed the child. The Lord met this man at the limit of his faith. This is reassuring to those seeking something of the Lord. Note the important part of this story that is not spelled out—the man was actively conversing with the Lord. This man was receiving the *rhema* of God—he was hearing God speak to him and was in active dialog with God. Many people came to the Lord with less doubt, such as the woman who touched the hem of His garment. She believed completely that this would heal her, and she was instantly healed. The Lord commended her for her faith (Luke 8:48).

One can ask of the Lord, as did the disciples, for an increase in their faith (Luke 17:5). The Lord's answer is very interesting. He talks about the need for the disciples to serve Him first. After they have done all that they should do, they should view themselves as unprofitable since they have done only what they should. Therefore, the implication in increasing one's faith is that we must go beyond the reasonable expectation of the Lord. We have to go beyond simply being a servant in our relationship with Him. This means that we have to be part of the family with the viewpoint of a son. We have to put the Father first in all things. We have to start living for God and serving Him with all of our heart, soul, mind, and strength. Then He will increase our faith; we can certainly expect this, based on His word. In addition, in Romans 10:17 we read: "So then faith *cometh* by hearing, and hearing by the word of

God." This tells us that we have to be able to talk reliably to and fro with God in order to get faith for a situation. *Word* in this Scripture is *rhema* in the Greek. This tells us that for faith to increase, we have to be able to hear the *rhema* of God.

As I was talking with the Lord while driving home from the office one day, I was asking Him why we are seeing so little healing based on faith. He answered me with a *rhema*. It was one that is consistent with the written Word, but one would have to bring a lot of Scripture together to synthesize the answer. (God, when He speaks a *rhema* frequently does this; He brings diverse issues together into a cohesive whole.) His answer to me was that many people come to Him wanting healing, and they try to muster the faith for this. The problem is that they do not know Him well enough. There is not the relationship with Him that allows them to trust His answer. It is not that He would withhold healing, but a person must be able to receive it. The lack of more frequent miracles in our society stems from a lack of depth in our society's relationship to the Lord. We cannot expect suddenly to have faith for healing, when we have not matured in the inner man to the point where we can receive it. The devil plays on this, making healing seem a "hit or miss thing;" and this even more undermines a person's ability to receive healing. The bottom line is that to receive divine healing or to understand why it is delayed or not available, one must be able to communicate with God and be able to hear His voice. This is exactly how the people were healed by the Lord in His earthly ministry. They could watch Him; they knew His powers; and they could speak with Him; and they could believe and trust for healing.

Unfortunately, many people leave the development of a vital relationship and friendship with God (John 15:14: "Ye are my friends, if ye do whatsoever I command you") until it is too late. It takes time, effort, sacrifice, and desire from both parties to build any inter-personal relationship. Building a relationship with our Creator is no different. One cannot expect to have a problem and run to God for help, when he has not submitted to Him. Do not be in the position of those that the Lord Jesus talks about in Matthew 7:22-24.

HOW IMPORTANT IS FAITH?

Faith is so important to God that He tells us in Romans 14:23 that whatever we do that is not done in faith is sin. This is a very powerful statement. It means that, when we do something for which we do not have the express approval of the Lord, we are in sin. We may attempt a seeming "good work;" but if it originates in our flesh and not with God, then it is sin. Most of the time the people of God are going about business as usual without any idea at all whether a particular activity is God's will for them. It is sin, if for no other reason, because it fails to put the Lord first in all things and thus violates the First Commandment.

Faith can vary from person to person regarding what may result in sinning. Romans 14 speaks about this whole issue. One person, for example, could eat meat sacrificed to idols in faith because he knew God had cleansed all things. Another person would violate his faith with the same actions, because he does not know the Lord in that issue as well as the other person. The Lord meets us regarding faith according to our growth experiences.

IN WHAT MAY WE HAVE FAITH?

Paul expresses the concern that faith in God should rest on knowledge of His power and not in the spoken wisdom of men: "That your faith should not stand in the wisdom of men, but in the power of God" (1 Corinthians 2:5). This need to have our faith based on seeing the power of God in action is the same today as it was in Paul's day. If we are not having our faith in God for the right reason (seeing power in action), then it will be an inferior faith, or even worse since it will be based on the wisdom of men. We can have faith in the Scripture; we can have faith in the words of men; we can have faith in such things as medicines; we can have faith in the familiar, such as night following day; and we can have faith in the "power of God." It is the last that God wants for us.

RESULTS OF HAVING FAITH IN THE POWER OF GOD

There are many results of having faith in the power of God.

Increase of Responsibility

Matthew 25:21 shows the increase of responsibility: "His lord said unto him, Well done, *thou* good and faithful servant: thou hast been faithful over a few things, I will make thee ruler over many things: enter thou into the joy of thy lord."

Luke 16:10-13 affirms this also: "He that is faithful in that which is least is faithful also in much: and he that is unjust in the least is unjust also in much. If therefore ye have not been faithful in the unrighteous mammon, who will commit to your trust the true *riches*? And if ye have not been faithful in that which is another man's, who shall give you that which is your own? No servant can serve two masters: for either he will hate the one, and love the other; or else he will hold to the one, and despise the other. Ye cannot serve God and mammon."

These Scriptures tell us that the Lord wants us to have trust in Him (faith) in order for us to put His things first (First Commandment). When we do this to His satisfaction, He will promote our area of authority and responsibility in His works. We have to perform all of our activities unto Him, including in our secular work (Ephesians 6:5-7, Colossians 3:22-25). This is what He has given to us. We are to give thanks to Him in all things (1 Thessalonians 5:18).

Money is a huge issue with the Lord. Our attitude is to be that all we have is from Him and should be for His use. We should not spend a penny without His approval. This will seem hard for everyone, but it is a critical attitude. The Lord regards this issue as critical in testing our hearts.

Forgiveness of Sins and Healing

The following passages show that healing and forgiveness of sins are linked.

Mark 2:5: "When Jesus saw their faith, he said unto the sick of the palsy, Son, thy sins be forgiven thee."

James 5:14-15: "Is any sick among you? let him call for the elders of the church; and let them pray over him, anointing him with oil in the name of the Lord: And the prayer of faith shall save the sick, and the Lord shall raise him up; and if he have committed sins, they shall be forgiven him."

Psalm 103:1-5 is one of the strongest Scriptures showing the connections between sins and healing: "Bless the LORD, O my soul, and forget not all his benefits: Who forgiveth all thine iniquities; who healeth all thy diseases" (vs. 2,3).

There are scores of other Scriptures attesting to this relationship.

Being used for releasing His Power

The Scriptures show that the early deacons had much power. Acts 6:8, for example, mentions Stephen: "And Stephen, full of faith and power, did great wonders and miracles among the people."

Gaining insight into the faith of others

Many of the early disciples showed insight into the faith of others. Acts 14:9 relates: "The same heard Paul speak: who stedfastly beholding him, and perceiving that he had faith to be healed." Paul's faith gave him the spiritual discernment to see that the man had faith to be healed. We have viewed this Scripture above to note it as an example of needing enough faith to be healed.

Hearts purified

Faith is the instrument by which hearts are purified. Acts 15:9 tells us: "And put no difference between us and them, purifying their hearts by faith." This is a very important principle for purifying one's heart.

Men justified before God

Most importantly, we are justified by faith. Romans 1:17 is a key passage: "For therein is the righteousness of God revealed from faith to faith: as it is written, The just shall live by faith."

Paul adds in Romans 3:28: "Therefore we conclude that a man is justified by faith without the deeds of the law."

Romans 5:1 states: "Therefore being justified by faith, we have peace with God through our Lord Jesus Christ."

Hebrews 10:38 discusses that the Lord will have no pleasure in any man who draws back from faith. "Now the just shall live by faith: but if *any man* draw back, my soul shall have no pleasure in him." This is the situation in which a person who has been through the second birth draws back and tries to live under the law. Such a person tries to use rules for his behavior. It can be very subtle. It avoids the effort of relationship and accountability.

Faith allows justification; and, in turn, those who are justified will live by faith. This explains that one goes from faith for justification to living by faith (faith to faith [Romans 1:17]). Faith works this without the law. This issue of "without the law" highlights the fact that in the law a person is operating under the First Covenant, and in faith a person is operating under the Second "superior" Covenant. Galatians 3:11 emphasizes that no man is justified by the law.

Having the Lord Jesus dwelling in our hearts

Ephesians 3:17 mentions Jesus' dwelling in our hearts. In the context this is something beyond the usual experience of the believer who already has the Holy Spirit living in his heart since the second birth. It occurs only when the inner man is strengthened in might by God's

Spirit. It is appropriated by faith. It is not something that is going to occur unless we are showing the fruit of the indwelling "might." We will also be rooted and grounded in the love of God, expressing this as an emanation from the inner man.

Unity of faith

Ephesians 4:13 speaks of this as a maturing of the body of the Lord Jesus, His Church. It has not occurred yet in Church history.

A defense to the devil

Ephesians 6:16 speaks of faith as a shield in our warfare. 1 Thessalonians 5:8 speaks of faith as a breastplate. Both are defense instuments in our fight with the devil.

OTHER ASPECTS OF FAITH

There are other aspects of faith that need to be mentioned briefly.

Faith is not sufficient for maturity in the inner man.

Faith is necessary, but not sufficient, for maturation in the inner man. Obedience to the *rhema* that God speaks to us will allow maturation over time.

1 Corinthians 13:2 and 13:13 discuss that faith, hope, and charity (love) are measures of maturity (implied) in the inner man. The greatest is charity, and without this the others are nothing.

We see the progression of these things more in 1 Timothy 1:5: "Now the end of the commandment is charity out of a pure heart, and *of* a good conscience, and *of* faith unfeigned." Charity depends on purity of heart, good conscience, and unfeigned faith.

2 Peter 1:4-9 describes the progression of maturity that comes as a result of obeying the Lord. One must go beyond just mere obedience, as we see in Luke 17:5-10. This was discussed above under the heading "How can we increase our faith?"

Faith and Conscience are linked.

We see this in 1 Timothy 1:5: "Now the end of the commandment is charity out of a pure heart, and *of* a good conscience, and *of* faith unfeigned." 1 Timothy 1:19 adds: "Holding faith, and a good conscience; which some having put away concerning faith have made shipwreck." The link is that we cannot have trust in God when our conscience convicts us of any sin in our life. This awareness of sin separates our inner man from God. 1 Timothy 3:9 and Hebrews 10:22 also speak of this link.

Faith can be overthrown.

2 Timothy 2:18: "Who concerning the truth have erred, saying that the resurrection is past already; and overthrow the faith of some." Those people who believed this were demonstrating more faith in the wisdom of men, were not listening to the *rhema* of the Lord, and hence were led astray into believing falsehood. It shows the utter importance of staying by the Lord as a sheep huddling close to its Shepherd—as Father and son, and as friend.

The relationship of faith and work

James addresses this relationship between faith and works in great detail. Read James 2:14-26. Essentially faith is not alive, if a person does not demonstrate it in his life by his work for the Lord. Performing works for the Lord in faith builds faith, which allows for performance of more work with increasing faith. The two go together, and the question of which is the egg and which is the chicken is irrelevant.

Faith and wavering

Hebrews 10:23 commands us to hold fast the profession of our faith without wavering. James 1:6 also addresses our asking in faith with nothing wavering. James then discusses at length how the Lord views those who waver. The Lord says that those who waver will receive nothing from Him (James 1:7). This nothing is at least in regard to wisdom. We have seen just how basic and important it is to get wisdom in Chapter 11.

Miscellaneous

Romans 1:12 shows that mutual faith comforts.

2 Corinthians 10:15 speaks of increasing faith. Jude 20 speaks also of building up ourselves on our most holy faith (recall that holy means separated to God).

Galatians 3:7 reminds us that people of faith in God are children of Abraham.

Galatians 5:22 mentions faith as one part of the fruit of the Spirit that grows in our heart. This fruit grows, as we follow our inner man as he hears from the Spirit of God. James 1:3 tells us that our faith works patience.

Peter tells us that our faith will be tried and that this is more precious than gold. It will result in honor, praise, and glory to the Lord Jesus Christ at His return. He states: "That the trial of your faith, being much more precious than of gold that perisheth, though it be tried with fire, might be found unto praise and honour and glory at the appearing of Jesus Christ" (1 Peter 1:7).

Part VI

20
SUMMATION OF HOW TO BE LED BY THE SPIRIT OF GOD

INTRODUCTION

In this chapter we will integrate all that we have studied and learned. In reading this one must keep in mind and use as an operational maxim that it is the Holy Spirit who leads us into all truth. The reason for this book is to help us to learn how to come to a point where we can reliably communicate with God, so that the Holy Spirit can be the one to lead us into all truth. God is far more able to understand how to develop and mature each one of His children than any teacher, even a teacher with a very generous anointing of the teaching ministry as described in Ephesians 4:11.

The Lord Jesus used the parable (story analogy) as one of His primary teaching methods. God speaks to us through types (the early tabernacle pointed to the Lord Jesus) and analogies. He has done this, because He designed us in such a way that we can understand concepts in the spiritual universe through these means, if we are seeking with open hearts. One of the greatest and most helpful analogies is that of the family. I suspect that it is for this reason that it is under such demonic attack at this point in time. If we take part in a traditional family structure, we can understand more of the things of God as we reflect on all of the daily issues with which we deal in this setting. We can look at the example of rearing children. We can see in the family context that parents desire the best for their children. They may have the wrong targets and motivations; but, nonetheless, they have a heartfelt desire to see their child succeed. The parents will, in love, discipline and train the child in order for him to grow into an independent adult with the ability to succeed. We can see this as a functional law in the human family. Remembering that man is made in the image of God, we can analogize that God wants the best for His children (Romans 8:28) and that He will train and discipline them in love (Hebrews 12:7-8). Therefore, as we study how to be led by the Spirit of God, keep in mind the following two principles.

1. God, who wants to see us mature as sons for eternal work, loves us with an everlasting love.

2. In order to reach maturity, we have to be disciplined.

We saw in previous chapters that in all circumstances in which we find ourselves we should seek to see the hand of God. This is a critically important concept to keep in the front of our minds always and to walk in it. We shall use this family analogy at times, although it is not of critical importance, since God certainly loves and teaches those who have not been raised in a traditional family.

FOUNDATIONS

We must understand the basic foundations that the Lord teaches us in Scripture. We have to get foundations correct in order to build and grow properly. If we do not get foundational concepts into our inner man by getting them into our heart, we will never mature in a co-ordinated and mature manner. The basic foundation is to understand how God relates to mankind in this age.

The Scriptures are obviously divided into two covenants (Testaments). In the Old Covenant God chose to reveal Himself to mankind by choosing a people group (Israel) who would be led by Him and thus be an example to other nations. Most of the Old Testament describes the issues in the relationship between man and God as experienced by Israel. All of these things are recorded for our benefits so that we can learn from them (1 Corinthians 10:11). In this relationship God chose to give Israel a set of Laws (the Ten Commandments and all of the Torah). By this Law came the knowledge of sin (Romans 3:20). He gave the Israelites a way of dealing with sin by sacrificing a "sin" offering. When in faith they believed that this sin offering took away their sin, they were cleansed from the remembrance of sin for a short period. They had to keep sacrificing at regular intervals and whenever they consciously sinned. Sin prevents us from talking with and hearing from God. We do not seek His presence when we are aware of sin. Note how Adam and Eve hid themselves from God. The Scriptures confirm many times that we must repent of our sin for adequate communication with God (*e.g.*, Psalm 66:18). In the Old Covenant people worshipped God by serving Him and by coming before Him at various times of the year for corporate worship (the feasts of the Lord) and praise. God's criteria are found in Psalm 29:2: "Give unto the LORD the glory due unto his name; worship the LORD in the beauty of holiness." If an individual in those days were to give the Lord the glory due Him, he would perfect holiness by separating himself from the "world system."

In the Old Covenant a Gentile could join himself to the God of Israel by committing to join in these same practices of sacrifice and corporate worship. There is a critical difference between these old ways and the current ways under the New Covenant. In the Old Covenant the people did not have a new spirit, a new heart, or the benefit of the indwelling Holy Spirit. They did not have God's law written on their heart and in their mind. These people did not have the ability to worship the Lord in spirit, but just in revealed truth. They had to worship with their all of their heart, mind, soul, and strength; but there was no mention of spirit. Of course, their soul contained a dying spirit; thus, they had to worship with their dying spirit. We have learned that this dying spirit lacked a lot of the functionality that it would have needed to worship God adequately (as Jesus tells Nicodemus in John 3).

In the current times we are operating under a New Covenant. For the individual this means that, when we go through the second birth, five things occur:

1. The Holy Spirit indwells our heart (and will lead us into all truth, and will comfort us).
2. We receive a new spirit that is born of God.
3. We receive a new heart.
4. God writes His laws on our heart.
5. God writes His laws in our mind.

God then expects us to worship Him in spirit and in truth: "But the hour cometh, and now is, when the true worshippers shall worship the Father in spirit and in truth: for the Father seeketh such to worship him.

God *is* a Spirit: and they that worship him must worship *him* in spirit and in truth" (John 4:23-24). We see from this that, to be a true worshipper of God, we must worship Him both in spirit and in truth. If we are going to fulfill this, then we will need to understand how to do so. Of course the first step is to obtain a new spirit at the second birth. Without this we cannot worship God properly in spirit.

We have learned earlier that the inner man is in constant communication with God. This inner man is our spirit. We have to worship God both through our inner man and through truth. We have to train our inner man to be a meek and quiet spirit, which is described as of great price to God (1 Peter 3:4). Remember that it is up to our soul to rule our spirit (Proverbs 25:28). Our spirit (inner man) becomes polluted (2 Corinthians 7:1) with filthiness by living in an unclean heart. We cannot worship God in spirit and in truth as we are commanded without going through a process of preparation. It is the purpose of this book to teach us how to do this in order for us to be fitted for God's service and responsive to God as He chooses what He wants of us. It is the purpose of this chapter to try to summarize the preceding chapters into an operational plan to allow you, the reader, to present yourself as a living sacrifice to the Lord God for His pleasure and for His service (Romans 12:1, Philippians 2:17).

As we look at the differences between the Old and the New Covenants, we can learn much from how the Holy Spirit described the New Covenant in Hebrews 8:6-13, Galatians 4:24-31, Matthew 5:17-18, John 1:17, Romans 6:14-15, Romans 7:6, Romans 8:4, Galatians 3:12, and Galatians 5:18. Reading these Scriptures and asking God to give us understanding will lead us to see that faith and the law are diametrically opposed. We saw in the chapter on faith that we cannot have faith, unless we can reliably hear the Lord God speaking to us (Romans 10:17). Therefore, until we can reliably hear from God, we cannot have reliable faith; and we, by default, have to live partly under the law. This results in the mixed fleshly carnal walk as displayed by the Corinthian church.

In this section where we are discussing foundations I would suggest that—until a person can see clearly those issues discussed in the paragraph above, can see the need to walk in them (as opposed to intellectually believing them), and will commit to walking in them—there will be an insufficient basis for growth; and that individual will struggle to have growth in the inner man. He may confuse growth for intellectual understanding of facts with the mind, but this is entirely different to seeing with spiritual vision and hearing with the ears of the inner man (Ephesians 1:17-18). Our inner man was not given to us as a baby at the second birth, but it came completely able to understand our soul (1 Corinthians 2:11). The issue is not that the inner man is a "babe," but rather that we allow ourselves to backslide; and then our flesh rules our spirit. Our flesh has made so much noise and has so impacted our heart that we have all sorts of structures and high and lofty things that we have erected against the Spirit of God. As a result we cannot hear or see the things that our spirit is telling us and showing us. The things we do see are dim and foggy. We have to spend much time and effort cleaning up the impurities that obscure our inner man's communications with the mind of the soul.

SOME RHETORICAL QUESTIONS

Since we are made in God's image, we are very like God in our attributes. Think of those attributes basic to men, which are not due to sin, and then consider the following two issues:

1. Many think that God does not communicate readily, since they find it hard to hear from Him. Is this consistent with a God who came every day to talk with Adam and Eve before the Fall? Is it consistent with the nature of man to be silent in the presence of others? Is it consistent with a God who talked with His prophets quite liberally? Even as Hebrews 1:3 tells us that Jesus is continually speaking to hold the universe together, just so God is always speaking. It is we who are not listening.

2. God presents two aspects of truth in His Word that often cause great problems for people as they try to balance them in their understanding—how free we are in our ability to act independently of God (known as free will) and how much all of our behavior

is pre-determined. Is it conceivable that a God who is able to make this universe and the human race could not balance these two issues so that both are equally true? We may not be able to understand it, but when we are able to talk to God and hear back from Him we certainly get an impression that we are free to choose. In fact on one occasion the Lord allowed my wife and me to choose between two condominiums at which we were looking. He told us that with one we would have some sorrows. He did not forbid us getting it, but He gave us His Fatherly advice. Do you think that a God who portrays Himself as our Father and asks us to love Him with all of our heart could possibly be content with a rigidly-forced love from a mechanical object that fits neatly into some automated life that is completely planned for it? How could such a God judge us and be fair? Fairness is such an innate concept that we surely have it as a characteristic from God.

We have to come to a balance on these issues, or we will drift into great error. The balance between free will and the mechanistic view is a narrow one that one has to walk as on a mountain ridge. On a mountain ridge deviation to the left or right will mean slipping down the slope and not being where one should be.

WE ARE GOD'S CHILDREN.

God adopts us as His children when He gives us the second birth experience (Romans 8:15, Ephesians 1:5). He desires us to grow in our inner man, beyond the experience in Hebrews 5:13 of being a babe, into mature sons (Romans 8:1), who are led by the Spirit of God. His whole purpose in that is to work good for us (Romans 8:28). While we are spiritual babes, we cannot understand much of the ways of God. We have a way that seems right to us (Proverbs 16:25), but the end of this way is death. In Exodus 33:13-23 we see Moses asking God to show him His ways so that he (Moses) might know Him. God allowed this. Generally, God tells us that His ways are above our ways; and His thoughts, above ours (Isaiah 55:9). God would show His ways only to someone whom He trusted. Moses by his life had earned God's trust.

It is common for us to expect God to give us important tasks to perform. Would you trust a babe with important work? Our intellectual skills do not translate into spiritual power (1 Corinthians 1:17-31). We must stop thinking that we are spiritually mature, until we see that the Lord trusts us with a release of His power through us. He does not trust true riches to us, until we are sufficiently mature enough to be capable of handling them (Ephesians 3:16). An analogy would be like equipping a two year old with weapons of war. The two year old is not even capable of following adult advice on when and how to use them. The enemy would have a field day with such a babe.

We must mature in the spirit, not in intellectual world wisdom within the mind of the soul, in order to follow the Spirit of God. When a baby is born, he has to learn to recognize the voice, appearance, and ways of his parents. It is the same with a soul who has been through the second birth. Our soul has a mature new inner man, but he has to learn how to relate to the new inner man and how to teach and train the inner man. Proverbs 25:28 states: "He (soul) that *hath* no rule over his own spirit *is like* a city *that is* broken down, *and* without walls."

ARE WE IN THE FLESH OR IN THE SPIRIT?

Our soul can be in the flesh or in the inner man. One can readily tell where the soul is just by observing what he is seeing (looking at), from whom he is hearing, and what he is thinking. The soul can focus on either the flesh or the inner man. The one on which the soul focuses will be the one that is strengthened in its impact on the soul. If we concentrate on the spirit, then we will be in a position to be led by the Spirit of God. We will hear from the Spirit of God, as our spirit bears witness to His Spirit. As we hear from the Spirit of God more reliably, then we can will to follow Him; or we can will not to follow Him. As our spirit becomes meek before God, we will submit our will to His will. We will then be in a state of being led by the Spirit of God. We will shortly look at the changes that we must make in ourselves for this to happen, but before doing so a note of caution is needed.

THE ENEMY

The devil does not like to see us go through the second birth at all. It is against his lusts. However, once this has occurred, he will then do all he can to prevent spiritual growth. As we purpose to grow in the knowledge and love of our Lord (it is a choice), the devil will send great attacks against us. We can rejoice in these, as we see them coming and as we are involved in them; for, as we look to see the hand of God in all things, we will see His purpose in these attacks is to let us learn how to stand against them. In doing so, we gain spiritual strength and spiritual world authority (Acts 19:15). As in Philippians 4:4 we should rejoice in the Lord always. In 1 John 4:4 the Lord assures us that He is greater than the devil. As we abide in the Lord and seek His leading in our spirit, we will not be overcome by the enemy. If we get into the flesh and are being led by the flesh down a wrong path, then the Lord may allow us to be harmed by the enemy in order for us to learn.

We read in Chapter 17 about how we appear five years after the second birth. We read about some of the errors into which we can fall, when we are not seeking the leading of the Spirit of God and the maturing that is necessary. When we are deliberately trying to mature in our inner man, then we will be subject to more sophisticated attacks from Satan. A prime method the devil will use is to try to confuse us about how God's leading takes place. Demons have sown many philosophies in the world about interactions with the spiritual world that are not God's leading.

If we wish to characterize these philosophies, we could place them on a graph of three dimensions. These dimensions would measure where we stand on the three aspects of all spiritual communication—the power axis, the state of the heart axis (emotion), and the control (information) axis. If we placed a zero point where these three axes intersect, then we could label this point as the place where we are spiritually unaware of anything. As we move along the power axis, we have growing awareness of the powers that are impacting our spiritual communications. As we move along the state of the heart axis, we have growing awareness of the impact these emotions have on our spiritual communications. Similarly, for the control and information axis we have a growing awareness of how our inner man and flesh battle for supremacy. Those people who ignore the impact of their emotions and ignore the understanding of the source of power in their communications and are looking only at the content of the thoughts of the mind are living in a one-dimensional spiritual world. They do not understand the things of the Spirit at all, since they do not perceive two of the axes that are present in all of their communications. They cannot, therefore, analyze the source of the spirit that they are receiving or emanating. They can worship only in what they perceive to be truth, but even in this perception of truth they can be badly deluded since they have erected barriers to the Spirit of God. They have fallen into the intellectualism of this age. They have made the mind supreme to the spirit. The evil spirits can readily make these people militantly self righteous in their interpretation of truth. We can see how easily the evil spirits can allow philosophies to be built up that are vain. Similarly, we can look at those people who do not worry about the knowledge and control axis and who ignore the power axis. They are one dimensional in that they think that they following their spirit when they are making decisions based only on the emotional state of their heart. If it feels right, they will do it. Again the devil leads these ones far astray from truth. They vainly think that they are worshipping God through their emotions, frequently tied to art and music. As we move further along these three axes in a balanced and co-ordinated way, analyzing each component of all communications, then our soul will grow in discernment, as our inner man responds to the movements of the Spirit of God and of evil spirits that try to influence it.

In this age we are being exposed to many religious beliefs, because there is so much more mixing of faiths, as people emigrate here and there from their native lands. Unfortunately, exposure to these faiths does not bring discernment. When we study these various faiths, we find many differences, for example, in how they teach that a follower relates to his god. If we do not have a very strong inner man, we can easily err by incorporating some of the practices and beliefs of these other faiths. We are right to have religious tolerance; God wants us to leave the tares until the end of the age. He is tolerant until then, but at that point His patience and long suffering are going to be set aside before His righteous judgment (Matthew 13:30). For the soul who has been through the second birth and who is learning to relate to the God who gave him the second birth, he must accept that he has to learn how He wants this to be done. Can you imagine a baby of age one year telling his parents how to relate to him? Be very careful not to fall into the error of taking the understanding of the mind as a spiritual maturity. It is not. We are not one-dimensional spiritual people.

GOD

Let us recall from Chapter 2 the names of God in the Old Covenant He used many names including "the God of Abraham, Isaac, and Jacob." In Matthew 28:19 we learn a New Covenant name: "Go ye therefore, and teach all nations, baptizing them in the name of the Father, and of the Son, and of the Holy Ghost." He is the Father, Son, and Holy Ghost." His triune nature is foundational. As we explore the implications for how we communicate with Him, we will review the following:

1. The Holy Spirit indwells the heart of the believer after the second birth. He will comfort us, will bear witness to the Lord Jesus Christ, will lift Him up, and will lead us into all truth.
2. The Lord Jesus describes the Father as greater then Himself (John 14:28), but He clearly tells us that He is equal to God and that He is God (Philippians 2:6).
3. In the Lord's Prayer the Lord Jesus Christ told us to pray to "Our Father who art in Heaven." In John 16:23 the Lord Jesus tells us not to ask anything of Him but to pray to the Father in His (the Lord Jesus') name.

Note once and for all that our God is not approached through an internal searching. He is in the Third Heaven, and His ear is beside our lips; but we do not see this in the natural realm. We do not have to be in a particular frame of mind or in a particular posture or setting. Our God is always ready for us to talk with Him. There are conditions on when He will hear: we must not regard iniquity in our heart, we must not hold a grudge against another, we cannot have a state in our heart of not forgiving, and we must not use vain repetitions. **We never ever, even as we mature, start seeking to talk with God within our heart.**

If we start seeking God within our heart or soul and if we start using vain repetitions, such as mantras, we are out of the will of our God and have opened our soul to being deceived and influenced by evil spirits. If we do not walk obediently, as our God commanded, instead thinking proudly that we know best, we will find in the long run that we have been greatly deluded and that our spiritual growth has been stunted.

God asks us to meditate in our hearts on His written word. This is not a turning off of the mind. We have to break His word down, realign it, and synthesize it until we see the Lord begin to teach us as the Holy Spirit here and there "quickens" something to us. Note that this is a prayerful process in that we will ask God to teach us and illuminate something over which we are puzzling. We should be very much aware that we do not know how, when, or where we may receive the answer. God controls the process. He will answer us as we ask in faith (James 1).

The Lord commands in Psalm 100:4: "Enter into his gates with thanksgiving, *and* into his courts with praise: be thankful unto him, *and* bless his name." This does not state that we do this by looking internally. We take it in faith that when we have a spirit of thanksgiving, we are able to come close to Him in the spiritual realm; and then, as we begin to praise, we will be in His courts in the spiritual realm. If we begin to mature in the inner man, He may be pleased to give us a sense in our spirit of being in those places; but we should never seek this out. We are not praising God, if we come seeking an experience; and the whole book of the "Song of Solomon" teaches us that the Lord will break us of this seeking for the self in order for us to mature. If we are to be like Him, we cannot ever be self-seeking.

Several Scriptures speak of the Lord Jesus and the Father abiding with the believer. This is never an internal abiding in the natural realm. The Father is not within us (just as King Solomon explained that he had built a house for God but it really would not contain Him [1 Kings 8:27]); but His Spirit is joined to us, just as the spirits of individuals are to be in unity with each other.

If we do not understand how the spiritual universe operates and if we do not follow the rules of our God for approaching this universe, we will be readily deceived and led into very grievous (to the Lord and eventually to us) pathways of error. The devil appeals to our intellectual pride and sets us up, while we are babes in our spiritual understanding, into paths that make us think that we can do things our way. It is so easy to be deceived in spiritual issues, if we do not know how to hear from God. If we allow the devil to stop us from learning to hear from God, then he has effectively closed down our ability to grow. It is so important that we humbly learn from God, if we are to grow. Let us now go back to our concept of the three axes.

LISTENING TO GOD—THE THREE AXES OF THE SPIRIT

On the power axis we, in maturing, must try to discern when the power of God is present, by reason of use. The devil will appeal subtly to the flesh and will try to get us, using our own soul power, to go through some flesh-led "mantra" to come into the presence of God. Even worse, he will try to supply his power by leading us to close down our own mind and will and to become like a medium for him to use our body for his purpose.

To listen to God, we have to come into the Lord's presence in the sense that we have to recognize Him. However, the Holy Spirit is always present in our heart after the second birth, and He does not need us to go through any special procedure other than to turn our attention to Him in order to hear from Him. There are no words, special procedures, or anything unnatural about it. Imagine coming into a room and seeing your friend Charlie sitting in the corner. Would Charlie expect some ritualistic approach to him where you felt you needed to keep repeating certain words, thoughts, or behaviors before you could talk to him? If you tried that, Charlie might go elsewhere for friendship. It is no different with the Lord. As we grow to know Him, we will naturally revere Him for who He is; as we learn what He is like in His dealings with us, then we will naturally come to love Him. When we turn our attention to the Lord, we will feel our heart and spirit rising in love; and we will sense His presence (as we would do with someone like Charlie above) because we are talking to Him. He does not ask us to be silent before Him, except that we should not allow ourselves to be noisy in a disrespectful way. Our mind should always be very active in listening to Him, as He communicates with us. We must sense the movement of His Spirit on us. The Lord asks us to wait on Him, but this is not in time of prayer with our trying to force Him to answer us. He may delay certain answers until another time, and waiting on the Lord is merely not acting in a particular issue until He chooses to tell us His answer. There is nothing mystical about this process. It is really no more difficult learning to know the Lord than it is learning to know a friend. All of the following Scriptures attest to the fact that we must learn to distinguish the voice and communications of God from the other voices in the world (John 10:3-5, John 10:27, 1 Corinthians 14:10, and Hebrews 3:7, 15). These other internal voices are of our own mind and soul, of our flesh, and of evil spirits.

When we listen to someone speak, we frequently have a problem trying to understand what he means, because we listen with just the intellect. We do not train ourselves to listen with the spirit. Therefore, sometimes we have to go back to try to reconstruct what was said; then we try to parse it through our mind, dissecting it for nuances. When we listen with the spirit, we will get all of the power (source), the heart desire behind the words, and the information that the speaker really wants to convey, regardless of what words he chooses. This is the difference between spiritual and physical listening. When we listen to God through the inner man, our soul matures in listening ability; and we will become able to discern much more readily the whole spiritual communication instead of just the limited spoken physical communication.

We must always test all three components of the communication to see if it comes from God. Regardless of how good it looks in two areas, if it fails in the third area, then it is not from God. Thus, communicating with God is a very "mind on" active listening and sorting out what is being said and testing it against God's written word. He expects this of us. Remember that the demons have access to hearing what God is telling us, and they can be great mimics. They will also try to talk with us while the Lord is talking with us. They have to be rebuked, and we can ask the Lord to do this.

Learning to listen to God takes active practice. Remember that the voices of your friends have various qualities at different times, and so does the Lord's voice. It takes time to learn all of this. Ask the Lord to teach you and to protect you. Your greatest asset is to know the Word of God thoroughly so that anything you hear and sense can be held up to this standard. Also remember, however, that we must be humble about knowing the Word of God. Being able to memorize it is helpful, but to integrate large parts of it requires the light of the Holy Spirit to lead us into all truth. Realize that the Scripture says that it is the Holy Spirit that leads us into "all truth." Our pride subtly appeals to us as we try to study the Word. We think that we can puzzle it out. This would be our leading ourselves into all truth, and this is not God's way. We must prayerfully read the Word and talk to God as we do so. We must ask Him to explain things to us, realizing that we cannot puzzle it out. As we allow ourselves to listen and receive of the Spirit of God, we will gain much richness in our understanding of the Word; and we begin to understand why we could never do it without this process. That is why the Scripture tells us that the Holy Spirit will lead us into all truth.

LISTENING TO GOD

We are called by God to a deeper relationship in order to be his friends and so that He can give us His work to do that He has ordained before the foundation of the world. In order for these things to occur, God must hear from us reliably, and we must learn to hear from Him reliably. As a spiritual babe we have to have our spiritual senses developed. Our inner man is not a baby, but we as a soul are babes in the spiritual universe right after the second birth. We shall now focus on how to learn to listen to God reliably. It involves removing those barriers which have been erected in our heart since our second birth, preventing our hearing from the Spirit of God. It is not due to God's failing to speak clearly. He is quite able to speak, but we are deaf to the voice of the Spirit and need healing in this area (John 12:29). This shows us that it is the condition of the hearer and not the speaker that is the problem. Our soul has to be healed in our ability to hear from the spirit. We have to go through the following steps:

1. We need to be delivered from regarding iniquity (sin) in our heart—our heart must be purified. As this happens, our inner man will be cleansed.
2. We have to forgive all men and hold nothing against another.
3. We have to come before God with praise and thanksgiving.
4. We must not come with vain repetitions.
5. We must come in faith.

As we do these things and as our heart and spirit are purified and cleansed, we will start to recognize what is coming to our mind of the soul from the soul itself, what is coming from the flesh, and what is coming from the inner man. This separation is the process that is described in Hebrews 4:12, and it is a foundational landmark that we must reach in our journey with the Lord. It is a place that can lead to spiritual rest. However, we can gain this rest only as we conquer the evil spirits opposing us and as we take control over our flesh. This process also takes time, but it is essential if we are to have spiritual rest.

THE PROCESS OF LEARNING TO BE LED BY THE SPIRIT OF GOD

In some respects this process follows the outline of this book. In other words, the chapters in this book show us in order what we need to do to mature in the inner man.

We need to believe and behave as if the spiritual universe is more important than the physical (Chapter 1 reviewed this). For us to mature in the spiritual universe, we have to learn about it and act on those things which we learn. An important fact is that our inner man lives on in eternity. If we act on its needs being greater than those of our physical comforts and lusts, then we are acting a behavior that demonstrates faith in this aspect of God's Word. Acting on this principle will, over time, put the flesh to a moment-by-moment crucifixion, and the inner man will grow at the expense of the flesh.

In Chapters 2-4 we reviewed who God is, who the devil is, and who man is. We need to understand God's perspective on these and then act on it. We must grow toward revering God and worshipping Him in truth and in spirit. To do this, we have to study His character and then walk with Him in faith. In order to succeed in spiritual growth, we have to be able to stand against the devil and overcome all fear. We can do this only as God strengthens us with might in our inner man.

We need to understand the details of how God has made us in the spiritual sense, as we have outlined in Chapters 9-15. There we examined the components of spiritual man.

Finally, as we read the closing chapters, we can begin to put it all together. We should try to keep this in the order and perspective from which it was presented in order to learn to communicate two ways with the Lord—God the Father, Son, and Holy Ghost.

It is only reasonable to state clearly that for growth and maturity to occur we will be held to God's standards, which are above man's standards. We have to commit our whole being to the service of God. We must come to love Him with all of our heart, soul, mind, and strength. Growth will accelerate, as we begin to move toward this goal. It will mean committing a vast amount of time. It will require changing our focus from those things that fulfill fleshly interests and comforts to finding out what God wants us to do with our time and resources. We have to empty our soul of self and become filled with the fullness of the Spirit of God. We have to undergo our own deliberate *kenosis* just as the Lord Jesus underwent His (Philippians 2:4-8). This book is for those few who will make the commitment that is required. It is these few who will be precious to the Lord, and through these and those like them He will work His work among the children of men.

THE DETAILS OF LEARNING TO BE LED BY GOD'S SPIRIT

We must start to take stock deliberately of our current beliefs, attitudes, and behaviors and hold them up to God's Word for their validation. This will require a great deal of time in the Word of God. We have to be taught by the Holy Spirit and not rely on other people for the vast majority of what we learn. What follows is broken out into individual steps for clarity. In reality, an individual will pursue many of them simultaneously; and in this manner God will coordinate spiritual growth. A fundamental skill that we must acquire as a spiritual neonate is that of seeing and hearing spiritual things as we abide in the inner man and not in the flesh. We shall look at the following steps that will help you as you seek to transition from a fleshly individual to one who is of use to the Lord because you know how to follow His Spirit. The steps are:

1. Learn to see the hand of God in all things (1 Thessalonians 5:18).
2. Walk in increasing faith as you trust the written promises in God's Word.
3. Learn to hear the voice of God in order to communicate with Him, and receive the *rhema* that will further increase faith.
   a. Meet the conditions for God to hear you.
   b. Purify your heart and cleanse your inner man.
   c. Test all the spirits that flow from your heart to the mind of your soul, analyzing the three components.
      i. Test the power.
      ii. Test the information and compare it to the *logos* of God.
      iii. Learn to recognize all of the emotions and states of the heart.
   d. Learn to distiguish between the voice of your conscience and a spirit of false guilt.
4. Undergo your *kenosis*, as you purify your heart and cleanse your inner man, by casting down vain imaginations and high things that exalt themselves against God. These are your heart beliefs, attitudes, and behaviors. They all have to be torn down actively and cast out.
5. Think only on the following things: "Finally, brethren, whatsoever things are true, whatsoever things *are* honest, whatsoever things *are* just, whatsoever things *are* pure, whatsoever things *are* lovely, whatsoever things *are* of good report; if *there be* any virtue, and if *there be* any praise, think on these things" (Philippians 4:8). If something is not in this Scripture, stop thinking about it and dwelling on it.

6. Take every single thought captive for the Lord Jesus Christ: "Casting down imaginations, and every high thing that exalteth itself against the knowledge of God, and bringing into captivity every thought to the obedience of Christ" (2 Corinthians 10:5).
7. Commit to put God first, and begin to tell Him that you love Him.
8. Become a person of very few words; for you are judged on what you speak, since it is spirit. Sift your planned words carefully before releasing them.
9. Carefully examine all doctrines of men's teaching; hold them up to the Scriptures; and, if necessary, ask God to explain (James 1:5-6). He is very willing to explain. He is your true teacher and not men, although God will use the right men for your needs.
10. Study the Scriptures daily, and do research on topics that the Lord brings before you, using a concordance or a software program.
11. Assemble yourself with other believers. Choose a congregation about which you have prayed and to which you have asked the Lord to guide you. He is the one who puts people into individual congregations. It is His right to choose for you.
12. Do not change your secular work, unless you are clearly led. This work should now be done with an attitude that you are doing it for the Lord.
13. You must pray constantly in the spirit without ceasing (1 Thessalonians 5:17) and maintain righteousness, peace, and joy in the heart.
14. You must praise God.
15. You are coming into relationship with a supernatural God, and there will be supernatural events in your life. You should expect and welcome them.
16. Never, ever compare yourself to another individual before God or in your own mind. This is a false spirit and must be vigorously rebuked (John 21:21-22).
17. Be humble toward all advice from counselors.
18. Always walk in truth.

As we begin to do all of these things, we should work on them together. They all have to be performed; and as we do so, we will find that we are growing in the inner man. Soon we will begin to feel very different. We will begin to find that old things will pass away and that we will no longer have anxiety and fear that motivate our actions. Instead, we will be walking in trust under God's love and looking to Him to fulfill His word to us in that He will supply all of our needs. We will begin to get a vision of what work He has for us in the Body of the Lord Jesus. He will see to it that we are equipped. We will find that there is a steady joy and peace within and a mounting sense of expectation about what the Lord is going to have us do. Only God can work with the individual, but His Word commands us to perform all of the above steps, and we must do them in order to relate to Him and to follow His Spirit.

As we do undergo the process of transformation, we will find ourselves following a roadmap that the Scripture sets forth for delivery from bondage to the world system and for entering into the rest of the Lord. This is the story of the Exodus and the journey to the Promised Land. It continues in the Old Testament, as we read about the battles to win the Promised Land. The individual believer has to progress from the Old Covenant to the New Covenant, as he is delivered by the Lord from bondage to the world system into the freedom that is in Christ Jesus our Lord. The Old Testament describes the shipwrecks that can occur due to disobedience. Do we really want to be sent into exile again if we refuse to rid ourselves of the idols in our heart (possibly material possessions, money, pride of life issues, lusts of the flesh, or lusts of the eyes—it is the attitude toward material possessions and money that make them idols or items of service to the Lord)? It can happen, if we do not continue to purify ourselves before the Lord. The Lord wants us to enter a New Covenant experience in which we have no rules except to follow His Spirit, to love Him with all of our heart, to love our neighbor as ourselves, and to love our brethren. In this New Covenant experience He will lead us into the work that He wants us to perform. He will challenge us to grow to the greatest of our potential. He will be beside us, and we will sense His presence. He will abide with/in us, and we will abide with/in Him.

As we walk in this way, the devil will do all that he can to thwart us; for the Lord will bless us with work that will attack demonic strongholds. We will grow in the anointing that the Lord will give us, and we will be able to stand and resist the devil. We will be fitted out with all of the armor of Ephesians 6. We will be separated from the world system. We may well come under persecution; but we will have the grace and strength to bear it, for God will supply His power to us.

As one partakes of this walk with the Lord, he has a great sense of fulfillment. There is nothing in the natural that can take the place of the relationship that has developed and that will grow even stronger as one comes into a dynamic living relationship with the God who created him. He will find multiple layers in Scriptures, since the whole document is alive. He will find that many things that he thought as a neonate are 180 degrees apart from reality.

We shall now ampilfy the individual sections discussed above.

1. Learn to see the hand of God in all things (1 Thessalonians 5:18).

It is very important to step back and dwell on who God reveals Himself to be in the Word. We have such a weak respect for Him in this age. We have to build up our reverence for Him. We have to develop a holy awe of Him. This can come only with time. Our heart must be emptied of self and of evil for this reverence to become resident within us. It can come over time only as we interact with God. One has to know Him for it to form. It is not sufficient to know about Him. We must walk with Him. As we become more accomplished at this, it is intimidating to realize that after 10-15 years we will perhaps only then be arriving at the beginning of wisdom. There are no short cuts to maturity. God would have to violate His character to allow this, for patience and long suffering are parts of His character that have to be formed in our hearts by process. Thinking it does not cause it to form. Do not be looking for short cuts—this is of a wrong spirit. That does not mean that we cannot avoid mistakes and wrong turns, if we will listen to advice from elders in the faith. That will shorten some of the time to maturity. A foundational step is beginning to ask God His purpose for us in every single thing that happens to us: "In every thing give thanks: for this is the will of God in Christ Jesus concerning you" (1 Thessalonians 5:18). As we begin to do this, we are learning to talk with God and to work with God. We will make mistakes, but we are on the way. Do not make the error of doing it just in the big things. This is man's way. It is the little things—line upon line, precept upon precept—that build up to the big things. If God cannot trust us in the little things, He will not trust us in the bigger things (Luke 16:11). That is His principle. At first it is awkward, looking at everything in this light. We will forget to do it; we will at other times be impatient and not wait on answers; at other times we will not believe in God's goodness and will go ahead of Him in the wrong direction or at the wrong time. This practice of prayerfully asking and seeking God's purpose in every event in which we are involved is a good start toward purifying the heart and cleansing the spirit. A note of caution is indicated before we go further.

We do not want to dwell on the devil and his angels, but we must recognize that we are in a lifelong battle with a foe who has no limits on his desire to steal, kill, and destroy. He does not hesitate to attack a babe. We must realize that he will try to prevent the second birth; and, if he fails in this, he will try to prevent growth. He and his followers are great mimics and will manifest as angels of light. They will work in half truth, and they have a greater power than we do. We must give them the respect that God gives them. They attack through the flesh and its lusts. If they cannot sidetrack us there, they will come against our spirit with spiritual force to bring about oppression, depression, anxiety, and confusion. They will try to intimidate through fear. They will use illness and the threat of death. They will motivate the world system to work against us, using it to attack our finances and physical comforts. If we do not think the devil and his angels are who God tells us they are, then they have neutralized us in the spiritual war in which we find ourselves. We can overcome these forces only as we abide in the Lord; in faith through our experiences with God we can learn to stand against these forces, as we prayerfully ask for and receive power in the inner man. The Lord has to deliver us from fear of them or their abilities in order for us to overcome them. It is only perfect love that casts out all fear, and we walk in perfect love only as we learn to trust the Lord experientially.

As we seek what God's purpose is in all events, we must be humble. We cannot elevate ourselves in our own mind, even if we have work from the Lord on the scope of the apostles Paul and Peter. We must always have a spirit of humility before God. If we are suffering, it is most likely for not waiting on the Lord or for disobedience. There is a need for us to suffer, and I would suggest that you do a word study on the word *suffer* in the writings of the Apostle Paul. This will help you to understand if you are suffering because of your godliness or because of disobedience. Have the attitude of looking first to see if there is something that you need to change or of which you need to repent. Seek the Lord, ask to be shown what the issues are, and then wait on the answer.

2. Walk in increasing faith as you trust the written promises in God's Word.

Until one gets used to hearing the individual *rhema* to him from the Lord and until one gets used to sorting out the Lord's voice from his own thoughts and from the voices of mimicking spirits, he can walk in faith on the written promises. There are thousands of these, and it would be wise to pick one as the Lord seems to "quicken" it to you as you read His Word. This process of the quickening of a passage of Scripture is one that you will soon experience, as you read the Word of God prayerfully. You will find that all of a sudden without any premonition on your part a particular passage will come into prominence in your mind in a way that is not natural. This is because the Holy Spirit is using it to show you something.

When you read the Word of God, it should be very actively read when you are alert and able to concentrate. You may have to ask God to give you the ability to concentrate at first. You should expect every reading of the Word to be a meeting with the Holy Spirit. He will communicate with your spirit, and this communication will rise from your heart into your mind. Since it is a spiritual flow, it will have a different power to it than that of a natural reading. It is this power to arrest your attention that you must learn to recognize. You then have to look at the content and pray over why God wants you to note this. At first, until you get used to this, it would be wise not to act in a major manner without the counsel of mature people of faith. God will not ask you to make life-changing decisions from a single reading of Scripture. There has to be a growing trend in other communications as well that seems to point to the same thing. Examine the structure behind the spirit of the passage that that got your attention. We see that the Scripture itself addresses what the emotion and thought content of a passage should be as one reads it: "All scripture *is* given by inspiration of God, and *is* profitable for doctrine, for reproof, for correction, for instruction in righteousness: That the man of God may be perfect, thoroughly furnished unto all good works" (2 Timothy 3:16-17). We must find that the content does not appeal to our pride of life but rather lays a new principle before us, rebukes us, or corrects us. If the communication comes with a feeling of lifting the self, it may not be from the Lord; or, if it was, we have allowed an evil spirit or a bad attitude in our own heart to overlay the original communication. There is nothing wrong with being joyful about receiving a message from the Lord, but this is different to self enhancement in a pride-of-life way that manifests as excitement. It will not feed a lust of the flesh or of the eyes.

As you grow in wisdom, you will have less difficulty in discerning what is from the Holy Spirit; but be careful at first. You should find this quickening to be a very common thing for you as you read the Scripture actively. Expect the Lord to point out areas where you can change in faith, for this is part of what the Holy Spirit will do. I try always to come to the Word to see what I am not doing that I should be doing; and then, when I see it, I commit immediately to changing my ways. This is so important for spiritual growth. It is this quickening of Scripture that will be an early way that you can reliably receive an individual communication from the Lord specifically for you in your relationship with Him.

3. Learn to hear the voice of God in order to communicate with Him, and receive the *rhema* that will further increase faith.

a. Meet the conditions for God to hear you.
b. Purify your heart and cleanse your inner man.
c. Test all the spirits that flow from your heart to the mind of your soul, analyzing the three components.

i. Test the power.
ii. Test the information and compare it to the *logos* of God.
iii. Learn to recognize all of the emotions and states of the heart.

d. Learn to distinguish between the voice of your conscience and a spirit of false guilt.

Learning to communicate with the Lord (both talking with Him in prayer and hearing from Him) is critical to the development of faith. We saw this in Chapter 19. If we do not have an increasingly broad faith, then we are not growing in our spirit. We have discussed the definition of the *rhema* in preceding chapters. It is the personal utterance of the Lord to His children and to the creation. The *logos* is the written Word of God, the Scripture. In Chapter 19 we saw that the *rhema* is the way that faith comes. The Holy Spirit can quicken the *logos*, as we discussed above. This then becomes a *rhema* for the individual.

Meet the conditions for God to hear you.

We shall look at Scriptures that define how God wants us to pray. If we do not follow His commands, then we cannot expect to hear clearly from Him. If you as a small child did not obey your Father, who had very good reasons for his commands to you, that would have hindered your relationship. The Scriptures tell us that God does not hear our prayer, if we regard iniquity in our heart: "If I regard iniquity in my heart, the Lord will not hear *me*" (Psalm 66:18).

If we have not forgiven someone, then we will be left with iniquity in our heart; and it will hinder our prayers and communication with God: "And when ye stand praying, forgive, if ye have ought against any: that your Father also which is in heaven may forgive you your trespasses. But if ye do not forgive, neither will your Father which is in heaven forgive your trespasses" (Mark 11:25). Jesus admonishes: "Therefore if thou bring thy gift to the altar, and there rememberest that thy brother hath ought against thee; Leave there thy gift before the altar, and go thy way; first be reconciled to thy brother, and then come and offer thy gift" (Matthew 5:23-24).

We must always pray in the Spirit: "Praying always with all prayer and supplication in the Spirit, and watching thereunto with all perseverance and supplication for all saints" (Ephesians 6:18). Jude 20 tells us the same: "But ye, beloved, building up yourselves on your most holy faith, praying in the Holy Ghost."

Other Scriptures address the constancy God wants from our prayers.

"And he spake a parable unto them *to this end*, that men ought always to pray, and not to faint" (Luke 18:1).

"Pray without ceasing" (1 Thessalonians 5:17).

"I will therefore that men pray every where, lifting up holy hands, without wrath and doubting" (1 Timothy 2:8).

Philippians 4:6 adds: "Be careful for nothing; but in every thing by prayer and supplication with thanksgiving let your requests be made known unto God."

In Matthew 6:5-9 Jesus gives instructions about prayer:

> And when thou prayest, thou shalt not be as the hypocrites *are*: for they love to pray standing in the synagogues and in the corners of the streets, that they may be seen of men. Verily I say unto you, They have their reward. But thou, when thou prayest, enter into thy closet, and when thou hast shut thy door, pray to thy Father which is in secret; and thy Father which seeth in secret shall reward thee openly. But when ye pray, use not vain repetitions, as the heathen *do*: for they think that they shall be heard for their

> much speaking. Be not ye therefore like unto them: for your Father knoweth what things ye have need of, before ye ask him. After this manner therefore pray ye: Our Father which art in heaven, Hallowed be thy name.

Peter adds: "Likewise, ye husbands, dwell with *them* according to knowledge, giving honour unto the wife, as unto the weaker vessel, and as being heirs together of the grace of life; that your prayers be not hindered" (1 Peter 3:7).

God is pleased when we can come to Him with thanksgiving in our heart and praise on our lips (Psalm 100:4), but it is not a pre-requisite for God to listen to us and hear us.

Therefore, we can conclude that in praying we must pray in the Holy Spirit. To do this we must be in our spirit, focusing our soul's attention on it instead of the flesh. We should pray without ceasing; we should not have any person that we have not forgiven; we should honor our wives; we should have nothing a brother can hold against us; we must pray in faith believing that God will answer; we should pray with thanksgiving; we must not regard iniquity in our heart; we must pray in secret; and we must not pray as the heathen do using vain repetitions (mantras). Thus, we have much to do in order to have our prayers heard and answered.

One of the most important requirements is not to regard iniquity in our heart. If we do not walk with a pure heart, perfect towards God, then we will have iniquity in our heart. We may not be regarding it, but we must ask God to cleanse us from all unrighteousness as we present our requests for forgiveness to Him (Psalm 19:12). Having a pure heart that is perfect toward God will increase the fellowship we have with God immensely. We should clarify that God knows everything and certainly hears all prayers from all people. In the Scriptures mentioned above He tells us that, while He may hear, He may not choose to respond. We shall turn to look at how we accomplish this purification below.

Purify your heart and cleanse your inner man.

As we begin our walk to take our soul back to the moment of the second birth in terms of purity of heart and of spirit, we will be following a path similar to that which the Israelites followed as God led them from bondage in Egypt to the Promised Land. This is a great roadmap for us. The Promised Land was to be a place of rest, but Israel never cleared the land of all of the people that she was supposed to. This journey is an analogy or a type of how we must walk with the Lord in our spiritual cleansing. Israel saw the works of God and saw Him leading His people and supplying their needs in terms of providing food, ensuring that their shoes and clothing did not wear out, and equipping them with riches as they began the journey. They wasted much time in the wilderness, and this is where we can save time, if we will, by being obedient to God. As they began their journey, the evil spirits attacked them constantly by stirring up dissension within their ranks and stirring up evil kings and peoples without. Despite all that God had shown them and done for them, they still, in large numbers, refused to walk in faith and in obedience. Once they got to the Promised Land, they never completely entered into rest, because they never completely took possession of it.

In just the same way as we begin our walk with God to purify our hearts and spirits, we will have evil attacks from without and from the flesh within the soul. Unless we walk in faith and obedience and allow God to deliver us of all fears, we will never enter the rest of Hebrews 4:12; and we will never mature.

The first landmark in maturing is beginning to take this walk. At first we do not see where we are going, but we eventually catch sight of the Promised Land. Our Promised Land in learning how to follow the Spirit of God is to be able to distinguish reliably the source of the leading that our soul is experiencing. In doing this we are beginning the separation of Hebrews 4:12. Note that to get to the Promised Land, we have to learn how to follow the Spirit of God by day and by night. This is an active process—it does not just happen. At this stage it is largely done by the Lord's giving revelation in the natural, "by His opening and closing doors," and by our being obedient not to rebel against this as we try to discern which way to go. To get to the Promised Land, we (our soul) has to learn to separate the leadings of the flesh, the soul, and the inner man. Eventually, we reach a place of discerning readily what is leading—our spirit, our soul, or our flesh. It is only as we do this that the Lord can lead us by His Spirit. When we cross into our Promised Land, we have to submit our will to His will voluntarily. In doing this, we will be led in the battles by the Lord as He tells us what to do in each situation to rid the enemies that are within our heart and thus purify our heart. This is what Joshua had to do (seek the Lord for battle plans before each battle). He did not always do this; and, thus, he had some losses. As we undergo this separation from self will, we are becoming more intimate with the Lord. We are getting to know Him and to love Him. At this point we begin an even greater battle and that is for the complete emptying of our own will. Once we can distinguish what is leading us, then we can choose to be led by it or not to be. By refusing to be led by anything other than our spirit as it bears witness to the Holy Spirit, then we will be led by the Spirit of God. In going through these changes, our heart will be purified.

We can read all of the prior chapters, and they will serve as a template for understanding in the soul's mind what we must become in our heart. Recall that man appears to God as what his heart is like. The soul must work with God to change the heart into an organ that is pleasing to the sight of God. As we change the heart, we must also control and cleanse our spirit. The two things will happen together since the inner man is in the heart and in constant interchange with the thoughts and content of the heart. We can look at some basic means for accomplishing this. It must all be done on God's schedule with us prayerfully asking God to show us what needs to be changed and then going about letting Him change it. There are two things that we must do, knowing them to be God's will, that will serve as the backbone for undergoing this transformation. They are closely linked.

1. We must begin "casting down imaginations, and every high thing that exalteth itself against the knowledge of God, and bringing into captivity every thought to the obedience of Christ; And

having in a readiness to revenge all disobedience, when your obedience is fulfilled" (2 Corinthians 10:5-6).

2. We must also test all of the spirits that emanate from us: "Beloved, believe not every spirit, but try the spirits whether they are of God: because many false prophets are gone out into the world" (1 John 4:1). We certainly do not want to emanate something false into the world.

We can be quite sure that God is expecting us to do these things, since they are commands. If we do not do these things constantly, then we do not love the Lord and abide in His love (John 15:9-15). In John 15:6 we read the dire consequences of not abiding in the Lord Jesus. We must be very sober minded about this—that is a result of the fear of the Lord. As we perform these things constantly, we begin to grow better at performing them and at recognizing impurity in ourselves. The process of cleansing the spirit and purifying the heart is very time consuming. As we begin to do this, our motivations are revealed to us; and we have to will to change them. We really see how desperately wicked and sick our hearts are. Those things that are hidden in the depths of our heart will be revealed to us by God, as He wants us to deal with them. He wants us to walk with a perfect heart toward Him. His definition of perfect is found in James 3:2. It deals with being perfect in word. Remember that man speaks out of the heart; and to speak perfectly, our heart will have to be pure.

In order to accomplish this work, we must perform a watching process. This is not an inward meditation but rather an analyzing of the spirits that are coming into the mind of the soul from the heart. These spirits bring the thoughts and intents of the heart to us. We have to deny expression to those spirits which are not of God and express those which are. This is not deceit but choosing who we will be before God. Deceit would be having a bad thought and intent toward another individual and cloaking it with something "more palatable" with the intent to mislead that person. In the process of not expressing something, we are not trying to mislead another person; for we are trying to purify our actions toward him by submitting to God.

In order to fulfill 2 Corinthians 10:5-6 and 1 John 4:1, we engage in an iterative process for the rest of our days on earth. We have to start to look at everything that we have become through our previous life experiences and put it on the altar before the Lord for change. We have to examine all of our attitudes, beliefs, and behaviors; for these are all expressions of spirit from our heart. It is a very comprehensive process that must leave no stone unturned, but it is not an inward meditation. Inward meditation is not a substitute for this process, if by that we mean trying to get in touch with the spiritual part of us. We do not need to meditate in this way, since our spirit is constantly expressing through our thoughts, attitudes, beliefs, and behaviors. We just have to observe what is coming out in our words and actions and also observe what we are suppressing.

We hold up these observations to the standards defined in Scripture; and we elect to make necessary changes in our beliefs, attitudes, and behaviors. Frequently, we must ask the Lord for strength in our inner man to overcome weakness in our will; and we may have to ask the Lord to rebuke an evil spirit and deliver us of that spirit. Note that even the Archangel Michael did not rebuke the devil himself (Jude 9). Sometimes the Lord will work through the body of believers to accomplish deliverance, but the individual believer can also petition the Lord to deliver him.

We should make a very formal process of emptying our hearts of self. This will accomplish the tearing down of strongholds, evil imaginations, and high things which exalt themselves against the knowledge of God. This will be discussed below under the next point. As we do this, it must not ever be an act of the will of the flesh. We must submit to God's timetable and method for purifying our heart. We cannot see enough in our heart even to know how to do it. We are commanded to take each thought captive by examining it for the spirit in it. At first we will need to make an analysis of almost everything, looking frequently at all three components of spirit to see if it is of the flesh, soul, inner man, or an evil spirit. As we grow in this process, our discernment will be sharpened; and we will start to identify to the Lord what needs to be changed. We will ask Him in faith to change it and trust that, in His time through the circumstances into which we are led, we will be changed. Our part is to capture the spirit of each thought and ask the Lord to cleanse us as needed. We should not express anything that is not of the Lord, but we are far from perfect; and to walk at this level will take great emptying of the self. Perfection in this is probably not possible for any of us, but that is not a reason not to work with the Lord to approach it. He will be greatly blessed by us, as we walk before Him in this manner.

It is always good, in looking at these spirits coming to our mind from our heart, to see who is being glorified by them. We should not allow a mixed walk—if a spirit is not glorifying God alone, then we should not release it. Our heart and our spirit are gradually cleansed through this continual process. Over time great purification and perfection can be achieved by the Lord as we submit. We cannot ever do this in the flesh because it would just build up sin in other areas, such as pride of life. It has to be done in Lord's power and timing.

Test all the spirits that flow from your heart to your mind of the soul, analyzing the three components.

a. *Test the power.*
b. *Test the information and how it compares to the logos of God.*
c. *Learn to recognize all of the emotions and states of the heart.*

There is a place for meditation in God's Word as we come before the Lord prayerfully and seek to know Him and to learn what He wants of us. This is a very active thing as we read the Word, asking God to bless this time. As we do this, we will hear God talking to our mind through our spirit and heart, as we learn to recognize His voice as opposed to other voices. We can know His voice from a testing of the content, emotion, and structure of the thought. It also helps to know the Lord's power and presence through training. It is not like coming into contact with an inner self or a spirit of the universe, nor is it a mystical experience. We must be very careful with all of these inward things to test the spirit behind every thought. The presence of the Lord will bring joy, peace, humility, and all of the other attributes of Him. We cannot expect to command His presence; but we must receive Him, as He comes to us. He will tell us things that we need to do and to change. Frequently, the Lord will delay His answer to our requests until our minds are at rest and not filled with noise and interruptions. Often answers will come as dreams or inward visions. We have to learn to recognize that God speaks to our spirits differently from the way men speak to us. We will experience His answers generally through revelation from His Scriptures. When God answers us, He frequently fills us with knowledge in which He brings together a number of Scriptures. It is very important to know Scripture and to study it comprehensively; for, if we do not, we have limited the Lord in how richly He can reveal Himself to us. The Scripture commands us to study and to keep God's Word as a frontlet before us. If we do not do this, then we are regarding iniquity in our heart; and He will not answer our prayers as much. He draws near to us as we draw near to Him. He does not force the issue. God is always gentle and is never controlling or manipulative. In fact, when we sense any spirit that is manipulative or controlling, then we know that this is not of God.

In learning to test the spirits always, we have to learn which ones are from God by experience. Most of the time we have a reasonably obvious choice, when we look at where a spirit is attempting to lead us or if we see that it is trying to control us; but there are some spirits, including a "spirit of false accusation" that can be very hard to discern. This discernment comes only by practice. We have to be very careful not to act on a spirit until we are sure about it.

Let us look in more detail at how we can recognize the voice of God. To do this, we must begin to observe consciously all of the thoughts and auditory voices that we have coming into our mind of the soul. We do not look within our soul, but we just observe what is happening in our mind. We do not have to sit still to do it. We do it as a part of all of our activities throughout the day and night. We do it constantly, just as we are always consciously taking every thought captive. This is the great difference between being led by the Spirit of God and being led by some evil spirit, who would call us to reflect inwardly and to come to some inner state-of-mind suspension. The Lord God wants our minds to be active; evil spirits want them turned off.

As we examine these spirits coming into our mind, we initially will take time to sort them out. They are going to be from the flesh, the Holy Spirit through our inner man, or an evil spirit (mostly masquerading as a spirit of light). We have to learn the difference in power between these three sources. This is not always easy; but as one becomes more aware of the spirits, one can discern the Lord's power. It is still and will not be moved. It comes as a sense of strength and permanence. We just have to practice sensing it. We will get used to it. An evil spirit will try to force us with a clamorous force that appeals to the lusts of our flesh. It may be very loud and will keep bothering us at inconvenient times until we have overcome it. Our own heart will speak to us of fleshly desires, pride of life issues, and lusts for things that we have seen. To hear the voice of your soul, ask yourself the question: what is the sum of two plus two? You will hear the answer four. That is the voice of your soul. This voice takes on different qualities under stress, and we have to learn them all. It is useful to look at what a spirit is trying to achieve and who is being glorified by this achievement if it occurs.

It will be helpful to look at an example. At one time I had been looking for a partner in my medical practice for many months. I had several candidates, but no match resulted. Another group of two doctors approached me to join them. This had an appearance of financial security. It had many benefits for my family and appeared to be a very good thing for all involved. I started to analyze the spirits involved. The offer came externally, not as a leading from within. That does not mean it is not from the Lord; but it should send up flags of caution, since the Lord will lead by the Spirit who dwells within us. I had, of course, been looking for a partner; but it was so far back in time that I could no longer analyze what spirit led me to begin this search. In reflecting back, I believe it probably was not from the Lord. As I prayed about the offer, a thought came gently to me that I was doing this for financial security; and this was a spirit of fear of the future. As soon as I saw that it was a spirit of fear at the bottom of the leading to join these other doctors, I rejected the offer. About two months later one of these doctors came to join me, and this resulted in a significant blessing. Not too much later the Lord led me to sell my practice to another physician, as He led my wife and me into what has turned into the greatest adventure of our lives, as we have sought to walk before Him in a manner pleasing to Him.

I shall give a simpler example. One morning I was preparing to leave home to drive to the office when I became aware that I would see a eunuch that day in the office. The information came from within; I had not been thinking about such issues. It was gentle and quiet, yet authoritative. There was a concern with it. I recognized the presence of the Lord quite clearly. My last patient that day in the office was a new patient to me. It was a young man who had a medical condition that rendered him functionally a eunuch. Prepared by the Lord's concern, I was able to give good advice based on Scripture which blessed both the patient and me.

There are hundreds of examples that I could go through, but the bottom line is that the only way to learn to recognize from where the spirit is coming is to start learning by observing. At times I have asked the Lord to teach me by giving me an example. He has always seemed willing to do this in short order. We learn as children before Him, and He is a very capable teacher.

After a while you will find a growing discernment. You will have experienced many situations and spirits. You will no longer have to go through the analytical process of looking at the components. You will just recognize the situation and the spirit, and you will be able to deal with it. Part of getting this experience is to focus on learning the various emotions and states of the heart that present the emotional component of the spirit. These have to come through practice, but eventually you will have built up discernment to the point at which you recognize which spirit is speaking to your mind— the Holy Spirit through your inner man, the flesh, or an evil spirit. Remember the fruits of the Holy Spirit and of the flesh as presented in Galatians 5. Learn these particularly, since you can hold almost any spirit up to these to identify the emotional component. If we are sensing impatience in our mind, then this is not of God and we should not act. If we are sensing peace, this is of God; but we must learn to distinguish this peace from God from the false peace that comes from making a decision and having the battle over.

Frequently, when we have an important decision to make, we have arguments from both sides coming into our mind. Pressure builds. We turn this over to the Lord and refuse to let anything make us think about it again. We tell the Lord that He can choose which way we go. We experience peace as the burden is taken by the Lord. This is His peace. If, instead, we say that we will choose course A over course B, then, when the decision is irrevocable, there is a sense of quietness that many would interpret as peace; but when we get to know the true peace, we will know the difference.

Concerning decision making we are commanded in Colossians 3:15: "And let the peace of God rule in your hearts, to the which also ye are called in one body; and be ye thankful." We must in all circumstances bring our hearts back to this point by turning over to the Lord decisions that are not obvious from past experience and by trusting Him to work out everything for our good (Romans 8:28).

Learn to distinguish between the voice of your conscience and a spirit of false guilt.

It took me a long time to detect reliably the presence of the enemy in this situation. Through experience we have to know the difference between the spirit from our conscience and an evil spirit trying to confuse us. It is very important to know the Word of God and to discern His Spirit in order to cleanse the conscience. Once cleansed and educated in the Word, it will become a better and more reliable guide. However, we must focus on being led by the Spirit of God and not by our conscience. The conscience serves to alert us, if we are in danger of going off track. The enemy will attempt to mix up our minds about choices, if we are not able to follow the Spirit of God from experience in hearing the voice of God and His various moods.

We must realize that God also speaks to us at times more audibly. I am not going to go into this in detail, but there are situations that may require that He "yell out to us" because we have not learned to walk in a more consistent manner. In my own experience these warnings have occurred mainly when I was insensitive to the leading of His Spirit. We must learn the different tones that God uses. We have to look at what God is saying to us in our circumstances; we have to be able to talk reliably with Him; and we have to prepare our hearts and spirits for this to occur.

We have to learn all of the moods and voices of God. It is frequently the still small voice that God uses. There is no emotional pressure with it; there is purity and kindness with it; the information comes quietly to our awareness when we are perhaps asleep, perhaps doing and thinking about something unrelated; and we just learn to recognize it as the Lord. It is gentle, and the wisdom fits the criteria in James 3:13-18.

Practice becoming aware of all of these spirits, as the Lord teaches you. Look to the Holy Spirit to teach you all of these things. This book can only make you aware that there is a process that any of us can undergo in order to hear the Lord talking to and fro with us. The Lord does not always give answers immediately; but when one seeks wisdom, there may be a period of preparation for being able to receive and understand an answer. As a person progresses along this path and the Lord becomes more of a friend, then one can converse with Him, expecting much more of the relationship.

The very important thing is that when you have learned to hear from God and can distinguish His voice and communications from those of self and those of evil spirits, then you can reliably choose to follow His Spirit if you will to do so.

4. Undergo your kenosis as you purify your heart and cleanse your inner man by casting down vain imaginations and high things that exalt themselves against God. These are your heart beliefs, attitudes, and behaviors. They all have to be torn down and cast out.

The Lord has told us that the servant is not greater than his master. The Lord Jesus emptied Himself of something far greater than we have, the attributes of His Godhead (Philippians 2). He expects us to empty ourselves of us. He tells us that if we lose our life, we will find it. When we can reliably distinguish God's voice witnessing to our spirit from the flesh, the soul, and evil spirits, then we have reached a state of separation such that we can fulfill Hebrews 4:12. We know now what is from spirit, flesh, and soul. Our soul is as our heart before the Lord. We now have to empty ourselves of our own will (lusts and desires). This is a much larger step than any we have had to date. In the past we could not tell even what came from our own will and what came from His will for us on a particular issue. Now, we can do this reasonably reliably; and we can then with His help, as He gives us power in our spirit, defeat the enemy and overcome our flesh and evil spirits. We have to search out those things that remain in our hearts that drive our evil desires and lusts, as the Lord identifies them to us.

We start to see in the spirit that we really are very limited in our abilities. We become meek before Him as we start to see the enormity of the spiritual powers arrayed against us. We seek His protection more and more. We defer to His judgment, knowing that He sees all and that our gaze is very limited.

We find that, as we determine to yield to Him, we grow in our spirit and start to see Him higher, more powerful, more capable, more loving, and more dependable. He was always these things; but, as our spirit grows, these characteristics take on a deep core reality by which we subconsciously operate. Our relationship deepens, and He begins to trust us with His work. It is a time of transition. We go from serving self to gradually abandoning self in the Lord. It will be a lifelong process that means continuing to crucify the flesh and to stand against evil spirits. He will give His power to us in order for us to do that. It is a time of growth in the inner man.

It happens imperceptibly from moment to moment, but over time we come to trust the spiritual universe more than the physical. It is not something at the level of the conscious mind, but rather an operation of the heart; for our heart is changed. Our spiritual awareness, judgment, and abilities grow. We carry an anointing with us. We communicate with the Lord continuously by focusing on keeping Him present in our awareness.

As we empty ourselves, we can look for the fruit of the Holy Spirit to remain in our heart and to take complete occupancy of it. We will be readily filled with a sense of the Lord's presence as we turn our attention to it. Our inner man will radiate peace, joy, and love into our heart; and those will be all that come to our mind. To be sure, the enemy will try to attack; but now we know immediately that he is coming against our spirit. We must strive to fight against the enemy by resisting anything in our heart that is not a fruit of the Holy Spirit. We must keep joy and peace at the center of our heart.

5. Think only on these things: "Finally, brethren, whatsoever things are true, whatsoever things *are* honest, whatsoever things *are* just, whatsoever things *are* pure, whatsoever things *are* lovely, whatsoever things *are* of good report; if *there be* any virtue, and if *there be* any praise, think on these things" (Philippians 4:8). If something is not in this Scripture, stop thinking about it and dwelling on it.

It is essential to follow this commandment of the Lord to purify the heart and cleanse the spirit. If we do not obey this, it will prevent us from purifying our heart; and we will not be able to hear from God. We have to separate ourselves from the world system. If we want to change but lack the power to change, we can ask the Lord to help us. This command covers everything that we see, hear, touch, smell, and taste. It is very comprehensive. It means being very selective about following news and even more selective about entertainment and relaxation. If you are uncertain about something, you can always ask the Lord about it. If there is conflict about these issues and your job, then you can turn to the Lord for counsel. He is quite able to answer you in a way that you will know that it is His answer. However, you cannot ask wavering, or you will not receive an answer (James 1:5-7).

6. Take every single thought captive for the Lord Jesus Christ: "Casting down imaginations, and every high thing that exalteth itself against the knowledge of God, and bringing into captivity every thought to the obedience of Christ" (2 Corinthians 10:5).

We have discussed this extensively above, but it is always relevant. Any new philosophy has to be examined and dealt with against Scripture and the leading of the Holy Spirit in your inner man (this is worshipping in spirit and in truth).

7. Commit to put God first, and begin to tell Him that you love Him.

At all times and in all ways submit to God. Begin as you start this walk by letting Him know that you love Him—it may be feeble and small, but you are committing to it. He must be the main individual in your life. All else comes second. You will have plenty of love left for your family—the amazing thing about love is that, when it is real, it is never insufficient for all who need it. It is very important that we speak these things out physically, for God's ear is close to our lips; and speaking them out brings a level of commitment.

8. Become a person of very few words; for you are judged on what you speak, since it is spirit. Sift your planned words carefully before releasing them.

This is a part of testing the spirit. It was discussed above.

9. Carefully examine all doctrines of men's teaching; hold them up to the Scriptures; and, if necessary, ask God to explain (James 1:5-6). He is very willing to explain. He is your true teacher and not men, although God will use the right men for your needs.

As we separate from the world system and tear down strongholds, vain imaginations, and high places, we will find that Satan and his demons have distorted much of the teachings in Scripture. There is much folklore in the church that needs to be destroyed, because it is based on error through half-truth. Never accept any teaching from man that you do not pass through your inner man and judge with him as you receive it. Listen with your inner man and not just your ears of flesh. Observe the spirits of what is being said. It may sound true; but if there is discomfort within your heart that comes from your inner man and not your conscience or false guilt, then it is teaching that is in error. You may not even understand the issues; but be guided by the Lord to learn more, so that you can understand what the Holy Spirit is saying about a particular teaching. Frequently, people who are teaching get a slightly wrong balance about important doctrines; and this will result in discomfort in your inner man as the Holy Spirit communicates with him.

10. Study the Scriptures daily, and do research on topics that the Lord brings before you, using a concordance or a software program.

A concordance or a software program is of great help in studying the Word of God. Word searches help you to examine all of the references to an issue, and the Lord will teach you through your greater knowledge. He will bring balance to complex issues. One can support anything he wants from a particular Scripture. When you study several hundred references in context prayerfully, you may be surprised by what you find. Always be prepared to change your ways before the Lord instantly on any aspect of the living of your life. Read the Word daily, for the Lord tells us that His Words are life and health to our flesh (Proverbs 4:20-22). This is an absolutely true statement. You can act in faith on it and find that your physical health will improve. A believer who has been through the second birth will not survive long without reading and meditating on the Word of God.

11. Assemble yourself with other believers. Choose a congregation about which you have prayed and to which you have asked the Lord to guide you. He is the one who puts people into individual congregations. It is His right to choose for you.

This is an area in which we must be obedient for our own growth in the inner man. The writer of Hebrews commands this, especially as end times approach (Hebrews 10:25).

12. Do not change your secular work, unless you are clearly led. This work should now be done with an attitude that you are doing it for the Lord.

Change your work only as the Lord leads you. You need to be absolutely certain to make sure it is the Lord leading you. The Scripture commands it: "Let every man abide in the same calling wherein he was called. Art thou called *being* a servant? care not for it: but if thou mayest be made free, use *it* rather. For he that is called in the Lord, *being* a servant, is the Lord's freeman. likewise also he that is called, *being* free, is Christ's servant. Ye are bought with a price; be not ye the servants of men. Brethren, let every man, wherein he is called, therein abide with God" (1 Corinthians 7:20-24).

13. You must pray constantly in the spirit without ceasing (1 Thessalonians 5:17) and maintain righteousness, peace, and joy in the heart.

When you keep your heart pure and in a state in which it is filled with the righteousness, peace, and joy of the Holy Spirit (Romans 14:17), you are in constant spiritual communication with the Spirit of God. The slightest spiritual frown or smile does not go unnoticed from either side. I think this is what to "pray without ceasing" means. It is the state of maintaining a meek and quiet spirit always before the throne of God. Spirits displace spirits; they do not kill them. When an evil spirit comes against one's spirit, it will displace it from the current position. We must therefore fight to stand our ground with the weapons of Ephesians 6. This command to pray without ceasing is a bedrock foundation for following the Spirit of God.

14. You must praise God.

Praising God must be by your obedience in keeping His commandments, in coming into His presence constantly and continuously with praise on your lips and thanksgiving in your heart, and in keeping your heart pure and perfect toward Him.

15. You are coming into relationship with a supernatural God, and there will be supernatural events in your life. You should expect and welcome them.

You are going to see and hear things in the spirit that will be quite new and strange. Test the spirit behind all of them. See whether it is God training you or the demons trying to puff you up with spiritual pride. It is so easy to fall from high spiritual places. Watch your footing at all times, and shelter meekly under the Lord's wings (Psalm 91:4). Do not self promote (Luke 14:8), but wait on the Lord always (Isaiah 40:31).

16. Never, ever compare yourself to another individual before God or in your own mind. This is a false spirit and must be vigorously rebuked (John 21:21-22).

The Lord tells us never to judge another's servant (Matthew 20:1-16). This is a command, and it must be observed. If a person does not observe it, he will fall into having a grievously judgmental spirit.

17. Be humble toward all advice from counselors.

If anyone gives you advice or a rebuke, take it and examine yourself before the Lord to see if it is correct. Do this in humility, esteeming others more righteous than yourself. The Lord tells us that there is much wisdom in a multitude of counselors. However, what the Lord says should determine the decision. You have to know that you have clearly heard from Him, and He may choose to keep you waiting. He is God, and He controls all of the variables in your situation.

Never try to be a "lone wolf;" you must be a part of the body of Christ. The devil may tempt you to think that you are more spiritual and can do without the others. If one does this, he has just violated a command of God and fallen prey to a form of spiritual pride.

18. Always walk in truth.

If one does not walk in truth at all times, he does not walk consistently with the Lord. God will never operate outside truth. We walk in so much half-truth that it takes a lot of effort to stop and examine spirits, beliefs, attitudes, and behaviors to discern which need changing. It is a hard, time-consuming reformation in our soul; but it must be done without compromise.

BEING CAREFUL ABOUT WHO OR WHAT IS LEADING US

Desires of the Heart

In Psalm 37:4-9: we read: "Delight thyself also in the LORD; and he shall give thee the desires of thine heart, Commit thy way unto the LORD; trust also in him; and he shall bring *it* to pass. And he shall bring forth thy righteousness as the light, and thy judgment as the noonday. Rest in the LORD, and wait patiently for him: fret not thyself because of him who prospereth in his way, because of the man who bringeth wicked devices to pass. Cease from anger, and forsake wrath: fret not thyself in any wise to do evil. For evildoers shall be cut off: but those that wait upon the LORD, they shall inherit the earth."

In this passage we see that we can be led by the desires of our heart; and some would interpret this to mean that, if we desire something, it is the Lord's will. This is not necessarily the case, for the qualification for this leading is that we delight ourselves in the Lord. This *delight* means that we do this with all of our being in all things. Some specific qualifications are listed in Isaiah 58:13-14: "If thou turn away thy foot from the sabbath, *from* doing thy pleasure on my holy day; and call the sabbath a delight, the holy of the LORD, honourable; and shalt honour him, not doing thine own ways, nor finding thine own pleasure, nor speaking *thine own* words: Then shalt thou delight thyself in the LORD; and I will cause thee to ride upon the high places of the earth, and feed thee with the heritage of Jacob thy father: for the mouth of the LORD hath spoken *it*." Note that this qualification involves "not speaking our own words on the sabbath." This all involves great intimacy with the Lord, and few there are who reach it. These people will be so unaware of self that they will not necessarily even be aware of being led in this manner. However, it is a wonderful way to be led; for then we have all of those things for which we yearn. This will almost certainly not involve material things, but it will involve spiritual matters. In being led by the desires of our heart, we must also put them to the testing of the spirit behind them. Eventually, as we fulfill the prerequisites listed in Isaiah 58:13-14, we can be led by the desires of our heart.

A very important caveat of this is that, when we are trying to make a decision, it will be the thing that we really wish to do least that frequently will be the thing that the Lord wishes us to do. Until you have walked closely before the Lord for a considerable time and during this time have submitted your will to His will, it is best to doubt strongly what you want to do and to look closely at that which you least wish to do. It will many times be His will for you to do that which you really do not want to do. Such is the requirement of His training and the strength of the flesh that must be broken.

Thoughts of the Mind

I have heard many people say that they ask God to guide their thoughts, and then they assume that their thoughts are from the Spirit of God. This whole book talks against this, for the thoughts are spirit and have to be tested. Also recall that the content of the thoughts is just one of the three components of spirit. A review of Daniel 7:15 will help us to see the difference. We must never be led by the thoughts of our mind. All of the people I know who have said this have run into a lot of trouble; some have been totally stopped in their maturation.

THE METAMORPHOSIS

As we learn to seek the leading of God's Spirit, we gradually mature to the point at which we become reasonably adept at knowing the source of all spirits entering the mind of the soul—those from the inner man, the flesh, or the soul. This is the Hebrews 4:12 benchmark in our maturing in our inner man. It is a place of rest to some degree, because we can much more readily defeat the flesh; but now we enter into a prolonged war with Satan who will try to wear us down. We can rejoice in this, since the Lord allows these attacks to cleanse us of impurity.

He uses it to refine us. We also have to wait continually on the Lord, as He develops patience in us. We are learning to submit our will to His will. These things are not easy, since the devil knows our fears and will play on them. The Lord, however, is turning this to good, as we learn to overcome our fears. It is only as we open our hearts to purification that the fullness of God's love abides with us and flows out of us. Remember: "There is no fear in love; but perfect love casteth out fear: because fear hath torment. He that feareth is not made perfect in love" (1 John 4:18). The Lord wants us to be completely fearless in order to radiate His love to a dying world. He will work to refine us by the situations in which we find ourselves. If we co-operate with Him, we will grow. Embrace those challenges that He gives to us; it is not easy, but it is so worthwhile.

In 2 Peter 1:4-7 we read: "Whereby are given unto us exceeding great and precious promises: that by these ye might be partakers of the divine nature, having escaped the corruption that is in the world through lust. And beside this, giving all diligence, add to your faith virtue; and to virtue knowledge; And to knowledge temperance; and to temperance patience; and to patience godliness; And to godliness brotherly kindness; and to brotherly kindness charity." Charity (love) is the final state that God wants for us, perfect love. We see in this passage a progress toward maturity, as we remove lust from our lives:

1. Faith is the foundation—we have discussed how to acquire this.

2. Diligence—we must put a one hundred percent effort into all spiritual things.

3. Virtue—we must always walk in truth, never deviating from seeking truth.

4. As we accomplish the preceding steps, we will start to grow in the knowledge of God.

5. As we gain knowledge of God, we will trust Him more and ourselves less, since we will see our limitations very clearly. This brings patience, since we cannot defeat or control the evil forces around us without being completely in God's perfect will.

6. As we rest in the growing knowledge of God and the spiritual universe, we will gain patience.

7. As we gain patience, we will start to see issues from God's perspective and the need to adhere to His timetable. We thus gain godliness.

8. As we see things from God's perspective, we start to see how trapped people are by the terrible forces of darkness and how much they need deliverance. Even our enemies take on a different perspective, since they are also trapped by evil. We develop brotherly kindness.

9. Finally, as the Lord refines our hearts further, we broadcast His love into the area of influence around us.

As we walk before the Lord in order to mature through these steps, some of the changes that occur in us come about through the following means.

Meditation on the Word in the Lord's presence will allow us to tear down the imaginations and high things that exalt themselves against the knowledge of God (2 Corinthians 10:5-6). We have to examine all of those philosophies that we have just soaked up from the world system and rid ourselves of these. We have to start believing God about His promises, and we have to start to know God through His interactions with us in our lives. This is not a knowing about God but a coming to know the very heart of God. We have to ask God to reveal to us His vision for our future. It will not be about our secular work goals as much as about His desire for us in terms of building up the body of Christ and preaching the gospel. We do that in whatever secular workplace He has us.

As we move through doing all of these things, we will gradually lose our own will as we submit to His will. This is undergoing a *kenosis*. Submitting to His will is a moment-by-moment decision and gradually becomes an attitude of heart, as we become meek before God. We cannot become meek just in the mind of the soul; it has to be by revelation from God to our spirit. It has to be by leading from the Sprit of God. It must be the bedrock of the new structures that we erect in the heart in order for the Lord Jesus Christ to be formed in our heart (Galatians 4:19). It is interesting to note that the Greek word for *formed* in this Scripture is that from which we get the word *metamorphosis*.

As we do these things, we gradually spend more time in the spirit. We are looking to the spirit for leading from the Lord. We are operating in the reality that the spiritual universe is foundational, and we are looking to see the Lord more clearly. We are lifting Him up as we defer to Him and as we give our will over to Him. As we do these things, we start to be led by the desires that He has placed in our heart. For us to know that a desire is from Him, it must pass the test of which spirit is behind it.

We go through a metamorphosis from focusing on the visible to walking in faith, trusting God's communications to us (the *rhemas*). Our focus becomes eternity and not temporal things. We still have to operate in the natural world, but the lusts of it have lessening influence on us. For this to occur, we have to begin this walk with the Lord in close association with Him. We have to give Him all of our time. He will test us in order for us to see whether our motives are real and whether we are going to persist. He will strengthen us in our resolve, as we ask Him to do so.

As we earn God's trust, He will release His power gifts through us; and we will have resident power built up in our inner man. We will gain spiritual authority. Demons recognized the apostle Paul and the Lord Jesus. We need to be in a position of authority for this to occur. The apostle Paul preached in demonstration of power. We must have the Lord's trust for this also.

An essential thing for growth is to understand and know the voice of God. This is foundational, and nothing else will occur unless we work with the Lord to allow this. A person must be able to hear from God in order to get faith (*rhema*).

We must begin by realizing that we have to go back to the state in which we were right after the second birth, when we had a pure heart and a new spirit (inner man). This spirit must be trained to work with our soul and must become obedient to our soul.

IN CONCLUSION

We can ask ourselves if it is worth emptying ourselves in this manner. It does not bring peace from spiritual conflict, but we have been given a very few short years on earth. These years are insignificant in terms of eternity. These years have been given us to prepare for eternity. It will be to your great cost in eternity, if you do not submit to the Lord's desires for you. He wants eternal good for each of us. Do not let your years on earth be ordinary. Let them be filled, as the Apostle Paul states in Philippians 3:14: "I press toward the mark for the prize of the high calling of God in Christ Jesus." Ponder the situation, and there can be no other rational response but to throw yourself on the ground before your Creator and say, as in Isaiah 45:9: "Woe unto him that striveth with his Maker! *Let* the potsherd *strive* with the potsherds of the earth. Shall the clay say to him that fashioneth it, What makest thou? or thy work, He hath no hands?" Then submit as the clay to be co-operatively molded and shaped to be a vessel of great use to the Lord.

Be as in 2 Timothy 2:20-21: "But in a great house there are not only vessels of gold and of silver, but also of wood and of earth; and some to honour, and some to dishonour. If a man therefore purge himself from these, he shall be a vessel unto honour, sanctified, and meet for the master's use, *and* prepared unto every good work." We must purge ourselves before the Lord of all iniquity, allow Him to purify and perfect our heart, and ask Him to cleanse our inner man of all impurity. We must work with Him in this process. Finally, count the cost of not walking before the Lord as He commands; and then say, as Joshua did: "Choose you this day whom ye will serve; ... but as for me and my house, we will serve the LORD" (Joshua 24:15). Choose to be another Joshua for the Lord—"as for me and my house, we will serve the LORD." And may God richly bless us in all of the riches of Christ Jesus as we commit ourselves to Him: "But my God shall supply all your need according to his riches in glory by Christ Jesus" (Philippians 4:19).

One final note is a searching question: are you compromising God's standards in any area? If you are, then in that area you do not have His protection, blessing, or companionship. You are vulnerable to the enemy's attacking you. God never, ever changes; and He will not compromise His standards. This means that for issues—such as the ones that occupy our current political and social endeavors—we, as believers, should not compromise ourselves (but we should never, ever judge those who do). By bringing the Spirit of the Lord through our own sanctification to people, we can cause them to fall to their knees in the presence of the Spirit of God and confess the Lord as their Savior. We win battles, not by public law (although it is right for this to be righteous) enacted by a clash of wills with those who hold other views, but by transmission of the Spirit of Holiness. As we turn hearts and as those who are called by His Name turn from their wicked ways and seek His face, then He will heal our land: "If my people, which are called by my name, shall humble themselves, and pray, and seek my face, and turn from their wicked ways; then will I hear from heaven, and will forgive their sin, and will heal their land" (2 Chronicles 7:14). We cannot do it through politics. That is a work of the flesh. The Lord Jesus did not ever get involved in politics as a means of change. Our time is to be spent before Him in prayer and meditating in His Word. He may lead us to be involved in politics as individuals but not as a church, for the Church is His body. Before getting involved in these political and social issues, make sure that it is God leading you into this involvement; otherwise, He will not bless your work. It is He who has set up the government that we have at any given time; our leaders are chosen by Him for His current purposes in history. That is why the Lord did not confront Roman power when he walked among us. He confronted evil powers and spiritual hypocrisy.

EPILOGUE

This book has examined the relationship of individuals to God. It has not focused on the Church. Surely few there are who do not see the weakness of the Church at this time in history. God wants it to be strong. The reason it is weak is that it has not put on the whole armor of God (Ephesians 6:10-18). Individual believers are weak for the same reason. These few key verses tell us not to wrestle with flesh and blood but to fight against spiritual wickedness. These powers deceive men into committing the sins that are so prevalent in our society. We can never purify our land by political power, for we are actually warring against the government that God has ordained. Our task is to displace spiritual powers. To do this successfully, we must put on the armor:

Our loins must be girded with truth.
Our breast must be protected by righteousness.
Our feet must be shod with the gospel of peace.
Our head must be covered with the helmet of salvation.
One hand must hold up the shield of faith.
Our other hand must carry the sword of the Spirit.

We should look at the state in our own lives of these six pieces of armor and ask God to help us to make them and to wear them daily. It would be helpful each day to reflect on what we have done that we could not have accomplished without God. We will see how little we actually use faith. We have to walk in increasing faith and expect power to be demonstrated after we speak the gospel (Mark 16:15-18).

Remember that Jesus came into the world to save the lost, not to condemn them. He came the first time in peace. We must carry that same spirit of humility. We must not condemn those in sin around us; but we should realize that, but for God's grace, we would be in their place. We must let them sense the joy, peace, and righteousness in our spirit; and they may be won. If not, it will not be our actions that add to their destruction. This is the putting on of the gospel of peace that carries us wherever we walk.

In putting on the armor of God, we must know God's Word in order to understand how to accomplish this. We have to know the *logos*—as taught by the Holy Spirit, not the philosophies of men. As individuals begin to grow into these things, revival can come and can be sustained. Then the Church will regain the power to influence heavenly bodies and to have victory over them.

www.ingramcontent.com/pod-product-compliance
Lightning Source LLC
LaVergne TN
LVHW010525100826
845148LV00001B/90

* 9 7 8 0 9 8 2 0 0 1 4 0 0 *